Stabilizing and Empowering Women in Higher Education:

Realigning, Recentering, and Rebuilding

Heidi L. Schnackenberg
SUNY Plattsburgh, USA

Denise A. Simard
SUNY Plattsburgh, USA

A volume in the Advances in Higher Education
and Professional Development (AHEPD) Book
Series

Published in the United States of America by
> IGI Global
> Information Science Reference (an imprint of IGI Global)
> 701 E. Chocolate Avenue
> Hershey PA, USA 17033
> Tel: 717-533-8845
> Fax: 717-533-8661
> E-mail: cust@igi-global.com
> Web site: http://www.igi-global.com

Copyright © 2023 by IGI Global. All rights reserved. No part of this publication may be reproduced, stored or distributed in any form or by any means, electronic or mechanical, including photocopying, without written permission from the publisher. Product or company names used in this set are for identification purposes only. Inclusion of the names of the products or companies does not indicate a claim of ownership by IGI Global of the trademark or registered trademark.

Library of Congress Cataloging-in-Publication Data

Names: Simard, Denise A., editor. | Schnackenberg, Heidi L., editor.
Title: Stabilizing and empowering women in higher education : realigning,
   recentering, and rebuilding / edited by Heidi L. Schnackenberg, and
   Denise A. Simard.
Description: Hershey, PA : Information Science Reference, [2023] | Includes
   bibliographical references and index. | Summary: "This volume is an
   essential read for women in leadership, faculty, administrators,
   professional staff, graduate students, and researchers. It provides
   valuable information and perspectives on creating access for
   marginalized groups, using roles as women leaders to create change, and
   nurturing and empowering women in leadership. Overall, it is a
   persuasive and powerful book that will help readers to realign,
   recenter, and rebuild in their personal and professional lives"--
   Provided by publisher.
Identifiers: LCCN 2023019791 (print) | LCCN 2023019792 (ebook) | ISBN
   9781668485972 (h/c) | ISBN 9781668486016 (s/c) | ISBN 9781668485989
   (ebook)
Subjects: LCSH: Women in higher education. | Women college teachers. |
   Women college students. | Feminism and higher education.
Classification: LCC LC1567 .S79 2023 (print) | LCC LC1567 (ebook) | DDC
   378.0082--dc23/eng/20230510
LC record available at https://lccn.loc.gov/2023019791
LC ebook record available at https://lccn.loc.gov/2023019792

This book is published in the IGI Global book series Advances in Higher Education and Professional Development (AHEPD) (ISSN: 2327-6983; eISSN: 2327-6991)

British Cataloguing in Publication Data
A Cataloguing in Publication record for this book is available from the British Library.

All work contributed to this book is new, previously-unpublished material. The views expressed in this book are those of the authors, but not necessarily of the publisher.

For electronic access to this publication, please contact: eresources@igi-global.com.

Advances in Higher Education and Professional Development (AHEPD) Book Series

Jared Keengwe
University of North Dakota, USA

ISSN:2327-6983
EISSN:2327-6991

Mission

As world economies continue to shift and change in response to global financial situations, job markets have begun to demand a more highly-skilled workforce. In many industries a college degree is the minimum requirement and further educational development is expected to advance. With these current trends in mind, the **Advances in Higher Education & Professional Development (AHEPD) Book Series** provides an outlet for researchers and academics to publish their research in these areas and to distribute these works to practitioners and other researchers.

AHEPD encompasses all research dealing with higher education pedagogy, development, and curriculum design, as well as all areas of professional development, regardless of focus.

Coverage

- Adult Education
- Assessment in Higher Education
- Career Training
- Coaching and Mentoring
- Continuing Professional Development
- Governance in Higher Education
- Higher Education Policy
- Pedagogy of Teaching Higher Education
- Vocational Education

IGI Global is currently accepting manuscripts for publication within this series. To submit a proposal for a volume in this series, please contact our Acquisition Editors at Acquisitions@igi-global.com or visit: http://www.igi-global.com/publish/.

The Advances in Higher Education and Professional Development (AHEPD) Book Series (ISSN 2327-6983) is published by IGI Global, 701 E. Chocolate Avenue, Hershey, PA 17033-1240, USA, www.igi-global.com. This series is composed of titles available for purchase individually; each title is edited to be contextually exclusive from any other title within the series. For pricing and ordering information please visit http://www.igi-global.com/book-series/advances-higher-education-professional-development/73681. Postmaster: Send all address changes to above address. Copyright © 2023 IGI Global. All rights, including translation in other languages reserved by the publisher. No part of this series may be reproduced or used in any form or by any means – graphics, electronic, or mechanical, including photocopying, recording, taping, or information and retrieval systems – without written permission from the publisher, except for non commercial, educational use, including classroom teaching purposes. The views expressed in this series are those of the authors, but not necessarily of IGI Global.

Titles in this Series

For a list of additional titles in this series, please visit: http://www.igi-global.com/book-series/advances-higher-education-professional-development/73681

Mentoring and Reflective Teachers in ESOL and Bilingual Education
JungKang Miller (Mercy College, USA) and Bahar Otcu-Grillman (Mercy College, USA)
Information Science Reference • © 2023 • 344pp • H/C (ISBN: 9781668483800) • US $215.00

Integrating TPACK and CALL in English Language Teaching
Mohialdeen Alotumi (Sana'a University, Yemen)
Information Science Reference • © 2023 • 256pp • H/C (ISBN: 9781668485460) • US $215.00

Co-Constructing and Sustaining Service Learning in Graduate Programs Reflections from the Field
Rabia Hos (University of Rhode Island, USA) and Brenda Santos (University of Rhode Island, USA)
Information Science Reference • © 2023 • 276pp • H/C (ISBN: 9781668465332) • US $215.00

Fostering Pedagogy Through Micro and Adaptive Learning in Higher Education Trends, Tools, and Applications
Ricardo Queirós (School of Media Arts and Design, Polytechnic of Porto, Portugal & CRACS INESC TEC, Portugal) Mario Cruz (School of Education, Polytechnic of Porto, Portugal & inED, Portugal) Carla Pinto (School of Engineering, Polytechnic of Porto, Portugal & CMUP, Portugal) and Daniela Mascarenhas (School of Education, Polytechnic of Porto, Portugal & inED, Portugal)
Information Science Reference • © 2023 • 376pp • H/C (ISBN: 9781668486566) • US $215.00

Cases on Teacher Preparation in Deaf Education
Nena Raschelle Neild (Gallaudet University, USA) and Patrick Joseph Graham (Rochester Institute of Technology, USA)
Information Science Reference • © 2023 • 352pp • H/C (ISBN: 9781668458341) • US $215.00

Sustaining Higher Education Through Resource Allocation, Learning Design Models, and Academic Development
Manyane Makua (Mangosuthu University of Technology, South Africa) and Mariam Akinlolu (London Metropolitan University, UK)
Information Science Reference • © 2023 • 322pp • H/C (ISBN: 9781668470596) • US $215.00

Addressing the Queen Bee Syndrome in Academia
Karis L. Clarke (Touro University California, USA) and Noran L. Moffett (Independent Researcher, USA)
Information Science Reference • © 2023 • 250pp • H/C (ISBN: 9781668477175) • US $215.00

701 East Chocolate Avenue, Hershey, PA 17033, USA
Tel: 717-533-8845 x100 • Fax: 717-533-8661
E-Mail: cust@igi-global.com • www.igi-global.com

Table of Contents

Preface xiii

Chapter 1
Stabilizing and Empowering Women in Higher Education: Aligning, Centering, and Building 1
    Natasha N. Johnson, Georgia State University, USA

Chapter 2
Unexpected Dreams 19
    Denise Demers, University of Central Arkansas, USA

Chapter 3
Toxic Femininity in Higher Education: Academia's Sting in the Tail – The Queen Bee 37
    Catherine Hayes, University of Sunderland, UK

Chapter 4
Informal Mentoring Among Women in Higher Education to Subvert Gender Bias 56
    Clair A. Stocks, Chapman University, USA

Chapter 5
Caveats to Accessibility: Does the Promise of On-Line Higher Education Programs Help
Minoritized Women in Higher Education? 72
    Carlene O. Fider, Pacific Oaks College, USA
    Camille Huggins, Pacific Oaks College, USA
    Eugenia Rodriquez, Pacific Oaks College, USA

Chapter 6
At the Crossroads: A Social-Ecological Model of Support for Women of Color in Higher
Education Leadership 87
    Lolita L. Kincade, SUNY Plattsburgh, USA

Chapter 7
Black Women Faculty Also Matter: A Paradigm Shift Toward Empowerment and Inclusion in
Higher Education 106
    Portia Allie-Turco, SUNY Plattsburgh, USA

Chapter 8
Gendered Cultures, Under-Representation, and the Career Challenges of Women Academics in a
South African University 143
    Yaw Owusu-Agyeman, University of the Free State, South Africa
    Reitumetse Mofana, University of the Free State, South Africa

Chapter 9
Nurturing and Empowering of Women in Leadership Positions: A Study With Special Reference
to the Indian Subcontinent 161
    Oindrila Chakraborty, J.D. Birla Institute, India

Chapter 10
Women and Universities: Determining Factors and Profiles of University Systems According to
Gender Composition 193
    Teodoro Luque-Martínez, University of Granada, Spain
    Nina Faraoni, University of Granada, Spain
    Luis Doña-Toledo, University of Granada, Spain

Chapter 11
Nobody Wants to Work Under These Conditions 216
    Ivania Delgado, Social Work Core Faculty, Pacific Oaks College, USA
    Nafiza Spirko, MSW Graduate Student, USA
    Saudia Rahamat, Community Project Manager/DEI Consultant, Canada

Chapter 12
The Trials and Triumphs of a Solo Mother-Academic 234
    Maureen E. Squires, SUNY Plattsburgh, USA

Chapter 13
A Tale of Two Universities: Primary Carers Working in Australian Universities 257
    Helen Hodgson, Curtin University, Australia
    Dorothea Bowyer, Western Sydney University, Australia

Chapter 14
Motherscholar and MotherLeader: The More Things Change, the More They Stay the Same 284
    Heidi L. Schnackenberg, SUNY Plattsburgh, USA

About the Contributors 296

Index 301

Detailed Table of Contents

Preface xiii

Chapter 1

Stabilizing and Empowering Women in Higher Education: Aligning, Centering, and Building 1
    Natasha N. Johnson, Georgia State University, USA

The importance of higher education in today's world and workforce cannot be overstated. It is well-known that higher education leads to better jobs, higher salaries, and elevated social status. Unfortunately, women have been historically underrepresented in the realm of higher education. In recent years, however, numerous efforts have been made to stabilize and empower women in this arena. As such, this chapter aims to provide an in-depth analysis of these progressive efforts. Stabilizing and empowering women in higher education is essential in promoting gender equality and generational social progress. While substantial gains have been made in recent years, much remains to be done. Universities must continue to support all women in higher education – students, staff, faculty, and leaders alike – through mentorship, work-life balance policies, and opportunities for advancement. Highlighted here is that these efforts will provide women with the support and opportunities necessary to succeed in and beyond the academic sphere.

Chapter 2

Unexpected Dreams 19
    Denise Demers, University of Central Arkansas, USA

Do dreams come true? Dream careers and dream lives? Sometimes yes, maybe no. With unforeseen challenges and detours in life, it is imperative to gain coping skills and a healthy individualized self-care routine. Mental health is of concern as the nation comes out of a global pandemic. It is time for the world to adjust, realign, and create a new system and culture at work as well as home. The author has adopted a motto that has served her well- "If you're not having fun, you're doing something wrong." However, this is not typically taught at home, nor at school, let alone in the workplace. This chapter is the author's story – how she continues to learn how to live authentically according to her values as a woman in higher education and an academic leader. She shares how she continutes to try to adapt, improvise, and overcome by shifting perspectives, creating personalized ways to thrive, and showing grace and acceptance to ourselves and others.

Chapter 3
Toxic Femininity in Higher Education: Academia's Sting in the Tail – The Queen Bee 37
    Catherine Hayes, University of Sunderland, UK

The metaphorical concept of the 'Queen Bee' now transcends situational contexts to such an extent that it has become a universal focus for both contexts of research and professional practice. Global crises provide a unique context of perspective for the manifestations of gender inequity to be revealed within the context of leadership and management in higher education. From an historical perspective a woman whose behaviours were identifiable as being characteristic of a queen bee, became associated with the notion of projected enmity towards other, typically younger women who may be able to compete with them professionally. This chapter will illuminate key aspects of the queen bee complex through a lens of perspective which permits a metacognitive consideration of gender-based standpoints in higher education.

Chapter 4
Informal Mentoring Among Women in Higher Education to Subvert Gender Bias 56
    Clair A. Stocks, Chapman University, USA

This chapter includes a summary of the current environment of higher education for women, an analysis of formal and informal mentoring opportunities and efficacy for women, and recommendations. Women in higher education continue to contend with significant disparities in representation in leadership, biased social norm expectations related to gender, and burdensome professional and personal invisible labor related to service and caretaking. As women face these ongoing and persistent impediments to career progress and ascension, they have created networks of informal mentoring relationships that provide them with support, resources, and resilience as they contend with the male-normed environment of higher education. Informal mentoring relationships are distinct from formal mentoring relationships, as the focus is on providing support for the whole person and not just professional strategy. Informal mentoring is also more accessible to women as the dearth of women in higher education leadership can create a lack of available same-gender formal mentors who have a lens of shared experience.

Chapter 5
Caveats to Accessibility: Does the Promise of On-Line Higher Education Programs Help
Minoritized Women in Higher Education? 72
    Carlene O. Fider, Pacific Oaks College, USA
    Camille Huggins, Pacific Oaks College, USA
    Eugenia Rodriquez, Pacific Oaks College, USA

This chapter explores the use of online education among minoritized women in pursuit of higher education. The chapter is scoped literature review of the current matters that minoritized women experience while pursuing an online education as well as anecdotal case studies of women's journeys of attending and working at online higher education institutions. Online education has made education accessible. Online education is flexible compared to the traditional format. As more minoritized women and non-traditional students utilized the advantages and convenience of online education, the more learning institutions are created. Since online education was instituted and became mainstream, it is available and accessible for all races, ethnicities, and genders. COVID-19 exacerbated issues of being able to access Wi-Fi in public spaces. Given that many online students are balancing multiple roles and responsibilities while pursuing their education, this balancing act illustrates the students' strength, persistence, and their commitment to obtaining an education.

Chapter 6
At the Crossroads: A Social-Ecological Model of Support for Women of Color in Higher
Education Leadership... 87
    Lolita L. Kincade, SUNY Plattsburgh, USA

The proportion of women of color faculty members in academia is on the rise, and they are also more visible in higher education leadership. Yet, systemic sexism and racism, coupled with other forms of intersectional oppression, makes it difficult to advance to senior level administration. This chapter explores the lived experiences of academicians with intersecting identities and proposes a social ecological model to guide the development of effective interventions through social environments. Knowledge applied from personal inquiry, practical examples, and empirical evidence have resulted in important recommendations that are organized into five nested, hierarchical levels. These recommendations can help to improve diversity and inclusion efforts, and to achieve structural and systemic transformation across colleges and universities.

Chapter 7
Black Women Faculty Also Matter: A Paradigm Shift Toward Empowerment and Inclusion in
Higher Education 106
    Portia Allie-Turco, SUNY Plattsburgh, USA

The upheavals caused by the COVID-19 pandemic continue to affect the lives of faculty across the globe. Inasmuch as the pandemic brought profound levels of anxiety, loss, and turmoil, it also created an opportunity to address ineffective and unjust policies in academia. For Black women academics, reflections on the pandemic do not linger on the realignment, reinvention, and reinvigoration of their professional lives because alignment, invention, and invigoration as fully accepted peers in the academy have never existed for them. Instead, the opportunity now is for Black women faculty to step into a space that has never been fully accessible to them as professionals. The pandemic provided an opportunity to recognize pervasive and systemic inequalities for minoritized individuals and communities that have always been reflected in the academy and to create an environment of inclusion and empowerment for everyone. Reimagining academia as an inclusive environment means intentionally challenging racial stereotypes and promoting spaces where Black women faculty feel included and connected.

Chapter 8
Gendered Cultures, Under-Representation, and the Career Challenges of Women Academics in a
South African University 143
    Yaw Owusu-Agyeman, University of the Free State, South Africa
    Reitumetse Mofana, University of the Free State, South Africa

The current study examines how gendered practices in a university in South Africa constrain the career progression of women academics. Drawing on feminist institutionalism, interview data were gathered and analysed from a sample of 20 men and women academics. The study revealed that gendered practices that constrain the career progression of women academics include weak academic nurturing culture, weak collegial relationships and networks among women academics, and preferences for men academics in leadership positions. The findings also revealed that while the women academics indicated that high academic workload, family responsibilities, and unfavourable promotion criteria constrain their career progression, some men participants believed that earmark scholarships and targeted mentoring arrangements for women could create a new class of elites. The study concludes by discussing the implications of the findings in relation to policy, practice, and future research.

Chapter 9
Nurturing and Empowering of Women in Leadership Positions: A Study With Special Reference
to the Indian Subcontinent 161
    Oindrila Chakraborty, J.D. Birla Institute, India

The philosophical dimensions of women's empowerment and nurture in all spheres of life will be addressed in this chapter. Additionally, there will be an effort to look at the problems and obstacles those women's empowerment faces both globally and on the Indian subcontinent. Another endeavor would be launched to examine the situation in the Indian Subcontinent with a small survey of women in senior roles across several industries. The chapter also provided instances of empowered women from the Indian subcontinent.

Chapter 10
Women and Universities: Determining Factors and Profiles of University Systems According to
Gender Composition 193
    Teodoro Luque-Martínez, University of Granada, Spain
    Nina Faraoni, University of Granada, Spain
    Luis Doña-Toledo, University of Granada, Spain

Nowadays, the presence of women in the university is the majority. The question is whether indicators of university results used in university rankings are linked to this presence. The aim of the article is to identify indicators considering different dimensions like teaching or volume of scientific production, analysing in what way the presence of women can be explained. The study involves six international academic rankings. The results showed that certain indicators, such as internationalization or industry income, were those that helped most to discriminate the unequal presence of women among university students. Universities should establish measures for the international recruitment of students and teaching staff, as well as designing measures that favour international collaboration. Likewise, the higher the income, the lower the presence of women, which highlights the scant presence of women following technical and technological courses, which are precisely those sorts of qualifications that capture more resources from industry.

Chapter 11
Nobody Wants to Work Under These Conditions 216
    Ivania Delgado, Social Work Core Faculty, Pacific Oaks College, USA
    Nafiza Spirko, MSW Graduate Student, USA
    Saudia Rahamat, Community Project Manager/DEI Consultant, Canada

This book chapter explores the history of capitalism in the United States and its roots in slavery. It reviews business organizational theories born under the exploitation and dehumanization of enslaved people. The chapter attempts to make the legacies of these systems visible in today's working conditions that have led to the great resignation exacerbated by COVID-19. The chapter, per the authors, uses the context of the education and training of helpers to highlight how these systems impact students in their academic journeys, career opportunities, and financial stability from an intersectional lens. Lastly, as a call to action for readers, it explores the Caremongering movement, a bottom-up mutual aid network that can teach industry management and decision-makers lessons on creating equitable, inclusive conditions that meet the needs of the people.

Chapter 12
The Trials and Triumphs of a Solo Mother-Academic 234
    Maureen E. Squires, SUNY Plattsburgh, USA

It is well documented in the literature that mothers in academia often work a "second shift," performing a majority of the uncompensated labor at home in addition to the compensated labor in the workforce. Further, this second shift is compounded by a "child tax," where mothers are penalized by the academy for caregiving responsibilities. Yet, much of the existing literature on gender disparity among faculty in higher education pertains to two-parent, heterogenous family structures. This results in a significant void and underrepresentation of other groups. The focus of this chapter is "solo parents," specifically solo-mother-academics. A solo parent is one who has no co-parent with whom to share caregiving responsibilities. In this chapter, the author presents a literature review, highlights of the author's experiences as a solo-mother in the academy, and ways to navigate both worlds. This work is influenced by qualitative research methods.

Chapter 13
A Tale of Two Universities: Primary Carers Working in Australian Universities 257
    Helen Hodgson, Curtin University, Australia
    Dorothea Bowyer, Western Sydney University, Australia

Returning to work after a career break can be challenging, accordingly employers implement a range of policies, practices, and strategies to support and retain working parents. This chapter analyses the work-family policies at two universities in the Australian university sector, through the eyes of academic parents. Grounding the discussion in the Australian industrial relations system, the authors examine the lived experience of academic parents drawing on two separate qualitative studies at two different Australian Universities. Initiatives in place to enhance career progression for academic parents are tested against lived experience. The authors find that policies and strategies need to be overhauled and suggest more feasible ones that universities can implement to enable the academic parent, who is juggling an academic career with parenting, to succeed in the post COVID uncertainty faced by the higher education sector.

Chapter 14
Motherscholar and MotherLeader: The More Things Change, the More They Stay the Same 284
    Heidi L. Schnackenberg, SUNY Plattsburgh, USA

For students in higher education, the pandemic brought about some lasting educational changes. There are more online courses and program options, more social-emotional support services, and increased resources to support student learning. Conversely, faculty lives are very similar to what they were before the pandemic, with some notable work-creep. In addition to traditional responsibilities, professors are doing more virtual meetings and online teaching, and devising ways to support students as they find their new normal. For motherscholars, this back-to-normal-plus-extras environment can be devastating. While the refrain to "get back to normal" gave many people comfort, "normal" wasn't such a great space for academic mothers in the first place. Has anything changed for motherscholars and MotherLeaders in higher education post-pandemic? If things haven't changed, then what does that say, about academic mothers and their value in higher education? This chapter will explore this issue and call for an implementation of much-needed practice and policy changes in the academy.

About the Contributors 296

Index 301

Preface

The recent decision by the U.S. Supreme Court to overturn Roe vs. Wade is just one of many events that has rocked women in the United States and across the world. Increased gun violence, the ongoing war in Ukraine, *Black Lives Matter,* the COVID-19 pandemic, the #metoo movement, and an array of other unanticipated occurrences have vastly changed the world we live in, and how we frame ourselves in it (Dodge, Elgert, & Paul, 2022). Since our surroundings, locally, nationally, and globally are currently in constant flux, essentially to the point of turmoil, how we see ourselves and understand who we are within the disarray is in a state of evolution as well (Malcolm, 2022). For most academics, centering themselves and finding stability within their own microcosm is necessary, and healthy, so that they can successfully function in a world in flux (Degn, 2018). Currently, finding stability within oneself often means realigning our priorities, ways of functioning, and goals (Clark & Carl, 2020; De Jong, Ziegler, & Schippers, 2020; Kuntz, 2021). Finding ways to make ourselves whole is empowering, and necessary, to help put our topsy-turvy world back on its axis again.

For women in higher education, recentering or realigning one's sense of self requires assessing primary concerns, desires, and responsibilities and situating them in a healthy way in both the personal and the professional (Puliatte, 2021; Zappala-Piemme, 2021). Given that higher education was founded on a culture of masculinity, the backbone of which still exists today, women struggle to find their voice and space in the academy at the best of times (Schnackenberg & Simard, 2017). Add to that a world in chaos, pushing in on the edges of higher education, and women academics have an expanded burden with which to contend (Schnackenberg & Simard, 2021). Reigniting empowerment for women currently working in colleges or universities requires realigning and recentering - essentially reforming identity - for a world that is reshaping itself before our very eyes.

Stabilizing and Empowering Women in Higher Education: Realigning, Recentering, and Rebuilding intends to inform readers and expand their understanding about specific challenges, issues, strategies, and solutions that are associated with women leaders in higher education, and the particular implications for realigning, recentering, and reinvigorating themselves both personally and professionally. The book includes a variety of emerging evidence-based professional practice and narrative personal accounts as written by administrators, faculty, staff, and/or students - anyone in a position of leadership who is keenly aware of the challenges faced by women leaders in the academy. The work is of value to women in leadership, faculty in higher education, administrators in higher education, higher education professional staff, researchers. instructors, administrators, professional personnel, and graduate students.

The current volume is different from other books currently published because it focuses on women leaders in education and the ways in which they've navigated the recent social, legal, cultural, and economic changes in society, and how these changes have brought about alteration and restoration to their sense of self, work-life balance, and identification and focus on priorities. While a host of other books and articles have focused on the effects of the pandemic and other social upheavals on the work lives of women, and women in higher education, this volume focuses on the process of the evolution of their identities during the crises. *Stabilizing and Empowering Women in Higher Education: Realigning, Recentering, and Rebuilding* brings to light and shares stories and research on how women academics create stability in their lives and empower themselves and others in times of uncertainty and confusion.

Heidi L. Schnackenberg
SUNY Plattsburgh, USA

Denise A. Simard
SUNY Plattsburgh, USA

REFERENCES

Clark, D., & Carl, P. (June 15, 2020). How to reset your goals during a crisis. *Harvard Business Review*. https://hbr.org/2020/06/how-to-reset-your-goals-during-a-crisis

De Jong, E. M., Ziegler, N., & Schippers, M. C. (2020). From shattered goals to meaning in life: Life crafting in times of the COVID-19 pandemic. *Frontiers in Psychology*, *11*, 577708. doi:10.3389/fpsyg.2020.577708 PMID:33178081

Degn, L. (2018). Academic sensemaking and behavioural responses - exploring how academics perceive and respond to identity threats in times of turmoil. *Studies in Higher Education*, *23*(2), 305–321. doi:10.1080/03075079.2016.1168796

Dodge, J., Elgert, L., & Paul, R. (2022). On the social relevance of Critical Policy Studies in times of turmoil. *Critical Policy Studies*, *16*(2), 131–132. doi:10.1080/19460171.2022.2060844

Kuntz, J. C. (2021). Resilience in times of global pandemic: Steering recovery and thriving trajectories. *Applied Psychology*, *70*(1), 188–215. doi:10.1111/apps.12296 PMID:33362330

Malcolm, D. R. (2022). The challenge of coming to terms with evolving priorities. *American Journal of Pharmaceutical Education*, *86*(2), ajpe8664. doi:10.5688/ajpe8664 PMID:35228200

Puliatte, A. (2021). Women academic leaders and self-care during a crisis. In H. L. Schnackenberg & D. A. Simard (Eds.), *Women and leadership in higher education during global crisis* (pp. 175–189). IGI Global. doi:10.4018/978-1-7998-6491-2.ch011

Schnackenberg, H. L., & Simard, D. A. (2017). *Challenges facing female department chairs in contemporary higher education: Emerging research and opportunities*. IGI Global. doi:10.4018/978-1-5225-1891-4

Schnackenberg, H. L., & Simard, D. A. (Eds.). (2021). *Women and leadership in higher education during global crisis*. IGI Global. doi:10.4018/978-1-7998-6491-2

Preface

Zappala-Piemme, K. E. (2021). Caring for yourself and keeping connected during the COVID-19 pandemic. In H. L. Schnackenberg & D. A. Simard (Eds.), *Women and leadership in higher education during global crisis* (pp. 147–158). IGI Global. doi:10.4018/978-1-7998-6491-2.ch009

Chapter 1
Stabilizing and Empowering Women in Higher Education:
Aligning, Centering, and Building

Natasha N. Johnson
https://orcid.org/0000-0001-8145-2153
Georgia State University, USA

ABSTRACT

The importance of higher education in today's world and workforce cannot be overstated. It is well-known that higher education leads to better jobs, higher salaries, and elevated social status. Unfortunately, women have been historically underrepresented in the realm of higher education. In recent years, however, numerous efforts have been made to stabilize and empower women in this arena. As such, this chapter aims to provide an in-depth analysis of these progressive efforts. Stabilizing and empowering women in higher education is essential in promoting gender equality and generational social progress. While substantial gains have been made in recent years, much remains to be done. Universities must continue to support all women in higher education – students, staff, faculty, and leaders alike – through mentorship, work-life balance policies, and opportunities for advancement. Highlighted here is that these efforts will provide women with the support and opportunities necessary to succeed in and beyond the academic sphere.

INTRODUCTION

"If you educate a man, you educate an individual. But if you educate a woman, you educate a nation."
– African Proverb[1]

The importance of higher education in today's world and workforce cannot be overstated (Johnson, 2014). It is a known fact that higher education leads to better jobs, better salaries, and better social status (Osterman & Shulman, 2011; Wiles, 1974). Unfortunately, women have been historically underrepresented in higher education (Alemán & Renn, 2002; Cronin & Roger, 1999; Krause, 2017). In recent

DOI: 10.4018/978-1-6684-8597-2.ch001

Copyright © 2023, IGI Global. Copying or distributing in print or electronic forms without written permission of IGI Global is prohibited.

years, however, numerous efforts have been made to stabilize and empower women in higher education (DiGeorgio-Lutz, 2002; Sharma & Afroz, 2014). Women's suffrage and civil rights movements marked significant milestones in the history and advancement of women's empowerment initiatives (Marino, 2019; Olson, 2001).

Figure 1. Women in higher education timeline

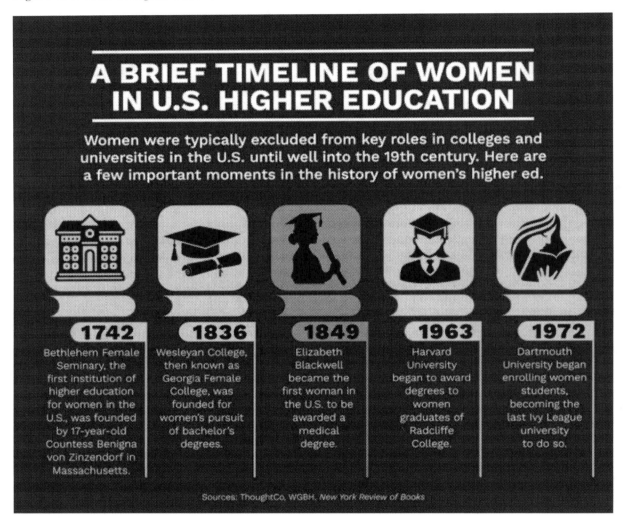

As shown in Figure 1 – *Women in Higher Education Timeline*, women were typically excluded from key roles in colleges and universities in the United States until well into the 19th century (Beard, 1916; Hill et al., 2016). Gender equity remains a challenge, even 100 years after recognizing women's right to vote (Perrons, 2009; Winchester & Browning, 2015). Although women have made noteworthy strides in advancing their status in various fields – including higher education – disparities remain extant (DeWitt, 2016; Noble & Moore, 2006). In higher education, women have successfully broken through the gender

Stabilizing and Empowering Women in Higher Education

barrier but are still underrepresented in specific disciplinary sectors and many top-level leadership positions (Johnson, 2021; Johnson & Fournillier, 2022, 2023).

Without question, gains have been made regarding the participation of women in society, politics, education, and employment. Nevertheless, the representation of women in positions of power and influence has been conspicuously less progressive (Goethals & Hoyt, 2017; Crowe et al., 2018; Slaughter, 2015). Although women have made noteworthy strides in advancing their status in various fields – including higher education – disparities remain extant. In higher education settings, women have been able to break through the gender barrier (Aiston, 2011; Eddy & Ward, 2017; Rosa & Clavero, 2022). However, they are still underrepresented in specific disciplinary sectors and in many top-level leadership positions across the board (Hoyt, 2010; Siemiatycki, 2019; Thomas, 2017).

The reasons behind women's underrepresentation in higher education vary, ranging from familial and cultural attitudes to financial issues. Women have long been viewed as less capable than men in specific fields (El-Amin, 2022; Smith & Johnson, 2019). Additionally, the cost associated with obtaining a higher education degree can be prohibitive for some women. However, there has been considerable progress in recent years. Many universities have implemented policies actively encouraging women to pursue higher education degrees. Scholarships and financial aid packages have also been introduced to help women overcome financial obstacles.

THEORIES ON WOMEN IN HIGHER EDUCATION

"Education is one thing no one can take away from you." – Elin Nordegren

Several theories attempt to explain the experiences and challenges faced by women in higher education, including the following five outlined below:

1. *Gender schema theory:* This theory suggests that individuals develop gender schemas or mental frameworks that influence their beliefs, attitudes, and behaviors. Women are often socialized to believe that specific fields or disciplines are unsuitable to and for them. Unfortunately, this may lead them to avoid pursuing these areas of study or encountering gender bias and discrimination when they do (see Bem, 1987; Davis & Wilson, 2016; Starr & Zurbriggen, 2017).
2. *Intersectionality theory:* Recognizes that women's experiences in higher education are shaped by the intersection of multiple social identities, such as race, class, sexual orientation, and ability. Women with various marginalized identities may face compounded barriers to success in higher education (see Carbado et al., 2013; Cho et al., 2013; Hancock, 2016; Nash, 2017).
3. *Stereotype threat theory:* This theory suggests that women who are cognizant of negative stereotypes about their gender may experience anxiety and decreased performance in academic settings. These experiences can contribute to lower retention rates and achievement levels for women in higher education (see Goff et al., 2008; Martens et al., 2006).
4. *Socialization theory* posits that individuals are socialized into gender roles and expectations from a very young age. Women may, over time, be socialized to prioritize caretaking and nurturing roles, which can conflict with the demands of academic work and make it more difficult for them to balance academic and personal responsibilities (see Carter, 2014; Grusec & Hastings, 2014; Stockard, 2006).

5. ***Structural theory:*** Focuses on the systemic and institutional factors that create barriers to success for women in higher education, such as biased hiring and promotion practices, lack of access to funding and resources, and insufficient support systems for balancing work and family responsibilities (see Arlow & Brenner, 1964; Friedkin, 1998; Wingood & DiClemente, 2002).

Together, these theories highlight the complex and multifaceted nature of the challenges faced by all women in higher education – students, staff, faculty, and leaders alike – and the need for systemic changes to address these issues (Parker, 2015; Shaukat & Pell, 2015).

The Importance of Equity

Equity in higher education is crucial because it ensures that all individuals have an equal opportunity to access and succeed in higher education, regardless of their socioeconomic background, race, gender, or other personal characteristics. There are several reasons why equity in higher education is essential. Firstly, equity promotes social mobility. Higher education can serve as a pathway to upward social mobility. However, certain groups may be left behind without equity in access and success, perpetuating social inequalities (Haveman & Smeeding, 2006; Navarette et al., 2017). Secondly, equity enhances economic growth. A diverse and well-educated workforce is essential for economic growth and development. Equity in higher education ensures that individuals from all backgrounds can contribute to and benefit from a thriving economy (Bourguignon & Dessus, 2009; Duflo, 2012).

Third, equity fosters a diverse and inclusive society. A multicultural, pluralistic academic body (i.e., students, staff, and faculty) can enrich the educational experience and promote cultural understanding. Equity in higher education promotes a more inclusive society that values and celebrates diversity (Allen, 2023; Winters, 2020). In addition, equity addresses systemic inequalities. Historically, certain groups have been excluded from higher education due to bias, nepotism, and large-scale systemic disparities. Equity in higher education is essential to addressing these inequalities and promoting social justice (Forcier et al., 2021; Richerme, 2021).

Thus, to achieve equity in higher education, institutions must address the various barriers that prevent equal access and success for all constituents. This work includes ensuring adequate financial support, providing academic and social support services, and addressing institutional biases and discrimination across the board (see Johnson, 2023; Schnackenberg & Simard, 2023; Thomas, 2019).

Equity for Women in Higher Education

Specific to women in higher education, equity for women is critical to achieving overall fairness and impartiality in higher education. Despite progress in recent years, gender inequalities persist in higher education, particularly in leadership positions and in certain academic disciplines (Eloy et al., 2013). Here, among others, are four reasons why equity for women in higher education is crucial: (1) *Equity for women promotes gender equality.* Women comprise roughly half of the population and should have an equal opportunity to access and succeed in higher education. Equity for women in higher education helps break down gender barriers and promote gender equality (De Welde & Stepnick, 2023). (2) *Equity for women increases diversity.* Women bring different experiences and perspectives to the classroom and academic research, enriching the educational experience for everyone. Equity for women in higher education promotes diversity in academia (Johnson, 2021; Johnson & Fournillier, 2022, 2023).

Stabilizing and Empowering Women in Higher Education

Further, (3) _Equity for women promotes economic growth._ Women with higher education degrees earn more and are more likely to contribute to economic growth. Equity for women in higher education ensures they have equal chances to access and benefit from the tools gained in higher education (Duflo, E. (2012). (4) _Equity for women specifically addresses systemic gender inequalities._ Women have historically been underrepresented in higher education, particularly in leadership positions and specific academic disciplines. Equity for women in higher education is necessary to address these and other systemic gender inequalities (Guthridge et al., 2022).

To promote the advancement of women in higher education, then, institutions can take several steps, including implementing policies to address gender bias, providing mentorship and support for women, and increasing the representation of women in leadership positions and in underrepresented academic disciplines (Graham, 2019). It is necessary to recognize that equity for women in higher education is not just a women's issue but an issue that affects society as a whole. Every constituency member has a role to play in achieving equity and justice.

STABILIZING AND EMPOWERING WOMEN IN HIGHER EDUCATION

"No country can ever truly flourish if it stifles the potential of its women and deprives itself of the contributions of half of its citizens." – Michelle Obama

One of the most efficient ways to stabilize and empower women in higher education is through mentorship programs. These programs provide women with access to experienced female academics in their field who can offer guidance, support, and motivation. They also provide networking opportunities, which can be invaluable in securing employment opportunities. These and related strategies ensure that women are afforded, at minimum, equal opportunities to pursue higher education degrees and advance in academia (De Welde & Stepnick, 2023).

In addition, universities have implemented policies that promote work-life balance for female academics. These policies include flexible scheduling, part-time options, and job-sharing. Such measures help women balance their academic pursuits with family responsibilities. Stabilizing women in higher education involves ensuring they have the resources, support, and opportunities to pursue their academic and professional goals without facing discrimination or barriers to advancement. Empowering women in higher education involves providing them with the tools, resources, and support required to succeed academically and professionally. Stabilizing and empowering women is crucial for achieving gender equality and promoting social and economic development.

Relevant leaders, researchers, academics, and community members agree that this can be accomplished by providing equal opportunities for women (Coles & Francesconi, 2019). Women should, naturally, be provided with equal access to higher education, scholarships, fellowships, and other resources. These opportunities enable them to pursue their academic goals without discrimination or barriers. Further, higher education institutions should actively encourage women to participate in research, conferences, and other educational activities (see Antoniou & Apergi, 2019). These and other actions will help create a more inclusive and diverse academic community. In this same vein, universities and colleges must continue promoting gender-sensitive policies (Stromquist, 2020, 2022). There should be palpable procedures sensitive to women's needs, including maternity leave, flexible working arrangements, and childcare support. These judgment-free actions go a long way to ensure that women are not disadvantaged in their academic pursuits due to family responsibilities.

Stabilizing and empowering women in higher education includes good, *active* relationship-building (Brown, 2005; Graham, 2019). Leaders must work to ensure that female students, faculty, and staff receive mentorship and guidance from senior women in their respective fields. This level of assistance helps build supportive networks and enables women to navigate the challenges of higher education. Overtly combating gender-based violence (Bosco Damous & Guillopé, 2021) is a primary example. Universities and colleges should have policies and procedures in place to address gender-based violence, including sexual harassment and assault. This intentionality will lead to the development of safe and supportive environments for women in higher education. Given the sheer importance of leadership, empowering women's leadership (see Longman & Madsen, 2014) is a must. Women should be encouraged and supported to take on leadership roles in academia. This support will help to break down gender stereotypes and promote women's voices in decision-making processes.

As outlined above, stabilizing and empowering women in higher education requires a large-scale and concerted effort from universities, governments, and society members. We all have a part to play in creating more inclusive and equitable academic environments for women. Stabilization and empowerment can be achieved by providing equal opportunities, encouraging participation, promoting gender-sensitive policies, providing mentorship, combating gender-based violence, and empowering women's leadership (Krause, 2017; Longman & Madsen, 2014; Lyness & Grotto, 2018).

Aligning with Women in Higher Education

"Women share this planet 50/50 and they are underrepresented—their potential astonishingly untapped." – *Emma Watson*

Gender equity strategies that respond to women's unique challenges in higher education must be developed and strengthened. Through research into gendered hierarchies, societal impositions on gender norms, and identification of such biases and stereotypes, perceptive institutional policies can be created to ensure equal access and opportunities for women. Policies and initiatives such as equitable access to funding, family-friendly benefits (such as support for parental duties and childcare), equal access to faculty positions, and salary parity can help realign higher education settings toward gender equity.

Figure 2 – *Women in Higher Education – The Numbers Behind the Story* covers a 40-year timeline between 1972 and 2014, in which Title IX (1972) ensured equal access to higher education for both sexes:

Stabilizing and Empowering Women in Higher Education

Figure 2. Women in higher education: The numbers behind the story[2]

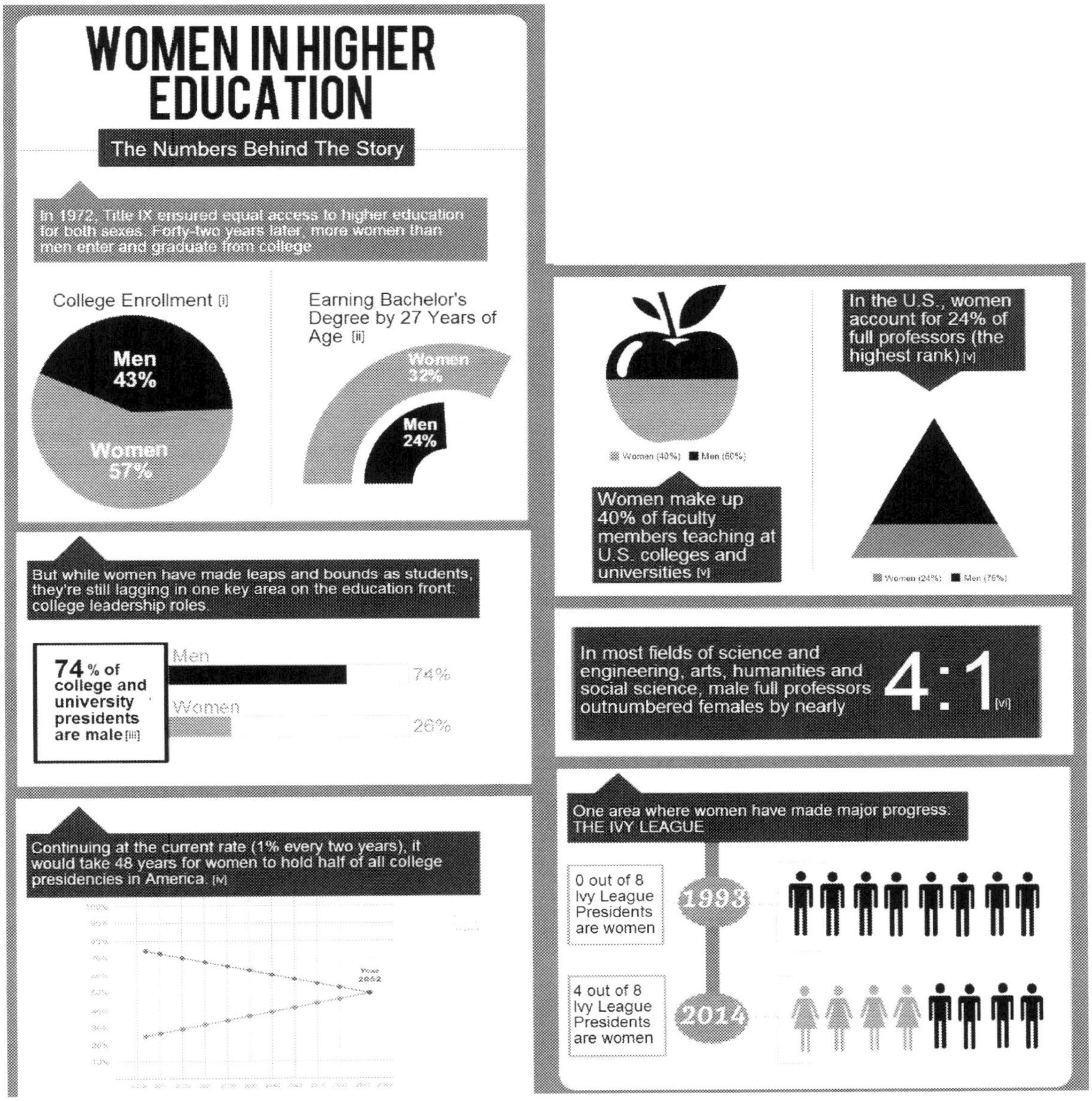

Over 40 years later (2014-present), more women than men enter and graduate from college. While women have made leaps and bounds in the academic sphere, they are still lagging in one key education area: top-level leadership roles. To date, roughly 74% of college and university presidents are male. Across all fields (e.g., science and engineering, arts, humanities, and social science, etcetera), male full professors have and continue to outnumber females by nearly 4 to 1 (David, 2015; Hill et al., 2016; Sheltzer & Smith, 2014).

Women continue to face numerous challenges, such as pay gaps, discriminatory policies and practices, the ongoing struggle to balance work, family, and other responsibilities (Johnson, 2021), and a lack of appreciation for their academic scholarship and teaching contributions. Realigning, recentering, and rebuilding efforts are necessary to tackle these challenges and ensure women thrive in higher education settings. This work, then, should focus primarily on aligning and forging alliances with women (Allan et al., 2006), centering women's voices and experiences (Osei-Kofi et al., 2010), and emphasizing and promoting community building (Sandmann & Jones, 2023), all in – and beyond – the context of higher education.

Centering Women in Higher Education

"We educate women because it is smart. We educate women because it changes the world." – Drew Faust

Centering women and women's experiences in the context of higher education is primary. Women must be recognized for their academic scholarship and teaching contributions as with any other subgroup. Creating spaces where women can have their voices heard and their concerns addressed is essential to making the progress we seek. Fewer academic women participate in publications, conference presentations, and reviews, which is a significant concern. Increasing academic recognition for women's work, such as instituting gender equity awards to appreciate women's research and teaching efforts and creating exclusive academic networks, can recenter women in higher education.

In the context of higher education, centering women involves prioritizing their needs, experiences, and perspectives in all aspects of the academic environment, from policies and practices to curriculum and pedagogy. Centering women can involve a variety of initiatives and strategies, including the following five supports:

1. ***Gender-responsive policies and practices*** (Wattanaporn & Holtfreter, 2014): Creating procedures and policies that are responsive to the needs of women students, faculty, and staff. This work can include policies related to sexual harassment and gender-based violence, parental leave, flexible work arrangements, and support for women in leadership positions;
2. ***Curriculum and pedagogy*** (Khalil et al., 2023): This means ensuring that the curriculum and pedagogy in higher education are inclusive and reflect women's experiences, voices, and perspectives. Strategies can include integrating feminist and gender studies into the curriculum, creating women's studies programs, and promoting women's voices in classroom discussions and research;
3. ***Support services*** (Pasque & Nicholson, 2011): Providing support services that are tailored to the needs of women students, such as career services, networking programs, and counseling services;
4. ***Diversity, equity, and inclusion (DEI)*** (Barnett, 2020): Creating a culture of diversity, equity, and inclusion that supports women students, faculty, and staff. This work can include promoting diversity in hiring and promotion practices, providing training on unconscious bias and microaggressions, and creating opportunities for dialogue and collaboration across different groups; and
5. ***Research and scholarship*** (Hart, 2006): Encouraging and supporting research and scholarship that explores issues related to gender and women's experiences in higher education. Strategies can include funding research on gender disparities in pay and promotion, researching and spotlighting women's experiences in STEM fields, and promoting interdisciplinary research focusing on women's issues.

Stabilizing and Empowering Women in Higher Education

In sum, centering all women in higher education requires a commitment to gender equity and recognizing women's unique challenges and opportunities in academic settings. By prioritizing women's needs, experiences, and perspectives, higher education institutions can create more inclusive and supportive environments that benefit all academic community members (Barnett, 2020; Hart, 2006; Khalil et al., 2023; Wattanaporn & Holtfreter, 2014).

Community Building in Higher Education

"Young women who want an education will not be stopped." – Freida Pinto

A culture of diversity and inclusion must be ingrained into higher education settings. Educators and other stakeholders in higher education must commit to rebuilding academic spaces that undermine gender equity efforts. Institutions must identify and eliminate harmful policies and cultures that hinder women's advancement. Coaching and relevant professional development programs that address gender biases and help women strive for tenure are not as common as they need to be in academia. Building a robust institutional culture that supports gender equity can help rebuild trust and relationships among female faculty members, helping to maintain a safe academic environment. Community building in higher education involves creating a sense of belonging and connection among students, faculty, and staff within the educational environment (Fitzgerald et al., 2020).

Building a sense of community can involve a combination of initiatives and strategies, including strengthening student organizations as a pipeline to navigating in and beyond academia. This work can include organizations focused on cultural identity, service, leadership, and academic interests. These programs can be particularly beneficial for women who may feel disconnected or isolated from the greater educational community as they continue traversing the sphere. Collaborative learning provides ample opportunity to encourage and facilitate collaborative learning opportunities among students, staff, and faculty alike (Sandmann & Jones, 2023). This work can include group projects, team-based assignments, and peer review sessions.

Incorporating service learning opportunities into academic programs can allow shareholders to engage with the larger community and build connections beyond the educational environment. Campus events offer numerous opportunities to bring together academic community members. Some examples can include cultural celebrations, guest speakers, and social events. Finally, the continued creation of inclusive cultures directly promotes community building and engagement. These efforts can move the needle beyond promoting diversity in hiring and promotion practices and unconscious bias and microaggressions training to actively support and create opportunities for collaboration and empowerment across all spectra (Sandmann & Jones, 2023).

Community building in higher education is critical for creating a supportive and inclusive academic environment. A most suitable climate involves those who intentionally promote academic success, personal growth, and advancement opportunities for all. By fostering a sense of belonging and connection, higher education institutions can create a culture that supports and empowers all academic community members (Sandmann & Jones, 2023; Welch, 2023).

SUPPORTING WOMEN AND WOMEN LEADERSHIP IN HIGHER EDUCATION

"We want the education by which character is formed, strength of mind is increased, the intellect is expanded, and by which one can stand on one's own feet." – Swami Vivekananda

Supporting Women in Higher Education

Empowering women in higher education involves providing them with the tools, support, and resources necessary to succeed academically and professionally. Stakeholders and institutions can support women in higher education by promoting leadership opportunities. Universities and colleges should actively promote leadership opportunities for women in academia. These efforts include encouraging women to take on leadership roles in student organizations, faculty governance, and other academic groups. In addition, it is essential to promote women's research and publication. Women in academia should be encouraged to pursue these and other related opportunities (e.g., funding). This work can help to build their academic credentials and promote their professional development. In this way, allies have a stake in uplifting and advancing women's voices in and beyond the academic sphere (Mayya et al., 2021).

Universities and colleges should have procedures in place that are sensitive to the needs of women (including, but not limited to, maternity leave, flexible working arrangements, and childcare support). We must ensure that women are not disadvantaged in their academic pursuits due to family responsibilities and other internal or external factors. Moreover, educational institutions should work to address gender bias in hiring, promotion, and tenure decisions (Fitzgerald et al., 2020). These efforts can include unconscious bias training for faculty and staff and promoting diverse representation in academic leadership positions. Finally, providing financial support for all remains a top priority. Women in higher education may face financial barriers due to systemic inequalities such as the gender pay gap. Universities and colleges can provide financial support through scholarships, grants, fellowships, and other resources to help women overcome these barriers.

Thus, empowering women in higher education requires a multifaceted approach. It must coalesce to address systemic inequalities, provide resources and support, and promote diversity and inclusion (Coles & Francesconi, 2019; Hoyt, 2010). By working to empower women in academia, we can create a more inclusive and equitable academic environment for all.

Supporting Women Leaders Higher Education

Women's leadership in higher education is critical for achieving equity and promoting diversity in academia. While progress has been made in recent years, women remain underrepresented in top-level leadership positions in higher education. There are four important reasons why women's leadership in higher education matters: (1) *Women in leadership promote and advance gender diversity*. Women bring unique perspectives and experiences to leadership roles, which can help to promote diversity and inclusion in higher education (Goethals & Hoyt, 2017); (2) *Women in leadership address gender inequalities*. Women continue to face barriers to leadership in higher education, including gender bias, structural inequalities, and lack of support. Women's leadership can help to address these inequalities and promote gender equity in academia (Lyness & Grotto, 2018).

Further, (3) *Women in leadership provide other women with role models*. Women leaders in higher education serve as role models for students, faculty, and staff, particularly for young women who may

Stabilizing and Empowering Women in Higher Education

be considering pursuing leadership positions in academia (Smith & Johnson, 2019; Thomas, 2019); and (4) *Women in leadership improve overall organizational effectiveness.* Diverse leadership teams have been shown to improve organizational effectiveness and decision-making. Women's leadership in higher education can help improve academic institutions' efficiency whole-scale (Gipson et al., 2017).

As such, institutions can take several steps to promote women's leadership in higher education. These actions include implementing policies to address gender bias in hiring and promotion, providing mentorship and support for women leaders, and increasing the representation of women in leadership positions (Guramatunhu-Mudiwa & Angel, 2022). It is necessary to recognize that women's leadership in higher education is not just a women's issue but an issue that affects the entire academic community (Mayya et al., 2021). Everyone, again, has a role to play in promoting and advancing equity by stabilizing and empowering women in higher education.

THE IMPORTANCE OF ALIGNING, CENTERING, AND BUILDING WOMEN IN HIGHER EDUCATION

"The education and empowerment of women throughout the world cannot fail to result in a more caring, tolerant, just, and peaceful life for all." – Aung San Suu Kyi

Among other areas in which direct growth is and continues to occur, women currently have higher college enrollment and completion rates than men. They outnumber men in undergraduate and graduate programs, with a ratio of 1.4 to 1 in undergraduate and 1.6 to 1 in graduate programs. However, despite their higher enrollment and completion rates, women often face more significant student loan debt than men. Women college graduates are more likely to have student loan debt and carry higher balances than their male counterparts. Other challenges and disparities unique to women in higher education include lower workforce pay and higher rates of mental health diagnoses. Despite making up the majority of college students, women are underrepresented among college faculty, in leadership, and they face disparities in various aspects of academia. Today's college completion rates speak to the growing gender gap in college completion, with young women being more likely to enroll in college and have a four-year college degree than young men. Women's educational gains have occurred alongside increased labor force participation and economic changes. College completion strongly correlates with higher lifetime earnings and more significant wealth accumulation (Alemán & Renn, 2002; DiGeorgio-Lutz, 2002).

Sociocultural Change and Women's Higher Education

Women's increased participation in higher education is both a force for and a consequence of sociocultural changes. The rise in women's higher education participation is linked to broader social transformations and has been studied concerning various variables, including social change indicators. Additionally, historical struggles continue to impact extant progress. For women, the journey toward higher education attainment and equality remains marked by historical inequities. Until the 19th century, for example, women were effectively barred from higher education, but they gradually gained access to education by establishing women's colleges and coed institutions. Progress continues to be made, but challenges such as pay equality and stereotypes persist.

Representation and Leadership in Higher Education

Achieving gender parity in higher education requires addressing issues of representation and leadership. Efforts are underway to increase the number of women leaders in higher education, such as promoting women's representation in high-ranking leadership positions and challenging the notion of a 'pipeline myth' suggesting a shortage of qualified women for leadership roles and responsibilities. For women of color, the ramifications of intersectionality remain ongoing. Women of color face additional challenges in higher education. Disparities exist in enrollment, graduation rates, advanced degree attainment, and representation in leadership positions. Addressing these disparities is essential for achieving equity and inclusivity in higher education (Krause, 2017; Longman & Madsen, 2014; Lyness & Grotto, 2018).

On a global scale, ensuring access to quality education for all girls and young women and providing leadership and advancement opportunities is more than a human right. Equity is (and should continue to be) an international development priority in this capacity. Educating and advancing the paths of girls and women has wide-ranging benefits, including improved health outcomes, reduced poverty, and increased social and economic empowerment. Moreover, recognizing the importance of women in higher education and addressing the challenges they face is crucial for achieving gender equality, promoting diversity and inclusion, and creating a more equitable and prosperous society.

CONCLUSION

"The more we pull together toward a new day, the less it matters what pushed us apart in the past." – *Johnnetta Cole, PhD*

Stabilizing and empowering women in higher education is essential in promoting gender equality and social progress. While sizable progress has been made in recent years, much remains to be done. Universities must continue to support women in higher education through mentorship programs, work-life balance policies, and opportunities for advancement (Graham, 2019). These efforts will provide women with the support and opportunities necessary to succeed in and beyond academia. Thus, creating a culture of gender equity and inclusion in higher education depends on realignment, recentering, and rebuilding efforts. These strategies focus on creating pool opportunities for women and creating safe spaces that appreciate and celebrate their work. Such an environment can strengthen women's career paths in higher education settings, eliminate gender biases and stereotypes, and prepare the way for the next generation of women in academia.

In recent years, various efforts have been made to stabilize and empower women in higher education. Stabilizing and empowering women in higher education is essential in promoting gender equality and social progress (Schnackenberg & Simard, 2023). While substantial progress continues to be made in recent years, there is still more work to do. The importance of higher education in today's world and workforce cannot be overstated, and university settings play a role in executing the school-work-advancement pipeline for women (Crowe et al., 2018; Welch, M. (2023). As such, this chapter highlights that these efforts will provide all women in higher education – students, staff, faculty, and leaders alike – with the support and opportunities necessary to continue succeeding in and beyond the academic sphere.

Stabilizing and Empowering Women in Higher Education

REFERENCES

Aiston, S. J. (2011). Equality, justice and gender: Barriers to the ethical university for women. *Ethics and Education*, *6*(3), 279–291. doi:10.1080/17449642.2011.632721

Alemán, A. M. M., & Renn, K. A. (2002). *Women in higher education: An encyclopedia*. ABC-CLIO.

Allan, E. J., Gordon, S. P., & Iverson, S. V. (2006). Re/thinking practices of power: The discursive framing of leadership in The Chronicle of Higher Education. *Review of Higher Education*, *30*(1), 41–68. doi:10.1353/rhe.2006.0045

Allen, B. J. (2023). *Difference matters: Communicating social identity*. Waveland Press.

Antoniou, A. S., & Apergi, M. (2019). 6. Gender and leadership in education. *Women, Business and Leadership: Gender and Organisations*, 94.

Arlow, J. A., & Brenner, C. (1964). *Psychoanalytic concepts and the structural theory*. APA.

Barnett, R. (2020). Leading with meaning: Why diversity, equity, and inclusion matters in US higher education. *Perspectives in Education*, *38*(2), 20–35. doi:10.18820/2519593X/pie.v38.i2.02

Beard, M. R. (1916). Woman's work in municipalities. D. Appleton.

Bem, S. L. (1987). Gender schema theory and the romantic tradition. In P. Shaver & C. Hendrick (Eds.), *Sex and gender* (pp. 251–271). Sage Publications, Inc.

Bosco Damous, L., & Guillopé, C. (2021). Gender-based violence in higher education and research: A European perspective. *Pure and Applied Chemistry*, *93*(8), 899–905. doi:10.1515/pac-2021-0401

Bourguignon, F., & Dessus, S. (2009). Equity and development: Political economy considerations. *No Growth without Equity?*, *45*.

Brown, T. M. (2005). Mentorship and the female college president. *Sex Roles*, *52*(9-10), 659–666. doi:10.100711199-005-3733-7

Carbado, D. W., Crenshaw, K. W., Mays, V. M., & Tomlinson, B. (2013). INTERSECTIONALITY: Mapping the Movements of a Theory1. *Du Bois Review*, *10*(2), 303–312. doi:10.1017/S1742058X13000349 PMID:25285150

Carter, M. J. (2014). Gender socialization and identity theory. *Social Sciences (Basel, Switzerland)*, *3*(2), 242–263. doi:10.3390ocsci3020242

Cho, S., Crenshaw, K. W., & McCall, L. (2013). Toward a field of intersectionality studies: Theory, applications, and praxis. *Signs (Chicago, Ill.)*, *38*(4), 785–810. doi:10.1086/669608

Coles, M. G., & Francesconi, M. (2019). Equilibrium search with multiple attributes and the impact of equal opportunities for women. *Journal of Political Economy*, *127*(1), 138–162. doi:10.1086/700731

Cronin, C., & Roger, A. (1999). Theorizing progress: Women in science, engineering, and technology in higher education. *Journal of Research in Science Teaching*, *36*(6), 637–661. doi:10.1002/(SICI)1098-2736(199908)36:6<637::AID-TEA4>3.0.CO;2-9

Crowe, A. R., Collins, C., & Harper, B. (2018). Struggling to let our selves live and thrive: Three women's collaborative self-study on leadership. *Pushing boundaries and crossing borders: Self-study as a means for researching pedagogy*, 311-318.

David, M. E. (2015). Women and gender equality in higher education? *Education Sciences*, *5*(1), 10–25. doi:10.3390/educsci5010010

Davis, T., & Wilson, J. M. (2016). Gender schema theory. The Wiley Blackwell Encyclopedia of Gender and sexuality studies, 1-3.

De Welde, K., & Stepnick, A. (Eds.). (2023). *Disrupting the culture of silence: Confronting gender inequality and making change in higher education*. Taylor & Francis.

DeWitt, P. M. (2016). *Collaborative leadership: Six influences that matter most*. Corwin Press.

DiGeorgio-Lutz, J. (Ed.). (2002). *Women in higher education: Empowering change*. Greenwood Publishing Group.

Duflo, E. (2012). Women empowerment and economic development. *Journal of Economic Literature*, *50*(4), 1051–1079. doi:10.1257/jel.50.4.1051

Eddy, P. L., & Ward, K. (2017). Problematizing gender in higher education: Why leaning in isn't enough. *Critical approaches to women and gender in higher education*, 13-39.

El-Amin, A. (Ed.). (2022). *Implementing Diversity, Equity, Inclusion, and Belonging in Educational Management Practices*. IGI Global., doi:10.4018/978-1-6684-4803-8

Eloy, J. A., Svider, P. F., Cherla, D. V., Diaz, L., Kovalerchik, O., Mauro, K. M., Baredes, S., & Chandrasekhar, S. S. (2013). Gender disparities in research productivity among 9952 academic physicians. *The Laryngoscope*, *123*(8), 1865–1875. doi:10.1002/lary.24039 PMID:23568709

Fitzgerald, H. E., Bruns, K., Sonka, S. T., Furco, A., & Swanson, L. (2020). The centrality of engagement in higher education. In *Building the Field of Higher Education Engagement* (pp. 201–219). Routledge.

Forcier, M., Wagner, J., & Holland, S. (2021). Gender diverse youth: Opportunities to identify and address systemic inequities. *Pediatrics*, *147*(6), e2021050278. doi:10.1542/peds.2021-050278 PMID:34006617

Friedkin, N. E. (1998). *A structural theory of social influence*. Cambridge University Press. doi:10.1017/CBO9780511527524

Gipson, A. N., Pfaff, D. L., Mendelsohn, D. B., Catenacci, L. T., & Burke, W. W. (2017). Women and leadership: Selection, development, leadership style, and performance. *The Journal of Applied Behavioral Science*, *53*(1), 32–65. doi:10.1177/0021886316687247

Goethals, G., & Hoyt, C. (2017). *Woman and Leadership: History. Theories and Case Studies, Great Barrington*. Berskshire Publishing.

Goff, P. A., Steele, C. M., & Davies, P. G. (2008). The space between us: Stereotype threat and distance in interracial contexts. *Journal of Personality and Social Psychology*, *94*(1), 91–107. doi:10.1037/0022-3514.94.1.91 PMID:18179320

Stabilizing and Empowering Women in Higher Education

Graham, C. (2019). Literature review: The gap between mentoring theory and practice for diverse women faculty. *Mentoring & Tutoring, 27*(2), 131–143. doi:10.1080/13611267.2019.1611273

Grusec, J. E., & Hastings, P. D. (Eds.). (2014). *Handbook of socialization: Theory and research.* Guilford Publications.

Guramatunhu-Mudiwa, P., & Angel, R. (2022). Women and Professional Generativity: Voices from the Field. *Advancing Women in Leadership Journal, 41*(1), 112–127. doi:10.21423/awlj-v41.a324

Guthridge, M., Kirkman, M., Penovic, T., & Giummarra, M. J. (2022). Promoting Gender Equality: A Systematic Review of Interventions. *Social Justice Research, 35*(3), 318–343. doi:10.100711211-022-00398-z

Hancock, A. M. (2016). *Intersectionality: An intellectual history.* Oxford University Press. doi:10.1093/acprof:oso/9780199370368.001.0001

Hart, J. (2006). Women and feminism in higher education scholarship: An analysis of three core journals. *The Journal of Higher Education, 77*(1), 40–61. doi:10.1080/00221546.2006.11778918

Haveman, R., & Smeeding, T. (2006). The role of higher education in social mobility. *The Future of Children, 16*(2), 125–150. doi:10.1353/foc.2006.0015 PMID:17036549

Hill, C., Corbett, C., & St Rose, A. (2010). Why so few? Women in Science, Technology, Engineering, and Mathematics. American Association of University Women.

Hill, C., Miller, K., Benson, K., & Handley, G. (2016). *Barriers and Bias: The Status of Women in Leadership.* American Association of University Women.

Hoyt, C. L. (2010). Women, men, and leadership: Exploring the gender gap at the top. *Social and Personality Psychology Compass, 4*(7), 484–498. doi:10.1111/j.1751-9004.2010.00274.x

Johnson, J. (2014). Divided We Fail: Why It's Time for a Broader, More Inclusive Conversation on the Future of Higher Education. A Final Report on the 2013 National Issues Forums. Kettering Foundation.

Johnson, N. N. (2021). Balancing race, gender, and responsibility: Conversations with four black women in educational leadership in the United States of America. *Educational Management Administration & Leadership, 49*(4), 624–643. doi:10.1177/1741143221991839

Johnson, N. N., & Fournillier, J. B. (2022). Increasing diversity in leadership: Perspectives of four Black women educational leaders in the context of the United States. *Journal of Educational Administration and History, 54*(2), 174–192. doi:10.1080/00220620.2021.1985976

Johnson, N. N., & Fournillier, J. B. (2023). Intersectionality and leadership in context: Examining the intricate paths of four black women in educational leadership in the United States. *International Journal of Leadership in Education, 26*(2), 296–317. doi:10.1080/13603124.2020.1818132

Johnson, T. B. (Ed.). (2023). *The Experiences of Black Women Diversity Practitioners in Historically White Institutions.* IGI Global. doi:10.4018/978-1-6684-3564-9

Khalil, N., Aljanazrah, A., Hamed, G., & Murtagh, E. M. (2023). Teacher educators' perspectives on gender responsive pedagogy in higher education. *Irish Educational Studies*, 1–17. doi:10.1080/03323 315.2023.2174575

Krause, S. F. (2017). *Leadership: Underrepresentation of women in higher education*. Northcentral University.

Longman, K. A., & Madsen, S. R. (Eds.). (2014). *Women and leadership in higher education*. IAP.

Lyness, K. S., & Grotto, A. R. (2018). Women and leadership in the United States: Are we closing the gender gap? *Annual Review of Organizational Psychology and Organizational Behavior, 5*(1), 227–265. doi:10.1146/annurev-orgpsych-032117-104739

Marino, K. M. (2019). *Feminism for the Americas: The making of an international human rights movement*. UNC Press Books. doi:10.5149/northcarolina/9781469649696.001.0001

Martens, A., Johns, M., Greenberg, J., & Schimel, J. (2006). Combating stereotype threat: The effect of self-affirmation on women's intellectual performance. *Journal of Experimental Social Psychology, 42*(2), 236–243. doi:10.1016/j.jesp.2005.04.010

Mayya, S. S., Martis, M., Ashok, L., & Monteiro, A. D. (2021). Women in higher education: Are they ready to take up administrative positions?—a mixed-methods approach to identify the barriers, perceptions, and expectations. *SAGE Open, 11*(1), 2158244020983272. doi:10.1177/2158244020983272

Nash, J. C. (2017). *Intersectionality and its discontents*.

Navarette, L., Cooper, D., Howe, M., & Liahut-Sanchez, G. (2017). *Elevating Equity for Social Mobility: Examples of Equity-Focused Practices and Partnership*. Community College League of California.

Noble, C., & Moore, S. (2006). Advancing women and leadership in this post feminist, post EEO era: A discussion of the issues. *Women in Management Review, 21*(7), 598–603. doi:10.1108/09649420610692534

Olson, L. (2001). *Freedom's daughters: The unsung heroines of the civil rights movement from 1830 to 1970*. Simon and Schuster.

Osei-Kofi, N., Shahjahan, R. A., & Patton, L. D. (2010). Centering social justice in the study of higher education: The challenges and possibilities for institutional change. *Equity & Excellence in Education, 43*(3), 326–340. doi:10.1080/10665684.2010.483639

Osterman, P., & Shulman, B. (2011). *Good Jobs America*. Russell Sage Foundation.

Parker, P. (2015). The historical role of women in higher education. *Administrative Issues Journal, 5*(1), 3. doi:10.5929/2015.5.1.1

Pasque, P. A., & Nicholson, S. E. (2011). *Empowering women in higher education and student affairs*. Theory, Research, Narratives and Practice from Feminist Perspectives.

Perrons, D. (2009). *Women and gender equity in employment: patterns, progresses and challenges*.

Richerme, L. K. (2021). Equity via relations of equality: Bridging the classroom-society divide. *International Journal of Music Education, 39*(4), 492–503. doi:10.1177/02557614211005899

Rosa, R., & Clavero, S. (2022). Gender equality in higher education and research. *Journal of Gender Studies*, *31*(1), 1–7. doi:10.1080/09589236.2022.2007446

Sandmann, L. R., & Jones, D. O. (Eds.). (2023). *Building the field of higher education engagement: Foundational ideas and future directions*. Taylor & Francis. doi:10.4324/9781003443353

Schnackenberg, H. L., & Simard, D. A. (Eds.). (2023). *Stabilizing and Empowering Women in Higher Education: Realigning, Recentering, and Rebuilding*. IGI Global., doi:10.4018/978-1-6684-8597-2

Sen, A. (1995). Gender inequality and theories of justice. *Women, culture and development: A study of human capabilities*, 259-273.

Sharma, R., & Afroz, Z. (2014). Women empowerment through higher education. [IJIMS]. *International Journal of Interdisciplinary and Multidisciplinary Studies*, *1*(5), 18–22.

Shaukat, S., & Pell, A. W. (2015). Personal and social problems faced by women in higher education. *FWU Journal of Social Sciences*, *9*(2), 101.

Sheltzer, J. M., & Smith, J. C. (2014). Elite male faculty in the life sciences employ fewer women. *Proceedings of the National Academy of Sciences of the United States of America*, *111*(28), 10107–10112. doi:10.1073/pnas.1403334111 PMID:24982167

Siemiatycki, M. (2019). The diversity gap in the public–private partnership industry: An examination of women and visible minorities in senior leadership positions. *Annals of Public and Cooperative Economics*, *90*(2), 393–414. doi:10.1111/apce.12240

Slaughter, A. M. (2015). Why women still can't have it all (pp. 84-102). Bloomsbury: OneWorld.

Smith, T. T., & Johnson, N. N. (2019). Creating support systems for Black women in nontraditional STEM career paths. In *Women's influence on inclusion, equity, and diversity in STEM fields* (pp. 108–142). IGI Global. doi:10.4018/978-1-5225-8870-2.ch005

Starr, C. R., & Zurbriggen, E. L. (2017). Sandra Bem's gender schema theory after 34 years: A review of its reach and impact. *Sex Roles*, *76*(9-10), 566–578. doi:10.100711199-016-0591-4

Stockard, J. (2006). Gender socialization. Handbook of the Sociology of Gender, 215-227.

Stromquist, N. P. (2020). Girls and women in the educational system: The curricular challenge. *Prospects*, *49*(1-2), 47–50. doi:10.100711125-020-09482-1 PMID:32836422

Stromquist, N. P. (2022). Women's Education in the 21st Century. *Comparative education: The dialectic of the global and the local, 187*.

Thomas, U. (Ed.). (2017). *Advocacy in Academia and the Role of Teacher Preparation Programs*. IGI Global.

Thomas, U. (Ed.). (2019). *Navigating Micro-Aggressions Toward Women in Higher Education*. IGI Global., doi:10.4018/978-1-5225-5942-9

Wattanaporn, K. A., & Holtfreter, K. (2014). The impact of feminist pathways research on gender-responsive policy and practice. *Feminist Criminology*, *9*(3), 191–207. doi:10.1177/1557085113519491

Welch, M. (2023). *Engaging higher education: Purpose, platforms, and programs for community engagement.* Taylor & Francis. doi:10.4324/9781003444473

Wiles, P. (1974). The correlation between education and earnings: The external-test-not-content hypothesis (ETNC). *Higher Education, 3*(1), 43–58. doi:10.1007/BF00153991

Winchester, H. P., & Browning, L. (2015). Gender equality in academia: A critical reflection. *Journal of Higher Education Policy and Management, 37*(3), 269–281. doi:10.1080/1360080X.2015.1034427

Wingood, G., & DiClemente, R. (2002). *The theory of gender and power. Emerging theories in health promotion practice and research: Strategies for improving public health.* Jossey-Bass.

Winters, M. F. (2020). *Inclusive conversations: fostering equity, empathy, and belonging across differences.* Berrett-Koehler Publishers.

ENDNOTES

[1]   All epigraphs retrieved from https://yourdream.liveyourdream.org/2017/06/25-education-quotes/

[2]   Figure 2: *Women in Higher Education – The Numbers Behind the Story.* Retrieved from https://elearninginfographics.com/women-in-higher-education-infographic/

Chapter 2
Unexpected Dreams

Denise Demers

https://orcid.org/0009-0000-4263-7374

University of Central Arkansas, USA

ABSTRACT

Do dreams come true? Dream careers and dream lives? Sometimes yes, maybe no. With unforeseen challenges and detours in life, it is imperative to gain coping skills and a healthy individualized self-care routine. Mental health is of concern as the nation comes out of a global pandemic. It is time for the world to adjust, realign, and create a new system and culture at work as well as home. The author has adopted a motto that has served her well- "If you're not having fun, you're doing something wrong." However, this is not typically taught at home, nor at school, let alone in the workplace. This chapter is the author's story – how she continues to learn how to live authentically according to her values as a woman in higher education and an academic leader. She shares how she continues to try to adapt, improvise, and overcome by shifting perspectives, creating personalized ways to thrive, and showing grace and acceptance to ourselves and others.

INTRODUCTION

If you are reading this, you are most likely an academic leader, a woman in higher education. I applaud you for your strength, grit and determination to be the best academic leader that you can! I am one of you, and instead of a fully-academic-journal-type chapter, I want to just talk with you. I will use a very conversational tone throughout as I share my experiences as a woman leader in higher education. You may find portions that you identify with and can benefit from as we discuss what life is like for me, and quite possibly for you, and how we can both improve in all areas of our life!

Although we know that administration in higher education is a difficult job (Bebbington et al., 2018; Greenwald, 2012), it is especially so for women (Lester, 2015; Rosa, 2021) and mothers (Isgro & Caste-ñeda, 2015). But also for men (Greenwald, 2012). I am a woman and a mother and an academic leader, and maybe you are too. So, therefore we will talk about us!!

I hope that as you read this you are sitting on the couch or in a comfortable armchair, or even a recliner – sitting comfortably. I hope that you are taking some time for yourself to better yourself as an academic

DOI: 10.4018/978-1-6684-8597-2.ch002

Copyright © 2023, IGI Global. Copying or distributing in print or electronic forms without written permission of IGI Global is prohibited.

leader. More importantly, I hope that you are taking time to better yourself as a woman, as a wife (if you are), and as a mother (if you are). But most importantly, to better yourself as an individual because you are an individual. As a woman, you wear many hats – even if you are not an academic leader, you wear many hats (Hochschild, 1989; Yee, 2021)! It has been said that education and motherhood are the two greediest institutions (Burke, 2010). I believe it. Both never end. Your work is never done (Hochschild, 1989; Gerstel, 2000). Yet here we are, up to our eyeballs in all things.

Looking back, I was never much of a reader growing up. In fact, it wasn't until my third child, a daughter, was born that I even took an interest. I took my children to the local library, but I would only browse and watch one of my toddlers, making sure he or she (whichever year it happened to be) did not destroy anything. It was my birthday in 2003. I will never forget it, nor the book. A good friend of mine gave me Esperanza Rising by Pam Munoz. Never before had a book come to life for me, with characters and meaning beyond the characters on a page. But I saw myself in Esperanza, in her mother, and her friends. How is it that I never knew this type of reading growing up? From that point on, I could not get enough of fictional reading. I would transport myself to these far-off places, or the life of a fictional character in an historical time. I'm sure none of my students would believe this about me, someone I am sure they look to as knowledgeable and put together. Maybe it is this part of me that understands them. And I am grateful.

One of the books I read during this time was not one of those self-help books by any means, or even an academic leadership book. This was a book purely fiction, purely entertainment, purely for me. It was juvenile fiction, for that matter, and in that book one of the characters was a garbage collector. Most people think that a garbage collector is not a great career to have, but this man loved it because he had plenty of time to think about things that mattered to him, and then did not worry about taking any of his work home with him. I found some truth to that and found some welcomed solace, maybe even envy because in academia, work is never done! So is it likewise with motherhood and with the family. Life continues 24 hours a day seven days a week regardless of where you are, or how sick you are, how tired you are, or how much those for whom you are accountable dislike you, your decisions, and where they think you are leading them.

So, let's jump right in, hopefully from your armchair.

CHILDHOOD DREAMS

My journey to leadership in higher education was not a straight path. I never expected to get a graduate degree, let alone dreamt of being in higher education. I'm pretty sure every young child has dreams. Some are lofty, losing traction as time marches forward and life creeps into a young child's life. Some state they will be astronauts or the President of the United States one day. Others are funny. Take for instance my children, specifically my daughter. One day as we drove through the McDonald's line (again), she declared that when she grows up she wants to work at McDonald's. I chuckled inside at the lofty aspirations from my only daughter and off we went, chicken nuggets and french fries in hand (soon to add to the old fries that surely were under her car seat). But then again, some childhood dreams are fairly realistic and they stick. They gain traction as a child's passion for that specific dream increases. Maybe they want to be a firefighter just like Dad, or a professional athlete of some sort.

As a young child I remember loving softball. I used to watch my dad and I knew I would be great. I practiced and practiced and practiced. I even had dreams of playing professionally one day. As a child

Unexpected Dreams

growing up in the Bay Area of California, I loved the Oakland A's. My dad was a fan; his dad was a fan; and all of our family were fans. A few of the players lived in our extended neighborhood so we "kind of" got to know them … that was back in the day, of course. Lucky for me, my best friend growing up was the son of one of the catchers for the Oakland A's. He would take me to games and sitting in the stands right above the dugout fueled my fanhood. It was during my 6th grade year that I won an orange record player at our elementary school's fair. It was perfect. My dad had old records, the big ones, of games and commentary from the Oakland A's and I would sit under my bedroom window and listen to them at night … over and over and over again. I had them memorized. I knew ALL the players from Rollie Fingers (old timer) to Ricky Henderson. I loved Ricky Henderson. He was so fast. I would try to mimic the way he stood in the batter's box. One game I even got to sit by him in the dugout for a minute (perks of having my friend's dad on the team). Oh! If only we had cell phones back then. That would be the selfie of my lifetime - at least at THAT moment of my life.

Growing through puberty didn't change my love of the game, or my passion to continue playing. But it was at that time in high school that a new dream surfaced. Coming from a place at the center of my existence, it was difficult to define for a moment. In fact, I was not sure it actually was a dream. With time, its comfort settled within my soul as a welcomed and longtime friend. It was one of those sensations that if you stay with it long enough, it becomes you. All I really want to be is a mother, I felt, I knew. This I knew; I actually knew. At my deepest core, motherhood was my dream and what was most meaningful, important, and significant to me. It did not change my love for softball and the passion I felt there. Instead it grounded that determination and gave me purpose. I went on to play in college and learned tremendous lessons for my lifetime, which is a chapter and book for another day.

I wonder how many childhood dreams are actually realized. And I wonder how many people "end up" in places, careers, and events that they would have never imagined but it ended up being the most fulfilling "dream" they have ever experienced. According to a 2019 Perkbox Insights survey of over 1,500 people, only 4% of adults actually landed their childhood dream job (Ramsell, 2019). They also found some startling statistics:

- over 60% of adults wish they were in that childhood dream career
- 43% did not feel they were talented enough for that dream job, or that they had the opportunities and resources to work in that area. Sadly, a greater percentage of women felt this way than men (28% vs 15%)
- When people did not pursue their dream job from childhood, they were twice as likely to be unhappy.

These are surprising statistics, to be sure. Other research increases the odds to a whopping 6% of adults find their childhood dream job (Polavieja & Platt, 2014). We will not spend time on the whys of this phenomenon, as they are plentiful. But, suffice it to say, such was my case, I did not play professional softball (or baseball). But I learned early on to adapt, improvise and overcome. I believe it was my mother that taught me this as she told me that very rarely do things turn out as we first plan or expect.

As indicated at the beginning of this section, my journey to academic leadership was circuitous. Maybe it was for you too. I will not bore you with the details of how I gained the knowledge, but I have come to know that things rarely end up exactly as planned. However, those moments serve as experience and learning opportunities (when looked back on, of course). You have those moments and so do I. Everyone does - from choosing a major and a career to planning for an event where everything ends

Unexpected Dreams

up not working out at all the way it was supposed to, but it still was a wonderful experience. Don't get me wrong, some flop so hard that you find yourself in a heap in the corner crying. I can think of more than a few of those moments, as I am sure you can too. Remember the wedding cake that fell as you were taking it to the table to be displayed? Or the garbage truck that backed into you and those bars used to pick up dumpsters pummeled your small compact car as you were on your way with your fiancé to your father's house? The heap you may have been in under the clothing rack in the mall (hypothetically speaking, of course) served as your hiding place until it all went away. Bouncing back when life takes twists and turns can be of greatest benefit to you as life moves on. Knowing how to adapt, improvise, and overcome is essential in many areas of life.

Dreams really do come true, just watch Disney+ or Hallmark. Playing softball in college was such a dream for me. And becoming a mother was the icing on the cake. I had no idea I had such love within my little heart to love another tiny human being as I did. As more children entered our family, it was astounding to me how that love grew. When my oldest was just six months old, I retired and stayed at home with him. I was living the dream with no sleep, dirty diapers, and all the benefits of a tiny mobile little boy. I got next to nothing done as he never slept. The house I thought would be spotless because I was home, was far from that dream. All the extra time I envisioned would prove to be swallowed up in my son and taking care of his needs. Was this really my dream? Why was it so difficult? All my teaching and training and experience adapting to the circumstances, improvising when things went awry, and overcoming the obstacles that plopped in my way seemed to be substituted with exhaustion, brain fog, and frustration.

Thankfully, I was not a quitter since I had three more beautiful children, all of which tried my patience and stamina in more ways than I could count. However, as I continued this role I had dreamed about for so long, I felt better about things and began to learn to make the most of the pitfalls, mishaps, and seemingly unorganized days. Motherhood became my skill indeed. I found that I could do hard things, even difficult gut-wrenching things regardless of how it turned out, which was often different than I had anticipated. The key for me, the secret to success, was two-fold. Attitude and perseverance. Fake it til you make it, my mother always said. But she never really defined when I would actually MAKE IT. Hence, I have been trying and persisting my whole life.

This chapter is all about how I did so (or better yet, how I continue to try to do so, "make it," each day as my roles and stages change), and how others might be able to do so by learning how to adapt, improvise, and overcome in a world that would rather see you fail. We will cover shifting perspectives, developing your own definition of thriving, and finally, showing grace and acceptance of yourself (what the world now is calling self-care) throughout the process.

ADJUSTING SAILS

I don't think I really ever loved the idea of working. I wanted to be a mother. Consequently, my traditional storybook dream of what life would look like at 22 years old was drastically incorrect. I would graduate, get married, have children, and live happily ever after with a man who made lots of money and all was right in our world. I have NO IDEA where that thought came from since my parents were divorced before I was in kindergarten, and our blended family, the "yours, mine, and ours," was anything but perfect. We were a normal family with stresses and dysfunctional moments. Sure, my mom stayed home and dad provided, but that was more the norm in those days. I knew they fought. As siblings we

Unexpected Dreams

did our best to blend ourselves into one family unit. My step dad had boys and my mom had us girls. There was a natural division, at least in some ways, but we were all friends as siblings usually are. Still, my perfect picture had been painted and I knew to think of nothing else.

This path was so strong that after bouncing from major to major, I finally ended up with Physical Education because I was on the softball team at the small southwestern university and loved all things sport related. But I didn't want to be a teacher, especially a PE teacher. So many stories to unpack for a different time. So, with no advising whatsoever, I graduated with a Bachelor's Degree in Physical Education. No teaching certificate or endorsement. Now what? I found out quickly that there are not many jobs for a college graduate with a degree in Physical Education. Thus, my circuitous route to where I am today began.

After some time in northeast Canada serving a mission for my church, I returned and knew I needed to do something different if I wanted to get a job one day. No handsome young man was knocking on my door and I was too independent to sit around and wait. I knew I had to keep moving forward, whichever direction that was for me. It was in Canada that I found and memorized the poem by Edgar Albert Guest (1921).

When things go wrong, as they sometimes will,

When the road you're trudging seems all uphill,

When the funds are low but the debts are high,

And you want to smile but you have to sigh,

When care is pressing you down a bit,

Rest if you must, but don't you quit.

Life is strange with its twists and turns,

As every one of us sometimes learns,

And many failures turn about

When we might have won had we stuck it out.

Don't give up though the pace seems slow –

You may succeed with another blow.

Success is failure turned inside out –

The silver tint of the clouds of doubt,

Unexpected Dreams

You can never tell how close you are,

It may be near when it seems so far;

So stick to the fight when you're hardest hit –

It's when things seem worst that you must not quit.

Quitting just was not an option for me. It took me four years, but I received a Master's degree in Exercise Science with an emphasis in Health and Fitness Promotion. Just prior to graduation I married my husband. Those early inklings of motherhood as my dream came back. While working as a Fitness Instructor, we had our first child, a son. Although I loved my job and everything I was doing, and needed the income because my husband was still in school, the pull to stay at home with my son became almost insatiable. Within six months I was retired at the young age of 30. I loved life. We were poor but made ends meet. A move for graduate school for my husband, a new job for him, another son, and life felt like I had always imagined it should, and would. Another move for my husband's job and I was living the dream, as difficult as it sometimes was.

Cue the challenge of job losses and the ultimate need to shift my perspective, relinquish the dream that might now feel more like a nightmare. How often I recited and rehearsed those lines from Edgar A. Guest (1921), "When things go wrong as they sometimes will. When the road you're trudging seems all uphill, when the funds are low and the debts are high, … when care is pressing you down a bit, rest if you must, but don't you quit…" I took some time to process and then in the end, the adjusting, improvising, and overcoming transformed into the drawing board, which led me to a doctoral program a couple hours from home. It realigned my priorities, my dreams, and my goals and I began to study mother-students and how they balance the multiple roles and responsibilities of being a mother AND a student in graduate school. I would graduate and land the job I have now. From the first phone interview I knew it was where I would be, and even where I wanted to be. As hard as that may be to believe, it was a 'gut' thing and I have loved being in my new environment.

SHIFTING PERSPECTIVES

As life began (I mean continued) to take its topsy-turvy turns in my married with children life, I found myself numb to the distinct disturbances of the days, as well as the yearnings of my own heart. Following a call from my husband that he was let go from another job, no tears fell down my cheeks. I was numb. It wasn't the first time, but it surely would be the last if I had anything to do with it. Adapt, improvise, and overcome. How was I supposed to adjust this time? Adapting to this was almost second nature. I had improvised bills and grocery runs countless times. Overcoming this was hard, something I am not sure I ever accomplished. But, instead of wallowing, I went to work on a plan. I shifted my perspective. And please do not think that this was easy. Nothing about it was - except my resolve. I was already working as an adjunct professor, but it wasn't enough to sustain a family. Back to the drawing board. Securing a position in higher education with a Master's degree was more difficult than I imagined. Additionally, it was no longer just me that I had to think about. I had a husband and four children. Could I move my family for school just to move them again for a job? This may have been where I truly learned about

Unexpected Dreams

self-care, or at least the greater need I had for it. How was a middle-aged mother of four supposed to go back and get a PhD? While proficient in diapers, bottles, lunchboxes, and school pickup lines, I was prone to forget where my keys were and feared how I would get along and/or measure up with younger students. Friends assured me that all would be well. I had to trust, even when those words seemed so far from the truth.

Thankfully, it was true. I did know a lot. My level of work and drive was obvious (Demers, 2014; Leisure, 2007), even though I felt frumpy most of the time coming straight from my motherhood role. What I lacked in book knowledge and content experience, I more than made up in life experience and hard work. True to the findings of Burke (2010), often mothering skills are transferable, valued, and recognized when it comes to academia. Likewise, Cole (2010) also found that she was able to draw upon her own personal experience to excel in her graduate program. I was actually succeeding. And not just succeeding, but excelling. My life took on new meaning. Even my mother noticed. "It's good to have the old Denise back," she said to me one day. It baffled me. Where had she thought I had been? Or maybe more importantly, where had I let myself go? Evidently, I had lost part of myself in my dream of motherhood. That may be better said in this way. I had not allowed myself to flourish as Denise as I mothered my children. I thought I was; I guess I was wrong and had to once again adjust and change my perspective just a little bit. It was Mills (1970) who said,

You must learn to use your life experiences in your intellectual work: continually to examine it and interpret it. In this sense craftsmanship is the centre of yourself and you are personally involved in every intellectual product upon which you work (pg. 216)

And use my experiences, I did. A lot. When learning theories that I had only briefly touched upon prior to this time, I used my own life experiences to understand them. Going into Health Education made using my own lifetime of experiences, especially as a mother, much easier. I was grateful for the transferable skills of motherhood into school and work. Everything is about behavior change and modification. At first, I was very nervous because I knew that changing a toddler's behavior was difficult. Prepubescent's behavior was even more difficult to modify. Who knew there were evidence-based theories to help? My perspective changed and so did I. Little by little I was evolving.

But I didn't want to change drastically. I liked who I was and loved being a mother. That day I walked up the three flights of stairs (having to stop to catch my breath because I was no longer the fit undergraduate student, or graduate student for that matter), dressed in capris and a casual shirt, began my new life. The nostalgia of driving onto a college campus and remembering my undergraduate years was coupled with anxiety and fear. I began to doubt if I was good enough. Truthfully, along with the mush brain I thought I had, having to do research on something I did not really care about terrified me. If I was going to do a dissertation, I wanted it to be from my heart and something that I really cared about. Meeting with that first professor and an administrator across campus buoyed my spirits and it felt as though something inside had caught fire. I was really doing this, not going back to my well-established comfort zone of a stay-at-home mom. My visit with the Department Chair was the boost I needed. She was kind and seemed to care about me, rather than merely my student status. After the normal pleasantries of introductions, she asked why I wanted to go back to school. I told her that I wanted to make a difference in the world. Her comment directly after would sink deep into my heart, tears welled up, and I knew I was at the right place. "You've already made a world of difference to four people" (personal communication, Fetro, 2011), speaking of my four children. After my second evening as a 40+ year old new graduate student, I met with the professor after class. It was then that she suggested that I research people like me, moms who go back to school. Those two comments sealed the deal for me. I was going back to school and I would begin a four-year study about mothers who go back to school, mother-students.

UNEXPECTED DREAMS

A new unexpected dream was born! Life in school took on new meaning once again. Though my life seemed to be pulled in two opposing directions, not allowing me to fully live in either, I loved what I was learning and doing. Like Penny Burks (2012), I often felt like a "time and space traveler" with both worlds on colliding courses much of the time. As I read more about women like me going back to school, I realized that was a common theme - worlds colliding (Cole, 2010; Burke, 2010). Although more difficult than anything I had done up to that point, the limbo spurred me on. Like Cole (2010), it collided for sure, but it also synergized who I was, who I am, and who I am becoming. I found friends and a support group to help me. I relied heavily on my husband, babysitters (let me just say that this part of the process was difficult having never really had long time babysitters up to that point), and friends to get me through. Grace and acceptance began to share room with guilt as my middle name. They tugged for power, me fully on the grace and acceptance side, and my little girl and woman alter egos on the other. I hate to admit that all too often I found that guilt reigned supreme.

On my drives to school and back (a two-hour commute both ways), thoughts and feelings that this is what I was born to do took hold. Regardless of feeling like I lived only on the open road, the interstate between both lives, I began to believe that this could be my path, where I would feel comfortable and be able to make a difference. Heidi Mirza (2010) also felt this way (Mirza & Hoskins, 2010). Her PhD, like mine, was a pivotal moment in her life, one that would leave us both breathless and excited, depleted and empowered.

In my second semester in a seminar class I decided I needed to publish something. YIKES! My negative self-talk again reared its ugly head. "Who are you to write anything worth publishing? You are a fraud. You are just a mother and a middle-aged mother at that!" All I could think about was whether an over 40 year old stay-at-home mom could actually publish something, anything? I chose to review a book about women like me. Remember my conversation with my professor on day two? Again, I read. But this time I also wrote. I did publish that review. That book's contents settled deeply into my heart and mind. Some of the experiences did not seem to speak to me or relate, but other portions were exactly what I was feeling and needed at that time. One purpose of the book was to urge the writers and readers to see themselves differently (Cole and Gunter, 2010). I was definitely seeing myself in a different light, illuminated by other things without dimming the light of motherhood. Certain phrases jumped off the page. At other times, I could insert myself into the stories of the writers. Maybe I could do this! This might be a new and unexpected path, perhaps even a dream! Ratky (1990) uses a few phrases to describe me at the beginning of this newfound journey. She says,

coming to have a feminine conscience is the experience of coming to see things about oneself and one's society that were heretofore hidden. ... we begin to understand why we have such depreciated images of ourselves ... Understanding, even beginning to understand this, makes it possible to change (pg. 21).

Unexpected Dreams

After defending my dissertation all about mother-students balancing the two greediest institutions of both school and home life (Edwards, 1993), both that have a never-ending task list with nothing ever fully finished, I relaxed for a brief moment, only to have the onslaught of worry hit me about getting a job. What would it look like? How do I interview? I had mock interviews with trusted mentors who told me I'd be fine, but warned against the institution and family. Knowing my allegiance to my family and how they come first in my life, would researching and working toward tenure take me away from my family at the very time they needed me? While I thought I hated research, I found it to be quite fun when it was about something I felt passionate about. Would I continue to feel that way? Would I be able to make my way? Thankfully, I trusted in those thoughts and feelings that had taken hold and landed a job at a moderately sized university in the southern United States.

And we moved. I had prepared everyone in my family to handle this move after being in the same town for 14 years. Everyone but myself, that is! All those that I had gathered around me for support were now gone, and I cried. Remember the heap in a corner? Yes, that was me…again. Learning to show myself grace and acceptance took on a new meaning. Adapting to change and altering my perspectives became a mountain. Thriving became my goal, but only after I got myself together. Isn't that how it always seems to go? We think we learn something just to find out that we are now in the next level course trying to apply what we thought we learned in the first class. We fail an assignment or even a test, but we grow and we learn. And all the strategies we tell our students should be practiced in house. Fortunately, I loved teaching and buried myself in my happy place, the classroom. And happily, the department culture valued family almost as much as I did. Though they may have wondered how a middle-aged woman with four children at home would manage teaching and researching at the same time as serving on a multitude of committees, I was able to put my best foot forward and succeed.

THE INSTITUTION

Admittedly, several of the systems at any university are broken, especially for women and mothers, but I put my head down and worked hard. And it WAS hard! But I was old enough and set in my values enough that leaving work at work was not a problem. I put in the hours at work knowing that I wouldn't have time when I got home with four children ranging from 9 to 16 years old. The idea of the *Second Shift*, the classic study by Arlie Hochschild (1989) regarding women who work, was spot on. Most women do not just have one shift of work and then go home to relax. Instead, they go home to their "second shift" of work, some even a third shift (Gerstel, 2000; Yee, 2021). Raddon (2002) said that being a successful academic is in direct conflict of typical mothering activities. Expectations for women who work continue to be unrealistic (Connelly and Ghodsee, 2011; Sallee, Ward, Wolf-Wendel, 2016; Wolf-Wendel & Ward, 2015, Ward & Wolf-Wendel, 2012) because it remains true that women do the lion's share of the household chores, the unpaid work of keeping the household in order and running (somewhat) smoothly. Although some researchers propose that workloads are becoming more equal in the past few decades (Bianchi, Milkie, Sayer, and Robinson 2000; Craig 2007; Mattingly and Bianchi 2003; Milkie, Raley, and Bianchi 2009; Sayer, England, Bittman, and Bianchi 2009), my work did not end when I got home from the office. According to Kate Mangino's recent publication *Equal Partners: Improving Gender Equality at Home* (2022), women continue to shoulder the majority of the household (65%) and childcare work of a home. Since the mid-20th century, women have entered the workforce and continue to try to break the glass ceiling, the invisible hand, pay inequality, and the second shift.

Unexpected Dreams

Working in higher education poses a separate problem. It is relentless, demanding, and unending. In order to obtain the grants/research funding, publish the research, attend conferences, and do those activities considered crucial to building a career in higher education, nights and weekends off are not an option. Raddon (2002) found that what makes a successful academic is in direct conflict of typical mothering activities. Often, the barriers reported by women keeping them from progressing and having representation in the highest leadership positions are family demands (Howe-Walsh & Turnbull, 2016) As much as the push for gender equality in the home is happening, progress is slow. Women are working more, but the responsibilities are not decreasing (both at home and at work). Consequently, burnout is happening more often for women than men (Aldossari & Chaudhry, 2020). Such was also the case for me. Instead, because I knew my "second shift" would begin the moment I left the office, I went in early enough to get all my work done at the office because, as I often commented, the next hat I wear would appear the moment I left my office. Off to a game, or to fix dinner, or to pick something up for someone. To simply return home, plop down in my recliner, and turn on the television was not only foreign to my nature, but completely foreign to my reality.

A PATTERN WORTH LIVING BY

Although being a woman in higher education has both advantages and disadvantages, both are seen from a personal perspective only. Many women report feeling like a fraud, like they don't belong (Reay, 1997; Clancy, 1997; Morley, 1997; Demers, 2014; Perkins, 2011 dissertation). Yet others finally feel energized and more alive (Demers, 2014). In my own research (Demers, 2014), I found that there were a few principles that related to whether or not a woman thrived in an educational environment. Balancing the multiple roles of being a student is predicated on being a mother first. That is what holds her together and helps her to add weight to both sides. This was her primary role. Her attitude and knowing that she was 'driven, determined, and motivated' helped to balance both the stressful as well as the joyful. Lastly, letting go of a little of both the good and bad was what eventually led to greater abilities to balance the demands of multiple roles. Letting go of stress at times, but also sometimes letting go of hobbies and friendships for a time in order to get things done. No doubt this continues on into the workplace. After all, managing both education/academia and the home is difficult.

Getting a job shortly after finishing school was wonderful. I traveled that same long interstate I had traveled for almost four years. Only this time I did not turn off at the same place. Instead, I continued onward and forward to my new unexpected dream destination. I was sad as I drove, but thought about my dissertation and about how I would now learn to balance being a professor in higher education and a mother simultaneously. I knew that making sure I was a mother first would be paramount. Remaining driven, determined, and motivated would also remain high on the attribute and attitude scale. I would surely have to let some things go that I very much liked. But I would also be adopting a new lifestyle with new and exciting adventures. New relationships and learning awaited me, along with a chance to change and become something greater than I was.

I was pretty lucky, really. I did not know it at the time - I tend to think everyone is exactly like me when my head is down and I am working hard. I was not only fortunate to have a wonderful group of people to work with in my department, but I had a very understanding department chair who valued both family and autonomy. It wasn't until much later that I learned that is very uncommon in higher education.

Unexpected Dreams

My seat at many tables revealed toxic and dysfunctional departments full of animosity, competition, and working on the clock.

So, as I said, this chapter is about how I have made it thus far and continue to try as each stage of life comes. As I write this, my youngest son just barely (literally) graduated from high school. This wash of emotion, four children grown and graduated from high school, is something different than I at one time expected it to be. But that is another story for another book, another topic, and a different time. The remainder is how I-have learned… no, how I AM learning to adapt, improvise, and overcome as I have developed a greater ability to shift my perspectives as life's changes and challenges occurred; how to develop an individual definition of what it means to thrive; and, maybe most importantly, how to incorporate grace and acceptance into your life more authentically as well as more automatically, without having to work hard.

THRIVING IN AN UNEXPECTED ROLE

I love teaching! My happy place really is the room in which I teach. However, from the beginning of my time at this university, people began to talk to me about administration. I was dead set against it. I wanted nothing to do with it. Let me reiterate that for clarity and meaning. I wanted NOTHING to do with it. NOTHING! But I found that I had attributes that lent themselves easily to the role. Without much experience, I became Chair of a committee and found myself on the Faculty Senate. The whisper of administration kept taunting me, sometimes kindly but oftentimes it was unwanted. The stress and headache repulsed me, to be honest. The lack of flexibility deterred me. And the title was something I never aspired to. Some folks get into higher education to climb the ladder of administration. I was not one of those people. But I found myself hanging out with them, most of them at the university. They were not mentors, but friends. That was the group I found myself associating with the most, those with whom I predominantly fit. Hints of administration kept flitting and fluttering in and out of my consciousness, in and out of my thoughts. Seven years later I found myself actually entertaining the thought, the possibility of becoming the department chair. However, I thought it compromised who I was at my core. I wouldn't do it. Would it take me away from my family? If so, then there was no way. But the suggestions kept coming, now even stronger. No longer were they subtle and inkling-like, but a full-fledged onslaught of reason, thought, benefits, and desire. My kids are nearly grown and I was a soon-to-be empty-nester. It made sense and felt right. The transferable skills of motherhood and work (Burke, 2010) still apply. However, so do the imposter syndrome and collisions (Cole, 2012; Burke, 2012). After much thought and processing, I applied and was offered the position.

Now I am the department chair and I am trying to have a department where there is a culture of family and mental health as the foundation. Adapting, improvising, and overcoming remain my motto in life and in the department. Shifting our perspectives will be of greatest benefit when we individually and collectively learn how to adjust our sails and redefine what it means to flourish in our environment as we advance our goals and our department.

With the classroom as my happy place, I would much rather spend time improving my courses than doing research. At least that was then. I wanted to be successful and knew that research was part of that when I took the position as an Assistant Professor. During that first year, I reached out to a couple people, one of whom responded. She had graduated with her PhD the same time I had and was now teaching and researching in Asia. We began what has become a beautiful friendship and I found a passion for research.

29

Through the years we have published and presented many different times, all about motherscholars. One of the earliest was a project about art-based self-care and how it can help women in higher education reduce stress (CohenMiller & Demers, 2019). In the end, collaborative encouragement, sometimes guilted pressure, regarding a healthy self-care practice eventually led participants to increase self-awareness. These informal support networks really help women and mothers in higher education (Demers, 2014; CohenMiller & Demers, 2019), specifically to reduce conflict. It was during that project that I began to expand my definition of what it means to thrive. What the research says isn't always what should happen in an individual's life. The dynamic properties of a human being make it so that every living person responds differently, to an extent, to stimuli of any sort. Our research specifically targeted coloring each day. It did not take long to find out that some of our participants, while they did enjoy coloring at times, did not always have the time or energy to color. But they would do something that relaxed them individually. One would take sports pictures of her children and edit them. Another found writing poetry helped her. And yet another colored on the bathtub wall with her young daughter. It did not necessarily matter what they were doing, but HOW they were doing it. It was all about making sure a space was created in order to practice a self-care routine of any type. These included physical and emotional space, but also family/self-space and a supportive collective space (CohenMiller & Demers, 2019).

Research became fun, especially with friends and about what I loved and was passionate about. Motherscholars are not only plentiful but have begun to make a ripple in higher education. Since the 1990s, women have received more degrees than men (U.S. Department of Education, 2021). Moreover, mother-students also receive more degrees than males or father-students (U.S. Department of Education, 2021). Yet the system and brick and mortar of higher education remains focused on the male in most instances (Danell Y Hjerm, 2013; CohenMiller et al., 2022).

So what now?

That is what I asked myself when I began studying mother-students in my doctoral work. The excitement for me was in finding a way to make the situation in which I found myself better. I wanted to find a way to thrive, but also a way for others to thrive as well. Like Burke (2010), I desired my story to help others, women especially, in school and as a motherscholar, for my story may be their story. It may be your story. I ask the same question now as I do any research regarding mothers in higher education, whether they are students or scholars.

What is to come of my research? It is my sincerest hope that higher education will become more welcoming and inclusive of all people, especially for motherscholars. In fact, I got together with my friend and another friend to write about what those institutions that are viewed as good, or even ideal, provide for women and motherscholars (CohenMiller et al., 2022). Support was the first thing we found. Women in higher education need support. We found that support was a plentiful need. Not only is social support needed from family, friends, and support networks (Demers, 2014; CohenMiller & Demers, 2019), but instrumental support as well (Turvett, 2011). Turvett's (2011) interview with a single mother who stated, "I need a wife," speaks volumes. However, the support that motherscholars and women in higher education felt was most beneficial was systematic support (i.e. financial and mentoring opportunities, institutional resources focused on families, and open communication about families). With all the obstacles they face, having open communication about families and policies and procedures developed with mothers and women in mind facilitates success most often.

See? Fun, right? To make a difference in the world I began at home with my own children and sphere of influence. As I have branched out, I continue to desire to make an impact on the world. Ask the right questions. Seek for the right answers. And do it over and over and again and again. CohenMiller et al.

Unexpected Dreams

(2022) advocate for a "culture of inclusiveness valuing them [motherscholars] as complete people, with lives in and outside of the gendered organization of academia" (pg. 104). As a department chair, that is my goal - to create a culture of inclusiveness for all, family, and mental health.

Creating an individual prescription for mental health is something that has been in the literature for a long time. Self-awareness and self-care can easily be overlooked and overused. Finding the time and space is crucial (CohenMiller & Demers, 2019), as well as finding what you love to do. I'm not sure when this began, but within the last eight years for sure. Retiring to my bed early became a ritual of taking care of myself. With time to unwind unencumbered by work and the humdrum of the day with no one needing me became my personal flourishing practice. Falling asleep was not the purpose, but sometimes I did. My family knew where I was and knew they could come to me if they needed. It took some time, but they adjusted and I thrived in a different way. I was happier and better able to attend to the demands of both home and work. Finding your own rhythm and technique matters far more than going through the motions, getting places quickly but never finding joy in the journey (Demers, 2017).

After all, no one makes you happy, nor do they make you thrive. Both are individual choices. Others may ask why you do certain things, figuring they are weighing you down. But some trucks need a load in the back to gain traction and get themselves unstuck. Find precisely what that is for you personally. Although you must be particular about what you add to your plate, or put in the back of your truck, know that it is completely your choice. Roles and responsibilities will continue on as a mother and as a woman (CohenMiller et al., 2022) in higher education. Choose to participate in events that buoy your soul in ways that make sense to you and you alone. Some may say spending the extra time traveling across the region to sit through hours of soccer games is not necessary and only adds stress to my already busy schedule. But these are the times that bring me joy. Although they take an exorbitant amount of time, they rejuvenate me and give me the traction I need to succeed in my work life as well.

A list full of self-care and thriving practices is always welcome. However, those lists tend to box people in unnecessary and detrimental ways. This leads to the final way that I am learning to grow into my role as a woman in higher education and empower others as an academic leader.

GRACE AND ACCEPTANCE

To even begin to contemplate this section of the chapter causes a whole host of feelings within me. They range from contentment and Zen to utter imposter syndrome. How can someone that feels she can barely stay afloat in the world of academic leadership even begin to know how to do this? Better yet…how is it that I, one who has just begun this journey, not even a full year in yet, share anything worthwhile with the world?

And just like that, you can feel it, can't you? Although the thought that you, the reader, are now looking down at me and thinking less of me is automatic and strong, chances are high that, to some extent, you do understand [my experience], at very least, to some degree. And you're probably rooting for me from your desks and armchairs around the world within the academic leadership arena. Because you, too, are in the arena (Brene Brown, 2015) and you get it. It has taken me a very long time and a lot of hard work to get to this place of self-understanding and self-appreciation. Grace and acceptance were not easy to come by and to be completely honest, they are a slow work in progress for me.

Culture has not been kind to women for many years (Ortner, 1972; Minnow, 2000). The "supermom trap" (Sasaki et al., 2010) has been up and running for maybe even longer. It is that feeling that we need to have it all, do it all, and then do some more. We need to take care of everyone else and then with the leftovers, help our communities and churches. Previous director of policy planning for the U.S. State Department and Dean of the School of Public and International Affairs, Anne-Marie Slaughter, now CEO of New America, wrote in *The Atlantic* (2012) about why women still can't have it all. She had taken a two-year public service leave from a university and found that her university's rules stated that after two years away, faculty lose their tenure. But she wasn't hurrying home only to go back into higher education, but because she found that juggling the needs of her family (two teenage boys) and the demanding high-level government work just wasn't feasible anymore. I'd like to think she chose her heart and what was ultimately best for her personally, as well as her family. Believing she created her own paradigm and definition of what it means to thrive and flourish just makes me feel a whole lot better.

No doubt that she, nor I, and probably not you neither, have arrived at full blown grace and acceptance. It has only been in the last 5-7 years that I have even begun doing the work needed to allow myself time to take care of me. Longer yet has been the shift inside to giving myself grace and acceptance, to not saying ugly and hurtful words to myself in my head, worse than I would ever say to even an enemy.

I am ok. I am enough! Yes, I now have a daily gratitude journal I write in every night (part of retiring to my bed early) and one that I write in every morning as well. Each morning I add a reflection of what self-care goals went well the day before, new ones for the present day, and MORE affirmations. It seemed a little hokey at first, but my affirmations have become part of me and who I am. I will continue to do this. I have seen its effect on my life. From the sunshine in the spring and warm water in the bathroom at work on a cold day to the text that came in from a friend from years ago or a call on a gloomy day, scribbling a few words, phrases, or sentences can help boost a person's mood (Kurian and Thomas, 2023a; 2023b).

Most recently, Chen et al., (2023) found that when leaders show and express gratitude, those they lead are more proactive. In our department, we begin each of our faculty meetings with a little gratitude. At least two people share something that they are grateful for within the university and also at home (or just not classroom or university related). It may take time, but our meetings begin on a positive note. It is easy to complain and be bitter about the institution, how they do this and don't do that, how they should do that and should not do this. When such sentiments become pervasive throughout a group, negativity takes root so grace and acceptance are more difficult to come by. Creating an attitude of gratitude (Phillips and Klocksieben, 2020; Gabana et al., 2019) really does reap individual benefits thus allowing us to have more personal benevolence in our lives.

Circling back, I am learning day by day, just like you, to persevere. More importantly, I am learning to love it (and myself) as I persist. You can too. Begin with a little adapting and improvising, and soon you, too, will overcome. But please don't believe that it is a one-and-done occurrence. On the contrary, it resembles more of a mud-run marathon where you run (or let's be honest, walk) a few steps forward only to splat in the mud and fall back a little. However, this is life, and we better learn to embrace it fully. Entering the arena is a majority of the challenge. I invite you to enter, to come join those you know who are motherscholars, women in higher education, those who may look like they have it all together, but are struggling one day at a time, just like you, to shift their perspectives, create their own thriving, and show themselves the biggest part of grace and acceptance. For you are enough! And you are good! May you find strength where there seems little and perseverance when the rope seems to have vanished long ago.

Unexpected Dreams

REFERENCES

Aldossari, M., & Chaudhry, S. (2020). Women and burnout in the context of a pandemic. *Gender, Work and Organization, 28*(2), 826–834. doi:10.1111/gwao.12567

Bebbington, W., Dirks, N., Price, D., Rand, J., Stolker, C., O'Sullivan, H., & Yakes, L. (2018). What is it like to take a leadership role at a university? *Times Higher Education.* https://www.timeshighereducation.com/features/what-is-it-like-to-take-a-leadership-role-at-a-university

Bianca, S. M., Millie, M. A., Sayer, L. C., & Robinson, J. P. (2000). Is anyone doing the housework? Trends in the gender division of household labor. *Social Forces, 79*(1), 191–228. doi:10.2307/2675569

Burke, P. J. (2010). Accessing doctoral education: Processes of becoming an academic. In B. A. Cole & H. Gunter (Eds.), *Changing lives: Women, inclusion, and the PhD* (pp. 19–40). Trentham Books Ltd., https://eric.ed.gov/?id=ED511419

Chen, S., Zhu, Y., Guo, L., & Liu, W. (2023). The Impact of Leader Gratitude Expressions on Followers' Behaviours: Increasing Gratitude and Increases Proactivity. *Journal of Leadership & Organizational Studies, 30*(2), 15480518231151575. doi:10.1177/15480518231151575

Clancy, K. (1997). Academic as anarchist: Working class lives into middle-class culture. In P. Mahony & C. Zmroczek (Eds.), *Class Matters. Working Class Women's Perspectives on Social Class* (pp. 44–52). Taylor and Francis., doi:10.4324/9780203992159

Cohen-Miller, A. S., & Demers, D. (2019). Conflicting roles of mother and academic? Exploring the use of arts-based self-care activities to encourage wellbeing. *Art/Research International: A Transdisciplinary Journal, 4*(2), 611–645. https://doi.org/ doi:10.18432/ari29391

CohenMiller, A. S., Demers, D., Schnackenberg, H., & Izekenova, Z.CohenMiller. (2022). "You are seen; you matter:" Applying the Theory of Gendered Organizations to equity and inclusion for mother-scholars in higher education. *Journal of Women and Gender in Higher Education, 15*(1), 87–109. doi: 10.1080/26379112.2022.2025816

Connelly, R., & Ghodsee, K. (2011). *Professor Mommy: Finding work-family balance in academia.* Rowman & Littlefield Publishers, Inc.

Craig, L. (2007). Is there a second shift, and if so, who does it? A time diary investigation. *Feminist Review, 86*(1), 149–170. doi:10.1057/palgrave.fr.9400339

Demers, D. (2017, March 1). Much ado about nothing. Teaching Matters @ UCA. https://teachingmattersatuca.wordpress.com/2017/03/01/much-ado-about-nothing/#more-1384

Demers, D. M. (2014). *"I Am The Captain Of The Ship": Mother's Experiences Balancing Graduate Education And Family Responsibilities* [Doctoral dissertation, Southern Illinois University]. https://opensiuc.lib.siu.edu/dissertations/810/

Edwards, R. (1993). *Mature women students: Separating or connecting family and education.* Taylor and Francis.

Gabana, N. T., Steinfeldt, J., Wong, Y. J., Chung, Y. B., & Svetina, D. (2019). Attitude of gratitude: Exploring the implementation of a gratitude intervention with college athletes. *Journal of Applied Sport Psychology, 31*(3), 273–284. doi:10.1080/10413200.2018.1498956

Gerstel, N. (2000). The third shift: Gender and care work outside the home. *Qualitative Sociology, 23*(4), 467–483. doi:10.1023/A:1005530909739

Greenwald, R. A. (2012, August 7). *New kinds of leadership*. Inside Higher Ed. https://www.insidehighered.com/advice/2012/08/08/essay-leadership-higher-education

Hochschild, A. R. (1989). *The second shift: Working parents and the revolution at home*. Viking.

Howe-Walsh, L., & Turnbull, S. (2016). Barriers to women leaders in academia: Tales from science and technology. *Studies in Higher Education, 41*(3), 415–428. doi:10.1080/03075079.2014.929102

Isgro, K., & Castaneda, M. (2015). Mothering in U.S. academia: Insights from lived experiences. *Women's Studies International Forum, 53*, 174–181. doi:10.1016/j.wsif.2014.12.002

Kurian, R. M., & Thomas, S. (2023). Perceived stress and fatigue in software developers: Examining the benefits of gratitude. *Personality and Individual Differences, 201*, 111923. doi:10.1016/j.paid.2022.111923

Kurian, R. M., & Thomas, S. (2023). Gratitude as a path to human prosperity during adverse circumstances: a narrative review. *British Journal of Guidance & Counseling*, 1-14.

Leisure, T. M. (2007). *Female graduate students' experiences in an online doctoral degree program: A heuristic inquiry*. [Doctoral Dissertation, University of South Florida]. Retrieved from ProQuest Dissertations and Theses. (Order No. 3251343.)

Lester, J. (2015). Cultures of work–life balance in higher education: A case of fragmentation. *Journal of Diversity in Higher Education, 8*(3), 139–156. doi:10.1037/a0039377

Mattingly, M. J., & Bianchi, S. (2003). Gender Differences in the Quantity and Quality of Free Time: The U.S. Experience. *Social Forces, 81*(3), 999–1030. doi:10.1353of.2003.0036

Milkie, M. A., Raley, S. B., & Bianchi, S. M. (2009). Taking on the Second Shift: Time Allocations and Time Pressures of U.S. Parents with Preschoolers. *Social Forces, 88*(2), 487–518. doi:10.1353of.0.0268

Miller, C. C. (2019, April 26). Women did everything right. Then work got 'greedy.' *The New York Times*. https://www.nytimes.com/2019/04/26/upshot/women-long-hours-greedy-professions.html

Mills, C. (1970). *The sociological imagination*. Penguin Books.

Minow, M. (2000). About Women, about Culture: About Them, about Us. *Daedalus, 129*(4), 125–145. https://www.jstor.org/stable/20027667

Mirza, H. S., & Hoskins, K. (2010). Love in the cupboard: A conversation about success and sadness when race, gender and class collide in the making of an academic career. In B. A. Cole & H. Gunter (Eds.), *Changing lives: Women, inclusion, and the PhD* (pp. 119–136). Trentham Books Ltd., https://eric.ed.gov/?id=ED511419

Unexpected Dreams

Misra, J., Lundquist, J. H., & Templer, A. (2012). Gender, work time, and care responsibilities among faculty. *Sociological Forum, 27*(2), 300–323. doi:10.1111/j.1573-7861.2012.01319.x

Morley, L. (1997). A class of one's own: Women, social class and the academy. In P. Mahony & C. Zmroczek (Eds.), *Class Matters. Working Class Women's Perspectives on Social Class* (pp. 109–122). Taylor and Francis. doi:10.4324/9780203992159

Offer, S., & Schneider, B. (2011). The gender gap in time-use patterns: Multitasking and well being among mothers and fathers in dual-earner families. *American Sociological Review, 76*(6), 809–833. doi:10.1177/0003122411425170

Ortner, S. B. (1972). Is Female to Male as Nature Is to Culture? *Feminist Studies, 1*(2), 5–31. doi:10.2307/3177638

Perkins, K. (2011). *A Case Study of Women Educational Administrators and Their Perspectives on Work and Life Roles*. [Graduate Theses, USF Tampa]. https://digitalcommons.usf.edu/etd/3290

Phillips, A. C., & Klocksieben, F. A. (2020). Attitude of gratitude: Evaluation of a wellness program to improve dispositional gratitude among medical students. *Journal of Wellness, 2*(2), 9. doi:10.18297/jwellness/vol2/iss2/9

Polavieja, J. G., & Platt, L. (2014, September). Nurse or mechanic? The role of parental socialization and children's personality in the formation of sex-typed occupational aspirations. *Social Forces, 93*(1), 31–61. doi:10.1093fou051

Raddon, A. (2002). Mothers in the Academy: Positioned and positioning within discourses of the 'successful academic' and the 'good mother.'. *Studies in Higher Education, 27*(4), 387–403. doi:10.1080/03075070220000011516

Ramsell, H. (2019, Oct. 11). When I grow up I want to be…. *Perkbox*. https://www.perkbox.com/uk/resources/blog/when-i-grow-up-i-want-to-be

Ratky, S. L. (1990). *Femininity and dominion: Studies in the phenomenology of oppression*. Routledge.

Reay, D. (1997). The double-blind of the 'working-class' feminist academic: The success of failure or the failure of success? In P. Mahony & C. Zmroczek (Eds.), *Class Matters. Working Class Women's Perspectives on Social Class* (pp. 18–29). Taylor and Francis., doi:10.4324/9780203992159

Rosa, R. (2021). The trouble with 'work–life balance' in neoliberal academia: A systematic and critical review. *Journal of Gender Studies, 31*(1), 55–73. doi:10.1080/09589236.2021.1933926

Sallee, M., Ward, K., & Wolf-Wendel, L. (2016). Can anyone have it all? Gendered views on parenting and academiccareers. *Innovative Higher Education, 41*(3), 187–202. doi:10.100710755-015-9345-4

Sasaki, T., Hazen, N. L., & Swann, W. B. Jr. (2010). The supermom trap: Do involved dads erode the moms' self-competence? *Personal Relationships, 17*(1), 71–79. https://psycnet.apa.org/doi/10.1111/j.1475-6811.2010.01253.x. doi:10.1111/j.1475-6811.2010.01253.x

Sayer, L. C., England, P., Bittman, M., & Bianchi, S. M. (2009). How Long is the Second (Plus First) Shift? Gender Differences in Paid, Unpaid, and Total Work Time in Australia and the United States. *Journal of Comparative Family Studies, 40*(4), 523–545. doi:10.3138/jcfs.40.4.523

Slaughter, A. (2012, July/August). Why women still can't have it all. *The Atlantic*. https://www.theatlantic.com/magazine/archive/2012/07/why-women-still-cant-have-it-all/309020/

Turvett, B. (2011). Life under construction. *Working Mother, 34*(5), 42.

Ward, K., & Wolf-Wendel, L. (2012). Academic motherhood: How faculty manage work and family. Rutgers University Press; 2012.

Wolf-Wendel, L., & Ward, K. (2015). Academic mothers: Exploring disciplinary perspectives. *Innovative Higher Education, 40*(1), 19–35. doi:10.100710755-014-9293-4

Yee, L. (2021, October 19). *Workplace evolution: The 'third shift' matters - and women do more of it.* Fast Company. https://www.fastcompany.com/90687404/the-third-shift-matters-and-women-do-more-of-it

Chapter 3
Toxic Femininity in Higher Education:
Academia's Sting in the Tail – The Queen Bee

Catherine Hayes
(iD) https://orcid.org/0000-0003-3870-2668
University of Sunderland, UK

ABSTRACT

The metaphorical concept of the 'Queen Bee' now transcends situational contexts to such an extent that it has become a universal focus for both contexts of research and professional practice. Global crises provide a unique context of perspective for the manifestations of gender inequity to be revealed within the context of leadership and management in higher education. From an historical perspective a woman whose behaviours were identifiable as being characteristic of a queen bee, became associated with the notion of projected enmity towards other, typically younger women who may be able to compete with them professionally. This chapter will illuminate key aspects of the queen bee complex through a lens of perspective which permits a metacognitive consideration of gender-based standpoints in higher education.

INTRODUCTION

'People must not turn into bees and kill themselves in stinging others....'

Sir Francis Bacon (1561-1626)

Identification of the 'Queen Bee' manifestation in organisational hierarchies, where predominantly male focused organisational culture is common are not unusual and have been documented in the published evidence base for decades (Rossi, 1965). Operationally defined, for the purposes of this chapter, the phenomenon refers to the intrinsic attitude and articulated behavioural responses of women who have

DOI: 10.4018/978-1-6684-8597-2.ch003

Copyright © 2023, IGI Global. Copying or distributing in print or electronic forms without written permission of IGI Global is prohibited.

Toxic Femininity in Higher Education

regularly faced gender-based discrimination and barriers to career progression who as a consequence of this then project similar gender-based discrimination and barriers upon their female counterparts, whether as an unconscious by-product of their own negative experience or as a deliberate intervention to ensure their own perceptible sense of superiority. The impact of this phenomenon is not only negative for fellow women on the receiving end of it, but it also impacts on overall organisational cohesion and can lead to a workplace culture within which discriminatory behaviour and barriers to progression are the social norm and where high rates of female staff turnover are demonstrable (Hussain, 2022). The published literature is filled with exemplars of how women are disadvantaged within the context of organisational hierarchies which are traditionally the preserve of older white men, with a recognisably negative impact on the agency of women and the opportunities afforded to them consequently (Derks, Van Laar & Ellemers, 2016). Whilst these patriarchal patterns perpetuate the myths of discrimination and reinforce workplace cultures which further consolidate negative attitudes, they are not the sole cause of the Queen Bee Phenomenon in practice (Mavin, 2006). The potential for emergence of the Queen Bee Phenomenon is exacerbated when women, who have become immersed in these cultures, as an integral part of having to directly compete with men and allude to the same behaviours, fail to support their female counterparts, and widen the gap in opportunity for progression for other women. If this remains unaddressed at an organisational level, this too becomes an embedded part of organisational culture and the reinforcement of concepts such as the glass ceiling and the whole concept of the 'Queen Bee' (Baumgartner & Schneider, 2010). Added to the context of a global crisis such as the global COVID-19 pandemic, the visibility of inequity and inequality becomes even more apparent in the context of Higher Education, which is what this chapter serves to illuminate.

BUILDING AND MAINTAINING THE HIVE

The impact of the COVID-19 pandemic has ensured not only that humanity has dealt with a sudden and harsh reminder of its own position relative to the risks man lives with on an everyday basis, but also the opportunities to initiate and manage change that these bring, specifically for women in business (Peters et al, 2020). The existential crisis facing HEIs as a direct consequence of 2020 has served as a lens through which other facets of ambiguity and contingency also influence meta-thinking concerning their strategic governance and operationalisation of policies in practice (Pellegrini et al, 2020). Facing ethical dilemmas, institutional leaders also must grapple with compounding intraneous and extraneous variables which exacerbate the current crisis situations HEIs now face (Rapanta et al, 2020).

Whereas the majority of HEIs across the globe work within specific methodological and management methodologies, the capacity for flexible adaptation, creativity, and innovation in crisis, arguably manifests more commonly amongst women leaders than their male counterparts (El-Besomey, 2020). The gender balance and diversity that women bring to executive leadership positions during times of crisis provides a correspondingly more diversified epistemic standpoint through which crises can be considered (Aldrich & Lotito, 2020). These often subtle but diverse differences in knowledge positionality serve to be more transformative than transactional and as such are often more contextually and situationally relevant to immediately pressing issues, offering a wider lens through which to present, frame and articulate considered solutions. This is particularly relevant in relation to the emergence of the organisational Queen Bee (Choo, 2020). Crises impact upon the theoretical underpinnings of the institutional rationales, designs, and operations of these contexts – within HEI and in parallel fields of praxis, where women have been

Toxic Femininity in Higher Education

witnessed at executive leadership levels, coping better and more appropriately than their male peers, almost as if facing a hypothetical wartime battle (Benziman, 2020; Maas et al, 2020).

The malalignment of the theoretical framework of HEI relative to the disciplinary perspectives of education has long been annotated as an issue for address (Barnett, 1990), however this was framed at a particularly politically volatile time as a means of highlighting larger ethical issues of concern, rather than crisis as an independent concept (Jandrić et al, 2020). The most recent challenge, presented by COVID-19, is to ensure that pedagogic practice across HEIs can adapt to new teaching and assessment methodologies, whilst at the same time ensuring an optimal quality and student experience for those joining academic programmes of study at HEIs (Rapanta et al, 2020) These experiences will potentially form the foundational bedrock which will ultimately underpin their future careers, personal lives, and capacity for wider civic societal contributions.

PYRAMIDAL ORGANISATIONAL HIERARCHIES

The formal administration structures of HEIs have altered little in a century (Kezar & Posselt, 2019). Still featuring a pyramidal structure where women notoriously occupy the bottom rung of the organisational hierarchy, remains a typical profile for the majority of global HEIs. In European and American HEIs, initiatives aimed specifically at addressing gender equity in education, are thriving, which aim to provide transformational leadership opportunities and development for women (Thorpe, 2019). These provide bespoke training, education, and progression pathways for those who wish to further their academic career trajectories but are limited in availability and opportunity to access them is often lacking in equity of opportunity. The central issue of capacity for women leaders in HEIs is not actually the number of women in HEIs across the globe but rather the positions they occupy, which tend to be traditionally clustered at the bottom of the organisational hierarchy with minimal degrees of representation at higher levels, As a consequence, women rarely progress to the level of Dean, but do occupy their subordinate positions as Associate Deans, Directors or Pro Vice Chancellors, rather than linchpin positions at the top (Rogers-Adkinson & Feldhaus, 2022). This is a source of blocking women's access to powerful positions and thus exerting a vision for the next generation of female leaders. Perhaps the greatest danger in this dynamic is the sheer invisibility of organisational and gender-based bias, which serves to block female progression. As a key aspect of social justice and equity in action, as both process and goal this is a fundamental area for address across the globe where untapped potential and the provision of opportunity warrant redress (McNair, Bensimon, & Malcom-Piqueux, 2020; Okoli et al, 2020).

Men are far more likely to attribute the underrepresentation or lack of women in executive level positions to the breaks they necessarily take in relation to family caring responsibilities, career interruptions due to pregnancy and their comparative and relative lack of research impact in HEI praxis (García-González, Forcén & Jimenez-Sanchez, 2019). In contrast women's perceptions of the same experience are littered with reports of actively overt and covertly demonstrated workplace discrimination, fuelled by the basis of their gender. Unlike the successes of Merkel and Thatcher in a political setting, where transformative learning is valued, the opposite has been found to be largely true in the context of HEI settings, where the higher women climb within the organisational hierarchy, the more they assume the character traits represented by male leaders, where they become deliberately and overly transactional (Allen & Flood, 2018). As a direct consequence of this, they progressively develop the same perspectives, that recruitment based on gender is something that ought to be tokenistic rather than something addressed in global HEI professional practice (Gomes, Grangeiro & Esnard, 2022). These deficit models are potentially damaging, but even more so where this is often unintentionally reinforced by members of their own gender because of the cultural normalisation of gender stereotyping and hence the hatching and emergence of organisational 'Queen Bees' (Teelken Deem, 2013). Göransson, et al (2008) stated that gendered organisational cultures are in turn linked to gendered knowledge, which means the naturally occurring agentic qualities with which women are wired to lead, are often masked by the bureaucracy and culture of organisations, rather than anything else. Consequently, the hegemonic and often toxic masculinity which drives organisations pervades into the wider cultural climate and becomes entrenched and difficult to address since it also manifests in women as well as men. At the heart of addressing these issues is the nature of recruitment and the nature of actively retaining women through to the point where they have visibly recognisable opportunities to apply for promotion or at least seek a career trajectory reflective of their capacity and capability and which is then not jeopardised by the hostility of other women in the workforce. This is apparent across many professional disciplines out with the context of Higher Education (Hayes & Graham 2020; Bellini et al, 2019). The nature of women's participation is also an issue, since they need the basis of equity and inclusivity to participate on an equal footing with their male counterparts. Those pragmatic issues which serve as barriers to this, are often found in the institutional operational policies within which all staff are required to work, regardless of academic or professional discipline (Cardel et al, 2020).

THE VISIBLE REPRESENTATION OF WOMEN IN ACADEMIA

The agentic qualities that women do bring to the context of executive leadership within the context of Higher Education Institutions

(HEIs) are based around their capacity for creativity and as a direct consequence the bridge to innovation that this secures (Lipton, 2015). They are also widely reported as enhancing capacity for effective communication and an authentic approach to dealing with both the professional and personal needs of others.

Perhaps dwelling overly on long held debates of both the metaphorical glass ceiling and glass escalator ought to be diminished by the consideration of women, who whilst largely atypical of female representativeness across HEIs, provide important lessons surrounding the agentic qualities which have underpinned their success (Arriaga, Stanley & Lindsey, 2020).

Presenting these women as exemplars, however, runs two distinct risks which have important implications for professional practice (Jameson, 2019). Firstly, the situations and contexts within which all women operate as leaders are largely unique and therefore the opportunity to emulate success is limited and secondly, women who are unable to transfer approaches into the context of their own workplace have an increased potential to perceive they will fail. In relation to the concept of failure, there are far wider independent variables and contextual issues at play, which correspondingly align with the far wider cultural challenges of organisational norms (Benslimane & Moustaghfir, 2020). One of the most insightful set of perspectives are those presented by Syed (2019) whose perspectives on the need for accuracy rather than creativity in the progressive development of change on major world issues such as feminism. His debate that during COVID-19 some leaders have demonstrated a clear capacity to pivot between leadership styles via the integration of both diverse views and binary decision-making processes. Reconciling the perceived tension that arises when seeking to increase diversity within established meritocracies remains a pivotal debate in any consideration of women and their opportunities to use innate agency within crisis. Doubtless this will prevail, although the pandemic has provided a forum for the illumination of not just exceptional women from the higher echelons of society but all those coping in more everyday settings of the home, the office and beyond (Howie & Tauchert, 2019).

MYSOGYNISTIC CULTURAL IDENTITY

The focus on predominantly masculine cultures within male dominated professions has been central to developing an understanding of how women's lives are impacted upon during their rise to senior leadership positions and where self-preservation and the perpetuation of negativity around other women has become an equally embedded part of organisational culture (Boggs & Mitchell, 2018). Gender stereotyping is known to be the key factor in workplace contexts and settings where as a rule women are characterised as being nurturing, compassionate and understanding than men, and these characteristics are also associated with weakness in relation to their capacity to occupy senior management roles where being an empath, is not necessarily perceived as a positive attribution, either personally or professionally (Hentschel, Heilman & Peus, 2019).

Framing professional identity has then been separated for successful women, who may deliberately segregate themselves from other women for whom abandoning these expected norms is more difficult. Proving their deferential difference from these stereotypical women, therefore becomes part of the picture of success, can lead to the potential of alienation in terms of the psychological articulation of ambition, the consolidation of newly embedded attitudes and the result of their expressed behaviours.

What constitutes the masculine attributes of leadership is also open to critical debate. Typically, men fulfil their own social role expectations by demonstrating stereotypical characteristics of the corporate competitor, risk taker who is confident and unfazed by processes of complex decision making, which may be unpopular with the wider workplace hierarchy (Smith & Fredricks-Lowman, 2020). In contrast, female leaders are often to be the antithesis of this and consequently hierarchy of capacity and capability place women lower in the metaphorical pecking order of appropriateness for the most senior leadership roles and the sustainable impact of them. Certainly, this is an organisational issue for address since it is an outward expression of gender inequity that catalyses a cycle of reinvention which perpetuates in to future generations of workplace employees. Breaking the cycle of gender inequity, affording opportunity and valuing equality is a systemic series of aims, which has the potential to radically alter the perspective of men and women in the workplace and to disrupt and eventually destroy the typical norms of the 20th Century workplace and reflect those necessary for the 21st.

The centuries themselves have shaped and framed societal expectation – nowhere is this more evident than in the tangible impact that the COVID-19 pandemic had on organisational infrastructure where feminist perspectives on structure and agency have again been brought to the fore of applied practice in business and management.

Media reports that women in leadership roles have greatly outperformed men in the strategic management of the implications of COVID-19 globally, have become an everyday source of interest and intrigue. The positive lauding of female prime ministers, presidents and politicians has also been counterbalanced by accounts from women with more standard positions on career trajectories, for whom home working, home schooling and the attempted continuance of everyday norms amidst a global pandemic are, by their very nature, far more routine and mundane prospects (Whitty-Collins, 2020). On an even more negative

Toxic Femininity in Higher Education

and resonant note, the media have reported on the increased incidence and prevalence rates of domestic violence crimes committed against women, which further detail the challenges that some women (and their children) in 21st Century society also face (Wenham, Smith & Morgan, 2020).

The scope and parameters of this chapter do not permit a consideration of all issues that all women face, rather this chapter provides an insight into the agentic roles of women leaders in global crises, which have ensured their credibility and dependability in times of greatest challenge to the context of Higher Education (HE) leadership across the world. A collective insight into the roles of women leaders within the COVID-19 pandemic has featured widely in the international press, where multi-agency perspectives on their actions and reactions have been largely positive (Trent, 2020). Belying this media frenzy, however, lies a far deeper debate in just how representative these women leaders are of those working within diverse HE leadership contexts and settings and indeed how far transferable their situational skills of leadership are (Henley & Roy, 2020).

The individual positionality of all women is equally important to those who operate as strategic heads of state and whose lives are largely characterised by the privilege of hierarchical positions and the status accompanying them (Bright, Acosta & Parker, 2020; Inman, 2020). This chapter aims to provide an insight into the existing evidence base of how women leaders in Higher Education during a global pandemic, such as COVID-19, cope. Not only does this illuminate the reality of concepts such as emotional labour, mental health and wellbeing and authenticity, it also serves to delineate the personhood of women from the professional roles they occupy across our global societies, within the situational specificity of Higher Education (Tshivhase, 2020).

In its entirety, this chapter also serves to deconstruct the characteristic and agentic qualities of women leaders amidst global crises, which are also reflected in the traits of women managing in more recognisable and relatable leadership roles in the context of Higher Education leadership (Thomas, 2020). The core acknowledgements that on a global level the impact of crises inevitably leads to a disproportionate impact on women, a lack of prioritisation of global impetus to address levels of gender inequality and the embedded role of gender equity in relation to human progression and development on a macro level is apparent (Power, 2020; WHO, 2020). This global perspective illuminates the inequalities that women educators face and the impact that this has on the broader scope of professional development through educational impact (Barba & Iraizoz, 2020). Whilst situational specificity is significant in terms of the context of, HE leadership, the universality of human experience underpinning them remains the connecting thread, which enables the deconstruction of meaning making in applied educational leadership experiences.

ROOTING PROACTIVE RESPONSE IN CRISIS

Crisis management of any variety necessitates a proactive response, rooted in complex ambiguity, which is non-conventional and is underpinned by active application of cognition, metacognition, and epistemic cognition to practice. In terms of temporal issues, response times can necessitate an immediacy of thinking and correspondingly rapid response, all of which may have potentially long-term consequences, necessitating leaders to be both accountable and responsible for their actions. Parallel to this lies Mezirow's (2009) Perspective Transformation Theory, posited by Mezirow, in relation to transformative learning as,

Toxic Femininity in Higher Education

"... the epistemology of how adults learn to reason for themselves - advance and assess reasons for making a judgement - rather than act on the assimilated beliefs, values, feelings and judgements of others..."

In terms of overall cognitive processing in the contexts of crisis, how gender is of direct relevance is rooted in the increased capacity women have, relative to men, to think flexibly, adaptably and with compassion (Villiers, 2019). This is not to denigrate the gender attributable skill sets of male employees across HEIs but to acknowledge that how people engage with problem solving and react can often have its basis in concepts which are adjuncts to, rather than facets of gender. Whereas men are geared towards objective problem solving in binary 'black and white' fashions as opposed to the capacity to think in shades of grey, which women more clearly demonstrate, what is clear, is that situation and context are the pivotal deciding variables in terms of the need for immediacy of action (Cahdriyana, et al, 2019). These problematic frames of reference, described by Mezirow in the context of education, explain how humans monitor their problem-solving capacities, once engaged in contexts and settings of complex ambiguity, where contingency planning comes to the fore (Mezirow, 2009).

THE IMPACT OF COMPLEX AND DISRUPTIVE AMBIGUITY

Within the context of complex and disruptive ambiguity in crisis, the capacity for both critical reflection and critical reflexivity are paramount. Self-awareness features highly as one of the core aspects of being able to undertake either optimally and effective action, since how responsive behaviours may be viewed by others, and the interrelationship of this with the alternative perspective of others can be indicators of potential success in crisis management. Behaviour which discriminates against women is not the preserve of male dominated organisational hierarchies and also exists in female dominated professions such as nursing and the caring professions, where male counterparts generally occupy a higher percentage of managerial roles, but women predominate in leadership positions (Cortis, Foley & Williamson, 2022). Being able to separate formal from informal relationships between women in the workplace is central to the support women perceive. Being friends with managers and having close personal relationships with them influences positive career progression and the issue of partisanship or nepotism can arise. However, for most women who wish to have a purely professional working relationship with their female counterparts, then informal engagement with other women can further exacerbate barriers to progression up the organisational hierarchy and lead to a greater incidence in anxiety and depression in relation to the impact of workplace stress (Wheaton & Kezar, 2019). This is particularly evident in workplace conflict where hostile interactions lead to further exacerbations of the Queen Bee Phenomenon. Illuminating an awareness of complex ambiguity enables a further conceptual consideration of the gender delineation occurring naturally because of the agentic qualities and attributes of women in the context of crisis management, where the Queen Bee Phenomenon may also be apparent. What is pivotal in these incidences is the capacity for and subsequent integration of tacit knowledge to practice, which stems from not only an extant evidence base but also experiential learning and wisdom, rather than any certainty or concretisation of new knowledge (Dewey, 1933). It is this which is transformational rather than transactional in terms of application and use in leadership praxis and aligns directly with the traditional gender traits of women and men in executive leadership positions, respectively. Through the advancement of the body of work in cognitive psychology at the turn of the 21st century, and the understanding of epistemic assumptions, models such as 'The Reflective Judgement Model' posited by King and Kitchener (2004) (see Table 1 overleaf) lend themselves to adapted application in relation to gender delineation. Whilst all of these are evidence based on the extant literature, the issues of situational specificity and context are pivotal in any consideration of complex ambiguity in crisis, not least because of the relative certainty of knowledge within them.

Table 1. A gender delineation adaptation of the King and Kitchener (2004) reflective judgement model as applied to the impact of the queen bee phenomenon

THINKING STAGES	POTENTIAL IMPLICATIONS ON AGENTIC QUALITIES FOR ASPIRING FEMALE LEADERS
Stage 1 (Pre-Reflective)	**State of Knowledge**: Knowledge is absolute and concrete with no reason to ask the question 'why? For example, women believe only what they have observed or been exposed to and thus know it to be as part of a true-single category belief system with an associated exposure to diversity of thinking. **Implications**: If the basis of knowledge for women influenced by Queen Bee Phenomenon is such that in this phase of pre-reflection the phenomenon is the sociocultural norm, then this potential 'normalisation of deviance' can be regarded as an integral part of the organisational culture (Brown & Ramlackham, 2022).
Stage 2 (Pre-Reflective)	**State of Knowledge**: Knowledge is certain but not readily available to everyone, the right person in authority needs to be sought– some people hold right beliefs, and some people hold wrong beliefs, which is like Perry's dualism in being observed or taught by an authority figure. **Implications**: In contexts where women are unaware of the issues of equity and equality surrounding their roles within an organisational hierarchy, or a clear organisational stance on them is not apparent, this can encourage subcultures to emerge, which may sustain the Queen Bee Phenomenon.
Stage 3 (Pre-Reflective)	**State of Knowledge**: Knowledge is assumed to be certain or temporarily uncertain and believe that absolute truth will be manifest in concrete data sometime in the future. Implicitly they maintain that ultimately all problems have solutions. **Implications**: The perpetuation of Queen Bee Phenomenon at the heart of academic institutions, which remains evident but overlooked by senior management as being something transient or largely irrelevant to equity and equality.
Stage 4 (Quasi-Reflective)	**State of Knowledge**: Knowledge is no longer certain, there is always a layer of ambiguity, limitations of the knower are acknowledged and without certainty knowledge cannot be validated. Well-structured problems such as arithmetic can be described completely, and ill-structured problems are afforded legitimacy at this stage. **Implications**: The Queen Bee Phenomenon is regarded as a legitimate manner in which senior female leaders and managers can express outward behaviour as a reflection of their inner attitude towards fellow female colleagues.
Stage 5 (Quasi-Reflective)	**State of Knowledge**: Knowledge is contextual and subjective, interpretations are different, so knowledge is different. **Implications**: Different perceptions of the Queen Bee Phenomenon are evident across HEIs with varying reception and accommodation of the concept.
Stage 6 (Reflective)	**State of Knowledge**: Knowing is uncertain and knowledge must be understood in relation to the context from which it was derived. Knowledge is constructed through evaluation, comparing knowledge and opinions across contexts, an initial basis for forming judgement/solutions to ill-structured problems. **Implications**: The concept of the Queen Bee Phenomenon may become immersed in complex ambiguity and a deeper part of the accepted organisational culture.
Stage 7 (Reflective)	**State of Knowledge**: Knowing is uncertain and subject to interpretation and epistemically justifiable claims can be made about the best solution to the problem. Knowledge as an outcome and a process of evaluation. Re-evaluation, new methods of inquiry, or new perspectives become available over time. **Implications**: Queen Bee Phenomenon, if not challenged may be come a permanent feature of organisations with traditional male management routes and female leadership roles, with a correspondingly high female staff turnover rate or stagnation of female support and mentorship for women wishing to progress.

Toxic Femininity in Higher Education

THE CASE FOR GENDER BASED CAPACITY FOR PROCESSES OF CRITICAL REFLECTION AND REFLEXIVITY

Axiologically identifiably fixed and typically white male, middle-aged, middle-class mindsets have shaped the society within which corporate leadership operates, with global HEIs being no exception. The perspectives these fixed mindsets are rooted in, stems not only from professional bias, but the constraints of cultures which seek to categorise, label and define men and women in relation to biology rather than their capacity to function as leaders, where gender is and ought to be regarded as incidental. What is evident is that the characteristic agentic qualities of both genders differ but what is equally clear is that these have been socially constructed over the course of lifetimes and it is a change in the fixed mindset of modern society that is gradually enabling recognition and acknowledgement of this. Sadly, whilst the COVID-19 pandemic may increase access to educational opportunities and potentially widen participation, the economic effects will have a greater negative impact, restricting even basic access to educational opportunity. In May 2020 the World Bank estimated that 60 million people were at risk of being pushed into extreme poverty worldwide because of COVID-19; erasing all progress made to alleviate poverty over the prior 3 years. This will likely adversely impact women in particular, whose roles both personally and professionally are influenced to a far greater extent than their male counterparts and as a direct consequence increase the likelihood of the emergence of the Queen Bee Phenomenon.

WOMEN LEADERSHIP IN HIGHER EDUCATION CONTEXTS

Despite HEI's making formal recognition of barriers to women reaching senior management positions across their organisational hierarchies, their executives have done relatively little to address issues of structure and agency in relation to antiquated practices that perpetuate these identified inequities and consequently the emergence of the Queen Bee Phenomenon (O'Connor, 2020). The situational and contextual backdrops which influence these inequities globally are, of course, largely defined by sub-cultures and contexts at macro, micro and meso levels – the ecological perspectives of where change has been lost in translation to quite often tokenistically address gender inequity in the workplace is often clearly tangible (Grimson & Grimson, 2019). However authentic approaches to tackling the provision of opportunities for women are rooted too, in wider societal actions and agencies which women respond to prior to and in the early development of establishing a professional identity. The perpetuation of an underrepresentation of women in senior management positions within the labour market generally, and the higher education senior leadership market specifically, is an issue for address but not in isolation. Alongside this there must be the address of the agency afforded to women in relation to the development of non-discriminatory gender practice, which means the women for whom Queen Bee behaviour becomes a means of progression via hostility towards their female counterparts no longer need to express this in practice.

The commonality of issues surrounding women in HEI leadership positions within and between diverse countries, is widely reported as something which transcends cultural barriers and contextual specificities. What unites the relative framing and positioning of these roles is the inflexibility of organisational infrastructures to accommodate diversity beyond feminist tokenism, which contributes directly to a lack of accessibility to leadership roles for women. This is a historical legacy characterised predominantly by dated approaches to the integration of women into the labour market at executive leadership levels

(O'Connor, 2019). Remuneration levels are all too often aligned with this inequity and what is evident is that whereas globally most institutions are making moves to close the gender pay gap, they are doing relatively little to change the infrastructure and support for potential women leaders, which impacts on the degree of opportunity afforded to them during their career trajectories (Heymann et al, 2019; Taylor et al, 2017). These career trajectories, by virtue of biological function, are still inevitably interrupted by maternity leave and caring responsibilities to a larger extent than the careers of their male counterparts. Equality and diversity initiatives at national levels in the UK, now ensure that many organisations are designated the status of equal opportunities employers, which have seen the rise of initiatives such as the Athena Swann mark emblazoned across HEI provider websites, reflecting their articulated capacity to advocate and support equal opportunities in the workplace. Whether this impacts authentically on these wider issues of structures and agency is something only longer-term evaluation will reveal.

Whilst equality proofing quality initiatives serve well in the identification of the impact of policies which have unintentionally negative impacts on women in practice, one key challenge is being able to identify and filter out the factors underpinning them. In the context of wider professional practice measures these can potentially serve to identify unintended policy impacts but serve neither to identify mechanisms to monitor or reverse the ongoing masculinisation of HEI provision. It ought to be expected that those countries which implement these policy initiatives (e.g., UK, New Zealand, Australia and Sweden) have a greater degree of success in their levels of equal opportunity for women in HEIs but the published research evidence actually points to countries such as Turkey, Portugal and Cyprus having better success rates despite having no formal nationally applied gender based equality initiatives in formal operation (Tanova et al, 2008; Reay, 2004).

TRADITIONALIST LEGACIES ACROSS SIGNATURE PEDAGOGIES

The longevity of male dominance in particular disciplinary subjects such as mathematics, science and engineering has done little to positively enhance the quality and duration of HEI women leaders' career trajectories. An evidence-based insight into this reveals a clear deficit of female professors across these disciplines, which bears witness to the corresponding longevity and history of education locally, nationally, and globally. One of the first steps to deconstructing this inequality is, as the STEM initiative in the UK has focused upon, to encourage equity and new awareness of careers available in traditionally male dominated professions (Fitzgerald, 2020). Where gendered organisational culture and processes are evident in favour with male employees, it is apparent from the literature that, conformity is also more widely valued than attributes of creativity, and, as a by-product, innovation. This has been both historically and contemporaneously apparent in the body of literature available but amidst crisis with the advent of the COVID-19 pandemic, has never been more relevant. In HEIs which have demonstrably lower levels of women at senior executive levels across their organisations, this brings into question the purist epistemic assumptions which are clearly non diverse and non-aspirational in terms of equality, diversity and consequently creativity. The exponential reach afforded by a clear capacity for a diverse workforce, not merely constructed of ideological representation, but one of operationalised knowledge and skill, is immeasurable and has been clearly evidenced by the progression of parallel fields of practice (Baykal, Soyalp & Yeşil, 2020). As an active consequence of these dilemmas which have pervaded organisations for the best part of half a century, issues of gatekeeping, the impact of gendered cultures and infrastructures policies and initiatives are at last beginning to feature mechanisms of moving forward positively

Toxic Femininity in Higher Education

but they also indicate the extreme way to go that organisation have to correct these systemic imbalances. What is clear is that if central policy does not change to reflect these needs, the governments, which also reflect an imbalance in the representation of women in executive roles, will persist in influencing the macro levels of society at which meso and micro levels are then by default poised to remain indefinitely.

Research has been conducted which conclusively identifies that senior managers of HEI organisations believe or hold assumptions that women, from a signature pedagogy perspective, are far more likely to work in the context of disciplines such as the social sciences, arts and humanities - those often termed 'soft subjects' or those which are responsible in health and medical care in the remit of 'caring' such as nursing (Dilnot, 2018; Henderson et al, 2018). They also perceived those empirical sciences due to the cultural necessity of maintaining the status quo of daily operations would potentially be interrupted by career breaks and the accommodation of caring responsibilities. In contrast to this perspective though, remains the fact that women's choice of study during school and university years also demonstrates that relatively few young women wish to study subjects such as science, technology, engineering and mathematics and as the current initiatives in UK educational settings indicate, this has become an identified area for redress in terms of changing the misconceptions that girls have about academic study in the post-compulsory sector (Lannelli & Duta, 2018). At a macro level, the labour market dictates the value of subject disciplines by leaders of global societies, where the representation of women leadership is also comparatively low. Reflective of this, is the fact that a corresponding hierarchy of subjects and disciplines exist, which is positively reinforced by the masculine perspectives driving their need. Because of this, fewer women follow maths, technology and sciences in preferences to the arts, humanities and social sciences (Vooren et al, 2022). The visual presence of women at the top of organisational hierarchies also serves to break down the perceptions of negative stereotyping still evident across society. By encouraging early career professionals who may well also be balancing a career with caring responsibilities and the new roles of parenthood, visibilities of success do far more than give the current generation of women opportunities. Central to this is the address of the gender pay gap, which has been well evidenced over recent years and remains a challenge across professional organisations and which can also heavily influence the perceived attractiveness of top management and leadership positions for aspiring female academics.

Aligned with the capacity for maximal earning capacity in the labour market are the opportunities to work in disciplines of these empirical studies, hence widening the gap between men and women in the potential to gain highly paid roles. Again, the redress of this balance would serve to close the gender income gap which characterises global economies. Research also highlights that those disciplines with which women more readily engage, also contribute widely to the development of the skill sets which men are known to lack (Darwish, Alzayed & Ahmed, 2020). Gender segregation in the early stages of student learning at school can be regarded as a key cause of the gender gap, both economically and in terms of leadership opportunity that women experience throughout their academic careers. Where these are of greatest concern is in relation to the concepts of citizenship, which HEIs often claim to incorporate as an integral part of their organisational strength across global communities. Within this context, diversity and equality are two issues upon which capacity for citizenship and capacity for active civic reach, can hinge.

DEBUNKING THE DEFICIT MODEL MYTH

Within the current literature it is well established that the skills that leading in the context of HEIs entails are not actually gendered at all. These skills are centred around the capacity and capability for endurance in relation to hard work, strategic vision, evidence of reputational impact in research, the courage to manage in the context of taking measured risk and the resilience and integrity to operationalise what is necessary for success (McQuillan et al, 2020). From an axiological standpoint, it is more often the case that the value placed upon what women leaders do, stems from the value of the disciplinary perspectives from which they emerge, rather than any overt judgement surrounding gender (Devillard, Hunt & Yee, 2018). Within the context of male senior management there are far more likely to be male academics from traditionally masculine subjects such as science and engineering, whereas, due to the historical legacies and patterns of humanities and caring professions, women are far less likely to have worked with and alongside them.

Women leaders are far more likely to express a capacity for collective and relationship behavioural approaches in practice, than male leaders, who are more likely to adopt purely transactional leadership strategies and operationalise these in practice. Because of this approach, women are often deemed to be less effective since their capacity to deal with complex ambiguity often entails detailed critical thinking as opposed to the binary decision making associated with transactional approaches. This is wholly dependent on the situational specificity of organisational contexts, which ultimately provides a platform for leadership execution and the ethos evident within it, in relation to differing leadership styles and approaches (Pecci, Frawley & Nguyen, 2020).

CONCLUSION

This chapter has explored the issues that crisis management reveals in workplaces where the Queen Bee Phenomenon has become an integral part of organisational culture. Far from being attributable to misogyny in the workplace by individual men or collective groups who are sexist in their daily dealings with women, it is evident that how women function in the workplace in cultures of equity and inequality are as much of an issue in practice. The issue then is not with people but with the organisations in which they work and how the structure and agency of HEIs can really determine positive and negative working environments. There must be the address of the agency afforded to women in relation to the development of non-discriminatory gender practice, which means the women for whom Queen Bee behaviour becomes a means of progression via hostility towards their female counterparts no longer need to express this in practice. There is now an existential crisis facing HEIs as a direct consequence of the COVID-19 pandemic and this serves as just one lens through which facets of complex ambiguity and the need for contingency can be viewed. Queen Bee Phenomenon is not only an ethical dilemma for Higher Education Institutes, but also one which, in redressing the balance of traditional organisational hierarchies so that the skills of women are optimally represented, is a 21st Century necessity for the assurance of equity and equality.

Toxic Femininity in Higher Education

REFERENCES

Aldrich, A. S., & Lotito, N. J. (2020). Pandemic Performance: Women Leaders in the COVID-19 Crisis. *Politics & Gender*, *16*(4), 1–9. doi:10.1017/S1743923X20000549

Allen, T. G., & Flood, C. T. (2018). The Experiences of Women in Higher Education: Who Knew There Wasn't a Sisterhood? *Leadership and Research in Education*, *4*, 10–27.

Arriaga, T. T., Stanley, S. L., & Lindsey, D. B. (2020). *Leading While Female: A Culturally Proficient Response for Gender Equity*. Corwin.

Barba, I., & Iraizoz, B. (2020). Effect of the Great Crisis on Sectoral Female Employment in Europe: A Structural Decomposition Analysis. *Economies*, *8*(3), 64. doi:10.3390/economies8030064

Barnett, R. (1990). *The idea of higher education*. McGraw-Hill Education.

Baumgartner, M. S., & Schneider, D. E. (2010). Perceptions of women in management: A thematic analysis of razing the glass ceiling. *Journal of Career Development*, *37*(2), 559–576. doi:10.1177/0894845309352242

Baykal, E., Soyalp, E., & Yeşil, R. (2020). Queen bee syndrome: a modern dilemma of working women and its effects on turnover intentions. In *Strategic Outlook for Innovative Work Behaviours* (pp. 165–178). Springer. doi:10.1007/978-3-030-50131-0_9

Bellini, M. I., Graham, Y., Hayes, C., Zakeri, R., Parks, R., & Papalois, V. (2019). A woman's place is in theatre: Women's perceptions and experiences of working in surgery from the Association of Surgeons of Great Britain and Ireland women in surgery working group. *BMJ Open*, *9*(1), e024349. doi:10.1136/bmjopen-2018-024349 PMID:30617103

Benslimane, M., & Moustaghfir, K. (2020). Career development practices and gender equity in higher education. *International Journal of Management Education*, *14*(2), 183–211.

Benziman, Y. (2020). "Winning" the "battle" and "beating" the COVID-19 "enemy": Leaders' use of war frames to define the pandemic. *Peace and Conflict*, *26*(3), 247–256. doi:10.1037/pac0000494

Boggs, A., & Mitchell, N. (2018). Critical university studies and the crisis consensus. *Feminist Studies*, *44*(2), 432–463. doi:10.1353/fem.2018.0028

Bright, A., Acosta, S., & Parker, B. (2020). Humility Matters: Interrogating Our Positionality, Power, and Privilege Through Collaboration. In Handbook of Research on Diversity and Social Justice in Higher Education (pp. 19-40). IGI Global.

Brown, N., & Ramlackhan, K. (2022). Exploring experiences of ableism in academia: A constructivist inquiry. *Higher Education*, *83*(6), 1225–1239. doi:10.100710734-021-00739-y PMID:34366440

Cahdriyana, R. A., Richardo, R., Fahmi, S., & Setyawan, F. (2019, March). Pseudo-thinking process in solving logic problem. []. IOP Publishing.]. *Journal of Physics: Conference Series*, *1188*(1), 012090. doi:10.1088/1742-6596/1188/1/012090

Cardel, M. I., Dhurandhar, E., Yarar-Fisher, C., Foster, M., Hidalgo, B., McClure, L. A., & Willig, A. L. (2020). Turning chutes into ladders for women faculty: A review and roadmap for equity in academia. *Journal of Women's Health*, *29*(5), 721–733. doi:10.1089/jwh.2019.8027 PMID:32043918

Choo, E. K. (2020). COVID-19 fault lines. *Lancet*, *395*(10233), 1333. doi:10.1016/S0140-6736(20)30812-6 PMID:32334693

Cortis, N., Foley, M., & Williamson, S. (2022). Change agents or defending the status quo? How senior leaders frame workplace gender equality. *Gender, Work and Organization*, *29*(1), 205–221. doi:10.1111/gwao.12742

Darwish, S., Alzayed, S., & Ahmed, U. (2020). How Women in Science can Boost Women's Entrepreneurship: Review and Highlights. *International Journal of Innovation Creativity and Change*, *14*(1), 453–470.

Derks, B., Van Laar, C., & Ellemers, N. (2016). The queen bee phenomenon: Why women leaders distance themselves from junior women. *The Leadership Quarterly*, *27*(3), 456–469. doi:10.1016/j.leaqua.2015.12.007

Devillard, S., Hunt, V., & Yee, L. (2018). Still looking for room at the top: Ten years of research on women in the workplace. *The McKinsey Quarterly*, *2*, 106–115.

Dewey, J. (1933). *How We Think A Restatement of the Relation of Reflective Thinking to the Educative Process*. Heath & Co Publishers.

Dilnot, C. (2018). The relationship between A-level subject choice and league table score of university attended: The 'facilitating', the 'less suitable', and the counter-intuitive. *Oxford Review of Education*, *44*(1), 118–137. doi:10.1080/03054985.2018.1409976

El-Besomey, D. A. M. (2020). The Contemporary Vision of Universal Strategic Planning for Facing (COVID-19) Crisis in the Field of Higher Education Via Virtual Learning-Training. *European Journal of Education*, *3*(2), 151–164. doi:10.26417/869dvb85y

Fitzgerald, T. (2020). Mapping the terrain of leadership: Gender and leadership in higher education. *Irish Educational Studies*, *39*(2), 1–12. doi:10.1080/03323315.2020.1729222

García-González, J., Forcén, P., & Jimenez-Sanchez, M. (2019). Men and women differ in their perception of gender bias in research institutions. *PLoS One*, *14*(12), e0225763. doi:10.1371/journal.pone.0225763 PMID:31805114

Gomes, M. B., Grangeiro, R. R., & Esnard, C. (2022). Academic women: A study on the queen bee phenomenon. *RAM. Revista de Administração Mackenzie*, *23*(2). doi:10.1590/1678-6971/eramg220211.pt

Göransson, K. E., Ehnfors, M., Fonteyn, M. E., & Ehrenberg, A. (2008). Thinking strategies used by Registered Nurses during emergency department triage. *Journal of Advanced Nursing*, *61*(2), 163–172. doi:10.1111/j.1365-2648.2007.04473.x PMID:18186908

Grimson, J., & Grimson, W. (2019). Eliminating gender inequality in engineering, industry, and academia. In *The Engineering-Business Nexus* (pp. 315–339). Springer. doi:10.1007/978-3-319-99636-3_15

Hayes, C., & Graham, Y. N. (2020). Prophylaxis in Action:# MeToo for Women of Medical and Surgical Disciplines. In Gender Equity in the Medical Profession (pp. 270-279). IGI Global.

Henderson, M., Sullivan, A., Anders, J., & Moulton, V. (2018). Social class, gender and ethnic differences in subjects taken at age 14. *Curriculum Journal, 29*(3), 298–318. doi:10.1080/09585176.2017.1406810

Henley, J., & Roy, E. A. (2020). Are female leaders more successful at managing the coronavirus crisis. *Guardian.* https://www. theguardian. com/world/2020/apr/25/why-do-femal e-leadersseem-to-be-more-successful-at-managing-the-coronavi rus-crisis .

Hentschel, T., Heilman, M. E., & Peus, C. V. (2019). The multiple dimensions of gender stereotypes: A current look at men's and women's characterizations of others and themselves. *Frontiers in Psychology, 10*, 11. doi:10.3389/fpsyg.2019.00011 PMID:30761032

Heymann, J., Levy, J. K., Bose, B., Ríos-Salas, V., Mekonen, Y., Swaminathan, H., & Darmstadt, G. L. (2019). Improving health with programmatic, legal, and policy approaches to reduce gender inequality and change restrictive gender norms. *Lancet, 393*(10190), 2522–2534. doi:10.1016/S0140-6736(19)30656-7 PMID:31155271

Howie, G., & Tauchert, A. (2019). *Gender, teaching and research in higher education: Challenges for the 21st century.* Routledge. doi:10.4324/9781315254548

Hussain, M. (2022). Development And Validation Of Queen Bee Syndrome Perception Inventory (QB-SPI). *Webology, 19*(4).

Inman, A. G. (2020). Culture and Positionality: Academy and Mentorship. *Women & Therapy, 43*(1-2), 112–124. doi:10.1080/02703149.2019.1684678

Jameson, J. (Ed.). (2019). *International perspectives on leadership in higher education: Critical thinking for global challenges.* Routledge. doi:10.4324/9781315122410

Jandrić, P., Hayes, D., Truelove, I., Levinson, P., Mayo, P., Ryberg, T., & Jackson, L. (2020). Teaching in the Age of COVID-19. *Postdigital Science and Education*, 1-162.

King, P. M., & Kitchener, K. S. (2004). Reflective judgment: Theory and research on the development of epistemic assumptions through adulthood. *Educational Psychologist, 39*(1), 5–18. doi:10.120715326985ep3901_2

Lannelli, C., & Duta, A. (2018). Inequalities in school leavers' labour market outcomes: Do school subject choices matter? *Oxford Review of Education, 44*(1), 56–74. doi:10.1080/03054985.2018.1409970

Lipton, B. (2015). A New" ERA" of Women and Leadership: The Gendered Impact of Quality Assurance in Australian Higher Education. *Australian Universities Review, 57*(2), 60–70.

Maas, B., Grogan, K. E., Chirango, Y., Harris, N., Liévano-Latorre, L. F., McGuire, K. L., & Primack, R. B. (2020). Academic leaders must support inclusive scientific communities during COVID-19. *Nature Ecology & Evolution, 4*(8), 1–2. doi:10.103841559-020-1233-3 PMID:32493950

Mavin, S. (2006). Venus envy: Problematizing solidarity behaviour and queen bees. *Women in Management Review*, *21*(4), 264–276. doi:10.1108/09649420610666579

McNair, T. B., Bensimon, E. M., & Malcom-Piqueux, L. (2020). *From equity talk to equity walk: Expanding practitioner knowledge for racial justice in higher education*. John Wiley & Sons. doi:10.1002/9781119428725

Mezirow, J. (2009). Transformative learning theory. In J. Mezirow & E. W. Taylor (Eds.), *Transformative Learning in Practise: Insights from Community, 39 Workplace, and Higher Education* (pp. 18–32). Jossey Bass.

O'Connor, P. (2019). Gender imbalance in senior positions in higher education: What is the problem? What can be done? *Policy Reviews in Higher Education*, *3*(1), 28–50. doi:10.1080/23322969.2018.1552084

O'Connor, P. (2020). Why is it so difficult to reduce gender inequality in male-dominated higher educational organizations? A feminist institutional perspective. *Interdisciplinary Science Reviews*, *45*(2), 207–228. doi:10.1080/03080188.2020.1737903

Okoli, G. N., Moore, T. A., Thomas, S. L., & Allen, T. T. (2020). Minority Women in Educational Leadership. *Handbook on Promoting Social Justice in Education*, 1711-1727.

Pecci, A., Frawley, J., & Nguyen, T. (2020). On the Critical, Morally Driven, Self-reflective Agents of Change and Transformation: A Literature Review on Culturally Competent Leadership in Higher Education. *Cultural Competence and the Higher Education Sector*, 59-81.

Pellegrini, M., Uskov, V., & Casalino, N. (2020). Reimagining and Re-Designing the Post-COVID-19 Higher Education Organizations to Address New Challenges and Responses for Safe and Effective Teaching Activities. Law and Economics Yearly Review Journal-LEYR, Queen Mary University, London, UK, 9(part 1), 219-248.

Peters, M. A., Rizvi, F., McCulloch, G., Gibbs, P., Gorur, R., Hong, M., & Quay, J. (2020). Reimagining the new pedagogical possibilities for universities post-COVID-19: An EPAT Collective Project. *Educational Philosophy and Theory*, 1–44.

Power, K. (2020). The COVID-19 pandemic has increased the care burden of women and families. *Sustainability: Science. Practice and Policy*, *16*(1), 67–73.

Rapanta, C., Botturi, L., Goodyear, P., Guàrdia, L., & Koole, M. (2020). Online university teaching during and after the COVID-19 crisis: Refocusing teacher presence and learning activity. *Postdigital Science and Education*, 1-23.

Reay, D. (2004, January). Cultural capitalists and academic habitus: Classed and gendered labour in UK higher education. []. Pergamon.]. *Women's Studies International Forum*, *27*(1), 31–39. doi:10.1016/j. wsif.2003.12.006

Rogers-Adkinson, D., & Feldhaus, H. (2022). Understanding and Overcoming Female-to-Female Oppression in Higher Education. In *Voices from Women Leaders on Success in Higher Education* (pp. 95–105). Routledge. doi:10.4324/9781003219897-11

Rossi, A. S. (1965). Women in science: Why so few? Social and psychological influences restrict women's choice and pursuit of careers in science. *Science*, *148*(3674), 1196–1202. doi:10.1126cience.148.3674.1196 PMID:17748114

Smith, N., & Fredricks-Lowman, I. (2020). Conflict in the workplace: A 10-year review of toxic leadership in higher education. *International Journal of Leadership in Education*, *23*(5), 538–551. doi:10.10 80/13603124.2019.1591512

Syed, M. (2019). Rebel Ideas: The power of diverse thinking. Hachette UK.

Tanova, C., Karatas-Özkan, M., & Inal, G. (2008). The process of choosing a management career: Evaluation of gender and contextual dynamics in a comparative study of six countries: Hungary, Israel, North Cyprus, Turkey, UK and the USA. *Career Development International*, *13*(4), 291–305. doi:10.1108/13620430810880790

Taylor, L. L., Beck, M. I., Lahey, J. N., & Froyd, J. E. (2017). Reducing inequality in higher education: The link between faculty empowerment and climate and retention. *Innovative Higher Education*, *42*(5-6), 391–405. doi:10.100710755-017-9391-1

Teelken, C., & Deem, R. (2013). All are equal, but some are more equal than others: Managerialism and gender equality in higher education in comparative perspective. *Comparative Education*, *49*(4), 520–535. doi:10.1080/03050068.2013.807642

Thomas, S. (2020). Women in Higher Education Administration Leadership and the Role of Institutional Support. In *Accessibility and Diversity in the 21st Century University* (pp. 234–249). IGI Global. doi:10.4018/978-1-7998-2783-2.ch012

Thorpe, A. (2019). Educational leadership development and women: Insights from critical realism. *International Journal of Leadership in Education*, *22*(2), 135–147. doi:10.1080/13603124.2018.1450995

Trent, R. J. (2020). *Women's Perspectives on the Role of Organizational Culture in Their Career Advancement to Leadership Positions: A Generic Inquiry* [Doctoral dissertation, Capella University].

Tshivhase, M. (2020). Personhood: Implications for Moral Status and Uniqueness of Women. Handbook of African Philosophy of Difference, 347-360.

Villiers, C. (2019). Boardroom Culture: An Argument for Compassionate Leadership. *European Business Law Review*, *30*(2), 253–278. doi:10.54648/EULR2019012

Vooren, M., Haelermans, C., Groot, W., & van den Brink, H. M. (2022). Comparing success of female students to their male counterparts in the STEM fields: An empirical analysis from enrollment until graduation using longitudinal register data. *International Journal of STEM Education*, *9*(1), 1–17. doi:10.118640594-021-00318-8

Wenham, C., Smith, J., & Morgan, R. (2020). COVID-19: The gendered impacts of the outbreak. *Lancet*, *395*(10227), 846–848. doi:10.1016/S0140-6736(20)30526-2 PMID:32151325

Wheaton, M. M., & Kezar, A. (2019). Interlocking systems of oppression: Women navigating higher education leadership. In *Challenges and opportunities for women in higher education leadership* (pp. 61–83). IGI Global. doi:10.4018/978-1-5225-7056-1.ch005

Whitty-Collins, G. (2020). *Why Men Win at Work:...and How to Make Inequality History*. Luath Press Ltd.

World Health Organization. (2020). COVID-19 and violence against women: what the health sector/ system can do, 7 April 2020 (No. WHO/SRH/20.04). World Health Organization.

ADDITIONAL READING

Allen, T. G., & Flood, C. T. (2018). The Experiences of Women in Higher Education: Who Knew There Wasn't a Sisterhood? *Leadership and Research in Education*, *4*, 10–27.

Arvate, P. R., Galilea, G. W., & Todescat, I. (2018). The queen bee: A myth? The effect of top-level female leadership on subordinate females. *The Leadership Quarterly*, *29*(5), 533–548. doi:10.1016/j.leaqua.2018.03.002

Baykal, E., Soyalp, E., & Yeşil, R. (2020). Queen bee syndrome: a modern dilemma of working women and its effects on turnover intentions. In *Strategic Outlook for Innovative Work Behaviours* (pp. 165–178). Springer. doi:10.1007/978-3-030-50131-0_9

Derks, B., Van Laar, C., & Ellemers, N. (2016). The queen bee phenomenon: Why women leaders distance themselves from junior women. *The Leadership Quarterly*, *27*(3), 456–469. doi:10.1016/j.leaqua.2015.12.007

Faniko, K., Ellemers, N., & Derks, B. (2016). Queen Bees and Alpha Males: Are successful women more competitive than successful men? *European Journal of Social Psychology*, *46*(7), 903–913. doi:10.1002/ejsp.2198

Faniko, K., Ellemers, N., & Derks, B. (2021). The Queen Bee phenomenon in Academia 15 years after: Does it still exist, and if so, why? *British Journal of Social Psychology*, *60*(2), 383–399. doi:10.1111/bjso.12408 PMID:32696985

Luo, X., & Gu, Y. (2022). Only the Legislation is Insufficient. In *2022 7th International Conference on Financial Innovation and Economic Development (ICFIED 2022)* (pp. 1813-1817). Atlantis Press. 10.2991/aebmr.k.220307.298

Rogers-Adkinson, D., & Feldhaus, H. (2022). Understanding and Overcoming Female-to-Female Oppression in Higher Education. In *Voices from Women Leaders on Success in Higher Education* (pp. 95–105). Routledge. doi:10.4324/9781003219897-11

Stolz, C., Reinhard, M. A., & Ende, L. (2022). Mean girls, queen bees and iron maidens? Female leadership and accusations of workplace bullying. *Open Psychology*, *4*(1), 249–264. doi:10.1515/psych-2022-0127

KEY TERMS AND DEFINITIONS

Agency: Is the the capacity, condition, or state of acting or of exerting power within the context of situationally specific contexts.

Toxic Femininity in Higher Education

Complex Ambiguity: Is a lack of clarity or awareness about situations, complicated by an array of multifactorial issues or variables.

Gender Inequity: Is discrimination based on sex or gender causing one sex or gender to be routinely privileged or prioritized over another.

Leadership Capacity: Is the human capital necessary to gain the consensus of others in supporting strategic change to achieve optimal operational implementation.

Metacognition: Is the capacity to make meaning and have awareness and understanding of one's own thought processes.

Misogyny: Is the hostility towards, prejudice or contempt for the female gender.

Reflection: A process of identifying, questioning, and assessing our deeply held assumptions.

Reflexivity: The capacity to see one's own perspective and assumptions and understand how one's perspective, assumptions and identity are socially constructed through critical reflection.

Situational Specificity: Is the context specific response that people demonstrate in different situations and settings.

Stereotype: Is the often false and unfair attribution given to others based on the belief that all people with a particular characteristic are the same.

Chapter 4

Informal Mentoring Among Women in Higher Education to Subvert Gender Bias

Clair A. Stocks

https://orcid.org/0009-0006-8655-7791

Chapman University, USA

ABSTRACT

This chapter includes a summary of the current environment of higher education for women, an analysis of formal and informal mentoring opportunities and efficacy for women, and recommendations. Women in higher education continue to contend with significant disparities in representation in leadership, biased social norm expectations related to gender, and burdensome professional and personal invisible labor related to service and caretaking. As women face these ongoing and persistent impediments to career progress and ascension, they have created networks of informal mentoring relationships that provide them with support, resources, and resilience as they contend with the male-normed environment of higher education. Informal mentoring relationships are distinct from formal mentoring relationships, as the focus is on providing support for the whole person and not just professional strategy. Informal mentoring is also more accessible to women as the dearth of women in higher education leadership can create a lack of available same-gender formal mentors who have a lens of shared experience.

INFORMAL MENTORING AMONG WOMEN IN HIGHER EDUCATION TO SUBVERT GENDER BIAS

Women's participation in the workforce has been increasing steadily over the last 60 years and is expected to be nearly equal to that of men by the close of the decade (U.S. Department of Labor, 2020). Women also outpace men in educational attainment, earning 57% of bachelor's degrees, 61% of master's degrees, and 54% of doctoral degrees (U.S. Department of Education, 2019). Despite these gains, women continue to be underrepresented in leadership positions in all professional and political sectors, including higher education (American Association of University Women, 2016; Badura et al., 2018). In

DOI: 10.4018/978-1-6684-8597-2.ch004

Copyright © 2023, IGI Global. Copying or distributing in print or electronic forms without written permission of IGI Global is prohibited.

**Informal Mentoring Among Women to Subvert Gender Bias**

the academy, women make up the majority of the workforce, but they are cloistered in entry and mid-level positions facing a torrent of barriers and biases precluding them from career ascension (Cañas et al., 2019; Johnson, 2017; O'Connor, 2018).

Ongoing and persistent role congruence demands contribute significantly to the underrepresentation of women in the higher echelons of the academy (Carli & Eagly, 2016; Chrobot-Mason et al., 2019; Eagly & Karau, 2002; Goethals & Hoyt, 2017; Madsen & Longman, 2020). Role congruity is the social expectation that individuals within certain identity groups behave in prescribed manners. Social roles demand that women are communal, deferential caretakers and that leaders are independent, assertive, and agentic resulting in incongruence between the two identities (American Association of University Women, 2016; Eagly & Karau, 2002; Goethals & Hoyt, 2017). The result places women who aspire to leadership in a double bind whereby these two identities are incompatible, so they are seen as ill-suited for both roles (Bierema, 2016; Eagly & Karau, 2002). Men face no such quandary as the ideal qualities of masculinity are perfectly in sync with those ascribed to leaders.

As women contend with the myriad of unique challenges they face in the academy, they have been particularly skilled at building networks to support one another and share wisdom, guidance, and encouragement, allowing them to better navigate the labyrinth of the male-normed higher education environment (Harris & Lee, 2019; Hollander & Yoder, 1980; Madsen & Longman, 2020; Uhl-Bien, 2006; Yip et al., 2020). The networks provide natural conditions for mentoring relationships among women to develop and thrive. Mentoring relationships have been shown to have a significant impact on the success of women in the academy by providing not only support and insight but also by ameliorating the sense of isolation felt by many women in higher education (Ong et al., 2017).

Formal mentoring is a well-established construct that typically pairs an established senior leader with a novice protégé to provide career guidance and identify areas of opportunity (Harris & Lee, 2019). While these types of mentoring relationships can be useful, it is helpful for women to have same-gender mentors who understand the particular perils they face in their careers. However, the ongoing leadership gender gap and the abundance of additional personal and professional labor women contend with means there is a shortage of senior women to serve as mentors (Cross et al., 2019). In response, women have turned to informal mentoring as an alternative. Informal mentoring, which occurs organically and between women regardless of rank, can be even more impactful as it provides whole-person support and a whisper network that identifies and protects against potential harm in professional environments (Clayman Institute for Gender Research, 2019; Statti & Torres, 2019).

This chapter provides an examination of the current environment of higher education for women in faculty and administrative positions. The theoretical frameworks of role congruity theory and relational leadership theory guide the discussion about the role informal mentoring plays in supporting women as they pursue their professional aspirations and seek to dismantle long-standing systemic patriarchal norms that have historically placed them at a disadvantage. Recommendations to the academy are provided to cultivate a more inclusive environment that recognizes both the challenges women face and the essential contributions and value they bring to higher education.

THEORETICAL FRAMEWORKS

The theoretical frameworks of role congruity theory (Eagly & Karau, 2002) and relational leadership theory (Hollander & Julian, 1969; Uhl-Bien, 2006) provide the lenses through which the phenomenon of informal mentoring among women in higher education to subvert gender bias is considered. Role congruity theory identified incongruence between feminine gender role expectations and the agentic and masculine traits of the socially prescribed leader identity, resulting in gender bias and discrimination (Eagly & Karau, 2002). Role incongruity results in women not being considered suitable for leadership or, if they do rise to leadership, views them as suspect for failing to comply with the expectations of femininity (van Gils et al., 2018). A famous example of the ire women have faced when they attempt to assume leadership positions is former U.S. senator and presidential candidate Hillary Clinton, who faced intense public scrutiny, often related to her gender (Sorrentino et al., 2022).

Whether a woman's qualifications make her suited for leadership is secondary to perceptions of how the collective feminine identity is ill-suited for the socially constructed visage of the rugged, independent, and decidedly male leader assumed to be most adept at shepherding organizations to success and prestige. Whether these stereotypes are factual is inconsequential. And in fact, the stereotypes are not true, as women have been shown to be effective and capable leaders. Research shows female leadership is associated with improved financial and operational outcomes, improved worker morale, more corporate social responsibility, greater innovation, fewer workforce reductions, and improved equality and national wealth (American Association of University Women, 2016; Gloor et al., 2020; Goethals & Hoyt, 2017). Nonetheless, perceptions contrary to the reality of the efficacy of female leadership persist and continue to contribute to the leadership gap.

Role congruity theory also demonstrates how women are maligned and punished when they fail to meet the expected behaviors associated with the feminine social role. Men are given the latitude to deprioritize their familial role in favor of their work identity as this aligns with the masculine provider identity (Bierma, 2016). Women are expected to do the opposite and sacrifice their career ambitions to support their husbands' pursuits and focus on domestic responsibilities. When women deviate from these expectations, their choices are met with intolerance and disdain (Eagly & Karau, 2002). Women who show independence, decisiveness, and professional ambition are viewed with skepticism and aversion for their failure to conform to the social expectations associated with femininity (Goethals & Hoyt, 2017). The negative perceptions of female leaders extend to peers, followers, and even the women themselves, who fall prey to the public scrutiny associated with role incongruity (van Gils et al., 2018).

While role congruity theory gives a basis for understanding how social roles contribute to the gender bias and discrimination women contend with, relational leadership theory provides a potential antidote through its focus on relationship-building over stereotyping. Rather than bestowing a leader with power based on perceptions and assumptions, relational leadership theory views leadership as an exchange of rewards between leaders and followers (French & Raven, 1959; Hollander, 1992). Relational leadership theory is concerned with the relationships leaders and followers build together, the establishment of trust, and the ongoing exchange of power and esteem between those involved in the relationship (Hollander & Julian, 1969; Uhl-Bien, 2006).

Relational leadership provides a framework by which women can be assessed according to their merits rather than by social norms and conventions. Rather than nurturing long-held stereotypes associated with social norms, relationship-building disrupts harmful and outdated conventions by providing an opportunity to redefine what is expected. Relational leadership is rooted in empathy, understanding, and authenticity, which can challenge biased constructs and redefine how we consider the ideal leader (Jian, 2021; Yip et al., 2020). Mentoring, with its focus on interpersonal relationships and understanding, is a natural environment where relational leadership can grow and thrive, giving way to new ways of understanding.

THE ENVIRONMENT OF HIGHER EDUCATION FOR WOMEN

The academy is tasked with contributing to the social good through the proliferation of ideas and innovation and by contributing to the improved social and economic situations of students and graduates (Kornbluh et al., 2020). However, higher education is an entity conceived of for and by White men, and it remains beholden to patriarchal traditions and norms (Burkinshaw & White, 2017; Ford, 2016; Odell, 2020). Men hold the majority of full-time tenured faculty positions and are paid more than their female counterparts (Johnson, 2017). More than 70% of college presidencies are held by men, and at doctoral-granting institutions, that number rises to 90% (O'Connor, 2018). Women, conversely, are overrepresented in entry and mid-level positions, with their presence diminishing at every step up the leadership ladder. While there has been some suggestion that women languish in less prestigious positions because they lack the ambition for leadership, studies contradict this and indicate the true reason for the leadership gap is ongoing and systemic gender bias and the persistent underrepresentation that dissuades women from pursuing advancement (Cañas et a., 2019; David, 2015; Hannum et al., 2015). In their study of women university presidents, Hill & Wheat (2017) noted that participants did not even recognize the possibility of leadership being open to them until later in their careers as there simply was no representation to indicate otherwise.

Women as Professional and Personal Caregivers

In the academy, while men concern themselves with research and leadership, women are tasked with most of the caretaking work of higher education (Subbaye & Vithal, 2017). Women spend more time teaching, advising, and fulfilling service roles which are often unrecognized or undervalued when it comes time for promotion (Hannum et al., 2015). Despite the clear delineation of prestige work and caretaking work that falls along gender lines, men often fail to recognize the imbalance at play in the academy. Rather, they view the academy as a noble meritocracy where women are equally capable and have ample opportunity to ascend and lead (Wong et al., 2018).

Social expectations contributing to role incongruence are furthered and perpetuated by the historically male-normed environment of the academy (Eagly & Karau, 2002). Not only are leaders seen as possessing inherently male qualities, but the responsibilities for household and family caretaking still overwhelmingly fall to women (Eagly & Koening, 2021). Women report being responsible for as much as 88% of the physical and emotional labor of family life, with well-educated and highly paid women taking on even more responsibility to compensate for the perceived role incongruence between their gender expectations and career aspirations (Ciciolla & Luther, 2019). When professional work is coupled with domestic labor, women spend an average of 15 hours more per week working than men, and their free time is largely devoted to housework, whereas men spend their free time on leisure (Bierema, 2016; Cañas et al., 2019; Statti & Torres, 2019). However, because there is still such a persistent pay gap, in dual-income families, 71% of men continue to out-earn their female partners, which leads to women relocating in service of their husband's careers and at the peril of their own (American Association of University Women, 2016; Brower et al., 2019; White & Burkinshaw, 2019). Further, the biological imperative that necessitates women bear children and assume primary caretaking for them through infancy results in women limiting their involvement in the workforce or leaving and reentering, interrupting their progress toward advancement and promotion (Burkinshaw & White, 2017). Often this professional lapse cannot be overcome, leaving women to abandon their ambitions and languish in lower-level positions than those to which they originally aspired.

The so-called leaky pipeline that sees women fall out of contention for leadership roles is often viewed not as a failing of the system in which women struggle to operate but rather as an individual choice women make for themselves (O'Connor, 2018). The academy does not recognize its complicity in interrupting, stalling, and vanquishing the career aspirations of women as it conceives of itself as a meritocracy where opportunity is equally available. Merit is assessed according to availability, visibility, and centering all aspects of life around professional pursuits – constructs that were implemented at a time when women were largely absent from the workforce and relegated to the work of domestic life to ensure men could focus on their careers (Bierema, 2016; White & Burkinshaw, 2019). Working women are excluded from excellence because they are deemed less available and committed to their professional life when they must contend with domestic responsibilities. Yet to delegate those responsibilities to others would result in societal judgment and be deemed an irresponsible or unfeeling wife or mother. Though reimaging how we think about professional excellence and contributions might remedy some of the barriers women face, there is little impetus for the male-dominated academy to change a system from which they benefit or to acknowledge the profoundly unjust environment they have cultivated (Burkinshaw & White, 2017; van Gils et al., 2018).

Women in Leadership: The Benefits of Gender Parity

Though higher education clings to norms and traditions that create substantial burdens and disincentives for women, their presence and leadership in the academy are associated with positive and beneficial institutional outcomes. Women tend to use leadership styles that resonate with employees and lead to greater morale, satisfaction, and retention (Eagly et al., 2003; Stelmokienė &n Endriulaitienė, 2020; Wong et al., 2018). Organizations with greater gender parity also benefit from a higher return on investment and sales, improved profits, fewer workforce reductions, and enhanced workplace ethics (American Association of University Women, 2016; Bierema, 2016; Gloor et al., 2020). Beyond institutional benefits, more representative leadership is also associated with greater national wealth and more participation in philanthropic endeavors (American Association of University Women, 2016; Gloor et al., 2020; Goethals & Hoyt, 2017). Despite the benefits that investments in gender parity bring to individuals, families, organizations, communities, and the nation, there continues to be an unwillingness to recognize the problem and its potential solutions. The slow and meager progress has left women adrift while attempting to work within a system that leaves them underrepresented, undervalued, and unseen (Badura et al., 2018). In response, women have created mentoring networks with other women in an effort to build support, explore identity through the lens of authenticity, and contribute to greater representation in the academy by challenging and supplanting the system of barriers they have faced as a result of persistent gender bias (Brue & Brue, 2018; Harris & Lee, 2019; Madsen & Longman, 2020; Yip et al., 2020).

FORMAL AND INFORMAL MENTORING

Mentoring is not a new concept in higher education. In fact, it is not uncommon for individuals to be assigned mentors to help them acclimate to their institutions and the professional roles they inhabit. A study of female university presidents revealed that these women overwhelmingly reported having mentors and credited these relationships as being a crucial component of their success (Ginsberg et al., 2019). However, much of the recognized structure for mentoring relies on the establishment of formal mentoring relationships where a senior leader uses their positional power to provide counsel and create opportunities for a junior employee (Harris & Lee, 2019). While these types of relationships can be advantageous in that they can provide the mentee with credibility through their affiliation with their mentor, women also describe formal mentors who are uninterested in understanding them and instead give derisive advice that upholds the male-normed environment of the academy (Cañas et al., 2019; Meister et al., 2017; Stocks, 2022; Wong et al., 2018). In addition, the leadership gap and the disparate demands on women's time result in a scarcity of senior women able to act as mentors for other women (Cross et al., 2019). Though male mentors may provide women with an ally with power (Longman et al., 2019), women in same-gender mentoring relationships have a shared framework of experience that enhances inclusion and belonging and creates a more beneficial experience for both parties (Brue & Brue, 2018; Ginsberg et al., 2019).

To address the dearth of same-gender formal mentors, women have created organic support networks and informal mentoring relationships. Women generously define a mentor as anyone who has helped them, whether or not that individual knows they are acting in a mentoring capacity (Searby et al., 2015). Beyond climbing the proverbial ladder, women are interested in forming relationships that provide social support and professional advice that recognizes and validates their experiences (Harris & Lee, 2019; Madsen & Longman, 2020; Yip et al., 2020). Given the desire of women to engage in authentic relationships rooted in mutual understanding, informal mentoring can be even more powerful than formal mentoring. In these relationships, women are able to choose their mentors and mentees, create communities of practice, and give women access to professional social networks from which they are often excluded as these groups are often designed around the more leisurely male experience (Block & Tietjen-Smith, 2016; Brower at al., 2019; Cross et al., 2019; Ginsberg et al., 2019; O'Connor, 2018).

BENEFITS OF INFORMAL MENTORING

While informal mentoring can serve a practical purpose in providing access to important mentoring relationships in an environment where there may be a shortage of women in senior leadership positions, it also provides social and emotional benefits to both the mentor and protege. Women are particularly interested in forming relationships rooted in authenticity and understanding from a shared perspective, creating more representation through empowerment and the shifting of biased norms around social roles (Stocks, 2022).

Authenticity

Women in the academy must walk a tenuous tightrope, balancing how they are perceived as women with how they are perceived as leaders (Eagly & Karau, 2002). Deviations from accepted norms can have long-term reputational consequences that can inhibit the careers of women. As men and the academy itself are wont to feign ignorance about the gendered challenges women face (Badura et al., 2018; Gloor et al., 2020; van Gils et al., 2018), it is especially important that women are able to form relationships with other women who understand the complex labyrinth that they are navigating (Eagly & Koenig, 2021). Women understand that other women may not only need stereotypical career advice;

they also need to be able to speak freely about the practical and social challenges of family life and overt and subvert discrimination they experience in the academy (Kuebel et al., 2021; Stocks, 2022). The performative demands of professional life for women often leaves them feeling unseen and trapped in an environment where to be taken seriously requires they divest themselves of their personal identity. Through mentoring, the ability to integrate their identity and inhabit the role of both woman and leader allows women to begin to understand how to subvert the gender bias they encounter professionally and personally (Brue & Brue, 2018).

Empowerment

As women become more comfortable sharing their authentic selves in their relationships with one another, they seek and proffer a sense of empowerment. Same-gender-informal mentoring provides an opportunity to critically examine role congruence demands, gender bias, and unfair treatment arising from stereotypes such as the tendency to overwhelm women with service and secretarial work, hostile and negative views of motherhood in the professional context, and demeaning behavior based on appearance and gender (Block & Tietjen-Smith, 2016; Brue & Brue, 2018; Cross et al., 2019; Longman et al., 2019; Sklaveniti, 2020; Statti & Torres, 2019). The external and internal biases women contend with can lead them to question their competence and belonging as they perceive their inability to fulfill the role of the ideal woman and ideal leader as a personal and professional failing (Bierema, 2016; Meeussen & Van Laar, 2018; Meister et al., 2017).

Informal mentoring relationships provide an opportunity for women to assert their support of one another, develop confidence, and shed the uncertainty of their merit, granting each other recognition as leaders in accordance with the tenets of relational leadership theory (Early, 2020; Nicholson & Kurucz; Yip et al., 2020). This shift in perspective allows women to synthesize their feminine and leader identities, building greater resilience and leaning into their ambitions (Brue & Bruem, 2018; Sklaveniti, 2020). As women affirm their competency, value, and worth for one another, they are empowered to push back against harmful practices, using their voices to advocate for themselves and other women (Stocks, 2022). Women who have a network of supporters and advocates in other women feel more emboldened to call out unfair practices, demand recognition, and demonstrate the value of their contributions, refusing to capitulate to harmful norms.

Representation

As women find themselves more empowered, they are able to better see themselves serving as institutional leaders and understand that the deficits in the academy are heavily influenced by the male-normed system that has failed to recognize the lived experiences of women. The scarcity of women in senior roles can make successful women appear to be a novelty, contributing to the narrative that positions men as leaders as women in supporting roles (Meister et al., 2017). While navigating the treacherous landscape of expected and accepted social roles is complex work, organically developed mentoring relationships embolden women to push forward and persist, creating greater representation and a slow dismantling of oppressive norms (Badura et al., 2018).

As women begin to fill more and more leadership positions, their presence in the highest levels of the academy is normalized. This added representation allows other women to envision what might be possible for them, providing the impetus they require to press forward rather than succumbing to the

Informal Mentoring Among Women to Subvert Gender Bias

leaky pipeline or remaining in lower-level positions (Hill & Wheat, 2017; O'Connor, 2018). Not only does this create greater opportunity for gender parity, but it also increases the number of women in senior positions who are able to serve as mentors and role models for other women, illuminating a path toward what is possible and what is necessary to get there (Cross et al., 2019; Manzi & Heilman, 2021; Moreland & Thompson, 2019; Roberts & Brown, 2019). In fact, many women who have experienced the positive benefits of mentoring (and those who pointedly feel they have missed out on such opportunities) feel called to participate in the mentoring of other women in an effort to pay forward the gifts of their mentors and to contribute to rewriting the script about what is possible (Searby et al., 2015; Statti & Torres, 2019; Stocks, 2022). As women in leadership become more and more visible in the academy, the perceptions we have about how women and leaders behave begin to shift and commingle.

Shifting Norms

With greater representation of women in senior leadership in the academy comes an opportunity to reconsider the norms that have been the foundation for long-standing and structural gender bias. As women are mentored and serve as mentors, they are able to showcase the benefits of such relationships, which in turn creates greater communities of practice, support networks for women, and opportunities to influence outcomes for one another (Meister et al., 2017; Pascale & Ohlson, 2020; Searby et al., 2015). This ability to influence goes beyond individuals, departments, and institutions and can impact the entire higher education sector and society as demands for recognition and equity become more pervasive. Women who engage in informal mentoring relationships work together to dismantle stereotypes and redefine what it means to be a woman and a leader, showing how these roles are mutually inhabitable and not exclusive of one another (Manzi & Heilman, 2021; Roberts & Brown, 2019; Statti & Torres, 2019). The ability to question long-standing practices associated with a male-dominated workforce and a meritocracy that functions to serve the dominant group creates cracks in a flawed and unjust system and allows for collaborative innovation that recognizes value based on new metrics and considerations. And as the doors open to more women in the highest ranks of the academy, the benefits to the women themselves, their families, students, institutions, the academy as a whole, and society are plentiful and abundant.

RECOMMENDATIONS

There is no doubt that mentoring is not a substitution for robust laws and regulations that address gender bias and discrimination, mandating a revision to norms and traditions that have historically disadvantaged women (Allen & Flood, 2018; Brabazon & Schulz, 2018; Early, 2020; Harris & Lee, 2019; Longman et al., 2019). However, legal progress has been slow and stalled, with legislation as fundamental as the Equal Rights Amendment failing to pass since its introduction a century ago (England et al., 2020; National Archives, 2022). Absent a government mandate to ensure equity for women, the onus falls on organizations to interrogate their practices and develop a framework for eradicating bias. Higher education, with its purpose of advancing the social good, should be called on to lead the way forward. The following recommendations serve as a starting point for addressing gender bias in the academy.

Meritocracy

The meritocracy upon which value, success, and promotion are assessed in the academy is presumed to be neutral but, in reality, is calibrated toward standards that privilege the experiences of men (Cañas et al., 2019; O'Connor, 2018). Pointing out the deficits in current systems used to recognize and reward excellence results not in initiatives to address the biases inherent in the current meritocracy but rather on how women can be "fixed" and operate within a sexist framework (White & Burkinshaw, 2019). The meritocracy does not recognize the invisible labor of women, including home and office caretaking, or the biological imperatives that see women shift in and out of the workforce during childbearing years (Kossek & Buzzanell, 2018). A pointed and recent example of such expectations can be seen in the research produced during the COVID-19 pandemic. As long periods of mandatory quarantine necessitated working from home while also keeping children home and overseeing their virtual education, research submissions from women plummeted while those from men increased (Wright et al., 2021). Lockdowns gave men an abundance of additional free time during which they were able to engage in the prestige work of research and publishing, while women endured the opposite experience as they were tasked with managing their professional workload as they simultaneously cared for their children and supervised virtual schooling for them. In an environment where the number of publications, uninterrupted professional participation, and physical presence are signs of achievement, women are deprived of opportunities afforded to their male peers (Stocks, 2022).

Addressing the inherent bias built into the academy's meritocracy system is imperative for higher education institutions to begin to close the leadership gender gap. Women must be at the center of this work because the absence of their perspectives in the leadership domain has perpetuated definitions of merit aligned with male behaviors and privileges (Gloor et al., 2020; Mijs, 2016; Powell & Arora-Jonsson, 2022). Re-evaluating how success and value are defined for purposes of professional advancement is an opportunity to interrogate systems that have left women behind with their focus on quantifiable productivity rather than inputs and outcomes. Not only does this provide women with a more level playing field in the workplace, but it may also encourage men to assume more responsibility for family caregiving if the basis for merit is divested from uninterrupted physical presence and professional participation (Clavero & Galligan, 2021).

Shifting away from the current male-normed meritocracy can begin with initiatives such as establishing representative committees for setting criteria for hiring and promotion focused on standards that recognize the lived experiences of women and consider metrics that do not create a disparity in opportunity. Recognizing the value of diversity and inclusion in the academy and its leadership also makes this an appropriate criterion to include as part of the assessment process (Nielsen et al., 2017). Rubrics can also be an important tool for evaluating individuals for hire and promotion. There is a measure of intentionality inherent in the design of rubrics and the criteria upon which standards are established that can reduce the tendency to rely too heavily on subjective evaluation mired in overt and unconscious biases, which have been shown to be especially detrimental to women (Blair-Loy et al., 2022; Brower et al., 2019; Goethals & Hoyt, 2017; van Gils et al., 2018).

Policies and Practices

The policies and practices of the academy can also be used to reduce gender bias and create a more inclusive environment for women. While well-intentioned policies exist at many institutions, they often

Informal Mentoring Among Women to Subvert Gender Bias

only provide the illusion of equity. Family leave policies are one such example of this phenomenon. These kinds of policies are often directed toward or used by women, who are then punished for their absence in an environment where any period of inactivity is viewed as a weakness or lack of professional commitment (Allen et al., 2021). Meaningful change requires a shift in perspective and the adoption of a nuanced and intersectional lens through which both opportunity and opportunity deficits are considered.

It is important that the academy considers equity and not just equality. Equality in an environment where one group wields an inordinate amount of power and privilege is a misnomer. Regardless of the practices of the academy, the social dictate that sees women as more responsible for household and family labor is a matter of fact, and a shift of perspective has been stubbornly unmoving (Cañas et al., 2019; Ciciolla & Luthar, 2019; Statti & Torres, 2019). A false narrative that claims women have chosen to abandon their professional pursuits is rampant. But the reality is women have been forced out of their careers by unrelenting and persistent bias that has impeded their ability to make progress. In the face of this reality, it is appropriate for the academy to implement policies and procedures that seek to correct this imbalance and equalize opportunity. Providing women with the ability to recoup lost opportunities through programs that provide research funding and policies that give them lessened administrative and service burdens recognizes the value of their contributions and the reality in which they function (O'Connor & Irvine, 2020).

To make true strides toward equity, the academy must continuously reiterate and affirm its commitment to dismantling structures that disadvantage women and other marginalized groups (Hernández-Johnson et al., 2019; Zembylas, 2018). The disbursement of power from those who have it to those who do not may be fraught with resistance. Thus, representative groups must be engaged to establish, communicate, and assess progress toward goals that advance a more balanced and diverse academy, routinely collecting and disaggregating data and feedback (Hodgins et al., 2022). This includes evaluating policies, procedures, and opportunities for development that do not *other* women or seek to contort them to fit within the academy's flawed traditions. Instead, the academy must look for ways to fix itself and disavow the deep-seated structures of patriarchy upon which it was established and has continued to run.

Mentoring

Scrubbing gender bias and establishing equitable practices in the academy is likely the work of decades and generations. While pressing forward with this work is critical to the advancement of women in higher education and society, the reality is that women will continue to face discrimination, role incongruence, and copious amounts of unrecognized caretaking labor. As such, mentoring remains a crucial tool for support. Same-gender mentoring relationships allow women an opportunity to be seen as their whole authentic selves by others who have a similar lived experience, which builds capacity, confidence, resilience, and empowerment.

The proliferation of informal mentoring relationships among women in higher education is evidence that mentoring will occur whether or not the academy invests in them (Cross et al., 2019; Ginsberg et al., 2019; Wong et al., 2018). Within these relationships, women find ways to imbue themselves and other women with a power the academy has long denied them. As institutions seek to create more equitable environments, they should provide opportunities for women to engage together and support one another formally and informally. The academy can contribute to the success of women by providing support for networking groups for women, including giving women space to host meetings, financial resources, and time to participate. Rather than viewing these relationship-building opportunities as extracurricular or extraneous to their professional role, they should be seen as an essential component of personal and professional development that provide women with the necessary tools, resources and community of care necessary to thrive in the exacting and competitive environment of the academy.

CONCLUSION

Despite decades of participation in the workforce, women are still faced with a barrage of barriers and biases that often leave them in a no-win situation where professional advancement is simply incompatible with the demands of womanhood. The academy, with its focus on innovation, knowledge, and advancing the social good, is an environment where women might be expected to fare better than in other sectors. However, men continue to dominate leadership positions in higher education while women languish in entry and mid-level positions. The academy leans into a philosophy of merit and equality without recognizing the standards they have established to signify value are simply out of reach for many women, and the structures that have been built rely on the invisible caretaking labor of women which is often unrecognized and devalued.

Though this is a well-researched area with ample evidence to support the maltreatment of women, few solutions have helped women adequately address these challenges. Instead, women have turned to each other to form organic relationships rooted in recognition, shared experience, and the desire to empower each other. These informal mentoring relationships have been critical to women's success and confidence as they navigate a treacherous landscape. Women have shown care and commitment to one another, investing in the subversion of gender bias and deconstruction of patriarchal norms that hold them at a disadvantage. While these relationships give women resilience and have helped them persist toward their goals and aspirations, the academy is called upon to participate in providing an equitable environment where women and men can flourish and thrive.

REFERENCES

Allen, K., Butler-Henderson, K., Reupert, A., Longmuir, F., & Finefter-Rosenbluh, I. (2021). Work like a girl: Redressing gender inequity in academic through systemic solutions. *Journal of University Teaching & Learning Practice*, *18*(3), 3. doi:10.53761/1.18.3.3

Allen, T. G., & Flood, T. C. (2018). The experiences of women in higher education: Who knew there wasn't a sisterhood. *Leadership and Research in Education*, *4*, 10–27.

American Association of University Women. (2016). *Barriers and bias: The status of women in leadership*. AAUW.

Badura, K. L., Grijalva, E., Newman, D. A., Yan, T. T., & Jeon, G. (2018). Gender and leadership emergence: A meta-analysis and explanatory model. *Personnel Psychology*, *71*(3), 335–367. doi:10.1111/peps.12266

Bierema, L. L. (2016). Women's leadership: Troubling notions of the "ideal" (male) leader. *Advances in Developing Human Resources*, *18*(2), 119–136. doi:10.1177/1523422316641398

Blair-Loy, M., Mayorova, O. G., Cosman, P. C., & Fraley, S. L. (2022). Can rubrics combat gender bias in faculty hiring? *Science, 377*(6601), 35–37. doi:10.1126cience.abm2329 PMID:35771928

Block, B. A., & Tietjen-Smith, T. (2016). The case for women mentoring women. *Quest, 38*(3), 306-315. doi:10.1080/00336297.2016.1190285

Brabazon, T., & Schulz, S. (2018). Braving the bull: Women, mentoring, and leadership in/ higher education. *Gender and Education, 32*(7), 873–890. https://www.doi.org/10.1080/09540253.2018.1544362 . doi:10.1080/09540253.2018.1544362

Brower, R. L., Schwartz, R. A., & Jones, T. B. (2019). 'Is it because I'm a woman?' Gender-based attributional ambiguity in higher education administration. *Gender and Education, 31*(1), 117–135. doi:10.1080/09540253.2017.1324131

Brue, K. L., & Brue, S. A. (2018). Leadership role identity construction in women's leadership development programs. *Journal of Leadership Education, 17*(1), 7–27. doi:10.12806/V17/I1/C2

Burkinshaw, P., & White, K. (2017). Fixing the women or fixing the universities: Women in HE leadership. *Administrative Sciences, 7*(30), 1–14. doi:10.3390/admsci7030030

Cañas, C., Keeve, C., Ramos, C., Rivera, J., & Samuel, L. (2019). Women in higher educational leadership: Representation, career progression, and compensation. *American Journal of Undergraduate Research, 16*(3), 5–13. doi:10.33697/ajur.2019.026

Carli, L. L., & Eagly, A. H. (2016). Women face a labyrinth: An examination of metaphors for women leaders. *Gender in Management, 31*(8), 514–527. doi:10.1108/GM-02-2015-0007

Chrobot-Mason, D., Hoobler, J. M., & Burno, J. (2019). Lean In versus the literature: An evidence-based examination. *The Academy of Management Perspectives, 33*(1), 110–130. doi:10.5465/amp.2016.0156

Ciciolla, L., & Luthar, S. S. (2019). Invisible labor and ramifications for adjustment: Mothers as captains of households. *Sex Roles, 2019*(81), 467–486. doi:10.100711199-018-1001-x PMID:34177072

Clavero, S., & Galligan, Y. (2021). Delivering gender justice in academia through general equality plans? Normative and practical challenges. *Gender, Work and Organization, 28*(3), 1115–1132. doi:10.1111/gwao.12658

Clayman Institute for Gender Research. (2019, December 17). *Whisper networks: On media, digital technology, and protection against harassment.* Stanford University. https://gender.stanford.edu/news/whisper-networks-media-digital-technology-and-protection-against-harassment

Cross, M., Lee, S., Bridgman, H., Thapa, D. K., Cleary, M., & Kornhaber, R. (2019). Benefits, barriers, and enablers of mentoring female health academics: An integrative review. *PLoS One, 14*(4), e0215319. doi:10.1371/journal.pone.0215319 PMID:30998791

David, M. E. (2015). Women and gender equality in higher education? *Education Sciences, 5*(1), 10–25. doi:10.3390/educsci5010010

Eagly, A. H., & Karau, S. J. (2002). Role congruity theory of prejudice toward female leaders. *Psychological Review, 109*(3), 573–598. doi:10.1037/0033-295X.109.3.573 PMID:12088246

Eagly, A. H., & Koenig, A. M. (2021). The vicious cycle linking stereotypes and social roles. *Current Directions in Psychological Science*, *30*(4), 1–8. doi:10.1177/09637214211013775

Early, S. L. (2020). Relational leadership reconsidered: The mentor-protégé connection. *Journal of Leadership Studies*, *13*(4), 57–61. doi:10.1002/jls.21671

England, P., Levine, A., & Mishel, E. (2020). Progress toward gender equality in the United States has slowed or stalled. *Proceedings of the National Academy of Sciences of the United States of America*, *117*(13), 6990–6997. doi:10.1073/pnas.1918891117 PMID:32229559

Ford, L. E. (2016). Two steps forward, one step back? Strengthening the foundations of women's leadership in higher education. *Politics, Groups & Identities*, *4*(3), 499–512. doi:10.1080/21565503.2016.1170705

French, J. R. P. Jr., & Raven, B. (1959). The bases of social power. In D. Cartwright (Ed.), Studies in social power (pp. 150-167). Univer. Michigan.

Ginsberg, F., Davis, J., & Simms, A. (2019). Women in higher education leadership: Challenges are many while opportunities are few. In H. Schnackenberg & D. Simard (Eds.), *Challenges and opportunities for women in higher education leadership* (pp. 219–237). IGI Global. doi:10.4018/978-1-5225-7056-1.ch013

Gloor, J. L., Morf, M., Paustian-Underdahl, S., & Backes-Gellner, U. (2020). Fix the game, not the dame: Restoring equity in leadership evaluations. *Journal of Business Ethics*, *161*(3), 497–511. doi:10.100710551-018-3861-y

Goethals, G. R., & Hoyt, C. L. (Eds.). (2017). *Women and leadership: History, theories, and case studies*. Berkshire Publishing Group, LLC.

HannumK. M.MuhlyS. M.Shockley-ZalabakP. S.WhiteJ. S. (2015). Women leaders within higher education in the United States: Supports, barriers, and experiences of being a senior leader. *Advancing Women in Leadership, 35*(1), 65-75. https://doi.org/ doi:10.18738/awl.v35i10.129

Harris, T. M., & Lee, C. N. (2019). Advocate-mentoring: A communicative response to diversity in higher education. *Communication Education*, *68*(1), 103–113. doi:10.1080/03634523.2018.1536272

Hernández-Johnson, M., Fayazpour, S., Candel, S. L., & Singh, R. (2019). Mothering the academy: An intersectional approach to deconstruct and expose the experiences of mother-scholars of color in higher education. In Y. Martinez-Vu, J. Pérez-Torres, C. Vega, & C. Caballero (Eds.), *The Chicana m(other) work anthology* (pp. 129–145). University of Arizona Press. doi:10.2307/j.ctvcj2hz5.12

Hill, L. H., & Wheat, C. A. (2017). The influence of mentorship and role models on university women leaders' career paths to university presidency. *Qualitative Report*, *22*(8), 2. doi:10.46743/2160-3715/2017.2437

Hodgins, M., O'Connor, P., & Buckley, L. (2022). Institutional change and organisational resistance to gender equality in higher education: An Irish case study. *Administrative Sciences*, *12*(2), 1–20. doi:10.3390/admsci12020059

Hollander, E. P. (1992). The essential interdependence of leadership and followership. *Current Directions in Psychological Science*, *1*(2), 71–75. doi:10.1111/1467-8721.ep11509752

Hollander, E. P., & Julian, J. (1969). Contemporary trends in the analysis of leadership processes. *Psychological Bulletin*, *71*(5), 387–397. doi:10.1037/h0027347 PMID:4893725

Hollander, E. P., & Yoder, J. (1980). Some issues comparing women and men as leaders. *Basic and Applied Social Psychology*, *1*(3), 267–280. doi:10.120715324834basp0103_6

Jian, G. (2021). From empathic leader to empathic leadership practice: An extension to relational leadership theory. *Human Relations*, *00*(0), 1–25. doi:10.1177/0018726721998450

Johnson, H. L. (2017). *Pipelines, pathways, and institutional leadership: An update on the status of women in higher education*. American Council on Education. https://www.acenet.edu/news-room/Documents/HES-Pipelines-Pathways-and-Institutional-Leadership-2017.pdf

Kornbluh, M., Collins, C., & Kohfeldt, D. (2020). Navigating activism within the academy: Consciousness building and social justice identity formation. *Journal of Community & Applied Social Psychology*, *2020*(3), 151–163. doi:10.1002/casp.2434

Kossek, E. E., & Buzzanell, P. M. (2018). Women's career equality and leadership in organizations: Creating an evidence-based positive change. *Human Resource Management*, *57*(4), 813–822. doi:10.1002/hrm.21936

Kuebel, C., Waters, H., & Svec, C. (2021). The academic-support group: Peer mentoring experiences of early-career music teacher educators. *Visions of Research in Music Education, 38*. https://opencommons.uconn.edu/vrme/vol38/iss1/4

Longman, K. A., Drennan, A., Beam, J., & Marble, A. F. (2019). The secret sauce: How developmental relationships shape the leadership journeys of women leaders in Christian higher education. *Christian Higher Education*, *18*(1-2), 54–77. doi:10.1080/15363759.2018.1547031

Madsen, S., & Longman, K. (2020). Women's leadership in higher education: Status, barriers, and motivators. *Journal of Higher Education Management*, *35*(1), 13–24.

Manzi, F., & Heilman, M. E. (2021). Breaking the glass ceiling: For one and all? *Journal of Personality and Social Psychology*, *120*(2), 257–277. doi:10.1037/pspa0000260 PMID:33252976

Meeussen, L., & Van Laar, C. (2018, November). Feeling pressure to be a perfect mother relates to parental burnout and career ambitions. *Frontiers in Psychology*, *9*(9), 2113. https://doi.orh/10.3389/fpsyg.2018.02113. doi:10.3389/fpsyg.2018.02113 PMID:30455656

Meister, A., Sinclair, A., & Jehn, K. A. (2017). Identities under scrutiny: How women leaders navigate feeling misidentified at work. *The Leadership Quarterly*, *28*(5), 672–690. doi:10.1016/j.leaqua.2017.01.009

Mijs, J. J. B. (2016). The unfulfillable promise of meritocracy: Three lessons and their implications for justice in education. *Social Justice Research*, *29*(1), 14–34. doi:10.100711211-014-0228-0

National Archives. (2022, June 17). *Equal Rights Amendment*. National Archives. https://www.archives.gov/women/era

Nicholson, J., & Kurucz, E. (2019). Relational leadership for sustainability: Building an ethical framework from the moral theory of 'ethics of care.'. *Journal of Business Ethics, 156*(1), 25–43. doi:10.100710551-017-3593-4

O'Connor, P. (2018). Gender imbalance in senior positions in higher education: What is the problem? What can be done? *Policy Reviews in Higher Education, 3*(1), 28–50. doi:10.1080/23322969.2018.1552084

O'Connor, P., & Irvine, G. (2020). Multi-level state interventions and gender inequality in higher education institutions: The Irish case. *Administrative Sciences, 10*(4), 1–21. doi:10.3390/admsci10040098

Odell, S. (2020). "Be women, stay women, become women": A critical rethinking of gender and educational leadership. *The SoJo Journal: Educational Foundations and Social Justice Work, 6*(1/2), 57–67.

Ong, M., Smith, J. M., & Ko, L. T. (2017). Counterspaces for women of color in STEM higher education: Marginal and central spaces for persistence and success. *Journal of Research in Science Teaching, 55*(2), 206–245. doi:10.1002/tea.21417

Pascale, A. B., & Ohlson, M. (2020). Gendered meanings of leadership: Developing leadership through experiential community-based mentoring in college. *Journal of Experiential Education, 43*(2), 171–184. doi:10.1177/1053825920905122

Powell, S., & Arora-Jonsson, S. (2022). The conundrums of formal and informal meritocracy: Dealing with gender segregation in the academy. *Higher Education, 83*(5), 968–985. doi:10.100710734-021-00719-2

Roberts, S., & Brown, D. K. (2019). How to manage gender bias from within: Women in leadership. *Journal of Business Diversity, 19*(2), 83–98. doi:10.33423/jbd.v19i2.2057

SearbyL.BallengerJ.TripsesJ. (2015). Climbing the ladder, holding the ladder: The mentoring experiences of higher education female leaders. *Advancing Women in Leadership, 35,* 98-107. https://doi.org/doi:10.18738/awl.v35i0.141

Sklaveniti, C. (2020). Moments that connect: Turning points and the becoming of leadership. *Human Relations, 73*(4), 555–571. doi:10.1177/0018726719895812

Sorrentino, J., Augoustinos, M., & LeCouteur, A. (2022). "Deal me in": Hillary Clinton and gender in the 2016 US presidential election. *Feminism & Psychology, 32*(1), 23–43. doi:10.1177/09593535211030746

Statti, A. L. C., & Torres, K. (2019). Innovative approaches to traditional mentoring practices of women in higher education. In H. Schnackenberg & D. Simard (Eds.), *Challenges and opportunities for women in higher education leadership* (pp. 1–19). IGI Global. doi:10.4018/978-1-5225-7056-1.ch001

Stelmokienė, A., & Endriulaitienė, A. (2020). Congruence between real and ideal leader. What matters more in today's work world: Ethical behavior of a leader or productivity? *Business: Theory and Practice, 21*(1), 184–191. doi:10.3846/btp.2020.11800

Stocks, C. (2022). *The 'imperative' of informal mentoring to subvert gender role incongruence among women in higher education leadership: A qualitative study* (Publication No. 30244699) [Doctoral dissertation, American College of Education]. ProQuest Dissertations Publishing.

Subbaye, R., & Vithal, R. (2017). Gender, teaching, and academic promotions in higher education. *Gender and Education, 29*(7), 926–951. doi:10.1080/09540253.2016.1184237

Uhl-Bien, M. (2006). Relational leadership theory: Exploring the social processes of leadership and organizing. *The Leadership Quarterly, 17*(6), 654–676. doi:10.1016/j.leaqua.2006.10.007

U.S. Department of Education. (2019). *Table 318.10: Degrees conferred by postsecondary institutions, by degree level and sex of student: Selected years, 1869-70 through 2028-29.* National Center for Education Statistics. https://nces.ed.gov/programs/digest/d18/tables/dt18_318.10.asp

U.S. Department of Labor. (2020). *Labor participation rates.* US DoL. https://www.dol.gov/agencies/wb/data/latest-annual-data/labor-force-participation-rates

van Gils, S., Van Quaquebeke, N., Borkowski, J., & van Knippenberg, D. (2018). Respectful leadership: Reducing performance challenges posted by leader role incongruence and gender dissimilarity. *Human Relations, 71*(12), 1590–1610. doi:10.1177/0018726718754992 PMID:30473588

White, K., & Burkinshaw, P. (2019). Women and leadership in higher education: Special issue editorial. *Social Sciences (Basel, Switzerland), 8*(204), 1–7. doi:10.3390ocsci8070204

Wong, A., McKey, C., & Baxter, P. (2018). What's the fuss? Gender and academic leadership. *Journal of Health Organization and Management, 32*(6), 779–792. doi:10.1108/JHOM-02-2018-0061 PMID:30299222

Wright, K. A. M., Haastrup, T., & Guerrina, R. (2021). Equalities in freefall? Ontological insecurity and the long-term impact of COVID-19 in the academy. *Gender, Work and Organization, 28*(51), 163–167. doi:10.1111/gwao.12518

Yip, J., Trainor, L. P., Black, H., Soto-Torres, L., & Reichard, R. J. (2020). Coaching new leaders: A relational process of integrating multiple identities. *Academy of Management Learning & Education, 19*(4), 503–520. doi:10.5465/amle.2017.0449

Zembylas, M. (2018). The entanglement of decolonial and posthuman perspectives: Tensions and implications for curriculum and pedagogy in higher education. *Parallax, 24*(3), 254–267. doi:10.1080/13 534645.2018.1496577

Chapter 5

Caveats to Accessibility:
Does the Promise of On–Line Higher Education Programs Help Minoritized Women in Higher Education?

Carlene O. Fider
https://orcid.org/0009-0007-0484-3071
Pacific Oaks College, USA

Camille Huggins
Pacific Oaks College, USA

Eugenia Rodriquez
Pacific Oaks College, USA

ABSTRACT

This chapter explores the use of online education among minoritized women in pursuit of higher education. The chapter is scoped literature review of the current matters that minoritized women experience while pursuing an online education as well as anecdotal case studies of women's journeys of attending and working at online higher education institutions. Online education has made education accessible. Online education is flexible compared to the traditional format. As more minoritized women and non-traditional students utilized the advantages and convenience of online education, the more learning institutions are created. Since online education was instituted and became mainstream, it is available and accessible for all races, ethnicities, and genders. COVID-19 exacerbated issues of being able to access Wi-Fi in public spaces. Given that many online students are balancing multiple roles and responsibilities while pursuing their education, this balancing act illustrates the students' strength, persistence, and their commitment to obtaining an education.

DOI: 10.4018/978-1-6684-8597-2.ch005

Copyright © 2023, IGI Global. Copying or distributing in print or electronic forms without written permission of IGI Global is prohibited.

Caveats to Accessibility

INTRODUCTION

Delivery of higher education via online asynchronous and synchronous learning platforms has revolutionized the accessibility to education for millions of students. The importance of online learning platforms was most evident during the COVID-19 pandemic which accelerated the necessity of online education, as universities around the world were forced to transition to remote learning to comply with social distancing guidelines (Dhawan, 2020). As of 2022, most established on-ground learning institutions have resumed traditional classroom-based learning format, but there has also been a proliferation of online learning programs which have attracted non-traditional students such as older adults, disabled individuals, working professionals, single parents, racially minoritized persons, and people living in rural communities (Stofkova et al., 2022). As higher education has become more accessible through online learning platforms, there are questions of its legitimacy and if the degree obtained, benefits non-traditional students' careers, in particular the career trajectories of minoritized women. This chapter will examine the history of on-line education, the structural opportunities it presents, and barriers in legitimatizing this mode of education to benefit minoritized women towards upward mobility in their professional journey.

STRUCTURAL BARRIERS TO ACCESSING HIGHER EDUCATION

Prior to the advent of online learning, higher education was not obtainable for many. Goldin (1990) suggests that there are four historical periods that show women's participation in the workforce and their educational obtainment. In the first phase, from the 1800's to the 1920s, women who were primarily poor, uneducated and unmarried entered the labor market. These women were often employed as piece workers in manufacturing plants, or they were employed as domestic help in other people's homes. These single women often then exited the workforce when they got married. Goldin (1990) indicates during the second phase, from the 1930s to the 1950s, married women entered the workforce in significant numbers, with an increase from 10% to 25%. These increases were the result of the rise in offices requiring clerical workers and new information technologies. In addition, there was tremendous growth in the number of women attending high school in the early 20th century, and that made them more marketable. While married women during the first period often stayed home, married women in the second period had more opportunities to work outside of the home, however, their participation was negatively affected by their husbands' income. As such, the higher his income, the less she would "need" to work outside the home.

In the third phase, women's labor force continued to rise and was driven by married women (Goldin,1990). It became more common for married women to continue working even as their husbands' income increased. One reason that married women worked more was due to the increasing availability of part-time employment.

The fourth phase, also called the quiet revolution from the late 1970s up to the very early 21st century, women's engagement in the labor force rose mostly due to view of young women in their late teens that they did not want their careers to be cut short by marriage and children (Goldin,1990). This view encouraged women to invest more in their education, which meant attending higher education institutions. This prepared them for careers that gave them status closer to men in the workplace. When the Women's Education Equity Act (WEEA) was passed in 1974, it was a significant piece of legislation which accompanies Title IX, the legislation which prohibits any type of sex-based discrimination in a school or educational program receiving federal funding. The emphasis of WEEA was to explore gender equity legislation that is centered on establishing and supporting women's equal access to higher education which focused on how improvements in access to education can thereby open access in other parts of society (Conrad et al., 2014; Niemi & Weaver-Hightower, 2020). The three main goals of WEEA were to promote gender equity in education, offer funds to make women's equality a reality and to eradicate suffering from multiple forms of discrimination based on sex, race, and limited English proficiency.

Currently, 56% of college graduates are women compared to their male counterparts at 44% (National Center for Education Statistics, 2021). Despite this, there are still structural barriers that hinder women from obtaining qualifications in higher education such as, financial constraints that often limit the ability of persons with little to low means to afford tuition, textbooks, and related expenses. Another factor is the lack of access to high quality higher education in many underserved or rural communities (Thomas et al., 2019; Unterhalter, 2009). Furthermore, systemic inequalities such as racism, ageism and ableism create barriers to higher education, as marginalized individuals face discriminatory practices (Thomas et al., 2019; Unterhalter, 2009). Another significant barrier that impacts women relates to work-life balance. More than 66% of all informal caregivers are women, they are either caring for children, parents, or both. The Bureau of Labor Statistics (2021) indicate that women hold 50% of the jobs in the United States and these competing demands makes it difficult to prioritize time for studying, attending classes, completing assignments while also making time for family and work responsibilities. Online learning can be a viable option for women who want to obtain higher education without having to sacrifice their work and family commitments.

An essential piece of federal legislation that was passed in 1964 was the Civil Rights Act which protects civil rights by prohibiting discrimination based on race, color, and national origin in various setting including employment, housing, voting, public accommodations, and education (Jargowsky, 2019). According to De Brey et al. (2019) only 8% of institutions have at least equitable student representation comparable to the ethnic and racial United States composition while 92% of higher education institutions have underrepresented rates of African Americans, Latinx and Native Americans undergraduates. The intersecting identities of being a woman and a non-white person also indicate while more women pursue higher education then their male counterparts, only 14.5% are Black, 12.9% are Latinx, 6.7% are Asian and .9% are Native Americans (National Center for Education Statistics, 2021). Graduation rates are generally higher among white and Asian women overall while minoritized women vary widely depending on the specific community and institution. African American students are suspended and expelled at a rate three times greater than white students (National Center for Education Statistics, 2021). Black and Native American women have the lowest graduation rate and are more likely than white women to enroll in community colleges and other non-four-year institutions.

The Rehabilitation Act of 1973 section 504 is a federal law that bans discrimination against people with disabilities (Section 504, Rehabilitation Act of 1973). According to this Act, a disability is any condition of the body or mind impairment including vision, movement, thinking, remembering, learning, communicating, health or mental health concerns that makes it more difficult for the person with the condition to do certain activities such as maintaining social relationships, and mobility and interacting with the world around them. Many might consider a disability as a single population, yet it is a diverse group of people with a wide range of needs. The Act further states that two people with the same type of disability can be affected in very different ways. Some disabilities may be hidden or not easy to see therefore may hide their disability due to fear of stigmatization.

The Rehabilitation act of 1973 section 504 provides accommodations for persons with a physical or mental impairment to have access to education (Section 504, Rehabilitation Act of 1973). Since the

Caveats to Accessibility

inception of this Act, the six-year graduation rate of undergraduate students with disabilities is 49.5%, compared to the 68% of student without disabilities. Despite this, only 37% of students report their disability to their college because on-ground higher education institutions sometimes fail to provide adequate accommodations or provide a truly inclusive space for students to express their true selves (Section 504, Rehabilitation Act of 1973). Students with disabilities are twice as likely to receive an out-of-school suspension than their non-disabled peers. Online learning may be a more inclusive and accessible avenue to reduce barriers to higher education. It can be a powerful tool for addressing systemic inequalities in traditional education systems and help foster a more inclusive and supportive learning environment.

HISTORY OF ONLINE EDUCATION

Systemic Barriers That Impact Online Learning

In 1981, the Western Behavioral Sciences Institute in La Jolla, California embarked on a novel way to deliver a distance education program (Feenberg, 1993). It was the start of online learning, which was specifically intended to engage upper-level business executives, who were mostly middle-aged white men, in its School of Management and Strategic Studies. The goal was to provide a remote delivery method so that these men could attend classes while simultaneously managing their businesses (Feenberg, 1993). Students were able to get instruction from highly qualified instructors that came from institutions like Yale, Harvard, and the University of California (Feenberg, 1993).

In the 1990s, a few universities began experimenting with delivering courses online, using early versions of learning management systems (LMS) and video conferencing technology (Dhawan, 2020). Following that, in the early 2000s, for-profit institutions such as the University of Phoenix and DeVry University began offering online degree programs, which became popular due to their convenience and accessibility (Allen & Seaman, 2011). By the mid-2000s there was an expansion of online programs becoming available in traditional universities. The overall goal was to reach non-traditional students, such as working and older adults (Miller & Lu, 2003). This was the turning point for an increase in the popularity of online education, as over the past decade there have been several universities that now offer fully online degree programs and certificates.

Online learning is defined as learning experiences in synchronous and asynchronous environments using different devices (e.g., mobile phones, laptops, tablets) with internet access. In these environments, students can independently learn and interact with instructors and their peers (Singh & Thurman, 2019). The synchronous learning environment allowed students to attend live lectures, real-time interactions between educator and student with instant feedback. While asynchronous learning allows students to access the course material and complete assignments at their own pace and on their own schedule without being required to participate in real-time interactions. COVID-19 made higher education institutions go from classroom-based learning to online learning. This overnight shift of normal classrooms to e-classrooms debunked its illegitimacy of the modality and its ability to provide quality education (Dhawan, 2020).

Despite technological strides, there are systemic factors that continue to impact access to online education. The issue isn't availability as there are copious amounts of online degree programs, the issue is equity that continues to impact accessibility (Lee, 2017; Niemi & Weaver-Hightower, 2020). Technology deficits can significantly impact online learning such as lack of a reliable internet connection or a suitable device, such as a laptop or tablet which hinders full participation with online classes (Lee, 2017; Pettit,

2020). Digital deserts or the digital divide refers to areas where access to reliable high-speed internet and other digital technologies is limited or non-existent. These areas are often in rural or low-income areas where there is limited access to high-speed internet such as tribal lands or in urban areas due to the cost of internet access (Lee, 2017; Pettit, 2020). If the student's device does not meet the minimum requirements to run the online learning platform or software, they may experience technical difficulties such as slow loading times or crashes which can be frustrating and disruptive to the learning process.

This technology deficit has other impacts on online education experiences such as digital literacy. Students with lower levels of digital literacy and proficiency due to either not having early and reliable access or having outdated technology, which can make it more difficult for them to navigate online learning platforms, communicate with instructors and peers, and complete assignments (Roche, 2017). It may also be that smart phones are the only type of technology available and completing assignments on a phone comes with its own set of challenges. When individuals reside in areas that lack resources to enroll in online degree programs, a lack of constant and reliable internet access can have a significant impact on their ability to perform well and engage in the learning process.

THE BENEFITS OF ONLINE EDUCATION

With its flexibility that allows students to learn at their own pace and time, there are many benefits to online learning (Singh & Thurman, 2019; American Council on Education, 2012). The advances in technology have made this modality more effective and engaging, with the emergence of new tools such as virtual and augmented reality, gamification, and adaptive learning systems (Burke & Schwalbach, 2021). These technologies provide an interactive learning experience with virtual discussions, online group projects, and access to online resources and materials (Cojocariu et al., 2014). It provides opportunities for an individualized approach for better learning outcomes as well as enhance digital skills, which are becoming increasingly essential to the current job market (Stofkova et al., 2022). Online learning provides students, the ability to self-monitor their understandings, reflects, control interactions about the concepts they learn (Means et al., 2009). Students' pre-existing cultural dispositions associated with their ethnicity, or age or intellectual ability that can largely influence their learning actions and thoughts, which may an obstacle in an on-the ground environment becomes less of a problem in the regular online learning environments. Online courses can provide convenience, eliminating the need to travel to a physical classroom which provides greater accessibility to individuals with mobility or geographical restrictions (Dhawan, 2020). It is also more cost-effective than traditional classroom-based learning, reducing the financial burden on students (Lothridge et al., 2013). Online learning also provided access to diverse populations that was otherwise struggling for an opportunity.

Older Adults

The benefits of online learning for the non-traditional students are unique to their intersecting identities. For the middle aged and older adult that are still working and are in their middle career, access to higher education via the online learning platform provides more flexibility, allowing them to balance their education with work and other commitments such as child-rearing (Xu & Xu, 2019; Bryce 2021). Many older adults are managing their other commitments and responsibilities such as caring for family members or managing health issues. The online learning platform can be beneficial for older adults with

Caveats to Accessibility

mobility and accessibility issues because it is multi-modal in how the learning material is disseminated (Basilaia & Kvavadze, 2020; American Council on Education, 2017). Access to online courses allows older adults to explore new areas of interest and develop skills while enhancing cognitive functioning (Cinquin et al., 2019). It also provides an opportunity for social engagement without the stigmatization of being older.

Rural Communities

Data from the Bureau of Labor Statistics (2021) suggests that educational attainment of people living in rural communities is generally lower than that of people living in urban areas. In the rural communities in the United States only 21.6% had a Bachelor's degree or higher, compared to 35.2% in urban areas. Online learning delivers access to rural communities that is often only available in urban areas because it allows students to study without travelling to a physical classroom (Allen & Seaman, 2011). Access to education for rural populations provides prospects for rural development and the opportunity to address the systemic issues (e.g., poverty) that have long been perpetuated in these communities (American Council on Education, 2012 & 2017).

Disabled Individuals

Around one billion persons are born with a disability globally, and 13.5% of the United States population is disabled (National Center for Education Statistics 2021). Online learning provides greater flexibility, allowing disabled learners to study at their own pace and time. It offers a range of benefits for neuroatypical individuals including those with autism spectrum disorder, attention deficit hyperactivity disorder, dyslexia and other conditions that affect learning and attention. This flexibility is particularly beneficial for individuals with disabilities who may need to take breaks or adjust their schedule to manage their condition. Additionally, online learning eliminates many physical barriers that may prevent disabled individuals from accessing traditional classroom-based learning environments because it allows online courses to be accessed from anywhere with an internet connection. Another benefit of online learning for disabled individuals is personalized learning because online learning platforms offers a range of accessibility features such as text to speech capabilities, closed captions for videos, adjustable font sizes, and screen reader compatibility. Online learning also provides opportunities for social engagement with virtual discussions and online group projects (Allen & Seaman, 2011). Furthermore, online learning provides a less stressful format for learning for neuroatypical learners. Traditional classroom settings can be overwhelming for individuals who are sensitive to sensory stimuli such as loud noises, crowds, and bright lights. Online courses can offer a more controlled and predictable learning environment which helps to reduce stress and anxiety. This helps to combat social isolation which is a significant issue for many disabled people.

Bilingual Students

Many racial and ethnic minorities may be the first person in their family to be accepted to college, and their experiences during their elementary and high school years may have created distrust of educational institutions, resulting in them not knowing how to successfully navigate higher education, and where to seek and ask for resources. Online learning platforms make it easy to access pertinent material that may otherwise be elusive.

Online learning improves accessibility for bilingual students because they can be taught at their linguistic pace. Learning platforms can be adaptive to assist with improving their language skills in both their native language and language of instruction. This can be beneficial for students who may not have benefitted from bilingual or immersion programs in their local schools. It also provides bilingual students access to a wider range of resources including online dictionaries, language learning tools and digital materials in multiple languages. Online learning can assist in eliminating systemic inequities in terms of educational resources and support, which can limit their ability to succeed in online learning and exacerbate existing disparities in educational outcomes (Du et al., 2015).

Minoritized Women

There have been various iterations of the term to describe women belonging to marginalized and under-represented groups such as women of color, women from marginalized communities, underrepresented women, disadvantaged women, and minority women. The most recent restatement of this group has been labelled *minoritized women* which has been used in academic and social justice contexts to acknowledge the systemic and structural forces that create and maintain marginalization and inequality. The term minoritized emphasizes that the experiences of women from marginalized communities are not a result of individual choice or characteristics but rather are the result of historical and ongoing processes of exclusion and oppression. These terms are broad brush characterizations that have been created by dominant and oppressive structures to delude one's individualized self and story.

Intersectionality in higher education acknowledges that individuals may face multiple forms of oppression and marginalization, which can affect their academic success, career prospects, and overall well-being (Mitchell et al., 2014; Crenshaw, 1989). It recognizes that the experiences of marginalized individuals are shaped by complex and intersecting factors, and that solutions to inequities must be multifaceted. Some women with multiple identities attending higher education institution face several challenges such as being a part of minoritized groups like being immigrant or LGBTQIA+, BIPOC, or those who have chronic illnesses or are diagnosed with a disability.

Minoritized women represent an intersectionality of multiple identities that influence an individual's experiences during their higher education journey (Mitchell et al., 2014; Bryce 2021). It recognizes that individuals have complex identities that cannot be reduced to a single characteristic or trait, such as race, gender, or disability. As such, an individual's experience and opportunities are shaped by the intersection of their various identities. For example, a woman who identifies as part BIPOC with a disability may experience different barriers to success in higher education than a non-disabled white man. The BIPOC woman's experiences are shaped by the intersection of her race, gender, and disability, which may create unique challenges and opportunities.

For persons who identify as Black, indigenous and people of color (BIPOC) or lesbian, gay, bisexual, transgender, queer or questioning, intersex and asexual (LGBTQIA+) may face barriers to accessing educational resources such as discrimination, prejudice, and lack of representation, online learning can provide a solution by offering a safe and inclusive learning environment. Overall, of the 60.2% female undergraduate students are white, while 14.5% are Black, 12.9% are Latinx, 6.7% are Asian and .9% are Native Americans (National Center for Education Statistics, 2021). Graduation rates are generally higher among white and Asian women overall while minoritized women vary widely depending on the specific

Caveats to Accessibility

community and institution. Black, Latinx and Native American women with the lowest graduation rate are more likely than white women to enroll in community colleges and other non-four-year institutions (Okwumabua, et al., 2011). Online education programs can provide a sense of community and support with virtual discussions and online group projects. There are opportunities to share and incorporate their lived experience in assignments without experiencing harassment and microaggressions that is often reported in traditional classroom-based learning environments. Online learning can eliminate many concerns by providing a safe and inclusive learning environment for all students.

Online education can be supportive of individuals with overlapping identities in several ways. Flexibility, accessibility, and the opportunity to advance their career are some common benefits of online education for individuals who identify as LGBTQIA+, BIPOC, those with chronic illnesses, intellectual and developmental disabilities, and immigrants who may not be confident with speaking aloud due to language barriers. More specifically, online education supports LGBTQIA+ individuals by providing a safe and supportive learning environment, where they may not have to contend with looks or questions about their identity or lifestyle. Further, they may have more of an opportunity to maintain some anonymity. Similarly, BIPOC individuals may have opportunities to feel more included in online education as they may have classmates from various parts of the world, and with a variety of cultural experiences. This may also be true for students with chronic illnesses or for students with developmental and intellectual disabilities. They face less stigma from classmates as developmentally and intellectually disabled students may then be able to gain valuable skills and knowledge, to improve their overall well-being, and increase their opportunities for employment and independent living because of online education. Online education allows for opportunities to customize curriculum such as self-paced learning.

Since BIPOC, LGBTQIA+ and immigrant populations are overrepresented in the lower income bracket, they do not have access to financial resources and may benefit from the possible lower cost of an online education since they do not have to absorb extraneous costs that are attached to attending classes in a more traditional format, such as paying of parking.

Minoritized populations take out more student loans than their white colleagues (Havens, 2021) which indicates having more educational debt than their male counterparts. Reasons for this are because there may be other family members that they are required to care for, and school loans are one way to get financial assistance that doesn't have to be immediately paid back (Müller, 2008). This financial barrier before engaging in higher educational pursuits can persist even after the degree is earned, keeping in mind the minority women are the lowest earners in the workplace (Lin, 2016; Havens, 2021). Minority women are more likely to have caregiving responsibilities for children, elderly family members, or other relatives (Miller & Lu, 2003; Lin, 2016), which can make it challenging to balance online education with their other responsibilities.

The desire to have better work-life balance is just one reason that women seem to be the largest consumers of online education. When looking at minoritized women, who culturally hold a lot of responsibilities in families and have lower paying jobs, statistics further suggest that this demographic continues to take advantage of what may be considered the convenience of online education (Lin, 2016; Bryce 2021). While there may in fact be flexibility in this modality, it is necessary to look at how an institution that was not initially created to support this minoritized group is now attracting them in such high numbers.

To contextualize reasons why minoritized women are attracted online education, two women were interviewed about what attracted them to attending an online educational program. One person was Dr. Veronica Davis, who is an African American single mother, with a chronic illness. She was middle-aged when she decided to attend an online university. Initially, Dr. Davis obtained her Bachelors and Master of Social Work at Temple University in 2001 and 2004. She then decided to attend Strayer University, an online university in 2010 and then attended Capella University for her Ph.D. in Professional Studies in Education where she graduated in 2019. One of the contributing factors that attracted her to pursue her education online was:

My goal was to become a professor, but I was a single mom with a daughter who was a freshman in high school. I was also working full-time as a social worker. The online experience was helpful with to maintain the work life balance. I was also trying to juggle; the online education program allowed me to work independently as well as be able to devote the time when everyone else is sleeping to work on assignments. I remember being up at 2:30am finishing assignments and papers. I went to Temple University which is situated in an urban environment that is in low-income communities. Although the school was very good, and it was a great educational experience, it was dangerous during the commute and as a woman I was always concerned about my safety. When I went to Strayer Universities online program, they were supportive. Capella University offered a sense of freedom and made me feel important. They understood who I was as a student and respected my time and my struggles. They made every student feel accepted and wanted. Online professors were passionate and understanding. My Ph.D. chair was calm. She was there with me from the beginning to end.

Another person who also attended an online school was Dr. Constance Walsh, who is a single mom of two children, identifies as queer and biracial (Black and Latinx), and grew up in Oregon but currently lives in California. She also attended a traditional on-ground school at Portland State University for her Bachelor's and Master's degrees.

I remember I was attending school during the great recession of 2008. Portland State University was downtown Portland, and it was considered a commuter school. I would drive to campus 2 to 3 days a week for class and two days a week for my practicum experience. I also worked full-time, I found myself driving daily and finding funds for student parking and gas were additional challenges to navigate in addition to my studies. Oregon's population is 80% white, so at Portland State I was the only person of color in my master's program so whenever there was a question about race and specifically about Black people, everyone in the class would turn to me as the representative for the entire race. I wasn't familiar with the term microaggression at the time I was attending, but it was a regular occurrence at Portland. I attended Trevecca Nazarene University located in Nashville, Tennessee and did my Doctorate in Education (Ed.D.) in Leadership and Professional Practice online in 2020. And I know that had it not been for the accessibility of an online program; I would not have been able to complete my doctorate, which had been a lifelong dream of mine.

Both women expressed sentiments of not feeling safe while attending on-ground institutions whether it was physically or emotionally. Dr. Davis discussed attending courses late in the evening spending extraneous funds and experiencing microaggressions. While they also expressed feeling supported and seen in the online programs and the convenience these types of programs offer. Both women of color with intersecting identities of being older, single moms, queer, fully employed and experiencing both traditional on-ground institutions and online programs clearly demonstrated how the online program enabled them to manage their work life balance. Another aspect of the challenges and possibilities that online education offers were the rigor of the academic programs. Research indicates to be a successful

Caveats to Accessibility

online student it is important to possess high levels of self-regulation, self-discipline, and metacognitive skills, which often falls under the broad rubric of self-directed learning (Stephen et al., 2021). As both women went to traditional on-ground higher education institutions it was important to ask to compare the rigor of online academic programs to on-ground programs. Dr. Veronica Davis shared the following:

You put in what you get out of it, although in the online program it does not have the same context as a on the ground school, but you can get the same support and experience. But it depends on personality, you have some students that are introverted or extroverted. I'm more of a people person. I like to talk to folks and be able to have those moments where I can share my experiences. With the online programs I have met the most amazing professors and fellow students who I was able to connect with while working on projects and during online discussions. The online program was geared to working adults and all the students had familiar commitments. The online Ed.D. program itself was as challenging, if not more than my in-person MSW program experience. Because I had a learning disability, I needed support via tutoring services and the writing center. The benefits of having those services online were paramount to my success as a student.

Both women expressed both online and on-ground programs are similar in the rigor in academic learning, however, they both felt more access to support that aided them in their learning and academic success within the online programs. Online education offers several benefits, including accessibility, flexibility, convenience, and personalized learning. They both spoke about the support from instructors, classmates, and the learning support resources. This seems to be echoed by others who are obtaining their degrees online. It is estimated that more than 30% of American students are enrolled in at least one online course (Palvia, et al., 2018). About 99% of these students taking U.S. online degree programs are physically located in the country (Palvia, et al., 2018). At least 52% of graduate students in the U.S. found their online college-level education to provide a better learning experience than their college-level classroom education (Pettit, 2020).

JOB PROSPECTS WITH AN ONLINE EDUCATION

But what about job prospects? Does a minoritized woman with an online college education benefit from their education and excel in their careers? During the first ten years of the inception of online learning platforms, there was often a stigma attached to online higher education programs which is largely due to the perception that online courses were less rigorous and valuable than traditional on-campus courses. This was substantiated when a couple of the well-known on-line universities such as DeVry University and the University of Phoenix had to pay millions of dollars back to students for false advertisement of obtaining jobs once graduated. They were also accused of being diploma mills which are organizations that grant degrees without meeting academic standards. Some of these institutions claimed certain accreditation status but lacked any educational standards. They are also predatory on unsuspecting students, constantly targeting immigrants and the low-income population.

In the early 2000s, this sordid history made some employers hesitant to accept online degrees, because of the consensus that students who earned their degrees online may not have received the same quality of education or had the same level of engagement as those who completed their studies on campus. As an minoritized women, who historically have been relegated to the lowest socio-economic status and was thought to be of a lower intelligence, with an online degree did not present as an ideal prospective employee. Dr. Davis discussed her experience,

In 2006 and 2010, there was a stigmatization that people had about online learning, so you were not getting great working experience. I wanted to transition from being a practitioner to an academic teaching in higher education as an academic, but it was difficult to get my first teaching position because I was a person of color, a middle-aged female and slightly overweight. I think it is a struggle for many of us of color, to be taken seriously, especially among younger students. When I moved to California, I obtained a Community College Teaching Certificate in 2014-2015 at California State University, Dominquez Hills online program and after taking the first two courses the Chair of the Psychology Department offered my first adjunct position which I was so grateful.

Both testimonies demonstrated the struggle of obtaining a job with their online degree. Minoritized women are those who often stand outside of society's definition of an acceptable women as they are older, poor, Black, or queer (Waiters, 2011). The issues related to their experience are not reserved for the educational process, as minoritized women who may face discrimination and bias the job market after graduation (Altmann et al., 2018; Lin, 2016), which can affect their success in the field. Much of this bias and discrimination may be based in the fact that the degree was earned online.

If you are pursuing a degree to work in higher education institutions, minoritized women often have issues of isolation, underutilization, demoralization as they are excluded from the informal and social aspects of institutions (Waiters, 2011). Minoritized women are likely to face stereotyped interpretations of their behaviors, and this may often interfere with collegiality. They are often ignored in seminars, departmental meetings and are continually called upon to present the minority view. They more so than white women are often overburdened with advising minority students. The mindset about online education has changed drastically since 2020. It is now seen as a benefit to be technology savvy for the new job market. It assists with job-relevant skills that can be immediately applied in the workplace which include soft skills like proper email and technically etiquette, it helps to work collaboratively online, assists with problem solving. Digital skills are important and can help people succeed in the labor market and improve communication with public administration. Digitization and globalization have increased the importance to communicate through the Internet, applications, and other e-based gadgets. Digital skills are one of the essential parts of e-Government, so people can use e-Government services in communication with public administration.

CONCLUSION

Changing perspectives and advancements can often be facilitated by large changes in society. As we have seen the growth of online learning platforms facilitated by the COVID-19 pandemic, the impact has been wide and far reaching. Women, in particular, are experiencing opportunities that historically had been closed. Whether acknowledging the structural barriers to accessing higher education as a woman, or the impact of legislation such as the Women's Education Equity Act (WEEA), there is no way to ignore the movement forward and upward. Despite only having its beginnings in 1981, distance education and online learning platforms have brought in an era of new acceptable ways of learning. Whether synchronous or asynchronous, and through the use of different technological devices, women have moved forward

Caveats to Accessibility

through systemic barriers that have impacted online learning. Economics and accessibility continue to be barriers that beg for further study and examination of how to overcome its impact. It is important to further note that intersecting identities such as race, age, location, ability/disability, to name a few, further add to the marginalization of identities who can benefit from flexibility accessibility and the opportunity of advancement through online education (Amina, 2021).

It is important to understand this is not only about the advancement of technology and how important online learning is to education. This is a story about humans and how online learning has broadened access by improving one's life and perhaps elevating a person's family out of poverty. Dr. Davis reflected on her grandmother's experience, expressing that she only signed an 'X' where her name should be on documents, because she was unable to read and write. Despite this, all of her children are college educated. Dr. Davis is the first person in her family to complete a terminal degree and this has made her a pioneer of sorts for her family. Women of color continue to desire to find their seat at the academic table and have a desire to occupy administrative positions in higher education, given that the face of higher education is rapidly changing. Online education provides opportunities for women to get access to quality educational experiences that make them competitive in the workplace. As time passes, and online programs continues to be the preferred method of obtaining an education, one can hope that minoritized women will continue to enroll and that employers will see these degrees as equal in rigor to those obtained in person.

It is with the deepest gratitude that educators like Dr. Veronica Davis and Dr. Constance Walsh have allowed us to gain perspective from their experiences and insights from their past. Their stories along with other women who have gained mobility and access through online education continue to inspire and motivate others who will see some of their identities and opportunities represented in them.

REFERENCES

Allen, I. E., & Seaman, J. (2011). *Going the distance: Online education in the United States.* Babson College. Babson Survey Research Group. https://www.onlinelearningsurvey.com/reports/goingthedistance.pdf

Altmann, A., Ebersberger, B., Mössenlechner, C., & Wieser, D. (Eds.). (2018). *The disruptive power of online education: Challenges, opportunities, responses.* Emerald Publishing Limited. doi:10.1108/9781787543256

American Council on Education, Center for Policy Analysis. (2012, February). The American College president study 2012. https://www.acenet.edu/Documents/American-College-President-VII-2012.pdf

American Council on Education, Center for Policy Analysis. (2017). *The American College president study 2017.* American Council on Education. https://www.acenet.edu/Documents/American-College-President-VIII-2017.pdf

Amina, T. (2021). Online education and women's empowerment. In Oxford Research Encyclopedia of Education. doi:10.1093/acrefore/9780190264093.013.1592

Basilaia, G., & Kvavadze, D. (2020). Transition to online education in schools during a SARS-CoV-2 coronavirus (COVID-19) pandemic in Georgia. *Pedagogical Research, 5*(4), em0060. doi:10.29333/pr/7937

Bryce, N. (2021). A year in a faculty writing group: Equity for women academics in higher education. *Journal of Faculty Development, 35*(1), 70–76.

Bureau of Labor Statistics. (2021, April). *Women in the labor force: A databook.* BLS. https://www.bls.gov/opub/reports/womens-databook/2020/home.htm

Burke, L. M., & Schwalbach, J. (2021). *Housing redlining and its lingering effects on education opportunity. Backgrounder. No. 3594.* Heritage Foundation.

Cinquin, P. A., Guitton, P., & Sauzéon, H. (2019). Online e-learning and cognitive disabilities: A systematic review. *Computers & Education, 130*, 152–167. doi:10.1016/j.compedu.2018.12.004

Cojocariu, V. M., Lazar, I., Nedeff, V., & Lazar, G. (2014). SWOT anlysis of e-learning educational services from the perspective of their beneficiaries. *Procedia: Social and Behavioral Sciences, 116*, 1999–2003. doi:10.1016/j.sbspro.2014.01.510

Conrad, C., Dixson, A., Smooth, W., & Revilla, A. T. (2014). A discussion on gender equity and women of color. *Frontiers, 35*(3), 3–14. doi:10.5250/fronjwomestud.35.3.0003

Crenshaw, K. (1989). Demarginalizing the intersection of race and sex: A black feminist critique of antidiscrimination doctrine, feminist theory and antiracist politics. *University of Chicago Legal Forum, 1989*(1), Article 8. https://chicagounbound.uchicago.edu/uclf/vol1989/iss1/8

De Brey, C., Musu, L., McFarland, J., Wilkinson-Flicker, S., Diliberti, M., Zhang, A., & Wang, X. (2019). *Status and trends in the education of racial and ethnic groups 2018.* (NCES 2019-038). U.S. Department of Education. National Center for Education Statistics. https://nces.ed.gov/pubs2019/2019038.pdf

Dhawan, S. (2020). Online learning: A panacea in the time of COVID-19 crisis. *Journal of Educational Technology Systems, 49*(1), 5–22. doi:10.1177/0047239520934018

Du, J., Ge, X., & Xu, J. (2015). Online collaborative learning activities: The perspectives of African American female students. *Computers & Education, 82*, 152–161. doi:10.1016/j.compedu.2014.11.014

Feenberg, A. (1993). 11 Building a global network: The WBSI experience. In *Global networks: Computers and international communication* (pp. 185–197). MIT Press.

Goldin, C. (1990). Understanding the gender gap: An economic history of American women (No. gold90-1). National Bureau of Economic Research.

Havens, T. (2021). Educational redlining: The disproportionate effects of the student loan crisis on Black and Latinx graduates. *The Vermont Connection, 42*(1). https://scholarworks.uvm.edu/tvc/vol42/iss1/11

Jargowsky, P. A., Ding, L., & Fletcher, N. (2019). The fair housing act at 50: Successes, failures, and future directions. *Housing Policy Debate, 29*(5), 694–703. doi:10.1080/10511482.2019.1639406

Lee, K. (2017). Rethinking the accessibility of online higher education: A historical review. *The Internet and Higher Education, 33*, 15–23. doi:10.1016/j.iheduc.2017.01.001

Lin, X. (2016). Barriers and challenges of female adult students enrolled in higher education: A literature review. *Higher Education Studies, 6*(2), 119–126. doi:10.5539/hes.v6n2p119

Caveats to Accessibility

Lothridge, K., Fox, J., & Fynan, E. (2013). Blended learning: Efficient, timely and cost effective. *The Australian Journal of Forensic Sciences, 45*(4), 407–416. doi:10.1080/00450618.2013.767375

Means, B., Toyama, Y., Murphy, R., Bakia, M., & Jones, K. (2009). *Evaluation of evidence-based practices in online learning: A meta-analysis and review of online learning studies.* U.S. Department of Education, Office of Planning, Evaluation, and Policy Development, https://files.eric.ed.gov/fulltext/ED505824.pdf

Miller, M., & Lu, M. Y. (2003). Serving non-traditional students in e-learning environments: Building successful communities in the virtual campus. *Educational Media International, 40*(1-2), 163–169. doi:10.1080/0952398032000092206

Mitchell, J. D., Simmons, C. Y., & Greyerbiehl, L. A. (2014). *Intersectionality & higher education.* Peter Lang. doi:10.3726/978-1-4539-1407-6

Müller, T. (2008). Persistence of women in online degree-completion programs. *International Review of Research in Open and Distance Learning, 9*(2), 1–18. doi:10.19173/irrodl.v9i2.455

National Center for Education Statistics. (2021, August). *Percentage of 18- to 24-year-olds enrolled in college, by level of institution and sex and race/ethnicity of student: 1970 through 2020.* NCES. https://nces.ed.gov/programs/digest/d21/tables/dt21_302.60.asp

Niemi, N. S., & Weaver-Hightower, M. B. (Eds.). (2020). *The Wiley handbook of gender equity in higher education.* John Wiley & Sons. doi:10.1002/9781119257639

Okwumabua, T. M., Walker, K. M., Hu, X., & Watson, A. (2011). An exploration of African American students' attitudes toward online learning. *Sage, 46*(2), 241–250. doi:10.1177/0042085910377516

Palvia, S., Aeron, P., Gupta, P., Mahapatra, D., Parida, R., Rosner, R., & Sindhi, S. (2018). Online education: Worldwide status, challenges, trends, and implications. *Journal of Global Information Technology Management, 21*(4), 233–241. doi:10.1080/1097198X.2018.1542262

Pettit, E. (2020, May 26). Being a woman in academe has its challenges. A global pandemic? Not helping. *The Chronicle of Higher Education.* https://rb.gy/3t8j5

Roche, T. B. (2017). Assessing the role of digital literacy in English for Academic Purposes university pathway programs. *Journal of Academic Language and Learning, 11*(1), A71–A87. https://journal.aall.org.au/index.php/jall/article/view/439

Section 504, Rehabilitation Act of 1973, 29 U.S.C. § 794 (1973). https://www.dol.gov/agencies/oasam/centers-offices/civil-rights-center/statutes/section-504-rehabilitation-act-of-1973

Singh, V., & Thurman, A. (2019). How many ways can we define online learning? A systematic literature review of definitions of online learning (1988-2018). *American Journal of Distance Education, 33*(4), 289–306. doi:10.1080/08923647.2019.1663082

Stephen, J. S., & Rockinson-Szapkiw, A. J. (2021). A high-impact practice for online students: the use of a first-semester seminar course to promote self-regulation, self-direction, online learning self-efficacy. *Smart Learning Environments, 8*(1), 6. 10.118640561-021-00151-0

Stofkova, J., Poliakova, A., Stofkova, K. R., Malega, P., Krejnus, M., Binasova, V., & Daneshjo, N. (2022). Digital skills as a significant factor of human resources development. *Sustainability (Basel)*, *14*(20), 13117. doi:10.3390u142013117

Thomas, J., Thomas, C., & Smith, K. (2019). The challenges for gender equity and women in leadership in a distributed university in regional Australia. *Social Sciences (Basel, Switzerland)*, *8*(6), 165. doi:10.3390ocsci8060165

Unterhalter, E. (2009). What is equity in education? Reflections from the capability approach. *Studies in Philosophy and Education*, *28*(5), 415–424. doi:10.100711217-009-9125-7

Waiters, L. R. (2011). *The perceptions of African American women concerning the intangible cost(s) and/or benefit(s) of a post-baccalaureate education and career choices*. ProQuest LLC.

Women's Education Equity Act. H.R.11149 — 93rd Congress (1973-1974). https://www.congress.gov/bill/93rd-congress/house-bill/11149

Xu, D., & Xu, Y. (2019). *The promises and limits of online higher education. Understanding how distance education affects access, cost, and quality*. American Enterprise Institute.

Chapter 6
At the Crossroads:
A Social-Ecological Model of Support for Women of Color in Higher Education Leadership

Lolita L. Kincade
SUNY Plattsburgh, USA

ABSTRACT

The proportion of women of color faculty members in academia is on the rise, and they are also more visible in higher education leadership. Yet, systemic sexism and racism, coupled with other forms of intersectional oppression, makes it difficult to advance to senior level administration. This chapter explores the lived experiences of academicians with intersecting identities and proposes a social ecological model to guide the development of effective interventions through social environments. Knowledge applied from personal inquiry, practical examples, and empirical evidence have resulted in important recommendations that are organized into five nested, hierarchical levels. These recommendations can help to improve diversity and inclusion efforts, and to achieve structural and systemic transformation across colleges and universities.

INTRODUCTION

Women have proven to be powerful forces, knocking down barriers and breaking cycles of patriarchy in higher education. They are also being empowered and enraged to dismantle systems of domination in the larger society. Despite facing challenges, women continue to make gains as qualified and established professionals and leaders. Though women are customarily connected through a shared experience of being female, intersections of race and gender that influence the experiences of women of color cannot be collapsed into a singular identity. The combined effects of race and gender impact the experiences of professionals in higher education. The identities of minority women are made up of interconnected intersections of race and gender, which have created overlapping and interdependent systems of discrimination and disadvantage (Crenshaw, 1989).

DOI: 10.4018/978-1-6684-8597-2.ch006

Copyright © 2023, IGI Global. Copying or distributing in print or electronic forms without written permission of IGI Global is prohibited.

Recent U.S. Department of Education (2020) data provides a demographic profile that reflects these disparities among women of color in full-time tenured and tenure-track positions, as well as higher academic ranks. Women overall tend to be overrepresented in non-tenure track positions, while under-represented minorities make up less than 20 percent of full-time faculty members across the country (Colby and Fowler, 2020). The proportion of women of color faculty members in academia is on the rise, and women of color are also more visible in higher education leadership. Yet, systemic sexism and racism, coupled with other forms of intersectional oppression make it difficult to advance to senior-level administration. Women of color compared to their counterparts navigate especially unique challenges that further complicate their already demanding academic and administrative roles. Discriminatory behavior and attitudes have both personal and professional impact in ways that are critical to the experience of women of color in the academy. In lieu of this reality, there is value in fostering more diverse and equitable practices, structures, and societal institutions to support women of color faculty and administrators. Intersectional Theory is useful in describing the cultural and historical experiences of women of color employed in the context of higher education. Specifically, it is essential to increase one's understanding of racial and gender-based stressors experienced by women of color in the context of a capitalist society, as this lived reality informs the development and implementation of a Social-Ecological theory-based framework. This chapter provides an overview of relevant scholarship and draws from experiences that support the need for the proposed Social-Ecological Model (SEM) in mitigating challenges associated with the intersectional experience. The application of the model to women of color in the academy is organized into five nested, hierarchical levels:

1. The individual level consists of specific characteristics that combat race-based stress, including self-care practices and healthy work-life balance.
2. The interpersonal level promotes increased understanding of institutional culture and climate, as well as relationships and social networks among people of shared identities to foster a supportive and collegial workplace.
3. The organizational level considers practices that can be adopted by higher education institutions, including upholding protections for professionals victimized by discrimination and workplace bullying, providing professional development opportunities, and engaging in equity practices.
4. Community structures offer relationships with professionals across universities and opportunities to engage with organizations and networks geared specifically toward women of color.
5. Equal opportunity for women of color to advance in public sectors is important, as it relates to society and public policy.

Since institutions of higher education consist of complex structures that can foster or impede the success of faculty and leaders, it is essential to examine this social environment to identify and implement changes that are needed to better support women of color in the academy. This in turn can help to improve diversity and inclusion efforts, and to achieve structural and systemic transformation across colleges and universities. Addressing implications for support, advocacy and best practices also promotes the recruitment, retention, and advancement of women of color in higher education.

At the Crossroads

THE IMPACT OF RACIAL CAPITALISM

In the early 19th century, chattel slavery was at the core of the American Southern economy and made a major contribution to capitalist development in the United States. The passage of the Emancipation Proclamation of 1863 hampered the economic activity of the southern states since free slave labor was to no longer be a form of subsidy. Desperate to find new ways to continue a system of subjugation, "black codes" were eventually enacted to restrict and limit the freedoms and progress of African American men, women, and children, extending through Reconstruction, Jim Crow, and movements of the 21st century.

The impact of slavery still resonates with many Black Americans. Disparities in employment, voting, housing, healthcare, administration of justice, distributions of wealth and income, and education can be traced to the legacy of slavery, and any of numerous policies and laws implemented to assure the continuance of White supremacy. Moreover, a prevailing capitalist society is deeply rooted in the persistence of racism. Over time, however, issues of sexism also heightened. Particularly, division of domestic labor, and segregation in schools and colleges posed challenges for women and girls in education (Arao, 2016). Academic institutions designed by and for "elite" White men in a capitalist society routinely excluded all women, setting the stage for systemic and structural inequality in the academy that calls for transformation even today. Women of color especially were never meant to thrive in the ivory tower of academia. For these women, racism and sexism coexist, uniquely affecting their experiences in higher education and in every aspect of life. This distinct form of discrimination is what we have come to understand as intersectionality.

UNDERSTANDING INTERSECTIONALITY

From the earliest years of the women's suffrage movement in the 1800s, mainstream feminism has centered the most privileged groups of women, focusing on the historical and cultural experiences of upper- and middle-class White women. Black women joined efforts to work alongside White suffragists but became increasingly more marginalized as the universal suffrage movement continued racially discriminatory practices. Black women readily recognized that their struggles were two-fold, because of their race and gender. Their unique challenges were ignored both in the fight against racial discrimination and in efforts to change the status of women in American society. As a result, Black women began to form equal rights organizations led by former abolitionists and women's rights advocates, to focus on issues that were directly impacting them.

This history mirrors the period of "second wave" feminism and even more current movements focused on women's liberation, where many are still fighting to centralize the needs and struggles of women of color. As such, calls to broaden the definition and scope of mainstream feminism has resulted in Black activists and feminist scholars developing theoretical frameworks to serve as a model representative of their experiences.

Intersectional Theory is a notable paradigm that is useful in describing aspects of the social and political identities of women of color. This framework has gathered significance in law and social sciences over many years, and has been described as a lived experience, an aspiration, a strategy, a way to analyze inequality, and even a movement (Al-Faham, Davis, and Ernst, 2019.) Intersectional Theory describes how distinctive systems of oppression interact as one overarching structure of domination (Collins, 1990). Carastathis (2014) explains how intersectionality conceptualizes relations between systems of oppression, which construct our multiple identities and our social locations in hierarchies of power and privilege. The U.S. higher education system is one of these hierarchies. Multiple marginalities experienced by women of color across university campuses requires further exploration, as these issues can no longer be ignored.

LIVED EXPERIENCES OF WOMEN OF COLOR IN HIGHER EDUCATION

Many of the challenges experienced by women at the intersection of race and gender are well documented in existing literature and include issues of unequal pay, gendered racism, stereotypes, internal oppression, microaggressions, communication barriers, exclusion, isolation, and pressure to forfeit one's cultural identity to name a few. The subsequent section describes in greater depth the nuances of these challenges. The author also draws from personal and professional experiences to further highlight some aspects of the lived experiences of women of color.

Wage Gaps

Pay disparities are a large concern for women across the board, and there are persistent disparities across higher education (Chen & Crown, 2019; Dominguez-Villegas et al., 2020). According to Johns (2013) women working full-time and year-round earn about 77 percent as much as their male counterparts, and this pay gap holds across all educational levels. Not only are women not receiving equal pay for equal work, but they do not receive equal pay for work of equal value. Further, while the Integrated Postsecondary Education Data System (IPEDS) does not directly collect faculty salary data by race and ethnicity, Colby and Fowler (2020) explain that inferences can be drawn about the existence of a *racial* pay gap overall, given the lack of underrepresented minority individuals at higher academic ranks.

The College and University Professional Association for Human Resources (CUPA-HR) further explored this notion with the publication of three reports on equity and diversity among higher education administrators. Findings suggest that women and ethnic minorities, analyzed separately, continue to face disadvantages regarding representation and pay (McChesney, 2018). Unlike IPEDS, however, this prompted consideration of the intersection of gender and ethnic minority status, and the challenges faced by these individuals in the higher education workforce. It was determined that women of color experience a combination of challenges common to both White women and minority men. Their overall median pay remains low due to being overrepresented in lower paid positions and underrepresented elsewhere. Yet, even when women of color occupy higher paid positions, they are paid considerably less than men. Thus, they experience the intersection of two challenges as it relates to fair and equal pay (McChesney, 2018).

Gendered Racism

Experiences of gendered racism are also common among women of color faculty and leaders in higher education. Love and colleagues (2020) explored these experiences among a sample of doctorate-holding Black women, using personal narratives, monologues, and reflections. Their research described oppressive functions of the academy that stereotype Black women and silence their voices, rendering them invisible. Also described were challenges of intellectual and emotional labor, or race-based stress. The

At the Crossroads

researchers concluded that Black women lacked support and experienced advancing the academy in painful ways that negatively impact their well-being and professional trajectories.

This is an interesting contrast to studies which required White higher education professionals to reflect on how gender identity and cultural taxation impacted their experiences. Participants, even those who were asked specifically to reflect upon the influence of gender, did not describe experiences of taxation. On the other hand, faculty of color felt that their gender and racial group adversely influenced their experiences in academia. They identified identity and cultural taxation as an issue that impacted both their career progress and career satisfaction (Hirshfield & Jospeh, 2012; Joseph & Hirshfield, 2011). Hannum and colleagues (2015) conducted a statistical comparison of 35 women at the senior-most levels of higher education institutions in the United States. It was reported that 75% of women of color mentioned the lack of opportunities and support they received, compared to 35% of their White counterparts. Only 7% of women of color reported having role models; more women of color shared experiences of scrutiny and criticism, and challenges related to the broad scope of their work in higher education, including isolation, not being heard, or fitting in at all.

Several years ago, the author participated in a conference session geared toward promoting equity in education for women. Some participants shared their frustrations with working in the academy and being in positions of "power." It was common among members of the group to be the sole person of color in their respective departments or colleges, leading to feelings of invisibility or an "outsider" experience. Attendees also discussed presumptions of incompetence about their capacity to complete tasks associated with their higher education leadership positions. As such, they felt as though they were required to work harder than their counterparts to prove their knowledge, skills, and areas of expertise. They also described being judged more harshly by colleagues and put under a negative microscope. This is a prime example of the emotional labor, and race-based stress that results from gendered racism. Heightened experiences of being *different* from colleagues is an emotional tax, which requires a preoccupation with coping, enduring, and surviving, as opposed to thriving in one's career. The overall effects of gendered racism experienced by women of color is detrimental to their health, as well as their physical, psychological, and social well-being (Erskine, Archibold, and Bilimoria, 2020; Travis, Thorpe-Moscon, & McCluney, 2016).

Social Stereotypes

Negative stereotypes are regularly associated with the group identify of women of color. Again, the combined effect of being both female and of color results in being typecasts according to one or the other aspect of their identity (Beckwith, Carter, & Peters, 2016; Hill et al., 2016; Sanchez-Hucles & Davis, 2010). Black women, in particular, are commonly depicted as being difficult to work with. They may be characterized as being incompetent, aggressive, hostile, over assertive or overbearing. This controlling narrative can serve as a psychosocial underpinning to perpetuate marginalization and manipulation (Howard et al., 2016). Howard and colleagues (2016) explain how this behavior typically goes unchallenged, as there is no follow-through on complaints by protected classes and offenders are not held accountable. This presents barriers to the achievement and upward mobility of professional women of color.

Acceptance of negative stereotypes about one's racial group has been the focus of some researchers, who suggest that there are correlations between internalized racism and psychological distress consisting of anxiety and depression (Sosoo et al., 2019; Willis, et al, 2021). Willis and colleagues (2021) explain that internalized racism adversely impacts the behaviors and performance of women of color, manifesting as *imposter syndrome*, or doubts about one's own abilities. However, it is important to note how this phenomenon is often used to mask systemic bias and racism. Responsibility is redirected to the individual experiencing discrimination, rather than addressing the culture and structure of racism, and the byproduct of inequities. The concept of imposter syndrome implies a pathology of the individual. In turn, it absolves the systems that bring it about of any accountability. Modern day women of color in western society are grappling to eradicate intergenerational patterns, confirmation bias and normalized othering, which may be universally characterized as imposter syndrome.

Microaggressions

Gendered and racial microaggressions, including microassaults, microinsults and microinvalidations are examples of everyday racism experienced by historically marginalized groups (Johnson & Joseph-Salisbury, 2018). Such negative exchanges are reported by women of color as being a frequent experience in the context of higher education. These subtle, stunning, or even automatic exchanges transmit hostile, derogatory and/or negative messages. Perpetrators of microaggressions are often unaware that they engage in such communications when they interact with racial and ethnic minorities (Sue et al., 2007). Further, when confronted with these concerns, perpetrators frequently "fight, flight or freeze," or weaponize "hurt feelings," which only further punishes women of color, and essentially bullies them into silence (DiAngelo, 2016; DiAngelo, 2022). The combined effects of these experiences can be associated with substantial emotional toll and racial battle fatigue (Chancellor, 2019; Pittman, 2012). The term "racial battle fatigue," describes the collective experiences of people of color who are subjected to racial hostility like soldiers who experience combat stress. Both are believed to result from being in a hostile environment where there are regular threats and attacks (Chancellor, 2019). Moody and Lewis (2019) investigated relations between gendered racial microaggressions and traumatic stress symptoms. Results from a hierarchical multiple regression analysis indicated that a greater frequency of gendered racial microaggressions was significantly associated with greater traumatic stress symptoms. Other researchers found similar correlations between racial microaggressions and mental health, including depression and psychological distress (Lewis et al., 2017; Williams & Lewis, 2019).

The author's friendship network consists of many professional women from diverse backgrounds, who have regularly shared the challenges they face combating gendered and racial microaggressions in the workplace. A leader and research scholar named "Keena" presented at a local conference on the impact of systemic and structural racism in higher education. During the question-and-answer session, a White female colleague requested that Keena elaborate on one of the concepts. Only, she desired her to do so "without all the attitude." This example of pathologizing cultural values and communication styles is one type of racial microaggression.

In the wake of media headlines about police violence in America, a diverse group of higher education professionals had a dialogue over lunch about racism, policing, and protest. "Gwen" interjected that racism does not exist in policing: "I was taught to never pull out a gun unless you intend to use it, she said." She went on to explain how "*all* people have it hard, not just Black people." Color-blind racial attitudes and the negation or dismissal of the experiences of people of color is another source of microaggressions.

"Angela," a higher education leader between 35-44 years of age lives in the Western United States. She is employed as a program director and faculty member at a Predominantly White Institution (PWI). Angela was told by a colleague that she was an affirmative action hire. She also recounted instances of being microaggressed and verbally attacked in public meetings in ways that were derogatory and had

At the Crossroads

harmful effects. Deeming Angela a *diversity hire* reveals low expectations about her competency in her role and abilities. Further, public verbal attacks dismiss and demean Angela, while undermining her authority in her leadership role.

These kinds of experiences are more prominent for women like Keena and Angela, who are part of multiple marginalized groups. Both overt aggressions and microaggressions can manifest in various ways, but the lingering, negative impact on the overall well-being of women of color is the same.

Prototypicality and Intersectional Invisibility

If we think along traditional gender lines as it relates to differing communication styles of men versus women, women of color may experience communication challenges or barriers when they display too much, or too little assertiveness, competitiveness, or independence. This might also be true when women of color display differing behaviors or ways of socializing that contrast with women of European backgrounds, since White women are thought to stand apart as prototypical of "women" in general (Johns, 2013; Lewis & Neville, 2015; Sanchez-Hucles & Davis, 2010).

The concept of non-prototypicality has also been linked to experiences of *intersectional invisibility*. Purdie-Vaughns and Eibach (2008) explain that Black women are neither prototypical of "women" nor "Black people," rendering them metaphorically invisible. The study of Comparative Human Genomics suggests that Black women carry the 'Mitochondrial Eve' gene, one of the oldest DNA lineages on earth to which all of humanity can be traced (Cann et al, 1987). Yet, White women remain a model of prototypicality. This is an indicator of the invisibility of women of color, even on a scientific level. This level of erasure and exclusion influences perceptions and evaluations of individuals at the intersection of race and gender.

Other research suggests that women of color employed in higher education experience invisibility when they are the sole person of color in their department, college, or university. As highlighted previously, these professionals are frequently excluded from formal and informal networks. This may lead to isolation and inadequate mentoring for women of color leaders (Constantine, et al., 2008; Geyton, Johnson & Ross, 2022; Hall, 2012). Alternative experiences of exclusion and isolation among women of color are rooted in the belief that their contributions in higher education are commonly unrecognized or undervalued. Some report failing to receive credit for their work, or having their ideas, initiatives and suggestions dismissed (Constantine et al., 2008; Harris, 2020; Pitman, 2012). Expected to conform to the conventional prototype, women of color are pressured to ignore important aspects of their identity, beliefs, cultural competencies, and values to achieve success in their higher education roles (Ibarra, Ely & Kolb, 2013; Mainah & Perkins, 2015; McCluney & Rabelo, 2019). In contrast, when women of color *are* recognized and visible, they may be expected to be experts on discourse related to race and gender by default, or to be "representatives" for all women of their same ethnic and racial background.

ASSESSING THE COSTS

Given these potential stressors and barriers to the success of ethnic minorities, why might women of color endure careers in higher education? There exists an apparent duality of rewards and costs for women of color scholars and leaders. Historically, prominent women of color have utilized education as a vehicle to solve many of the burning issues in society, by engaging in highly trained, organized, and politically committed work. They demonstrated this strong will to positively impact the world around them, while facing insurmountable obstacles and adversity including fighting to gain access into an academy typically reserved for White males. Not only did these women make history for themselves, but they charted a path for future academicians to follow. Frierson (2011) explains that participation of women of color in leadership roles within higher education is so important because it informs changing demographics in the United States and in our global society at large. While women of the past paved the way for the onset of this change, those in the present are motivated by the possibility of an even more inclusive and socially just society. Women of color demonstrate a deep commitment to this charge and believe that their presence in higher education provides an opportunity to transform the institutional culture for those of racially diverse and ethnic backgrounds (Frierson, 2011). Further, women of color in academe also understand the power of intersectional representation on college and university campuses for students. They serve as models, mentors, and sources of support for marginalized students, who do not otherwise see themselves represented in professoriate or senior-level administrative roles.

The work of educators at intersections is transformative and impactful, as they are well positioned to positively influence students, academic institutions, and to make valuable contributions to the larger society. Yet, the benefits of their roles in the academy do not mask the varying issues and challenges they contend with on a regular basis. Racism in all its forms, including discriminatory behavior and attitudes have pervasive side effects, impacting women of color both personally and professionally in harmful ways.

Having worked across universities in various parts of the United States as both a faculty member and administrator, the author is all too familiar with the kind of "othering" that can be associated with an intersectional identity. Attributes including race, gender, and age have played a significant role in shaping attitudes and professional experiences with others. The pathway to senior level administration in academia has been rife with racism, microaggressions, mislabeling, and the drawbacks of being misunderstood. Women of color exist against a backdrop of myth and stereotype (Colon-Alverio, & Flowers, 2022) and issues like those outlined in this chapter exist at micro, meso and macrolevels. As such, Social-Ecological Theory can provide a framework for mitigating issues at multiple levels. Processes and models rooted in inclusivity and belonging are the only sustainable solutions to the critical issues described. There is value in promoting attitudes, beliefs, and behaviors that support representation and success of women of color in their academic and administrative roles. The SEM model proposed in this chapter can assist in accomplishing this.

A Social Ecological Theory-Based Framework

Murray Bookchin's Social Ecological Theory asserts the fundamental idea that existing ecological problems are rooted in deep-seated social problems (Golden & Earp, 2012). As an activist and educator, Bookchin rejected European and American radical traditions by promoting a school of thought that called for the replacement of unjust and hierarchical relationships in human society (Best, 1998). Like early African American ecological agents and authors who underscore the ecological burdens of living within human hierarchies in the social order (Ruffin, 2010), Bookchin understood the ethical, social, and political implications of ecology. Among the persistent ecological problems that permeate our society today are economic, ethnic, cultural, and gender conflicts.

The work of other researchers, such as Urie Bronfenbrenner, is an extension of this Social Ecological model. The Ecological Systems Theory, sometimes referred to as the Bioecological Model of Development, is one of the most widely accepted explanations of the influence of social environments on human

At the Crossroads

development. This model suggests that there are multiple levels of influence on behavior, and interactions between individuals and their environment shape development over time (Golden & Earp, 2012).

In 1980, theorist Rudolf Moos developed a Social Ecological Model (SEM) of Health Promotion, which was concerned with environmental change, behavior and policies that assist individuals in making healthy choices in their daily lives (Golden & Earp, 2012). McLeroy, Bibeau, Steckler and Glanz (1988) also later proposed an Ecological Model of Health Behaviors that identified multiple levels of influence as it relates to health choices made by individuals. These models were designed to both explain and change health behavior.

Generally, ecological models assume not only that multiple levels of influence exist, but also that these levels are interactive and reinforcing. A defining feature of any ecological model is that it considers the physical environment and its relationship to people at individual, interpersonal, organizational, community and societal levels. In essence, Social Ecological models assist us in understanding social systems and interactions between individuals and environments within the system. Moreover, this model considers the complex interplay between individual, relationship, community, and societal factors (CDC, 2019; Glanz et al., 2008; McLeroy et al., 1988).

Figure 1. The social ecological model (SEM)

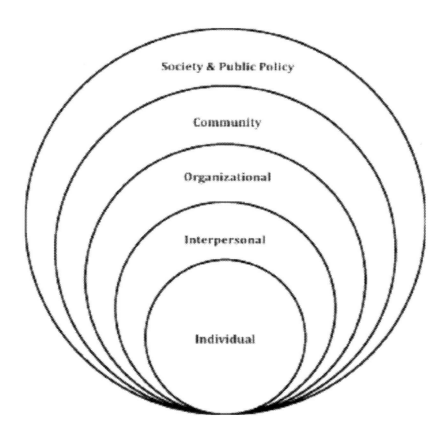

See *Figure 1*. The Social-Ecological Model is organized into five nested, hierarchical levels:

6. ***Individual***: Specific characteristics that may influence behavior change make up this level of the SEM model. These characteristics can include knowledge, skills, attitudes, behavior, self-efficacy and/or values.
7. ***Interpersonal:*** Relationships and social networks have the potential to influence behaviors. This level considers formal and informal social networks and social support systems.
8. ***Organizational***: Organizations or societal institutions often enforce behavior-determining factors. This level of influence is significant as it relates to practices that may be adopted regarding phenomena of interest.
9. ***Community***: Community structures may consist of relationships among organizations, institutions, and informational networks. This level emphasizes the *functions* of this "built environment."
10. ***Society & Public Policy***: Policies and laws implemented at local, state, national, and global levels have significant potential impact on people and varying systems.

As it relates to public health prevention and control interventions, consistent evidence shows that implementing multiple changes at various levels of the SEM model is effective in improving health-related behaviors. However, it is also important to consider the implications and potential effectiveness of this model in the context of social institutions such as colleges and universities, as there is limited information in this area of study.

Since colleges and universities are embedded in larger social and economic structures, the environmental context may influence individual people differently (e.g., women of color). A Social Ecological Model can assist us in understanding such nuances and provide guidance for developing successful interventions through social environments. Specifically, a Social-Ecological theory-based framework can be useful in understanding, exploring, and addressing factors impacting the experiences of women of color in higher education. This approach encompasses and targets a wide range of perspectives and can inform the development of long-term solutions to issues impacting the experiences of women at intersections of race and gender in their various roles in higher education.

Recommendations for Advocacy and Support

Transformative interventions can support representation and success of women of color faculty and administrators at varying levels of the Social-Ecological Model. A SEM model of support is useful in identifying points of leverage and intervention at individual, interpersonal, organizational, community and societal levels. See *Table 1*. Support at each level can aid women of color in reaching their full personal and professional potential in higher education.

At the Crossroads

Table 1. A social ecological model (SEM) of support for women of color in higher education

Level [1] *Individual*	Level [2] *Interpersonal*	Level [3] *Organizational*	Level [4] *Community*	Level [5] *Society & Public Policy*
1a. **Practice self-care** ■ Mindfulness ■ Meditation ■ Managing the amount of time devoted to work *1b.* **Address internalized oppression** ■ Relevant mental health services, including therapy with a focus on Race-Based Traumatic Stress	*2a.* **Increase knowledge & understanding of culture and climate of predominantly White institutions** *2b.* **Build social support networks** ■ Shared gender, racial/ethnic/ immigrant and class-based identities ■ Friendships with other faculty/research colleagues of color ■ Safe and private venting spaces to discuss similarities in experiences *2c.* **Demonstrated support in the workplace by women of color** *2d.* **Peer Mentoring** ■ Other women of color in higher education leadership/ administration	*3a.* **Greater representation of women of color** *3b.* **Address wage inequity issues** *3c.* **Uphold protections for those facing discrimination, bullying & verbal abuse** *3d.* **Professional development training addressing:** ■ Cultural humility ■ Unconscious bias ■ Collegiality ■ Intersectional experiences	*4a.* **Peer mentoring and support groups across universities** ■ Virtually or on social media ■ Face-to-face gatherings by region *4b.* **Empowerment seminars aimed at racially diverse women** *4c.* **Formal and professional organizations geared toward women of color employed in higher education**	*5a.* **Proactive plan of action to ensure equal opportunity in employment & university programs and activities** *5b.* **Support for women of color in politics** *5c.* **Acknowledge and address racial capitalism** ■ White allies to relinquish power and reallocate resources to minority populations.

Individual

Specific characteristics including self-care can positively influence the experiences of women of color at the individual level. Examples of self-care include engaging in mindfulness and/or meditation practices. Since daily challenges in higher education can impact the self-esteem, positive image and healthy decision making of women of color, mindfulness and meditation can counter negative experiences and empower women to address issues of race-based stress, and related physical and psychological effects. These practices allow women to overcome barriers affecting their hearts, bodies, and minds. Additionally, social organizations such as colleges and universities can develop opportunities to engage in healthy practices. Other examples of self-care may include managing the amount of time one devotes to work. Creating a delicate balance between home and work can be useful. It is common among women to be confronted with incompatible role obligations and stress associated with the ability to fulfill only a limited number of those obligations. Role compartmentalization and time management can assist in creating a healthier balance. Finally, therapy or other relevant mental health services can be beneficial in addressing internalized oppression. Only, culturally competent practitioners should be trained to recognize Race-Based Traumatic Stress, and the unique psychological and emotional distress that results from racism and discrimination.

Interpersonal

As a method of preparedness for working in Predominantly White Institutions (PWIs) it is essential to increase one's understanding of the culture and institutional climate, since it has the potential to significantly influence diversity experiences in higher education. A college or university's climate is its expression of identity and purpose; the impressions, beliefs and expectations held by students, staff, faculty, and administrators as it relates to the work and learning environment, and factors that represent expressions of the institution's identity and purpose (Piggot & Cariaga, 2019; Schneier, Ehrhart & Macey, 2013). Further, the institutional climate includes the explicit mission and policies that drive institutional goals. One should seek strong member-identification with the mission and goals of the institution to ensure a strong sense of belonging. Also, women of color can navigate their various roles in higher education more successfully when they have increased understanding of the institutional support that may be available to them. This can aid in combating the invisibility, isolation and racial stigma that is commonly experienced among women of color in higher education. Also, scholars and leaders will be able to identify if the institutional climate will be one that supports their identity, beliefs, cultural competencies and values, or if there will be pressure to ignore aspects of their identity to achieve success. This is essential, since women of color often draw from racial and cultural assets to achieve and maintain their success.

The importance of formal and informal networks and social support systems can also be helpful at the interpersonal level. While allies have an important role in offering mutual support, networks of persons with shared gender, racial, ethnic, immigrant and class-based identities is critical to establishing support, friendships, and professional collaborations. Also, members of these networks can be deliberate in creating safe spaces to share their experiences, vulnerabilities, needs, and most importantly to champion for the success and advancement of fellow colleagues and scholars. This will aid in developing a supportive and collegial community among women of color. Women of color who have already successfully navigated unique challenges and climbed the ranks of academia can serve as models, mentors, and leaders for others. They can help to build a bridge for new and rising professionals. These efforts should be committed and sustained over time. The networking and mentorship efforts identified at the interpersonal level are important to increasing the number of faculty and leaders of color in our colleges and universities, as well as the number of minority women who become leading professionals. This will lead to greater representation of women of color in higher education.

Organizational

Efforts to recruit and retain women of color in higher education positions should be a critical goal at the organizational level. Parity in pay might improve retention efforts. College and university administrators must be intentional about addressing wage inequity issues. There should be efforts made to recruit and retain women of color in positions where they are grossly underrepresented, particularly in higher paying faculty, professional and administrative roles. Institutions can plan strategically by evaluating internal equity as it relates to pay and representation, using accurate and detailed salary data, and establishing competitive salaries when competing for limited pools of minority candidates (College and University Professional Association for Human Resources, 2019).

Upholding protections for women of color and others victimized by discrimination, workplace bullying, harassment, verbal abuse, and similar destructive behaviors should be a consideration as it relates to retention of higher education professionals and cannot be minimized or ignored. Behavior that creates a

At the Crossroads

hostile work environment and that is based on factors such as race and gender overlaps with discriminatory harassment, covered under federal civil rights laws. Therefore, existing policies and interventions to address concerns of this nature are mandated and perpetrators must be held accountable. Abuse, bullying and harassment concerns should be addressed delicately so as not to force victims of misconduct into silence, or to enable continued bullying behavior.

Finally, professional development at the organizational level can be beneficial in teaching and encouraging practices that will lead to more favorable and equitable treatment for women of color in higher education. Explicit training on cultural humility, unconscious bias, collegiality, and experiences of intersectionality should be implemented to increase cultural competence. As it relates to cultural humility, it is essential to understand that women of color scholars and leaders desire to be seen as individuals, who are to be understood on their own terms, and not as representatives of their race, gender, or culture. Also, efforts to interrupt a tendency to categorize people or reinforce learned stereotypes that lead to discriminatory behavior is critical to addressing unconscious bias. While there are varying approaches to such diversity training, increasing self-awareness and changing automatic and deeply ingrained biases is not an event, but rather a process. As such, training efforts must be ongoing and long-term, if there is to be sustainable change. Fundamentally, collegiality encompasses respect, cooperation, and shared responsibility. Structural collegiality is also an important consideration as it relates to governance and organization. These values should be the underpinning of not only our moral code, but also our institutional code of ethics.

Professional development training must also aim to assist individuals and organizations in understanding how race and gender shapes one's experience in higher education. It is vital to consider factors related to individual identity and self-identification, and the effects of overlapping systems of discrimination and disadvantage. Since organizations and societal institutions can enforce behavior-determining factors, implementing these strategies can lead to more positive experiences and outcomes for women of color in the academy. Psychological benefits may include cross-cultural empathy and shared humanity. Further, increased knowledge of the lived experience of women of color can inform organizations on how to build creative initiatives toward inclusivity and better intercultural relationships among faculty, staff, and administrators.

Community

Peer mentoring and support groups *across* universities are appropriate at the community level. Examples included virtual, or face-to-face networking opportunities for mentoring, guidance, sponsorship and/or advocacy. For example, New England Humanities Consortium (NEHC) Mellon Mentors is a program that considers social barriers and the specific constraints faced by people of color in academia as scholars and administrators, which create obstacles to their retention and success. In this program, regional mentoring cohorts are established to alleviate unequal advancement through the ranks of academia. The American Association of State Colleges and Universities (AASCU) also provides various academies and affinity groups for tailored mentoring, learning and support.

While mentors advise and guide, sponsors are advocates. They may consist of leaders in academia or those in executive level positions who are well connected and established in their careers. Sponsorship focuses on rallying for specific opportunities; making phone calls and sending emails that would lead to promotion and career advancement. Women of color across networks should utilize their influence to advocate for other qualified staff, faculty, and higher education leaders. There are also existing sponsorship programs. The Mellon Faculty of Color Fellowship provides a financial resource that allows fellows to spend a full year at a NEHC host institution, where there are opportunities to focus their efforts on visibility, promotion, and professional development, while interacting with a broad intellectual community (New England Humanities Consortium, 2023). The additional support such opportunities can provide is invaluable.

Participation in empowerment seminars geared toward racially diverse women is another great way to establish *community* in higher education settings. These seminars or conferences are usually uniquely designed to fit the needs and values of women of color by addressing the complex issues experienced at the intersections (e.g., addressing imposter syndrome, the glass ceiling and unequal pay, managing barriers & biases, etc.) These events provide a space to meet, connect, inspire, and be inspired by women who have shared experience and who are also passionate about creating lasting change for racially diverse women. These conference opportunities may be hosted by professional organizations with the same or a similar mission, eliminating bias, enhancing diversity and inclusion, and the development of women in their professional roles. Continuous educational opportunities, prospective employment, networking, and increased access to resources in higher education are among the benefits of membership-based professional associations and organizations.

Society and Public Policy

At the fifth and final level of this proposed SEM model to support women of color in higher education is the implementation of effective structures and policies to ensure equal opportunity in employment, university programs, and activities. It is critical to ensure that colleges and universities follow the provisions of a written plan to proactively recruit, hire, promote and retain women and minorities. Preparation should be made to analyze and professionally address inconsistencies or concerns with existing plans when appropriate.

On a larger scale, supporting women of color in local, state, national and global politics has the potential to empower them to drive institutional and social change. Bynam & Gomez Stordy (2017) explain that training, mentorship, strong relationships, and supportive workplace environments contribute to advancement and success of women of color leaders. In these positions, women of color have a say in the policies that are up for discussion and in the legislation that is advanced (O'Connor & Yanus, 2004). Finally, White allies should not fail to acknowledge and address the legacy of racial capitalism. They can be proactive in relinquishing power and reallocating resources to minority populations. These efforts are important to shaping the overall landscape and well-being of our society.

CONCLUSION

Centering the experiences, perspectives, and voices of women of color in higher education is critical. This chapter shed light on racial and gender-based stressors experienced uniquely by women of color in higher education. In short, women of color face disadvantage and several challenges, relative to their counterparts (Dominguez-Villegas et al., 2020; Geyton, Johnson & Ross, 2022; Harris, 2020; Hill et al., 2016; Lewis & Neville, 2015; Love et al., 2020; McCluney & Rabelo, 2019; Moody & Lewis, 2019). As such, the SEM model presented provides recommendations to support women of color in the academy, and in mitigating challenges associated with the intersectional experience. Offered at varying levels are

At the Crossroads

methods of advocacy and support that address related issues, and that have the potential to contribute to important structural and systemic change across colleges and universities. Implementation of this model in a college or university setting will require opportunities to assess its direct impact on organizational culture and structure, as well as outcomes for the target demographic. The completion and analysis of a formal report that summarizes activities, as well as more detailed information about salient strategies that were implemented will assist in understanding the totality of model's impact. The report might focus on specific changes that were made at individual, interpersonal, organizational, community and societal levels. Identifying key components needed to apply the model most effectively can be generalized for use by others seeking to affect change. Achieving reform in higher education is both complex and challenging. However, the availability of a universal model to guide our efforts in supporting professionals at the intersection of race and gender presents a unique opportunity for sustainable change. Seeding the next generation of women of color leaders is vital to future advancement of the academy, and to the betterment of the world.

As we continue to seek to understand and support racially diverse scholars and professionals, the author strongly cautions against ignoring and/or minimizing the experiences of those at the intersections of race and gender. It is not helpful to shy away from or implode about discussions of race, systemic racism, discrimination, or White privilege. Outward displays of defensiveness and anger as a response to these challenges perpetuate a vicious cycle of oppression. Moreover, in the presence of racial stress such behavior continues to foster an insulated environment of racial protection and comfortability for the privileged, reinforcing racial interests and perspectives (DiAngelo, 2015). Researcher DiAngelo (2015) encourages letting go of racial certitude and reaching for humility. It is essential to use one's voice and privilege to advocate for diversity and to combat issues related to racism and sexism in higher education. We cannot afford the penalty of silence about things that matter. The time to do what is right is always now.

REFERENCES

Al-Faham, H., Davis, A. M., & Ernst, R. (2019). Intersectionality: From theory to practice. *Annual Review of Law and Social Science, 15*(1), 247–265. doi:10.1146/annurev-lawsocsci-101518-042942

Arao, B. (2016). Roles of Black women and girls in education. *Historical Reflections. Reflexions Historiques.*

Beckwith, A. L., Carter, D. R., & Peters, T. (2016). The underrepresentation of African American women in executive leadership: What's getting in the way? *Journal of Business Studies Quarterly, 7*(4), 115–134.

Best, S. (1998). Murray Bookchin's theory of social ecology: An appraisal of the ecology of freedom. *Organization & Environment, 11*(3), 334–353. doi:10.1177/0921810698113004

Cann, R. L., Stoneking, M., & Wilson, A. C. (1987). Mitochondrial DNA and human evolution. *Nature, 325*(6099), 31–36. doi:10.1038/325031a0 PMID:3025745

Carastathis, A. (2014). The concept of intersectionality in feminist theory. *Philosophy Compass, 9*(5), 304–314. doi:10.1111/phc3.12129

Centers for Disease Control and Prevention (CDC). (2019). The Social Ecological Model: A Framework for Prevention. CDC. https://www.cdc.gov/violenceprevention/overview/social-ecologicalmodel.html

Chancellor, R. L. (2019). Racial battle fatigue: The unspoken burden of Black women faculty in LIS. *Journal of Education for Library and Information Science, 60*(3), 182–189. doi:10.3138/jelis.2019-0007

Chen, J. J., & Crown, D. (2019). The gender pay gap in academia: Evidence from the Ohio State University. *American Journal of Agricultural Economics, 101*(5), 1337–1352. doi:10.1093/ajae/aaz017

Colby, G., & Fowler, C. (2020). *Data snapshot: IPEDS data on full-time women faculty and faculty of color*. American Association of University Professors.

Collins, P. H. (1990). Black feminist thought in the matrix of domination. *Black Feminist Thought: Knowledge. Consciousness and the Politics of Empowerment, 138*, 221–238.

Colon-Alverio, I. D., & Flowers, T. D. (2022). The Racial Battle Fatigue of Black Graduate Women in the Academy. In Black Women Navigating Historically White Higher Education Institutions and the Journey Toward Liberation (pp. 69-87). IGI Global. doi:10.4018/978-1-6684-4626-3.ch004

Constantine, M., Smith, L., Redington, R. M., & Owens, D. (2008). Racial microaggressions against Black counseling and counseling psychology faculty: A central challenge in the multicultural counseling movement. *Journal of Counseling and Development, 86*(3), 348–355. doi:10.1002/j.1556-6678.2008.tb00519.x

Crenshaw, K. (1989). Demarginalizing the intersection of race and sex: a black feminist critique of antidiscrimination doctrine, feminist theory and antiracist politics. *University of Chicago Legal Forum*. University of Chicago. https://chicagounbound.uchicago.edu/uclf/vol1989/iss1/8

DiAngelo, R. (2015). White fragility: Why it's so hard to talk to White people about racism. *The Good Men Project, 9*.

DiAngelo, R. (2016). *White fragility* (Vol. 497). Counterpoints.

Dominguez-Villegas, R., Smith-Doerr, L., Renski, H., & Sekarasih, L. (2020). Labor Unions and Equal Pay for Faculty: A Longitudinal Study of Gender Pay Gaps in a Unionized Institutional Context. *Journal of Collective Bargaining in the Academy, 11*(1), 2. doi:10.58188/1941-8043.1793

Erskine, S. E., Archibold, E. E., & Bilimoria, D. (2020). Afro-diasporic women navigating the black ceiling: Individual, relational, and organizational strategies. *Business Horizons, 64*(1), 37–50. doi:10.1016/j.bushor.2020.10.004

Frierson, H. T. (2011). *Women of color in higher education: Turbulent past, promising future*. Emerald Group Publishing.

Geyton, T., Johnson, N., & Ross, K. (2022). 'I'm good': Examining the internalization of the strong Black woman archetype. *Journal of Human Behavior in the Social Environment, 32*(1), 1–16. doi:10.1080/10911359.2020.1844838

Glanz, K., Rimer, B. K., & Viswanath, K. (Eds.). (2008). *Health behavior and health education: theory, research, and practice*. John Wiley & Sons.

Golden, S. D., & Earp, J. A. L. (2012). Social ecological approaches to individuals and their contexts: Twenty years of health education & behavior health promotion interventions. *Health Education & Behavior*, *39*(3), 364–372. doi:10.1177/1090198111418634 PMID:22267868

Hall, J. C., Everett, J. E., & Hamilton-Mason, J. (2012). Black women talk about workplace stress and how they cope. *Journal of Black Studies*, *43*(2), 207–226. doi:10.1177/0021934711413272 PMID:22457894

Hannum, K. M., Muhly, S. M., Shockley-Zalabak, P. S., & White, J. S. (2015). Women leaders within higher education in the United States: Supports, barriers, and experiences of being a senior leader. *Advancing Women in Leadership Journal*, *35*, 65–75. doi:10.21423/awlj-v35.a129

Harris, A. P. (2020). *Presumed incompetent II: Race, class, power, and resistance of women in academia*. University Press of Colorado.

Hill, C., Miller, K., Benson, K., & Handley, G. (2016). *Barriers and bias: The status of women in leadership*. American Association of University Women. https://www.aauw.org/resources/research/barrier-bias/

Hirshfield, L. E., & Joseph, T. D. (2012). 'We need a woman, we need a black woman': Gender, race, and identity taxation in the academy. *Gender and Education*, *24*(2), 213–227. doi:10.1080/09540253.2011.606208

Howard, A., Patterson, A., Kinloch, V., Burkhard, T., & Randall, R. (2016). The Black women's gathering place: Reconceptualizing a curriculum of place/space. *Gender and Education*, *28*(6), 756–768. doi:10.1080/09540253.2016.1221895

Johns, M. (2013). Breaking the glass ceiling: Structural, cultural, and organizational barriers preventing women from achieving senior and executive positions. *Perspectives in Health Information Management*, *1*(11). PMID:23346029

Johnson, A., & Joseph-Salisbury, R. (2018). 'Are You Supposed to Be in Here?' Racial microaggressions and knowledge production in higher education. In *Dismantling race in higher education* (pp. 143–160). Palgrave Macmillan. doi:10.1007/978-3-319-60261-5_8

Joseph, T. D., & Hirshfield, L. E. (2011). 'Why don't you get somebody new to do it?' Race and cultural taxation in the academy. *Ethnic and Racial Studies*, *34*(1), 121–141. doi:10.1080/01419870.2010.496489

Lewis, J. A., & Neville, H. A. (2015). Construction and initial validation of the Gendered Racial Microaggressions Scale for Black women. *Journal of Counseling Psychology*, *62*(2), 289–302. doi:10.1037/cou0000062 PMID:25867696

Lewis, J. A., Williams, M. G., Peppers, E. J., & Gadson, C. A. (2017). Applying intersectionality to explore the relations between gendered racism and health among Black women. *Journal of Counseling Psychology*, *64*(5), 475–486. doi:10.1037/cou0000231 PMID:29048194

Love, B. H., Templeton, E., Ault, S., & Johnson, O. (2021). Bruised, not broken: Scholarly personal narratives of Black women in the academy. *International Journal of Qualitative Studies in Education : QSE*, 1–23. doi:10.1080/09518398.2021.1984607

Mainah, F., & Perkins, V. (2015). Challenges facing female leaders of color in U. S. higher education. *International Journal of African Development*, *2*(2), 5–13.

McChesney, J. (2018). Representation and pay of women of color in the higher education workforce. *College and University Professional Association for Human Resources [CUPA-HR].* https://www.cupahr. org/surveys/research-briefs/2018-representation-pay-women-of-color-higher-ed-workforce

McCluney, C. L., & Rabelo, V. C. (2019). Conditions of visibility: An intersectional examination of Black women's belongingness and distinctiveness at work. *Journal of Vocational Behavior, 113*, 143–152. doi:10.1016/j.jvb.2018.09.008

McLeroy, K. R., Bibeau, D., Steckler, A., & Glanz, K. (1988). An ecological perspective on health promotion programs. *Health Education Quarterly, 15*(4), 351–353. doi:10.1177/109019818801500401 PMID:3068205

Moody, A. T., & Lewis, J. A. (2019). Gendered racial microaggressions and traumatic stress symptoms among Black women. *Psychology of Women Quarterly, 43*(2), 201–214. doi:10.1177/0361684319828288

New England Humanities Consortium. (n.d.). *Faculty of color working group.* FOCWG. https://www.focwg.org/

Pittman, C. T. (2012). Racial microaggressions: The narratives of African American faculty at a predominantly White university. *The Journal of Negro Education, 81*(1), 82–92. doi:10.7709/jnegroeducation.81.1.0082

Purdie-Vaughns, V., & Eibach, R. P. (2008). Intersectional invisibility: The distinctive advantages and disadvantages of multiple subordinate-group identities. *Sex Roles, 59*(5-6), 377–391. doi:10.100711199-008-9424-4

Ruffin, K. N. (2010). *Black on earth: African American ecoliterary traditions.* University of Georgia Press. doi:10.1353/book11452

Sanchez-Hucles, J. V., & Davis, D. D. (2010). Women and women of color in leadership: Complexity, identity, and intersectionality. *The American Psychologist, 65*(3), 171–181. doi:10.1037/a0017459 PMID:20350016

Sosoo, E. E., Bernard, D. L., & Neblett, E. W. (2019). The Influence of internalized racism on the relationship between discrimination and anxiety. *Cultural Diversity & Ethnic Minority Psychology, 26*(4), 570–580. doi:10.1037/cdp0000320 PMID:31886684

Sue, D. W., Capodilupo, C. M., Torino, G. C., Bucceri, J. M., Holder, A., Nadal, K. L., & Esquilin, M. (2007). Racial microaggressions in everyday life: Implications for clinical practice. *The American Psychologist, 62*(4), 271–286. doi:10.1037/0003-066X.62.4.271 PMID:17516773

Travis, D. J., Thorpe-Moscon, J., & McCluney, C. (2016). *Emotional tax: How Black women and men pay more at work and how leaders can take action.* Catalyst.

U.S. Department of Education. (2020). IPEDS, HR Survey component (provisional data). National Center for Education Statistics.

Williams, M. G., & Lewis, J. A. (2019). Gendered racial microaggressions and depressive symptoms among Black women: A moderated mediation model. *Psychology of Women Quarterly, 43*(3), 368–380. doi:10.1177/0361684319832511

At the Crossroads

Willis, H. A., Sosoo, E. E., Bernard, D. L., Neal, A., & Neblett, E. W. (2021). The Associations Between Internalized Racism, Racial Identity, and Psychological Distress. *Emerging Adulthood*, *9*(4), 384–400. doi:10.1177/21676968211005598 PMID:34395061

Chapter 7
Black Women Faculty Also Matter:
A Paradigm Shift Toward Empowerment and Inclusion in Higher Education

Portia Allie-Turco
SUNY Plattsburgh, USA

ABSTRACT

The upheavals caused by the COVID-19 pandemic continue to affect the lives of faculty across the globe. Inasmuch as the pandemic brought profound levels of anxiety, loss, and turmoil, it also created an opportunity to address ineffective and unjust policies in academia. For Black women academics, reflections on the pandemic do not linger on the realignment, reinvention, and reinvigoration of their professional lives because alignment, invention, and invigoration as fully accepted peers in the academy have never existed for them. Instead, the opportunity now is for Black women faculty to step into a space that has never been fully accessible to them as professionals. The pandemic provided an opportunity to recognize pervasive and systemic inequalities for minoritized individuals and communities that have always been reflected in the academy and to create an environment of inclusion and empowerment for everyone. Reimagining academia as an inclusive environment means intentionally challenging racial stereotypes and promoting spaces where Black women faculty feel included and connected.

PANDEMIC WITHIN A PANDEMIC

The challenges of the pandemic affected all faculty at all institutions; however, Black women faculty at large were disproportionately affected because the pandemic magnified already existing consequences of structural racism, persistent health disparities, and pervasive inequalities (Njoku et al., 2021). Black faculty faced increased personal and professional pressure due to the pandemic's effects on Black communities dealing with rampant illness, unemployment, and death. In fact, rates of infection, hospitalization, and death from COVID-19 were twice as high for Black Americans, and the underlying conditions contrib-

DOI: 10.4018/978-1-6684-8597-2.ch007

Copyright © 2023, IGI Global. Copying or distributing in print or electronic forms without written permission of IGI Global is prohibited.

Black Women Faculty Also Matter

uted to the staggering rates of mortality associated with race for hospitalized patients with COVID-19 (Rubin-Miller et. al., 2020; Yehia et. al., 2020.)

In addition, as a result of the racially charged experiences that fueled the #Black Lives Matter movement, Black faculty, professional staff, and students suffered collective racial trauma (Sosoo et al., 2022). Black women were at the forefront of the racial storm that had been brewing for decades. Black women have always been at the center of the liberation movement and felt compelled during the pandemic to continue in the struggle through protest, marching, teaching, and supporting the Black community in this time of intense racial crisis (Njoku & Evans, 2022).

The COVID-19 pandemic openly revealed to the larger society the underlying disparities and injustices that the Black community has always known, and that gave rise to the disproportionate impact of COVID-19 on People of Color (Centers for Disease Control, 2021; Dubay et al., 2020; Sneed et al., 2020). The multi-layered plight of Black Americans during the COVID-19 pandemic has been called "a pandemic on a pandemic" (Laurencin & Walker, 2020), and American society could no longer simply look the other way. Further, amid the tumult following George Floyd's murder, racial issues could no longer be avoided because the shocking images permeated the media. America had to confront the racial reckoning that unfolded in real-time during an unfolding mass health crisis (Reny & Newman, 2021; Powell, 2022).

In the academy, the upheaval also reverberated. Perhaps counter-intuitively, the pandemic also created an opening for broader ways of thinking, enriched worldviews, and new methods of teaching, service, and scholarship. There have been opportunities to discuss race and racism in a new way, and this has opened the door for new alliances with other faculty members who wish to join in solidarity against systemic racism that became so evident to the world. In order to allow this crucial work to continue, however, it is important to understand the complexities that currently exist and the underlying conditions that gave rise to the inequities in the first place.

RACIAL CHALLENGES IN THE ACADEMY

Patriarchy and the Controlling Images of Black Women

The White patriarchy has been responsible for dictating the nature of womanhood for all women and positioned womanhood to be defined by idealized notions of White womanhood. In this depiction, a feminine woman is White, pure, virtuous, and obedient. White feminists strived to challenge this paternalistic view of White womanhood as fragile and powerless, yet it continues to inform what is considered the most valuable, idealized, and true nature of womanhood (Gilligan, 1982). The idealized White woman stands in stark contrast to depictions of Black women who have been caricatured by negative stereotypes due to their lower status since slavery (Hernandez & Rehman, 2019; Collins, 2000; hooks, 1982). These ideal White societal norms have designated an impossible standard through which racially minoritized women are evaluated and ways in which society responds to their attributes even though the standards are impossible to meet.

Blackness as an artificially created social attribute has been contrasted against Whiteness to represent what is considered the deviant underbelly of American society. As people of African descent, Black Americans have been chained by this construction of race since slavery to reflect their personhood as uncivilized, unintelligent, criminal, or inferior (Collins, 2011). For Black women, historical and ongoing racial oppression intersects with gender inequities, which in turn compound this notion of deviance or otherness as reflected by several controlling images that subjugate Black women. These include the Angry Black Woman and the Mammy (perpetual caregiver), two tropes that are especially impactful in the professional sphere (Collins, 2011; Harris-Perry, 2011).

The prevailing White patriarchal values that continue to be dominant in Western society promote a view of womanhood that is obedient, fragile, nurturing, sweet, friendly, and soft-spoken (Frankenberg, 1993; Tong, 2018). Women, including women leaders, are expected to manifest these traits regardless of their positions and are negatively evaluated when they fail to meet these standards (Brescoll, 2016). Female educators are also expected to engage students in these stereotypical depictions of idealized womanhood (hooks, 1986; 2014; Maher & Tetreault, 2001), and gain favorable student ratings when they are warm, friendly, and nurturing (Chávez & Mitchell, 2020; MacNell et al., 2015; Tisdell, 1998). However, since slavery, Black women's femininity has long been contrasted with this idealized White femininity and has been found lacking by such unjust standards (Ringrose et al., 2019). Studies indicate that as early as elementary school, Black girls are conventionally viewed as "loud" and "out of control" (Carter Andrews, et. al., 2019; Morris, 2007). These pejorative stereotypes stemming from slavery have dire consequences for Black girls at school and have been associated with suspensions and the school-to-prison pipeline (Morris, 2016).

The perception of uncontrolled anger follows Black girls into adulthood so that when Black women stand up for themselves, they are characterized as overly assertive, aggressive, and combative. Historically and in the present day, this stereotype of the Angry Black Woman has permeated the media and depicts Black women as irrational, masculine, and unworthy of male protection that is afforded to White women (Ashley, 2014; Corbin et al., 2018). However, this stereotype does account for the righteous indignation and heightened need for self-protection that gets activated as a survival skill during difficult social interactions (Ashley, 2014). The Angry Black Woman trope is directed especially toward Black women who assertively advocate against systemic injustice and intentionally disrupt color-blind inequity, White privilege, and supremacy (Motro et al., 2022). In the same way, the Angry Black Woman trope has been at the center of racial marginalization in academia, where they fight against being seen as "angry disruptors" (Doharty, 2020).

Another stereotype that also contributes to the disenfranchisement of Black Women faculty and prevents their careers from gaining real traction is the "Mammy" trope of uncomplaining selfless caregiving. Historically, caretaking has been delineated as the role of underprivileged poor, or non-White women. When discussing controlling images of Black womanhood, (Collins, 2009) argues that Black women have been confined to the role of caretaker since slavery. This caretaker idea carries into college classrooms, where Black female educators are expected to provide warm and supportive care to their students, in addition to teaching the substance of their courses. It is perpetuated in expectations for a myriad of other thankless tasks for Black women faculty in the academy as well.

Teaching While Black

The idea of "Teaching While Black" underscores the notion that teaching can be soul-destroying for Black faculty members who critically engage with and challenge racism at any level, due to racial and gendered social positionality in their profession (Daniel, 2019, Young & Hines, 2018). As context, positionality refers to an individual's identity based on their social position and power in any given society and is based on an intersectional understanding of their race, gender, class, sexual orientation, ability,

Black Women Faculty Also Matter

and other aspects of their group membership. Despite achieving the relatively elevated status of professional faculty, Black women's racialized and gendered status negatively influences their experiences in the classroom (Blackshear & Hollis, 2021; Rideau & Robbins, 2020).

Because of the positionality of Black women faculty existing at the intersection of race and gender, their expertise and authority as professionals is often delegitimized. Black women have made great gains in educational attainment in the United States and are being colloquially celebrated as the most educated gender per capita. Despite Black women's great achievements in educational attainment, the academy at large, as a microcosm of society, continues to reflect the racism in the majority White society when Black faculty are viewed through racial lenses that hinder their progress and empowerment. Black women faculty account for only 3% of college faculty and tend to be concentrated in the junior ranks or non-tenured faculty tiers (National Center for Education Statistics, 2018). Given their scarcity in higher education, they face considerable barriers in being perceived as subject experts in their fields of study or being legitimized as sources of knowledge because of commonly held bias.

Scholars note that despite academic achievement or attaining professional competence, authority in the classroom is harder to gain for Black women faculty (Sivasubramaniam, 2022). When Black women are in positions of leadership, a lack of societal power and authority impedes their ability to influence the classroom environment (Johnson-Bailey, 2015; Maher & Tetreault, 2001). The concept of authority in the classroom involves the negotiation between an educator and students that encompasses the complex skills of inviting cooperation, willingness, and assent to learn. Classroom authority is influenced by numerous factors including credibility, trust, institutional expectations, cultural and societal factors, and student disposition (Metz, 1978; Pace, & Hemmings, 2006). The institutionalized racial lens interrupts students from seeing Black faculty as knowledgeable experts regardless of Black faculty's ostensible position of authority in the academy.

Presumption of White Male Faculty Expertise

As with every other faculty member and student, Black women faculty positionalities impact the teaching and learning environment. Research supports the notion that an educator's traits, including physical attractiveness, are associated with students' perceptions of the faculty's credibility (Fisher et al., 2019). Further, research studies on students' perceptions of the idealized characteristics of professors have uncovered that 'the ideal teacher' is male, White, and has an authoritative and knowledgeable disposition. As a result of systemic racism and sexism, White male professors occupy a favored social position that has deemed them as the originators of knowledge, and their teaching is most often associated with objectivity, fact, and elevated intellectualism (Cheryan & Markus, 2020; Smith & Lander, 2012). This favored status has been associated with greater leeway in the classroom, most especially when teaching about issues pertaining to race and racism. Because of his position as a critical and objective source of knowledge, a White male professor exudes a detached and knowledgeable demeanor, which contradicts the role expected of women.

By contrast, stereotypes related to Black professors reinforce the notion that Black people are not intellectually capable, or they lack appropriate credentials and training (Davis & Brown, 2017; McCoy-Wilson, 2020). Additionally, the level of scrutiny for Black women faculty is in stark contrast to male faculty (McCoy, 2021). When men are in charge, they are presumed to be competent and are seldom accused of being bossy (Allen & Stewart, 2022; Hentschel et al., 2019). When Black women are direct, their behavior is translated into a narrative that they are abrasive, bossy, or aggressive. Therefore, the same traits that are admired in White male professors can be damaging for Black women faculty due to the perception that as women they are aggressive, argumentative, loud, and mean (Amott & Matthaei, 1996; Harris-Perry, 2011; Motro et al, 2022; Weitz & Gordon, 1993). These characteristics in Black female faculty influence students' negative assessment of faculty behavior in the classroom, leading to the differential and biased negative evaluation of the same trait based on gender and race (Chesler & Young, 2007; Young et al., 2015).

The Pandemic and Teaching About Race and Racism

During the pandemic, heightened and racialized societal experiences surrounding the murder of George Floyd made their way into the classroom. Black faculty have long reported that discussions of race and racism have a damaging impact on promotions and tenure, and yet they are often called upon to address issues of race, diversity, and inclusion, often with limited support regarding student reactance or resistance. This can lead to Black faculty choosing to self-silence on issues of race to prevent negative career repercussions. Following George Floyd's murder, the need to have discussions about race became even more urgent, however, this in itself was an added stressor because of the differing political and cultural views within classrooms (Simien & Wallace, 2022). Professors felt the need to meet the moment but also had to consider the inordinate emotional and psychological quagmire presented. For some, keeping silent seemed the wisest choice.

The intense racial focus heightened the distress of Black faculty who were grieving in real-time as members of the Black community. They were also trying to support Black students who were similarly experiencing shock and grief. In addition, Black faculty strove to create an equitable classroom in a racially charged environment. Black faculty faced the tortured choice to continue self-silencing or to disrupt the status quo by joining in and elevating Black voices in the struggle toward equity.

The notion that an ideal classroom is a safe space for sharing and exchanging ideas is widely supported in literature. Educators understand that classroom safety and caring promote critical thinking skills and learning (Stanfill & Klean-Zwilling, 2023). However, Black female faculty emphasize that the classroom is rarely safe for faculty or students of color (Closson et al., 2014; hooks, 1999; Thomas, 2020; Wong et al., 2022). This is due in large part to the understanding that the classroom replicates the complex racial dynamics of the wider society. This is particularly evident when teaching about issues of diversity and inclusion (Layne et. al., 2022). Scholars highlight the considerable challenges experienced by faculty of color when teaching about race and racism (Rideau & Robbins, 2020). Student resistance to discussing race and racism is expressed in the form of hostile silence (Ladson-Billings, 1996), interrupting, questioning, or engaging in other behavior that disrupts meaningful dialogue. This behavior has the outcome of silencing and interrupting the teacher and making the classroom a stressful and unsafe place for the teacher who is the "other."

Student Reactions to Diversity Courses

Black faculty are more likely than White faculty to teach classes that explore societal inequities (Ahluwalia et al., 2019). The minoritized status of Black women faculty is further complicated when they teach about issues that question typically accepted or controversial knowledge. White educators who teach about inequity are considered progressive and equity-minded experts who are imparting factually sound knowledge. In contrast, due to their racialized positionality, Black faculty teaching diversity and equity-focused courses face an increased risk of being regarded as sharing biased and subjective knowledge that is rooted in a personal agenda (Truong et. al., 2014). Further, discussion of racism can often activate students' defense mechanisms or even open hostility (Sue et al., 2011; Burton & Furr, 2014). Students, especially White male students (Thomas, 2020; Evans-Winters & Hines, 2020; Pittman, 2010), are more likely to engage in conscious and unconscious acts of resistance, including challenging the authority, credibility, or teaching effectiveness of Black women faculty. These disruptive actions are even more pronounced when Black women faculty are teaching about diversity and can manifest as disrespect, open hostility, and student pursuit of punitive action to administration all of which significantly impact the teaching and learning environment (Thomas, 2020 Louis et al., 2016; Martinez & Welton, 2017).

Student Teaching Evaluations of Black Faculty

Teaching evaluations form the bedrock of professional assessment and are foundational to the career trajectory of academic faculty. However, student evaluations of educators are not objective, more often they are based on the likeability of the instructor or how positively students feel about themselves in the classroom and are strongly influenced by race and gender (Baker & Copp, 1997; Black, 2021; Lazos 2012; Mitchell & Martin, 2018). A dilemma for Black faculty invested in teaching about oppression and inequity centers around the understanding that professor likeability and charisma rarely emerge for Black faculty in White spaces and promote the conspiracy of watering down racial inequities to avoid student backlash (Daniel, 2019). Student evaluations of teaching are traditionally lower for courses that promote equity, inclusion, and diversity (Ross & Edwards, 2016). Faculty of Color who teach diversity-related content are more likely to have significantly lower teaching evaluations due to student rejection of the course content. Students voice their disapproval by rating the instructor lower on course evaluations (Young et al., 2016). These weaponized lower ratings have damaging implications for tenure and promotion; against Black faculty.

Black Women and Academic Service

Service is another area that increases the marginalization of Black women in higher education (Domingo et al., 2020; Misra et al., 2021). The notion that Black women faculty are uniquely positioned to respond to service work in response to the diversity, equity, and inclusion needs of college campuses has been documented in the phenomenon of cultural or identity taxation, which links to other intersectional experiences of marginalization, such as contingent status (Guillaume & Apodaca, 2020; Rideau, 2019). Scholars such as Porcher and Austin (2021), underscore the prevailing notion that Black women "are the Mules of the World," toiling under the harshest environments with minimal resistance, doing what needs to be done without recognition.

Data shows Black women are more likely to be the lowest-paid faculty members in non-tenure track or contingent positions (McChesney, 2018). Contingent or non-tenure track faculty hold the majority of faculty positions in higher education (Pryor, 2020), with Black women and other Women of Color representing almost 41% of all women in these faculty positions (Boss et al., 2019; Finkelstein et al., 2016). Contingency status increases marginalization due to a lack of job security, pay inequity, and lack of resources to engage in scholarship that is needed to gain a chance for advancement into tenure-track status (Allison et al., 2014; Kezar & Maxey, 2012; McNaughtan et al., 2017). Furthermore, non-tenure track positions typically have higher teaching and service loads, which further prohibit research and other scholarship opportunities.

Women in contingent faculty roles also face the dilemma of being at-will employees so job instability is often a normal experience for them. They are documented to face inordinate pressure and obligation to assume additional service responsibility in order to maintain job security in higher education (Haviland, 2017). This is especially true for Black women faculty, where contingent status exacerbates already existing marginalization in the academy (Hirshfield & Joseph, 2012). Due to experiences with oppression, Black women have already internalized the cultural expectation that they have to work twice as hard to succeed in professional and academic spaces (DeCuir-Gunby et al., 2020). While this belief in itself is oppressive and destructive, it has been critical for Black survival in White spaces, and letting go of the idea is rife with risk. Thus, it is understandable that "just saying no" to unending demands for unpaid additional service does not seem like a viable option, given how tenuous the employment situation often is within the academy.

Tokenized University Service

Relatedly, tokenism has been recognized as a serious drain on the emotional and psychological well-being of minoritized faculty, including Black women faculty. Although Kanter (1993) conceptualized the phenomenon of tokenism to describe the experiences of women who were employed in male-dominated industries, this concept has been expanded to include the unique experiences of Black Indigenous and People of Color (BIPOC) working in White dominated environments. Tokenism delineates three characteristics that racially minoritized faculty encounter when working in historically White institutions (Kanter, 1993). The first is the visibility associated with being a numerical minority and the de facto visibility in predominantly White spaces. This heightened visibility adds a layer of scrutiny for tokenized faculty and alters the typical conditions that other faculty operate under (Kanter, 1993). Tokenized faculty also suffer from the pressure to assimilate the dominant standards and norms of the institution, which renders their selfhood invisible (Dobbs & Leider, 2021; Settles et al., 2019). Assimilated Black faculty who are tokenized suffer from the phenomenon of role entrapment by being required to be a spokesperson and expert of their Black racial group (Settles et al., 2019). The final characteristic as delineated by Kanter (1993) reflects boundary heightening, which occurs when tokens challenge the status quo, leading members of the dominant group to exaggerate their group norms to exclude the token. In this role, the token becomes a threat to the natural order and may be purposely excluded from the rituals and customs of the dominant group.

Marginalization of Scholarly Contributions

Black faculty are negatively impacted by the devaluation and exclusion of their academic scholarship particularly when centered on issues of race and oppression (Gutierrez et al., 2012). Studies have already revealed the gendered and racialized aspects of academic research. When it comes to academic research, women receive less credit and visibility and are cited less often than men (Buchanan, 2020; Bell et al., 2021). Furthermore, they are less likely to make an impact with their scholarship when their scholarship explores topics that are not traditionally associated with, or do not resonate with, White men (Dion, et al., 2018; Key & Sumner, 2019; Lundine et al., 2018). For Black faculty, scholarly marginalization occurs both formally and informally within the academy. Black women educators note that their scholarly

Black Women Faculty Also Matter

interests and contributions are disrespected and are perceived to lack scientific rigor, as a result, they are less likely to be cited or credited (Smith & Garrett-Scott, 2021). Informally, exclusion occurs when faculty colleagues dismiss research based on a lack of understanding of the value or appreciation of the focus (Buchanan, 2020; Gutierrez et al., 2012). Even before the height of the pandemic, equity-minded Black scholars such as Christen Smith (Smith et al., 2021) were calling for the recognition of Black women's intellectual contributions in the academy. This advocacy effort culminated in the founding of the #CiteBlackWomen movement. During the pandemic, and as protests against anti-Black racism, this movement joined the wider # Black Lives Matter movement to call for an end to discrimination and marginalization of faculty researchers who center race and racism in their academic scholarship (Makhulu, 2022; Smith et al., 2021)

WORKING WITH WHITE COLLEAGUES

Microaggressions

Black women's experiences in working with White colleagues in higher education are characterized by continuous encounters with racism and racial microaggression (Allison., 2018; Louis et al., 2016; Ross-Sheriff, 2012; Warren, 2021). Microaggressions are subtle, yet often unconscious slights that can evoke racism, hostility, sexism, homophobia, and other problematic thoughts or behaviors (Sue, 2010; Sue & Spanierman, 2020). The idea of microaggressions emerged in the 1970s by Psychologist Chester Pierce, who found that although microaggressions could be unintentional, the impact that they had on the targeted person was still hurtful (Pierce, 1970).

The stress associated with routine exposure to racial microaggressions has been linked to mental, emotional, and physical strain (Moody & Lewis, 2019). This stress has real physiological ramifications, including suppressed immunity and increased risk of illness. Given the ubiquitous presence of racism in the United States, Black Americans face an emergency stress-response system that is constantly engaged, resulting in cumulative emotional, physical, and psychological stress.

These microaggressions can have a substantial negative impact on the experiences of Black Professors at predominantly White institutions (Nadal et al., 2014; 2015; Pittman, 2012). Routine events of microaggression, such as having authority and credentials questioned, being thought to be intellectually inferior, or being disrespected, reflect chronic racism (Davis & Brown, 2017; Sykes, 2021; Woods-Jaegar et al., 2021). Racial microaggressions have been associated with physical, emotional, and mental exhaustion (Gray & Brooks, 2021; Mickey et al., 2020; Nadal et al., 2017), and race-based traumatic stress (Carter et al., 2007; 2010; 2011). The damaging effects of the stress associated with frequent exposure to racism (Novacek et al., 2020), are correlated with debilitating health conditions such as heart disease, hypertension, strokes, diabetes, anxiety, depression, disordered sleep, and low self-esteem (Erving et al., 2023; Woods-Jaegar et al., 2021; Hicken et al., 2013).

Being the Race Expert With Colleagues

During the pandemic, the need to center racial discussions became urgent. Black faculty often have to engage in racial dialogue during times when they themselves are emotionally vulnerable as members of the Black community (Hawkins, 2022). Black faculty who are expected to take on the role of teaching about race and racism in the classroom often do so without training or additional financial or other resource allocations from the academy.

Because Black women faculty are typically the sole Persons of Color in academic departments, they frequently find themselves unwillingly at the center of discussions about race and racism, whether they are called upon to serve as race experts or to assuage White guilt during times of racial upheaval. Additionally, they are expected to devote a significant amount of time to planning and facilitating faculty training, often without compensation or reduction of their faculty roles.

Unequal Care-Taking Burdens

During the pandemic, caretaking became even more critical, and a student-facing focus became intensified throughout higher education to prevent further academic disruption and to maintain enrollment in an economically risky climate. Faculty had to scramble to create courses online in modalities for which very few were trained. Women faculty, particularly, were also tasked with recognizing and supporting the psycho-social well-being of students who were exhibiting high levels of stress. Women faculty have traditionally been the front line for this type of student support, and the cost to them is rarely recognized (Guarino & Borden, 2017). Interestingly, women researchers have noted that this phenomenon of being seen as naturally suited to service is akin to functioning "twice as housewives" (Docka-Filipek & Stone, 2021). Engaging in invisible domestic labor in the academy and holding domestic duty at home has detrimental outcomes on women's academic career success (Hanasono et al., 2019. In the pandemic, however, the load became especially difficult as all these expectations amplified, even though women faculty themselves were also experiencing increased stress; Docka-Filipek et al., 2023).

For Black women faculty, the burden of emotionally supporting students became exceedingly heavy. Black feminist scholars emphasize that caretaking has different connotations for women of color and that being cared for is associated with White privilege. Black women have historically occupied the stereotypical role of a natural caretaker and surrogate mother to other women's children (Harris-Perry, 2011). During slavery, Black women's servitude was repackaged and portrayed as dutiful and willing mothering. In this controlling "Mammy" trope, Black women continue to be expected to perform as tireless and self-sacrificing caregivers.

In higher education, Black women faculty are praised for not only demonstrating maternal care for students but they are also expected to draw from a perceived innate and culturally bound obligation to give back (Mawhinney, 2011). When service to students is viewed as a moral obligation, this taxing labor can minimize the structural obligation inflicted on Black women and camouflage the harm to their tenure and professional status in the academy. Universities penalize women of color because their work with students and in the university is presumed to be heart-driven, rather than research-based. The fact that scholarship by women of color documenting these complex dynamics is delegitimized is part of the same problem (O'Meara et al., 2018).

The socially constructed view that women and women of color are naturally suited to caregiving has been recognized as detrimental to women faculty well-being in higher education including their ability to refuse or to ask for shared responsibility in this area (Acker & Feuerverger, 1996; Macfarlane & Burg, 2019; Reid, 2021). Furthermore, when women faculty set limits to caring work, students punish them for not meeting their gendered expectation for caring regardless of the evidence that women faculty spend more time in caring activities such as meeting with students.

Black Women Faculty Also Matter

Taking Care of Minoritized Students

Faculty support is, indeed, an invaluable resource for students; however, there is a general expectation that Black faculty will take care of Black students, even if the students belong to other departments in an institution. Further, there is little to no recognition that Black women faculty undertake the majority of efforts for sustaining the needs of Black students. Research validates that Black students perform better when their professors engage in the dual role of faculty and other mothering (Collins, 2022). This means in practice that a Black female faculty member must hold up high expectations for success in academic work, but also be deeply invested in nurturing each student's personal life and emotional well-being, especially students of color. With university counseling departments inundated during the pandemic, faculty became de facto counselors trying to respond to high levels of student distress, particularly Black students who were activated by traumatic race-based events in the culture.

The caregiver stereotype is re-enacted most intensely during times of political and racial upheaval. For Black women faculty, racial tensions required that they spend inordinate amounts of time providing healing emotional work to students who otherwise might not have had other racially specific sources of support in academia (Njoku & Evans, 2022). Although most Black faculty report that giving back through this type of service is fulfilling, most recognize that there is an institutional obligation to provide it without reward or recognition. During the COVID-19 pandemic and including the racial upheaval that boiled to the surface following George Floyd's murder, faculty of color reflected that the emotional labor of supporting BIPOC students increased (Wilson et al., 2023) yet, BIPOC faculty were not excused from additional faculty demands, such as research, despite this additional demand (Simien & Wallace, 2022).

A Triple Tax

During the height of the pandemic, many faculty wrestled with a lack of available childcare, unexpected home-schooling responsibilities, decreased income, and many other COVID-19-related stressors. The closure of daycare facilities and schools and the shift to online learning, including other challenges of parenting, took a toll on the lives of working parents. However, despite these stressors, the academic process continued to demand excellence in teaching, research, and scholarship. For female faculty, academic responsibilities have long required juggling the demands of household duties and professional obligations, and these pressures were multiplied during the pandemic (Skinner et al., 2021). Furthermore, it is widely accepted that most women carry a disproportionate load of caregiving responsibilities often referred to as the "mommy tax." This impacts the professional and personal well-being of women generally and extends directly to women faculty too (Morgan et al., 2021; Fulweiler et al., 2021).

For Black female faculty, these demands exist and are compounded by additional stressors. Even before the COVID-19 pandemic, Black female faculty were most at-risk for career disruptions, especially women who are single heads of households and tasked with caring for extended family, without support for themselves. In fact, these stressors have long been linked to the commonly held notion that Black women can handle inordinate amounts of work, without relief or help – the Mammy trope. This has real-world implications in poor health outcomes and the internalization of distress for Black women generally, but also for Black women faculty in higher education.

In addition to the "mommy tax" that Black women faculty shoulder if they are parents, they also suffer from the pressure of the "Black Tax," a second form of social taxation that includes the expectation that they will spend more time on household and community activities in support of others as an obligation and expectation of the roles they perform. In the academy, they then also pay a triple tax as Black women faculty members who tend to hold the rank of junior faculty, and who thus have more service requirements and clinical responsibilities as instructors and assistant professors. This results in a lesser likelihood of holding leadership positions and it also makes Black women more professionally vulnerable, especially during times of uncertainty like the COVID-19 pandemic. Given this triple taxation, the burden is heavy, and it is unfairly borne by Black women academics.

BLACK WOMEN'S EFFORTS TO GAIN

Respectability and Acceptance in White Academic Spaces

Strong Black Women Faculty

In an attempt to disrupt derogative stereotypes, the Black community's attempt to heal the generational trauma inflicted on Black womanhood resulted in the promotion of femininity characterized by an unyielding strength, and concern for the wellbeing of the community. This created an expectation of a Black woman who can maintain multiple roles and remain unfazed, a pillar of the community, one who can work without tiring, and most importantly demonstrates all these attributes without complaint or need for support (Harris-Perry, 2011). Termed "Strong Black Woman" (SBW), this archetype prescribes feminine expectations for "good" Black women (Watson & Hunter, 2016), and challenges derogative stereotypes of deficient or oversexualized womanhood. However, endorsement of this schema has inadvertently promoted emotional suppression, increased anxiety, stress, and isolation (Abrams & Maxwell, 2018; Watson & Hunter, 2015; Watson & Singleton, 2017; Woods-Giscomb´e, 2010). According to Collins (2000, 2011) Black women are influenced by the SBW schema and it exerts control on their everyday functioning with damaging consequences. The hallmark of the SBW schema is a lack of vulnerability or fear of enacting the Angry Black Woman trope. This leads to the suppression of emotion, which is a vicious cycle that promotes the notion that Black women possess inordinate human strength or are invulnerable to distress (Carter & Rossi, 2019). White women's tears are acknowledged and legitimized, whereas Black women's tears are invisible and pathologized based on historical and ongoing oppression (Accapadi, 2007).

Dealing With Racial Microaggressions

In a desire to disprove prevalent racist stereotypes and tropes, Black people seeking respectability and acceptance in American society have found it necessary to employ a panoply of survival strategies. This has often involved changes to personal presentation in language and appearance in order to fit in with the majority culture and to mitigate biases. Known as code-switching or identity shifting, it is essentially a strategy to whitewash one's own Blackness to circumvent stereotypes and to conform to norms as a Black person in a majority White culture. In the microcosm of academia, identity shifting is commonplace as the conscious or unconscious process of changing one's language, and/or cultural behaviors to fit Eurocentric ideals of professionalism. Being a Black professor in a White academic space has involved this psychologically exhausting and soul-destroying strategy as a crucial aspect of professional academic acceptance.

Code Switching as the Quest for Professional Respectability

For Black Americans, language and speech patterns have been another avenue for oppression in White spaces, therefore survival strategies to mitigate oppression have been a necessary tool for advancement. Code-switching is an example of an oppression survival strategy and involves the deliberate act of altering one's vernacular, to fit into or adapt to a more desirable or acceptable social situation (McCluney et al., 2021; Young et al., 2014). For Black Americans, code-switching is an attempt to gain distance from the damaging stereotypes surrounding Blackness and being perceived as unintelligent or deemed 'ghetto' by forsaking African American Vernacular English in favor of Standard American English in the presence of members of White majorities.

While code-switching was typically associated with changing one's speech patterns, including accents, it is now recognized that code-switching encompasses a broad range of behaviors and actions, such as appearance and mannerisms (McCluney et al., 2021), that are meant to accommodate the dominant traits of a preferred culture in any given society. Enacting the preferred White norms is needed for survival in White spaces; essentially, code-switching is a buffer against microaggressions that tell Black people being themselves is not good enough (Harris, 2020).

Code-Switching Black Women's Physical Appearance

The pandemic provided an opportunity for most professionals to relax professional standards for attire, and this was certainly true in the academy as well. Most people enjoyed the idea of a casual and relaxed atmosphere and a chance to showcase personal living spaces. However, Black people faced the threat of heightened exposure to judgment and stereotypes rather than an opportunity to be themselves. They continued to protect their professional image, with some opting to conceal identity and lifestyle traits that reveal an Afrocentric life.

The physical characteristics that Black women bring to the academy are often unique and counter to the physical appearance norms of White women faculty. Moreso, Black physicality is historically racialized and depicted as deviant (Collins, 2009). Black women, who strive for respectability and inclusion in professional spaces, including the academy, are tasked with masking their natural selves in public spaces, and hair is one of the most politicized ways to ensure this happens (Dickens & Chavez, 2018; Donaldson, 2015). Black hair in its kinky and coiled state often triggers stereotypes and challenges dominant White ideals of professionalism, refinement, and scholarship. It is most often associated with rebellion, lack of control, or militancy (Bryant, 2013). Because straight hair appears tamed and presentable, it most closely aligns with White qualities associated with intelligence and beauty (Award et al., 2015). Respectability politics dictate that to counter this stigma, Black women have to choose between self-authenticity or the ramifications of a lack of social respectability Dawson et al., 2019). Black women understand that they need to assimilate within the academy in spaces such as classrooms to mitigate oppressive beliefs about their competence. (Allison, 2018; Donahoo, 2019).

Researchers such as Dabiri (2014), emphasize that most White people lack an understanding of the everyday realities of maintaining Black hair in White spaces or the oppression surrounding its expression. The idea that "hair is just hair" disregards the invisible embedded socialization and oppression that Black women endure when presenting themselves to society, and ignores the fact that self-altering processes are stressful and expensive social challenges that some Black women feel they need to engage in to gain acceptance and respect in the academy (Allison, 2018). Cultural humility requires an understanding of the social and historical connection that Black women have with their hair, as part of the intersectional understanding of their Black female experience.

Racial Battle Fatigue

Code-switching and other self-masking strategies, such as self-silencing, are trauma responses and have been necessary tools to survive in academic life. While such measures have been strategic for professional survival, they also cause emotional and psychological pain associated with "Racial Battle Fatigue," the cumulative impact of dealing with racism and microaggressions (Sue et al., 2008; Smith 2014). The cost of this type of silencing to fit in has enormous mental health implications (Jones et al., 2021).

It was William Smith (2004; 2014) who conceptualized the phenomenon of Racial Battle Fatigue to provide a theoretical framework for studying and understanding the complex and damaging impact of racism on African Americans working in predominantly White educational institutions. Smith (2004) used a trauma lens to relate the experiences of Black faculty to those of combat trauma-impacted soldiers. According to Smith (2004), Racial Battle Fatigue results from routine distressing experiences with racism that encompass microaggressions, or life-threatening events. In academic circles, Racial Battle Fatigue can include experiences with racism that lead to hypervigilance, social and professional withdrawal, and self-censorship. Racial Battle Fatigue has emotional, psychological, and physical impacts, including heightened anxiety and emotional dysregulation, such as anger or anger suppression, helplessness, hopelessness, and depression. The physiological impacts include increased hypertension, sleep disruption, changes in appetite, and extreme fatigue.

Racial Battle Fatigue can be a lethal condition when left untreated. Black women in America have the highest prevalence of hypertension (46%) and cardiovascular disease (47%) in the United States, and Black female faculty carry this vulnerability with them into the workplace (Felix et al., 2019; Jones et al., 2020). For Black female faculty to survive, let alone thrive, a paradigm shift is necessary, and, thankfully, such change is possible now more than ever.

PARADIGM SHIFT: MEETING GOALS FOR DIVERSITY, EQUITY, AND INCLUSION

Most academic institutions in the United States have publicly declared the goal of increasing diversity awareness as part of their strategic goals. This declaration comes with increased pressure to realize these institutional goals in the classroom. While all faculty have been tasked with integrating the necessary diversity work in academic courses, Faculty of Color are most often called upon to lead this work. Ahluwalia et al. (2019) conducted a phenomenological study to explore the lived experiences of Faculty of Color teaching multicultural courses. The researchers uncovered that most diversity-related courses are taught by marginalized faculty, including Faculty of Color or non-tenure track faculty. These faculty are often presumed to be diversity experts due to their race, and they discuss experiencing racial microaggressions related to their identity and faculty status, i.e., being perceived as "diversity hires" who lack merit.

Identity taxation occurs when faculty members are expected to shoulder the bulk of diversity and equity work due to their membership in historically minoritized groups beyond what is expected of White faculty members (Padill, 1994). Teaching courses that are centered on diversity and inclusion impacts Black faculty in negative ways that are not often visible. Faculty of Color report that teaching

Black Women Faculty Also Matter

multicultural courses has detrimental personal and professional implications (Sue et al., 2011). Still, it falls to the Faculty of Color to fill the gap needed to achieve the institutional goals of inclusion (Hirshfield & Joseph, 2012).

Transforming academia requires an intentional disruption of prevailing policies and procedures to align with more inclusive and equitable practices. Critical scholars have offered recommendations toward this goal (Ash et al., 2020; Davis et al., 2020; Kendi, 2019). At its core, the work of transformation requires a strong commitment to being anti-racist, from academic institutions, from colleagues within the academy, and from Black women faculty themselves.

TRANSFORMING ACADEMIC INSTITUTIONS

Reframe the Image of the 'Typical Professor'

The changing demographics in the United States require all members of the campus community to commit to diversity, equity, and inclusion. This includes examining and expanding the conventional image of what is considered professional and interrogating implicit biases of how 'ideal professors' look and behave. Belonging in the academy means that Black women professors truly feel like they can be their authentic selves and reveal their professional Black identity without penalty. They can be themselves in the academy and are valued for the unique aspects of this Black identity that contribute to diversity in the professoriate.

Recruit and Retain Diverse Faculty

Academic institutions can lead the way in this transformation. Authentic commitment to diversity, equity, and inclusion requires a clear and intentional goal to recruit and retain diverse faculty, staff, and students. This includes having strategic plans that are measurable to ensure diverse representation within the academic community as a whole. Academic institutions have an obligation to ensure that faculty embrace cultural humility and receive appropriate training and mentoring in the areas of diversity, equity, and inclusion from appropriately trained experts in the field. Such measures must be thorough and ongoing in order to build the kind of intellectual community that will provide the best education for its members.

Representation Matters

Expanding the number of diverse faculty will prevent Black faculty isolation caused by being the only one or one of a few other Persons of Color at an institution. Consequently, the presence of Black women will not satisfy mere numerical tokenism (Kanter, 1977; Dickens, et al., 2020). This will avoid the dual problems of being hyper-visible (Buchanan & Settles, 2019), and the pressure to perform due to marginalized status (Dickens et al., 2020). Increased diversity, academic connection, and inclusion will allow Black female faculty to bring their whole selves to the academy without masking or code-switching.

Representation matters especially in hiring and retaining diverse faculty, but non-superficial representation also encompasses intentional efforts to highlight diversity and celebrate the successes of diverse contributions across academia to disrupt the grip of negative stereotypes (Keane et al., 2022). Universities should use deliberate visual representation of Black women faculty in all aspects of campus activity. This allows Black students to imagine themselves in positions of leadership in advanced education. Additionally, the representation of racially minoritized faculty also allows increased exposure and comfort to different accents, mannerisms, and appearances and legitimizes them. Most importantly, these efforts empower racially marginalized faculty to be their authentic selves in the classroom and reduce the likelihood of code-switching.

Redesign Methods for Evaluating Tenure and Promotion

A significant disparity in promotion exists between White and Black faculty (Davis et al., 2011). Black faculty are promoted at significantly lower rates than their White faculty (Porter et al., 2020. Critical scholars such as Aly and colleagues (2022) have called for a redesign of the tenure and promotion process by highlighting that the accepted norms are not impartial but are shaped by the White majority who created it to the detriment of inclusion and advancement of Faculty of Color.

Throughout the COVID-19 pandemic, the desire to engage in critical dialogue within the university context was juxtaposed with the pressure to avoid sensitive subjects and placate students. Students have considerable power in determining the professional trajectory of academic faculty. One way in which students exert influence is through anonymous and formal feedback in the form of course evaluations. Faculty are aware that student evaluations of faculty reflect students' conscious and implicit bias (Kezar et al., 2019; Heffernan, T. 2022).

Critical scholars have called to attention the detrimental impact of faculty evaluation as one of the mechanisms of determining tenure and promotion for Faculty of Color. Studies indicate that because of the potential for anonymous evaluations to be weaponized, Faculty of Color are confronted with career-threatening decisions regarding pedagogy related to transformative or emancipatory teaching. Students' conscious and unconscious biases impact the ways they perceive, respond to, and evaluate Black women faculty particularly (Basow et al., 2013). Nonetheless, these biases are not considered in the interpretation of teaching evaluations, which may negatively affect the reappointment or promotion of these faculty members.

Academic leadership must explore multiple avenues for the interpretation of faculty teaching effectiveness as a part of the evaluation for tenure and promotion. Teaching evaluation is one method of gaining knowledge about students' experiences in the classroom, however, a more balanced approach is necessary for effective measurement. This requires open dialogue that is contextualized within an intersectional and sociopolitical lens. Academic leaders must be willing to review teaching effectiveness from a multi-dimensional approach (Kreitzer & Sweet-Cushman, 2021), including peer teaching evaluations, letters of recommendation, and samples of teaching materials, particularly in those courses that reflect a strong focus on diversity, equity, and inclusion. By using these multiple data points, rather than simply relying on what may amount to unfairly biased student evaluations, administrators can glean a more accurate view of their faculty's competence and excellence.

Recognize and Reward Faculty Service

Institutional commitment to diversity, equity, and inclusion should be reflected in the reward structures for tenure and promotion in the academy. Although labor- and time-intensive, service is not typically a valued or acknowledged aspect in the faculty review process. Service obligations fall disproportionately on women, including women of color (Domingo et al., 2020). Further, engagement in service precludes opportunities to participate in research and publication, which are prized over service contributions. In this way, participating in service has detrimental impacts on tenure, forcing women to choose between more service or their advancement.

A paradigm shift in the academy would acknowledge this uneven load in service expectations. If higher education's commitment to supporting diversity, equity, and inclusion is to be realized, the service obligation overload of Black women faculty must be recognized and dismantled. This process starts with the recognition of the hidden labor and uneven service workload expected of Faculty of Color (Hart, 2016). Academic leaders must interrupt the identity taxation experienced by Black women faculty by developing equitable academic loads that integrate the expectation and call to provide service, which in turn would reduce the overburdening of Black women faculty (Blackshear & Hollis, 2021). Service must be rewarded by incorporating it in faculty evaluation for promotion and tenure. This move would ensure that meeting the institutional goals for equity and inclusion also elevates the status of Black faculty.

Recommit to Supporting Diverse Faculty

A caring and supportive community increases the emotional and psychological safety of racially minoritized faculty. Community support for faculty is a powerful moderator for isolation (Kastens & Manduca, 2017) and contributes to increased learning, professional invigoration, and reciprocal emotional and practical support. Support for Black faculty is critical to professional and personal survival. Supportive environments have been associated with empowerment for Black faculty, which increases their productivity as scholars (Wenger-Taylor, 2015) and creates the necessary foundation for them to have meaningful relationships with students. Black women faculty benefit from community support through interdepartmental relationships and affinity or co-support groups (Baldwin & Johnson, 2018).

All too often institutions take initial steps to provide spaces for diverse voices, but these result in mere performative gestures because these initiatives are not sustained by sufficiently allocated time or financial support and compete with other academic demands. Re-envisioning adequate support would require that organizational interventions intentionally foster supportive and networking opportunities for Black women faculty by allocating appropriate financial and service resources to ensure their sustainability (Bellamy et al., 2020; Davis et al., 2020; Penny et al., 2015), and by promoting affinity groups. Ratifying this would mean commitments such as hiring and retaining a coordinator to organize, implement, and facilitate these efforts so that faculty do not need to do so in their overburdened schedules.

Retrain to Disrupt Racism

Institutional commitment to disrupt racism must include developing a strategic focus and policies to engage faculty and staff in racial awareness training regarding colorblind racism in academia (Bonilla-Silva, 2006). The focus must provide holistic training beyond the typical implicit bias training, which has not been found to reliably reduce bias despite increasing knowledge (Dover et al., 2016). Onyeador and colleagues offer strategies for improving racial awareness training and emphasize the necessity of being prepared to deal with negative reactions to diversity efforts, supporting the correction of previously held misperceptions; and developing institutional opportunities for meaningful intergroup contact.

Racial awareness and cultural humility training improve personal growth (Carter et al., 2020), which in turn can result in curricular changes that promote social justice. Furthermore, when faculty improve their awareness, knowledge, and understanding of racism and oppression, an increased commitment and ability to integrate this into student learning in the classroom is evident. This has the benefit of improving classroom dynamics surrounding racial dialogue and has a positive effect on academic growth for students as learners and social justice change agents (Devine & Ash, 2022).

WHITE COLLEAGUES AS CHANGE AGENTS

Reimagine Allyship

White colleagues within the academy can also invite transformation by leveraging their privilege and position in service of social justice. A sense of belonging in the institution is essential for the success and career satisfaction of Black women faculty, and White colleagues can bring their considerable influence to bear to create a welcoming environment in the academy.

Critical racial scholars acknowledge that teaching about race and racism, including calling out racist policies and practices, contributes to the backlash against Black faculty by labeling them as disruptive and or problematic (Johnson-Bailey, 2015). The fallout from this hostile response has been oppressive strategies to subdue or reprimand the maligned faculty in various ways including tenure denial, employment termination, or limiting their options for advancement, instead of addressing institutionalized racism in the academic environment.

In this environment, allies have been an increasingly invaluable shield that can protect the psycho-emotional well-being of Black faculty. To be inclusive, allies must speak up against bias and shield Black faculty in academic and professional settings. The importance of partnering against racism is widely researched, but the lessons we learn from that research must be implemented accordingly. Studies indicate that White Americans who actively confront bias are viewed as more credible than Black Americans (Rasinski & Czopp, 2010). White faculty members must leverage their power and privilege to join in the struggle for equality and inclusion of Black faculty members.

Reimagining allyship encompasses many forms. In the areas of scholarship, seasoned scholars in the role of an ally can invite collaboration with Black female junior faculty to support their credibility in the field. They can legitimize scholarship rooted in equity and inclusion (Ashburn-Nardo, 2018; Ashburn-Nardo et al., 2020; Bell et al., 2021) and intentionally disrupt perceptions that publication in certain journals is less prestigious than others, especially journals that tend to publish content from Black American scholars (Bell et al., 2021; Özbilgin, 2009; Settles, et al., 2019). Furthermore, allyship requires monitoring and lobbying to ensure that reviewers, editors, and authors in peer review are also more diverse to address these systemic issues (Roberts et al., 2020). When White faculty members join in the struggle for equality and inclusion of Black faculty members, they live into their own highest values to advocate for equity and social justice (Bowleg, 2021).

Raising Race in Dialogues

Black feminist scholars recognize that schools are institutions that maintain and reproduce the oppression of BIPOC by choosing to focus only on Eurocentric education rather than including diverse and culturally sustaining knowledge. This promotion of Eurocentric knowledge normalized White education as the idealized standard of education (Gay, 2002; 2010; 2015; Ladson-Billings, 1995; 2000; 2022), therefore when students are presented with information that is contrary to Eurocentric ideology, they have strong or negative reactions to the content and the messenger. Students who are challenged to consider views from diverse and marginalized groups may react with emotions ranging from anger, and denial to resistance (Evans-Winters & Hines, 2020). These emotions are an expected and crucial part of recognizing and understanding the systemic and structural aspects of racism. For White students, this understanding is a deeply transformational process that requires acknowledgment, understanding, and support. Students need to be prepared to address both the cognitive and emotional aspects of integrating information that may be contradictory to what they have known. Some may need to be supported as they navigate feelings of disorientation and betrayal as they challenge the nature of interlocking and complex systemic racism. Therefore, all faculty members who are invested in equity and social justice must play an equal part in the educational experience to maximize this transformational experience and mitigate backlash against Faculty of Color who are teaching about race and racism.

Intentional dialogue about the nature of power, privilege, and oppression requires a commitment from all members of the campus community. To ensure effective communication, campus community members benefit from restorative and self-monitoring skills to engage in difficult dialogue. Everyone must understand their sociopolitical positionality and how they inhabit marginalized and privileged identities. This recognition impacts conversations about the nature of oppression and mitigates self-defensive postures. Furthermore, self-evaluation allows for better interruption of implicit bias when stereotypes are activated in relationships with diverse communities.

Redefining allyship also means an intentional realignment of diversity work so that all faculty share the responsibility to uphold diversity initiatives on campus, including teaching and mentoring students about race and racism. White ally faculty can take the initiative to become informed on issues of race and racism and step up to be change agents in academia.

Re-Examine and Decolonize the Curriculum

An ideal curriculum reflects the contributions of diverse populations and centers comprehensive knowledge drawn from a broad base of cultural perspectives. This curriculum broadens students' knowledge by challenging them to understand and accept that knowledge is socially constructed, and therefore reflects political and social power. The ability of faculty to develop courses and plan such curricula reflects their earned position of power due to the ability to influence the direction of learning toward certain content or material. From a sociopolitical standpoint, this power to determine the inclusion or exclusion of content is often informed by an individual instructor's positionality.

When faculty are committed to diversity, equity, and inclusion, they are intentional about designing and selecting course content that is reflective of diverse communities. Furthermore, they promote critical inquiry about how diverse groups are reflected to promote empowerment and challenge stereotypes. Tatum (1994) pointed out that while students benefit from having Faculty of Color teach them about racism, she emphasized the value of White allies teaching about racism and modeling that teaching about inclusivity is not the sole responsibility of BIPOC faculty (Tatum, 1994). In addition, when White allies intentionally support the research and scholarship of Black women faculty and understand that race and gender-based research are fraught with marginalization, they understand that citation matters (Craven, 2021; Mott & Cockayne, 2017) and are committed to intentionally elevating diverse scholarship.

Re-Envision and Redesign Mentorship

Mentorship, where a senior member of a learned community helps a junior apprentice with skill acquisition and knowledge transition, is a proven method of professional support going back to ancient Greece. Mentorships are still indispensable; in the academy, they help faculty feel that they belong to the academic institution and help them navigate the complex process of academic promotion and tenure.

Ideally, a junior tenure track faculty professor starts with doctoral socialization regarding what the process of tenure entails. This includes passing along expectations for research, teaching, and service, as well as "navigation capital," which is advice from a senior tenured faculty member on how to negotiate demands to meet institutional requirements (Robinson et al, 2022). Unfortunately, this is rarely the experience of racially marginalized faculty (Ross & Edwards, 2016; Zambrana et al., 2015). Most Black women junior faculty tend to graduate as non-traditional doctoral students, which means that they are generally older, with marriage and family commitments, and self-funded. As such, transitioning to the academy allows for very limited opportunities for interacting with seasoned faculty in graduate assistantships and apprenticing or even for informal avenues of observation, communication, and learning (Kniess et al., 2017; Cole et al., 2017).

Having mentors and role models is crucial for success, yet research indicates that there are inadequate numbers of mentors for Black female faculty in higher education. Additionally, research also shows that faculty tend to mentor students who follow the mentor's professional research interests (King & Upadhyay, 2022). Given the scarcity of minority faculty in the academy, this creates a vicious cycle of lack for Black women seeking meaningful mentorships, especially in the areas of equity research, critical studies, race-related studies, or research involving political scholarship. Additionally, though Black women faculty are less likely to have mentors, they are more likely to be actively mentoring others (Davis et al., 2022). This reinforces the "all giving; no receiving" legacy of one-way caregiving with which Black women faculty struggle. Rather, they are left to self-generate a patchwork of second-hand mentorships through whatever other avenues might exist, such as social media, mentors of other peers, or conferences (Baldwin & Johnson, 2018).

To address this issue, the academy must re-envision and redesign mentorship opportunities for Black female faculty that will invite a space for collegiality, mutual understanding, respect, and support (Bertrand Jones et al., 2020). Financial resources can make available a variety of creative models supporting Black women faculty, such as the intensive academic mentoring bootcamp offered by the Sisters of the Academy (SOTA) where senior and junior members are paired for a variety of workshops designed to foster the academic success of Black women in the academy in teaching, scholarly inquiry, and service to the community. This engagement is designed to advance identity-building and empowerment, promote academic success, and allow for other important social advantages, including networking, access to resources, and providing a safe space to process racialized experiences (Davis & Sutherland, 2008; Jones et al., 2023).

Additionally, affinity mentorship and collaboration has been found to improve collegiality and scholarship and generally leads to decreased isolation for Black women faculty (Bertrand Jones et al., 2020). Accordingly, affinity groups, such as Sistah Network, are making a difference in social-emotional support through an authentic celebration of the unique contributions of Black women and by affirming the importance of identity as a remedy for destructive aspects represented in code-switching and self-silencing (Allen & Joseph, 2018). These uplifting experiences feed the soul of Black women and offer fresh perspectives for rejuvenation, perseverance, and emotional accompaniment in the difficult sphere

Black Women Faculty Also Matter

of the academy. Breaking through isolation through connection with Black women faculty will increase opportunities for collaboration and professional growth and also benefit the academy with a greatly enriched exchange of scholarly viewpoints among colleagues.

TRANSFORMATIVE BLACK WOMEN FACULTY

Restoring Vibrancy in the Aftermath of Racial Battle Fatigue

Physical, mental, and emotional exhaustion has been identified as the leading reason why Black women faculty leave the academy. This fatigue results from the cumulative effects of Black women faculty neglecting their emotional well-being to fulfill the extensive needs of the academy. While all women surpass men in this and take the lion's share of the labor of caring, supporting, and mentoring students (Constanti & Gibbs, 2004; Reid, 2021), the stereotypical view that Black women are uniquely positioned to be default caregivers in higher education collides with cultural and racist pressure to engage in their hyper-performance of caring behaviors. This endless demand for emotional labor carries a heavy price that ultimately destroys the well-being of Black women. In higher education, the emotional labor of faculty carries the mission of the academy of being student-focused, however, when Black faculty are presumed to engage in caring behaviors out of a sense of moral obligation, they face an increased risk of having this service work being undervalued, unrecognized, and unrewarded (Acker & Feuerverger, 1996), adding to their physical, emotional, and spiritual exhaustion.

To survive and thrive in the face of racism, Black people must develop strategies for taking care of themselves and coping. Although Black people are not responsible for the racism they experience, prioritizing their self-care is essential for healthy well-being. Self-care can exist individually and in supportive circles with other Black women (Allen & Joseph, 2018). Black women rely on informal social networks to cope with life demands and challenges. Throughout history, the notion of sisterhood has been at the core of what it means to be a Black woman and is reflected in the concept of Sister Circles (hooks, 1999; Burnette, 2019). Most recently, Sister Circles is a model for creating and promoting supportive networks for Black women professionals. Similar to other affinity groups such as SOTA, they build upon a sense of community that naturally occurs among Black women both inside and outside of higher education. They incorporate culturally relevant and race-specific strategies to address the impact of stress and anxiety that are a result of living in a racist society. Emerging research on Sister Circles documents that these informal networks have beneficial impacts on the health and mental health of Black women and mitigate risk factors through improved engagement in healthy nutrition, exercise, and sleep.

Rest and Restoration as Resistance

During slavery, Black American's labor as a commodity was used to determine their value, and this generational trauma still plagues Black American communities as reflected in the value of having to work twice as hard to prove worth. Rethinking the relationship with rest as a political action against the over-demanding work ethic can empower Black women faculty. Intentional decisions to take a restorative posture and to resist the characterization of self-care as "laziness," is in fact, exceedingly brave. The health-promoting aspects of stress reduction have long been proven. Human beings achieve a state of wellness when they have opportunities to take a break from the demands of life and find relief from exertion (SAMSA). Rest has the beneficial quality of supporting rejuvenation, calming the central nervous system, and improving mental and emotional well-being.

While rest is important for all people, it is crucial for Black Americans due to a legacy of historical and generational trauma and stress that is pervasive within the Black community. Rest is an act of liberation against systemic racism, and the grinding work ethic that has punished Black Americans since slavery (Hersey, 2022). Since the pandemic and the upheaval following George Floyd's murder, this need for restorative rest has become even more critical. Black women faculty themselves can become powerful agents for transformation when they can rest, redirect energies from endless dissipation, and instead, tap into their internal resources to recover and heal.

The COVID-19 pandemic threw the world into a state of chaos and turmoil, and this was certainly felt in the academy as well. For Black women faculty, finding stability and empowerment in this tumultuous time has been challenging due to the current climate of flux and confusion, but also because of the longstanding and pervasive racial inequalities that were compounded during the pandemic. A paradigm shift toward inclusion is possible despite all of it. This ultimately benefits the entire academy because institutions will no longer be paying mere lip service to the idea of diversity, equity, and inclusion but will actively implement a strategic choice to disrupt the deeply entrenched legacy of structural racism in higher education (Boykin et al., 2020). Now, more than ever before, institutions have the chance to support Black women faculty in elevating their voices, by creating greater opportunities for mentorship, and in celebrating Black women faculty's ability to be fully and unapologetically themselves on campuses across the country. White colleagues can stand up in allyship, intentionally creating community and collaboration for Black women faculty within the academy. Black women faculty, themselves, can exercise the ultimate resistance to oppressive tropes of the past by refusing to internalize the messages of subordinated value, choosing instead to rest, recover, and nurture their authentic selves.

REFERENCES

Abrams, J. A., Hill, A., & Maxwell, M. (2019). Underneath the mask of the strong Black woman schema: Disentangling influences of strength and self-silencing on depressive symptoms among US Black women. *Sex Roles*, *80*(9-10), 517–526. doi:10.100711199-018-0956-y PMID:31086431

Accapadi, M. M. (2007). When White Women Cry: How White Women's Tears Oppress Women of Color. *The College Student Affairs Journal*, *26*(2), 208–215.

Acker, S., & Feuerverger, G. (1996). Doing good and feeling bad: The work of women university teachers. *Cambridge Journal of Education*, *26*(3), 401–422. doi:10.1080/0305764960260309

Ahluwalia, M. K., Ayala, S. I., Locke, A. F., & Nadrich, T. (2019). Mitigating the "powder keg": The experiences of faculty of color teaching multicultural competence. *Teaching of Psychology*, *46*(3), 187–196. doi:10.1177/0098628319848864

Allen, A. M., & Stewart, J. T. (Eds.). (2022). *We're Not Ok: Black Faculty Experiences and Higher Education Strategies*. Cambridge University Press. doi:10.1017/9781009064668

Allen, E. L., & Joseph, N. M. (2018). The sistah network: Enhancing the educational and social experiences of Black women in the academy. *Journal About Women in Higher Education*, *11*(2), 151–170. doi:10.1080/19407882.2017.1409638

Allison, D. C. (2018). Free to be me? Black professors, White institutions. *Journal of Black Studies*, *38*(4), 641–661. doi:10.1177/0021934706289175

Allison, M., Lynn, R., & Hoverman, V. (2014). *Indispensable but invisible: A report on the working climate of non-tenure track faculty at George Mason University*. Department of Sociology and Anthropology, George Mason University.

Aly, M., Colunga, E., Crockett, M. J., Goldrick, M., & Gomez, P. YH, F., Kung, P.C., Pérez, M., Stilwell, S.M., & Diekman, A.B. (2022). Changing the culture of peer review for a more inclusive and equitable psychological science.

Amott, T. L., & Matthaei, J. A. (1996). *Race, gender, and work: A multi-cultural economic history of women in the United States*. South End Press.

Arday, J., & Mirza, H. S. (Eds.). (2018). *Dismantling race in higher education: Racism, whiteness and decolonising the academy*. Palgrave Macmillan. doi:10.1007/978-3-319-60261-5

Ash, A. N., Hill, R., Risdon, S., & Jun, A. (2020). Anti-racism in higher education: A model for change. *Race and Pedagogy Journal: Teaching and Learning for Justice*, *4*(3), 2.

Ashburn-Nardo, L. (2018). What can allies do? In A. Colella & E. King (Eds.), *The handbook of workplace discrimination* (pp. 373–386). Oxford University Press.

Ashburn-Nardo, L., Lindsey, A., Morris, K. A., & Goodwin, S. A. (2020). Who is responsible for confronting prejudice? The role of perceived and conferred authority. *Journal of Business and Psychology*, *35*(6), 799–811. doi:10.100710869-019-09651-w

Ashley, W. (2014). The angry Black woman: The impact of pejorative stereotype on psychotherapy with Black women. *Social Work in Public Health*, *29*(1), 27–34. doi:10.1080/19371918.2011.619449 PMID:24188294

Awad, G. H., Norwood, C., Taylor, D. S., Martinez, M., McClain, S., Jones, B., Holman, A., & Chapman-Hilliard, C. (2015). Beauty and body image concerns among African American college women. *The Journal of Black Psychology*, *41*(6), 540–564. doi:10.1177/0095798414550864 PMID:26778866

Baker, P., & Copp, M. (1997). Gender matters most: The intersection of gendered expectations, feminist course content, and pregnancy in student course evaluations. *Teaching Sociology*, *25*(1), 29–43. doi:10.2307/1319109

Baldwin, A. N., & Johnson, R. (2018). Black women's co-mentoring relationships as resistance to marginalization at a PWI. In O. N. Perlow, D. I. Wheeler, S. L. Bethea, & B. M. Scott (Eds.), *Black women's liberatory pedagogies: Resistance, transformation, and healing within and beyond the academy* (pp. 125–140). Palgrave Macmillan. doi:10.1007/978-3-319-65789-9_7

Basow, S., Codos, S., & Martin, J. (2013). The effects of professors' race and gender on student evaluations and performance. *College Student Journal*, *47*(2), 352–363.

Bell, M. P., Berry, D., Leopold, J., & Nkomo, S. (2021). Making Black Lives Matter in academia: A Black feminist call for collective action against anti-blackness in the academy. *Gender, Work and Organization, 28*(S1), 39–57. doi:10.1111/gwao.12555

Bellamy, P. L., Mosely, D. V., Green, C. E., Neville, H., Hargons, C., Lewis, J. A., Burdine, K., Whittaker, V. A., French, B. H., Steverson, D., Adames, H. Y., Busey, C., Adam, S., Mejia, J., Ross, G., Lewis, A., Lee, L., Emerson, M., Abiodun, S., Samanez-Larkin, G. (2020, June). Academics for Black survival and wellness anti-racism training. Academics for Black Survival and Wellness.

Bertrand Jones, T., Ford, J. R., Pierre, D. F., & Davis-Maye, D. (2020). Thriving in the academy: Culturally responsive mentoring for Black women's early career success. *Strategies for supporting inclusion and diversity in the academy: Higher education, aspiration and inequality*, 123-140.

Bhalla, N. (2019). Strategies to improve equity in faculty hiring. *Molecular Biology of the Cell, 30*(22), 2744–2749. doi:10.1091/mbc.E19-08-0476 PMID:31609672

Bhattacharyya, B., & Berdahl, J. L. (2023). Do you see me? An inductive examination of differences between women of color's experiences of and responses to invisibility at work. *The Journal of Applied Psychology, 108*(7), 1073–1095. doi:10.1037/apl0001072 PMID:36780282

Black, M. D. (2021). Exploring relationships between a teacher's race-ethnicity and gender and student teaching expectations. *Education Inquiry, 12*(2), 202–216. doi:10.1080/20004508.2020.1824343

Blackshear, T., & Hollis, L. (2021). Despite the place, can't escape gender and race: Black Women's faculty experiences at PWIs and HBCUs. Taboo. *The Journal of Culture and Education, 20*(1), 28–50.

Bonilla-Silva, E. (2006). *Racism without racists: Color-blind racism and the persistence of racial inequality in the United States* (2nd ed.). Rowman & Littlefield.

Boss, G. J., Davis, T. J., Porter, C. J., & Moore, C. M. (2019). Second to none: Contingent women of Color faculty in the classroom. In *Diversity, equity, and inclusivity in contemporary higher education* (pp. 211–225). IGI Global. doi:10.4018/978-1-5225-5724-1.ch013

Bowleg, L. (2021). "The master's tools will never dismantle the master's house": Ten critical lessons for Black and other health equity researchers of color. *Health Education & Behavior, 48*(3), 237–249. doi:10.1177/10901981211007402 PMID:34080476

Boykin, C. M., Brown, N. D., Carter, J. T., Dukes, K., Green, D. J., Harrison, T., Hebl, M., McCleary-Gaddy, A., Membere, A., McJunkins, C. A., Simmons, C., Walker, S. S., Smith, A. N., & Williams, A. D. (2020). Anti-racist actions and accountability: Not more empty promises. *Equality, Diversity and Inclusion, 39*(7), 775–786. doi:10.1108/EDI-06-2020-0158

Brescoll, V. L. (2016). Leading with their hearts? How gender stereotypes of emotion lead to biased evaluations of female leaders. *The Leadership Quarterly, 27*(3), 415–428. doi:10.1016/j.leaqua.2016.02.005

Bryant, S. L. (2013). The beauty ideal: The effects of European standards of beauty on Black women. *Columbia Social Work Review, 4*(1), 80–91.

Buchanan, N. T. (2020). Researching while Black (and female). *Women & Therapy, 43*(1-2), 91–111. doi:10.1080/02703149.2019.1684681

Burnette, L. M. (2019). *The Love of My Sisters: Exploring Black Women Academics' Narratives on the Uses and Benefits of Sister Circles*. Georgia State University.

Burton, S., & Furr, S. (2014). Conflict in multicultural classes: Approaches to resolving difficult dialogues. *Counselor Education and Supervision, 53*(2), 97–110. doi:10.1002/j.1556-6978.2014.00051.x

Butler, B. R. (2021). Ain't IA Woman: Black Women's Endurance in Higher Education, the Implications of Linked Fate, and the Urgent Call for Greater Cultural Responsiveness. *Journal of African American Women and Girls in Education, 1*(3), 1–9. doi:10.21423/jaawge-v1i3a97

Byrd, A. D., & Tharps, L. (2014). *Hair story: Untangling the roots of black hair in America*. St. Martin's Print.

Carter, E. R., Onyeador, I. N., & Lewis, N. A. Jr. (2020). Developing & delivering effective anti-bias training: Challenges & recommendations. *Behavioral Science & Policy, 6*(1), 57–70. doi:10.1177/237946152000600106

Carter, L., & Rossi, A. (2019). Embodying strength: The origin, representations, and socialization of the strong Black woman ideal and its effect on Black women's mental health. *Women & Therapy, 42*(3-4), 289–300. doi:10.1080/02703149.2019.1622911

Carter Andrews, D. J., Brown, T., Castro, E., & Id-Deen, E. (2019). The impossibility of being "perfect and white": Black girls' racialized and gendered schooling experiences. *American Educational Research Journal, 56*(6), 2531–2572. doi:10.3102/0002831219849392

Cartwright, A. D., Avent, J. R., Munsey, R., & Lloyd-Hazlett, J. (2018). Interview experiences of minority counselor education faculty from underrepresented groups. *Counselor Education and Supervision, 57*(2), 132–146. doi:10.1002/ceas.12098

Center for Disease Control (2021). *United States COVID-19 Cases and Deaths by State*. CDC.

Chávez, K., & Mitchell, K. M. (2020). Exploring bias in student evaluations: Gender, race, and ethnicity. *PS, Political Science & Politics, 53*(2), 270–274. doi:10.1017/S1049096519001744

Cheryan, S., & Markus, H. R. (2020). Masculine defaults: Identifying and mitigating hidden cultural biases. *Psychological Review, 127*(6), 1022–1052. doi:10.1037/rev0000209 PMID:32804526

Chesler, M., & Young, A. A. Jr. (2007). Faculty members' social identities and classroom authority. *New Directions for Teaching and Learning, 2007*(111), 11–19. doi:10.1002/tl.281

Closson, R. B., Bowman, L., & Merriweather, L. R. (2014). Toward a race pedagogy for Black faculty. *Adult Learning, 25*(3), 82–88. doi:10.1177/1045159514534192

Cole, E., McGowan, B. L., & Zerquera, D. D. (2017). First-year faculty of color: Narratives about entering the academy. *Equity & Excellence in Education, 50*(1), 1–12. doi:10.1080/10665684.2016.1262300

Collins, P. H. (2022). *Black feminist thought: Knowledge, consciousness, and the politics of empowerment*. Routledge.

Constanti, P., & Gibbs, P. (2004). Higher education teachers and emotional labour. *International Journal of Educational Management, 18*(4), 243–249. doi:10.1108/09513540410538822

Corbin, N. A., Smith, W. A., & Garcia, R. (2018). Trapped between justified anger and being the strong Black woman: Black college women coping with racial battle fatigue at historically and predominantly white institutions. *International Journal of Qualitative Studies in Education : QSE*, *31*(7), 626–643. do i:10.1080/09518398.2018.1468045

Craven, C. (2021). Teaching antiracist citational politics as a project of transformation: Lessons from the Cite Black Women movement for White feminist anthropologists. *Feminist Anthropology*, *2*(1), 120–129. doi:10.1002/fea2.12036

Croom, N. N. (2017). Promotion beyond tenure: Unpacking racism and sexism in the experiences of Black womyn professors. *Review of Higher Education*, *40*(4), 557–583. doi:10.1353/rhe.2017.0022

CROWN Act of. 2019, 116 USC §§ 3-6 CROWN Act of 2019, Cal. Education Code § 212.1 Crown Coalition. (2019). https://www. thecrownact.com

Crumb, L., Cartwright, A. D., Hammonds, D. S., & Harris, J. A. (2023). Code-switching 101: Black women counselor educators' personal and professional identity development. *Counselor Education and Supervision*.

Dabiri, E. (2014, January). The politics of Black hair. NewStatesman. *Teaching while Black: Racial dynamics, evaluations, and the role of White females in the Canadian academy in carrying the racism torch. Race, Ethnicity and Education*, *22*(1), 21–37.

Davis, D. J., Reynolds, R., & Bertrand Jones, T. (2011). Promoting the inclusion of tenure earning Black women in academe: Lessons for leaders in education. *Florida Journal of Educational Administration & Policy*, *5*(1), 28–41.

Davis, D. J., & Sutherland, J. (2008). Expanding access through doctoral education: Perspectives from two participants of the Sisters of the Academy Research Boot Camp. *Journal of College Student Development*, *49*(6), 606–608. doi:10.1353/csd.0.0041

Davis, D. J., & Sutherland, J. (2008). Expanding access through doctoral education: Perspectives from two participants of the Sisters of the Academy Research Boot Camp. *Journal of College Student Development*, *49*(6), 606–608. doi:10.1353/csd.0.0041

Davis, S., & Brown, K. (2017). Automatically discounted: Using Black feminist theory to critically analyze the experiences of Black female faculty. *The International Journal of Educational Leadership Preparation*, *12*(1), n1.

Davis, T. J., Greer, T. W., Sisco, S., & Collins, J. C. (2020). "Reclaiming my time" amid organizational change: A dialectical approach to support the thriving and career development for faculty at the margins. *Advances in Developing Human Resources*, *22*(1), 23–40. doi:10.1177/1523422319885115

Davis, T. M., Jones, M. K., Settles, I. H., & Russell, P. G. (2022). Barriers to the successful mentoring of Faculty of Color. *Journal of Career Development*, *49*(5), 1063–1081. doi:10.1177/08948453211013375

Dawson, G. A., Karl, K. A., & Peluchette, J. V. (2019). Hair matters: Toward understanding natural black hair bias in the workplace. *Journal of Leadership & Organizational Studies*, *26*(3), 389–401. doi:10.1177/1548051819848998

DeCuir-Gunby, J. T., Johnson, O. T., Womble Edwards, C., McCoy, W. N., & White, A. M. (2020). African American professionals in higher education: Experiencing and coping with racial microaggressions. *Race, Ethnicity and Education*, 23(4), 492–508. doi:10.1080/13613324.2019.1579706

Devine, P. G., & Ash, T. L. (2022). Diversity training goals, limitations, and promise: A review of the multidisciplinary literature. *Annual Review of Psychology*, 73(1), 403–429. doi:10.1146/annurev-psych-060221-122215 PMID:34280325

Dickens, D., Jones, M., & Hall, N. (2020). Being a token Black female faculty member in physics: Exploring research on gendered racism, identity shifting as a coping strategy, and inclusivity in physics. *The Physics Teacher*, 58(5), 335–337. doi:10.1119/1.5145529

Dion, M. L., Sumner, J. L., & Mitchell, S. M. (2018). Gendered citation patterns across political science and social science methodology fields. *Political Analysis*, 26(3), 312–327. doi:10.1017/pan.2018.12

Dobbs, C. L., & Leider, C. M. (2021). "Does this happen to everyone?": Women professors of color reflect on experiences in the academy. *International Journal of Qualitative Studies in Education : QSE*, 1–15.

Docka-Filipek, D., Draper, C., Snow, J., & Stone, L. B. (2023). 'Professor Moms'& 'Hidden Service'in Pandemic Times: Students Report Women Faculty more Supportive & Accommodating amid US COVID Crisis Onset. *Innovative Higher Education*, 1–25. PMID:37361116

Docka-Filipek, D., & Stone, L. B. (2021). Twice a "housewife": On academic precarity, "hysterical" women, faculty mental health, and service as gendered care work for the "university family" in pandemic times. *Gender, Work and Organization*, 28(6), 2158–2179. doi:10.1111/gwao.12723

Doharty, N. (2020). The 'angry Black woman'as intellectual bondage: Being strategically emotional on the academic plantation. *Race, Ethnicity and Education*, 23(4), 548–562. doi:10.1080/13613324.2019.1679751

Domingo, C. R., Counts Gerber, N., Harris, D., Mamo, L., Pasion, S. G., Rebanal, R. D., & Rosser, S. V. (2020). More service or more advancement: Institutional barriers to academic success for women and women of color faculty at a large public comprehensive minority-serving state university. *Journal of Diversity in Higher Education*.

Domingo, C. R., Gerber, N. C., Harris, D., Mamo, L., Pasion, S. G., Rebanal, R. D., & Rosser, S. V. (2022). More service or more advancement: Institutional barriers to academic success for women and women of color faculty at a large public comprehensive minority-serving state university. *Journal of Diversity in Higher Education*, 15(3), 365–379. doi:10.1037/dhe0000292

Donahoo, S. (2019). Owning Black hair: The pursuit of identity and authenticity in higher education. In *Navigating micro-aggressions toward women in higher education* (pp. 73–95). IGI Global. doi:10.4018/978-1-5225-5942-9.ch004

Donaldson, C. (2015). *Hair Alteration Practices Amongst Black Women and the Assumption of Self-Hatred*. Online Publication of undergraduate studies.

Dover, T. L., Major, B., & Kaiser, C. R. (2016). Members of highstatus groups are threatened by pro-diversity organizational messages. *Journal of Experimental Social Psychology*, *62*, 58–67. doi:10.1016/j.jesp.2015.10.006

Dubay, L., Aarons, J., Brown, K. S., & Kenney, G. M. (2020). How risk of exposure to the coronavirus at work varies by race and ethnicity and how to protect the health and wellbeing of workers and their families. *Urban*. https://www.urban. org/sites/default/files/publication/103278/how-risk-ofexposure-to-the-coronavirus-at-work-varies.pdf

Erving, C. L., Zajdel, R., McKinnon, I. I., Van Dyke, M. E., Murden, R. J., Johnson, D. A., Moore, R. H., & Lewis, T. T. (2023). Gendered Racial Microaggressions & Black Women's Sleep Health. *Social Psychology Quarterly*, *86*(2), 01902725221136139. doi:10.1177/01902725221136139

Evans-Winters, V. E., & Hines, D. E. (2020). Unmasking white fragility: How whiteness and white student resistance impacts anti-racist education. *Whiteness and Education*, *5*(1), 1–16. doi:10.1080/23 793406.2019.1675182

Felix, A. S., Lehman, A., Nolan, T. S., Sealy-Jefferson, S., Breathett, K., Hood, D. B., Addison, D., Anderson, C. M., & Cene, C. W., ´Warren, B. J., Jackson, R. D., & Williams, K. P. (2019). Stress, resilience, and cardiovascular disease risk among Black Women: Results from the women's health initiative. *Circulation*, *12*(4), e005284. PMID:30909729

Finkelstein, M. J., Conley, V. M., & Schuster, J. H. (2016). *The faculty factor: Reassessing the American academy in a turbulent era*. JHU Press. doi:10.1353/book.48021

Fisher, A. N., Stinson, D. A., & Kalajdzic, A. (2019). Unpacking backlash: Individual and contextual moderators of bias against female professors. *Basic and Applied Social Psychology*, *41*(5), 305–325. do i:10.1080/01973533.2019.1652178

Fox Tree, J. E., & Vaid, J. (2022). Why so few, still? Challenges to attracting, advancing, and keeping women faculty of color in academia. *Frontiers in Sociology*, *6*, 238. doi:10.3389/fsoc.2021.792198 PMID:35118155

Frankenberg, R. (1993). *White women, race matters: The social construction of whiteness*. U of Minnesota Press. doi:10.4324/9780203973431

Fulweiler, R. W., Davies, S. W., Biddle, J. F., Burgin, A. J., Cooperdock, E. H., Hanley, T. C., Kenkel, C. D., Marcarelli, A. M., Matassa, C. M., Mayo, T. L., Santiago-Vàzquez, L. Z., Traylor-Knowles, N., & Ziegler, M. (2021). Rebuild the Academy: Supporting academic mothers during COVID-19 and beyond. *PLoS Biology*, *19*(3), e3001100. doi:10.1371/journal.pbio.3001100 PMID:33690708

Gaston, M. H., Porter, G. K., & Thomas, V. G. (2007). Prime Time Sister Circles: Evaluating a gender-specific, culturally relevant health intervention to decrease major risk factors in mid-life African-American women. *Journal of the National Medical Association*, *99*, 428–438. PMID:17444433

Gay, G. (2002). Preparing for culturally responsive teaching. *Journal of Teacher Education*, *53*(2), 106–116. doi:10.1177/0022487102053002003

Gay, G. (2010). *Culturally responsive teaching: Theory, research, and practice*. Teachers College Press.

Gay, G. (2015). The what, why, and how of culturally responsive teaching: International mandates, challenges, and opportunities. *Multicultural Education Review*, *7*(3), 123–139. doi:10.1080/200561 5X.2015.1072079

Gilligan, C. (1982). *In a different voice: Psychological theory and women's development.* Harvard University.

Godlee, F. (2020). Racism: The other pandemic. *BMJ (Clinical Research Ed.)*, *369*, m2303. doi:10.1136/ bmj.m2303

Gordon, H. R., Willink, K., & Hunter, K. (2022). Invisible Labor and the Associate Professor: Identity and Workload Inequity. *Journal of Diversity in Higher Education*. Advance online publication. doi:10.1037/ dhe0000414

Gray, K. J., & Brooks, L. B. (2021). Give yourself permission to rest. *Genealogy*, *5*(17), 1–7. doi:10.3390/ genealogy5010017

Griffin, K. A., & Reddick, R. J. (2011). Surveillance and sacrifice: Gender differences in the mentoring patterns of Black professors at predominantly White research universities. *American Educational Research Journal*, *48*(5), 1032–1057. doi:10.3102/0002831211405025

Guarino, C. M., & Borden, V. M. H. (2017). Faculty service loads and gender: Are women taking care of the academic family? *Research in Higher Education*, *58*(6), 672–694. doi:10.100711162-017-9454-2

Guillaume, R. O., & Apodaca, E. C. (2020). Early career faculty of color and promotion and tenure: The intersection of advancement in the academy and cultural taxation. *Race, Ethnicity and Education*, *23*(1), 1–18.

Gutierrez y Muhs, G., Neimann, Y. F., Gonzalez, C. G., & Harris, A. P. (Eds.). (2012). *Presumed incompetent: The intersections of race and class for women in academia.* The University Press of Colorado.

Hanasono, L. K., Broido, E. M., Yacobucci, M. M., Root, K. V., Peña, S., & O'Neil, D. A. (2019). Secret service: Revealing gender biases in the visibility and value of faculty service. *Journal of Diversity in Higher Education*, *12*(1), 85–98. doi:10.1037/dhe0000081

Harris, A. P. (2020). *Presumed incompetent II: Race, class, power, and resistance of women in academia.* University Press of Colorado.

Harris-Perry, M. V. (2011). *Sister citizen: Shame, stereotypes, and Black women in America.* Yale University Press.

Hart, J. (2016). Dissecting a gendered organization: Implications for career trajectories for mid-career faculty women in STEM. *Journal of Higher Education (Columbus, Ohio)*, *87*(5), 605–634. doi:10.1353/ jhe.2016.0024

Haviland, D., Alleman, N. F., & Allen, C. C. (2017). Separate but not quite equal: Collegiality experiences of full-time non-tenure-track faculty members. *Journal of Higher Education, c88*, 1–24.

Hawkins, D. S. (2022). "After Philando, I had to take a sick day to recover": Psychological distress, trauma and police brutality in the Black community. *Health Communication*, *37*(9), 1113–1122. doi:10.1080/10410236.2021.1913838 PMID:33902344

Heffernan, T. (2022). Sexism, racism, prejudice, and bias: A literature review and synthesis of research surrounding student evaluations of courses and teaching. *Assessment & Evaluation in Higher Education*, *47*(1), 144–154. doi:10.1080/02602938.2021.1888075

Hernández, D., & Rehman, B. (Eds.). (2019). *Colonize this! Young women of color on today's feminism*. Hachette.

Hersey, T. (2022). *Rest is Resistance: A Manifesto.*

Hicken, M. T., Lee, H., Ailshire, J., Burgard, S. A., & Williams, D. R. (2013). Every shut eye, ain't sleep: The role of racism-related vigilance in racial/ethnic disparities in sleep difficulty. *Race and Social Problems*, *5*(2), 100–112. doi:10.100712552-013-9095-9 PMID:23894254

Hirshfield, L. E., & Joseph, T. D. (2012). 'We need a woman, we need a black woman': Gender, race, and identity taxation in the academy. *Gender and Education*, *24*(2), 213–227. doi:10.1080/09540253.2011.606208

Hooks, B. (1981). *Ain't I a woman: Black women and feminism*. Pluto Press.

hooks, b. (1999). *Sisters of the yam: Black women and self-recovery*. South End Press.

Johnson-Bailey, J. (2015). Academic incivility and bullying as a gendered and racialized phenomenon. *Adult Learning*, *26*(1), 42–47. doi:10.1177/1045159514558414

Jones, H. J., Ibemere, S., Gaillard, T., Harris, A., Anthony, J., & Shambley-Ebron, D. (2020). Factors Associated with Self-Reported Hypertension Among Black Women. *Journal of National Black Nurses' Association. Journal of National Black Nurses' Association*, *31*(2), 32–38. PMID:33617705

Jones, M. K., Davis, S. M., & Gaskin-Cole, G. (2023). An integrative review of sistah circles in empirical research. *Psychology of Women Quarterly*, *47*(2), 03616843231154564. doi:10.1177/03616843231154564

Jones, M. K., Gaskin-Cole, G., & Reynolds, A. (2023). Masks Off: A Community-Based Psychoeducational Group Intervention with Black Women. *Journal for Specialists in Group Work*, *48*(3), 1–17. doi:10.1080/01933922.2023.2170506

Jones, M. S., Womack, V., Jérémie-Brink, G., & Dickens, D. D. (2021). Gendered racism and mental health among young adult US Black women: The moderating roles of gendered racial identity centrality and identity shifting. *Sex Roles*, 1–11.

Kanter, R. M. (1993). *Men and women of the corporation*. Basic Books.

Kastens, K., & Manduca, C. (2017). Leveraging the power of a community practice to improve teaching and learning about the earth. Change, Vol. 49, Issue 6, p.14-22. Kelly, B. T., Gayles, J. G., & Williams, C. D. (2017). Recruitment without retention: A critical case of black faculty unrest. *The Journal of Negro Education*, *86*(3), 305–317.

Keane, E., Heinz, M., & Mc Daid, R. (2022). Diversifying the Teaching Profession: Representation Matters. In Diversifying the Teaching Profession (pp. 3-21). Routledge.

Kendi, I. X. (2023). *How to be an antiracist*. One world.

Key, E. M., & Sumner, J. L. (2019). You research like a girl: Gendered research agendas and their implications. Political Sci. *Politics*, 1–6.

Kezar, A., & Maxey, D. (2012). Missing from the institutional data picture: Non-tenure-track faculty. *New Directions for Institutional Research*, *2012*(155), 47–65. doi:10.1002/ir.20021

King, N. S., & Upadhyay, B. (2022). Negotiating mentoring relationships and support for Black and Brown early-career faculty. *Science Education*, *106*(5), 1149–1171. doi:10.1002ce.21755

Kniess, D., Benjamin, M., & Boettcher, M. (2017). Negotiating faculty identity in the transition from student affairs practitioner to tenure-track faculty. *The College Student Affairs Journal*, *35*(1), 13–24. doi:10.1353/csj.2017.0002

Kreitzer, R. J., & Sweet-Cushman, J. (2021). Evaluating student evaluations of teaching: A review of measurement and equity bias in SETs and recommendations for ethical reform. *Journal of Academic Ethics*, 1–12.

Ladson-Billings, G. (1995). Toward a theory of culturally relevant pedagogy. *American Educational Research Journal*, *32*(3), 465–491. doi:10.3102/00028312032003465

Ladson-Billings, G. (1996). Silences as weapons: Challenges of a Black professor teaching White students. *Theory into Practice*, *35*(2), 79–85. doi:10.1080/00405849609543706

Ladson-Billings, G. (2000). Racialized discourses and ethnic epistemologies. In N. K. Denzin & Y. S. Lincoln (Eds.), *Handbook of qualitative research* (2nd ed., pp. 257–277). Sage.

Ladson-Billings, G. (2022). *The dreamkeepers: Successful teachers of African American children*. John wiley & sons.

Laurencin, C. T., & Walker, J. M. (2020). A pandemic on a pandemic: Racism and COVID-19 in Blacks. *Cell Systems*, *11*(1), 9–10. doi:10.1016/j.cels.2020.07.002 PMID:32702320

Layne, T. M., Clark, U. S., Mohamed, N. E., Miller, S. J., Sly, J. R., Kata, H. E., Astha, V., Lawrence, S. A., Hutson, Y., Campbell, K. N., & Benn, E. K. (2023). Undue burden: Black faculty, COVID-19, and the racial justice movement. *Journal of Clinical and Translational Science*, *7*(1), e14. doi:10.1017/cts.2022.460 PMID:36755534

Lazos, S. R. (2012). Are student teaching evaluations holding back women and minorities? The perils of "doing" gender and race in the classroom. In G. Gutierrez y Muhs, Y. Niemann, & C. Gonzalez (Eds.), *Presumed incompetent: The intersections of race and class for women in academia* (pp. 164–185). University Press of Colorado. doi:10.2307/j.ctt4cgr3k.19

Lester, Y., Owens, D., & Tadros, E. (2021). The experiences of Black female faculty in counselor education. *Journal of Professional Counseling, Practice, Theory, & Research*, *48*(2), 76–90. doi:10.1080/15566382.2021.1948769

Louis, D. A., Rawls, G. J., Jackson-Smith, D., Chambers, G. A., Phillips, L. L., & Louis, S. L. (2016). Listening to our voices: Experiences of Black faculty at predominantly White research universities with microaggression. *Journal of Black Studies*, *47*(5), 454–474. doi:10.1177/0021934716632983

Lundine, J., Bourgeault, I. L., Clark, J., Heidari, S., & Balabanova, D. (2018). The gendered system of academic publishing. *Lancet*, *391*(10132), 1754–1756. doi:10.1016/S0140-6736(18)30950-4 PMID:29739551

Macfarlane, B., & Burg, D. (2019). Women professors and the academic housework trap. *Journal of Higher Education Policy and Management*, *41*(3), 262–274. doi:10.1080/1360080X.2019.1589682

MacNell, L., Driscoll, A., & Hunt, A. N. (2015). What's in a name: Exposing gender bias in student ratings of teaching. *Innovative Higher Education*, *40*(4), 291–303. doi:10.100710755-014-9313-4

Maher, F. A., & Tetreault, M. K. T. (2001). *The feminist classroom: Dynamics of gender, race, and privilege*. Rowman & Littlefield Publishers.

Makhulu, A. M., & Smith, C. (2022). # CiteBlackWomen. *Cultural Anthropology*, *37*(2), 177–181. doi:10.14506/ca37.2.01

Martinez, M. A., Chang, A., & Welton, A. D. (2017). Assistant professors of color confront the inequitable terrain of academia: A community cultural wealth perspective. *Race, Ethnicity and Education*, *20*(5), 696–710. doi:10.1080/13613324.2016.1150826

Mawhinney, L. (2011). Othermothering: A personal narrative exploring relationships between Black female faculty and students. *Negro Educational Review*, *62/63*(1–4), 213–232.

McChesney, J. (2018). Representation and pay of women of color in the higher education workforce. College and university professional association for human resources. *Education*, *3*(4), 245–256.

McCluney, C. L., Durkee, M. I., Smith, R. E. II, Robotham, K. J., & Lee, S. S. L. (2021). To be, or not to be… Black: The effects of racial codeswitching on perceived professionalism in the workplace. *Journal of Experimental Social Psychology*, *97*, 104199. doi:10.1016/j.jesp.2021.104199

McCoy, H. (2021). What do you call a black woman with a PhD? AN*****: How race trumps education no matter what. *Race and Justice*, *11*(3), 318–327. doi:10.1177/2153368720988892

McCoy-Wilson, S. (2020). We have a Black professor?" Rejecting African Americans as disseminators of knowledge. *Journal of Black Studies*, *51*(6), 545–564. doi:10.1177/0021934720925777

McNaughtan, J., García, H. A., & Nehls, K. (2017). Understanding the growth of contingent faculty. *New Directions for Institutional Research*, *2017*(176), 9–26. doi:10.1002/ir.20241

Metz, M. H. (1978). Clashes in the classroom: The importance of norms for authority. *Education and Urban Society*, *11*(1), 13–47. doi:10.1177/001312457801100102

Mickey, E. L., Kanelee, E. S., & Misra, J. (June 5, 2020). 10 Small steps for department chairs to foster inclusion. *Inside Higher Ed*. https://www.insidehighered.com/advice/2020/ 06/05/advice-department-chairs-how-foster-inclusion among-faculty-opinion

Minnett, J. L., James-Gallaway, A. D., & Owens, D. R. (2019). Help A Sista Out: Black Women Doctoral Students' Use of Peer Mentorship as an Act of Resistance. *Mid-Western Educational Researcher*, *31*(2).

Mitchell, K. M., & Martin, J. (2018). Gender bias in student evaluations. *PS, Political Science & Politics,* *51*(3), 648–652. doi:10.1017/S104909651800001X

Moody, A. T., & Lewis, J. A. (2019). Gendered racial microaggressions and traumatic stress symptoms among Black women. *Psychology of Women Quarterly, 43*(2), 201–214. doi:10.1177/0361684319828288

Morgan, A. C., Way, S. F., Hoefer, M. J., Larremore, D. B., Galesic, M., & Clauset, A. (2021). The unequal impact of parenthood in academia. *Science Advances, 7*(9), eabd1996.

Morris, E. W. (2007). "Ladies" or "loudies"? Perceptions and experiences of Black girls in classrooms. *Youth & Society, 38*(4), 490–515. doi:10.1177/0044118X06296778

Morris, M. (2016). Pushout: *The criminalization of Black girls in schools.* New Press.

Motro, D., Evans, J. B., Ellis, A. P., & Benson, L. III. (2022). Race and reactions to women's expressions of anger at work: Examining the effects of the "angry Black woman" stereotype. *The Journal of Applied Psychology, 107*(1), 142–152. doi:10.1037/apl0000884 PMID:33793257

Mott, C., & Cockayne, D. (2017). Citation matters: Mobilizing the politics of citation toward a practice of 'conscientious engagement'. *Gender, Place and Culture, 24*(7), 954–973. doi:10.1080/0966636 9X.2017.1339022

Nadal, K. L., Davidoff, K. C., Davis, L. S., Wong, Y., Marshall, D., & McKenzie, V. (2015). A qualitative approach to intersectional microaggressions: Understanding influences of race, ethnicity, gender, sexuality, and religion. *Qualitative Psychology, 2*(2), 147–163. doi:10.1037/qup0000026

Nadal, K. L., Griffin, K. E., Wong, Y., Davidoff, K. C., & Davis, L. S. (2017). The injurious relationship between racial microaggressions and physical health: Implications for social work. *Journal of Ethnic & Cultural Diversity in Social Work, 26*(1-2), 6–17. doi:10.1080/15313204.2016.1263813

Neal-Barnett, A., Stadulis, R., Murray, M., Payne, M. R., Thomas, A., & Salley, B. B. (2011). Sister circles as a culturally relevant intervention for anxious Black women. *Clinical Psychology: Science and Practice, 18*(3), 266–273. doi:10.1111/j.1468-2850.2011.01258.x PMID:22081747

Nicol, D. J., & Yee, J. A. (2017). "Reclaiming our time": Women of color faculty and radical self-care in the academy. *Feminist Teacher, 27*(2–3), 133–156. doi:10.5406/femteacher.27.2-3.0133

Njoku, A., & Evans, M. (2022). Black women faculty and administrators navigating COVID-19, social unrest, and academia: Challenges and strategies. *International Journal of Environmental Research and Public Health, 19*(4), 2220. doi:10.3390/ijerph19042220 PMID:35206408

Njoku, A., Joseph, M., & Felix, R. (2021). Changing the narrative: Structural barriers and racial and ethnic inequities in COVID-19 vaccination. *International Journal of Environmental Research and Public Health, 18*(18), 9904. doi:10.3390/ijerph18189904 PMID:34574827

Novacek, D. M., Hampton-Anderson, J. N., Ebor, M. T., Loeb, T. B., & Wyatt, G. E. (2020). Mental health ramifications of the COVID-19 pandemic for black Americans: Clinical and research recommendations. *Psychological Trauma: Theory, Research, Practice, and Policy, 12*(5), 449–451. doi:10.1037/ tra0000796 PMID:32525370

O'Meara, K., Templeton, L., & Nyunt, G. (2018). Earning professional legitimacy: Challenges faced by women, underrepresented minority, and non-tenure-track faculty. *Teachers College Record, 120*(12), 1–38. doi:10.1177/016146811812001203

Olzmann, J. A. (2020). Diversity through equity and inclusion: The responsibility belongs to all of us. *Molecular Biology of the Cell, 31*(25), 2757–2760. doi:10.1091/mbc.E20-09-0575 PMID:33253074

Onyeador, I. N., Hudson, S. K. T., & Lewis, N. A. Jr. (2021). Moving beyond implicit bias training: Policy insights for increasing organizational diversity. *Policy Insights from the Behavioral and Brain Sciences, 8*(1), 19–26. doi:10.1177/2372732220983840

Özbilgin, M. (2009). Equality, diversity, and inclusion at work: yesterday, today and tomorrow. *Equality, diversity and inclusion at work: a research companion*, 1-16.

Pace, J. L., & Hemmings, A. (Eds.). (2006). *Classroom authority: Theory, research, and practice.* Routledge. doi:10.4324/9781410617163

Padilla, A. M. (1994). Ethnic minority scholars, research and mentoring: Current and future issues. *Educational Researcher, 23*(4), 523–440. doi:10.2307/1176259

Penney, S., Young, G., Badenhorst, C., Goodnough, K., Hesson, J., Joy, R., McLeod, H., Pelech, S., Pickett, S., Stordy, M., & Vaandering, D. (2015). Faculty writing groups: A support for women balancing family and career on the academic tightrope. *Canadian Journal of Higher Education, 45*(4), 457–479. doi:10.47678/cjhe.v45i4.184396

Perlow, O. N., Wheeler, D. I., Bethea, S. L., & Scott, B. M. (2018). *Black women's liberatory pedagogies: Resistance, transformation, and healing within and beyond the academy.* Palgrave MacMillan. doi:10.1007/978-3-319-65789-9

Pierce, C. (1970). Offensive mechanisms. In F. Barbour (Ed.), *The Black seventies* (pp. 265–282). Porter Sargent.

Pittman, C. T. (2010). Race and gender oppression in the classroom: The experiences of women faculty of color with White male students. *Teaching Sociology, 38*(3), 183–196. doi:10.1177/0092055X10370120

Pittman, C. T. (2012). Racial microaggressions: The narratives of African American Faculty at a predominantly White university. *The Journal of Negro Education, 81*(1), 82–92. doi:10.7709/jnegroeducation.81.1.0082

Pitts, B. (2021). "Uneasy lies the head that wears a crown": A critical race analysis of the CROWN Act. *Journal of Black Studies, 52*(7), 716–735. doi:10.1177/00219347211021096

Porcher, K. M., & Austin, T. (2021). "Black Women are the Mules of the World": Black Women Professors of Practice in Teacher Education Programs. *Journal of African American Women and Girls in Education, 1*(3), 109–129. doi:10.21423/jaawge-v1i3a54

Porter, C. J., Boss, G. J., & Davis, T. J. (2023). Just because it don't look heavy, don't mean it ain't: An intersectional analysis of Black women's labor as faculty during COVID. *Gender, Work and Organization, 30*(2), 657–672. doi:10.1111/gwao.12820

Porter, C. J., Moore, C. M., Boss, G. J., Davis, T. J., & Louis, D. A. (2020). To be Black women and contingent faculty: Four scholarly personal narratives. *The Journal of Higher Education, 91*(5), 674–697. doi:10.1080/00221546.2019.1700478

Powell, A. (2022). Two-step flow and protesters: Understanding what influenced participation in a George Floyd protest. *Communication Quarterly, 70*(4), 407–428. doi:10.1080/01463373.2022.2077122

Pryor, K. N. (2020). Thriving, Surviving, or Striving? A Part-Time Non-Tenure-Track Faculty Typology for the New Era of Faculty Work. *Teachers College Record, 122*(11), 1–40. doi:10.1177/016146812012201104

Rasinski, H. M., & Czopp, A. M. (2010). The effect of target status on witnesses' reactions to confrontations of bias. *Basic and Applied Social Psychology, 32*(1), 8–16. doi:10.1080/01973530903539754

Reid, R. A. (2021). Retaining women faculty: The problem of invisible labor. *PS, Political Science & Politics, 54*(3), 504–506. doi:10.1017/S1049096521000056

Reny, T. T., & Newman, B. J. (2021). The opinion-mobilizing effect of social protest against police violence: Evidence from the 2020 George Floyd protests. *The American Political Science Review, 115*(4), 1499–1507. doi:10.1017/S0003055421000460

Richards, B. N. (2019). Faculty assessments as tools of oppression: A Black woman's reflections on color-blind racism in the academy. In Byrd, W. C., R. Brunn-Bevel, J., & Ovink, S. M. (Eds.), Intersectionality and higher education: Identity and inequality on college campuses. Rutgers University Press. doi:10.36019/9780813597706-009

Rideau, R. (2019). "We're just not acknowledged": An examination of the identity taxation of full-time non-tenure-track Women of Color faculty members. *Journal of Diversity in Higher Education*. doi:10.1037/dhe0000139

Rideau, R. (2021). "We're just not acknowledged": An examination of the identity taxation of full-time non-tenure-track Women of Color faculty members. *Journal of Diversity in Higher Education, 14*(2), 161–173. doi:10.1037/dhe0000139

Rideau, R., & Robbins, C. K. (2020). The Experiences of Non-Tenure-Track Faculty Members of Color with Racism in the Classroom. *To Improve the Academy: A Journal of Educational Development, 39*(2).

Ringrose, J., Tolman, D., & Ragonese, M. (2019). Hot right now: Diverse girls navigating technologies of racialized sexy femininity. *Feminism & Psychology, 29*(1), 76–95. doi:10.1177/0959353518806324

Roberts, S. O., Bareket-Shavit, C., Dollins, F. A., Goldie, P. D., & Mortenson, E. (2020). Racial inequality in psychological research: Trends of the past and recommendations for the future. *Perspectives on Psychological Science, 15*(6), 1295–1309. doi:10.1177/1745691620927709 PMID:32578504

Robinson, D., Adams, T. R., Williams, B. K., & Williams, N. N. (2022). Surviving higher learning: Microinvalidations of Black junior faculty in higher education. *We're Not OK: Black Faculty Experiences and Higher Education Strategies, 75-93.*

Ross, H. H., & Edwards, W. J. (2016). African American faculty expressing concerns: Breaking the silence at predominantly white research oriented universities. *Race, Ethnicity and Education, 19*(3), 461–479. doi:10.1080/13613324.2014.969227

Ross-Sheriff, F. (2012). Microaggression, women, and social work. *Affilia, 27*(3), 233–236. doi:10.1177/0886109912454366

Rubin-Miller, L., Alban, C., Artiga, S., & Sullivan, S. (2020). COVID-19 racial disparities in testing, infection, hospitalization, and death: analysis of epic patient data. *Kaiser Family Foundation,* 2020916.

Settles, I. H., Buchanan, N. T., & Dotson, K. (2019). Scrutinized but not recognized:(In) visibility and hypervisibility experiences of faculty of color. *Journal of Vocational Behavior, 113*, 62–74. doi:10.1016/j.jvb.2018.06.003

Settles, I. H., Jones, M. K., Buchanan, N. T., & Brassel, S. T. (2022). Epistemic exclusion of women faculty and faculty of color: Understanding scholar (ly) devaluation as a predictor of turnover intentions. *The Journal of Higher Education, 93*(1), 31–55. doi:10.1080/00221546.2021.1914494

Simien, E. M., & Wallace, S. J. (2022). Disproportionate service: Considering the impacts of George Floyd's death and the coronavirus pandemic for women academics and faculty of color. *PS, Political Science & Politics, 55*(4), 799–803. doi:10.1017/S1049096522000580

Sivasubramaniam, M. (2022). Interrogating the Relationship Between a Teacher's Race and Classroom Authority. In The Complexities of Authority in the Classroom (pp. 201-208). Routledge. doi:10.4324/9781003140849-21

Skinner, M., Betancourt, N., & Wolff-Eisenberg, C. (2021, April 14). The disproportionate impact of the pandemic on women and caregivers in academia. *Chronicle of Higher Education.* https://sr.ithaka.org/wp-content/uploads/2021/03/ SR-Issue-Brief-Impact-Pandemic-Women-CaregiversAcademics-033121.pdf

Smith, B. P., & Hawkins, B. (2011). Examining student evaluations of black college faculty: Does race matter? *The Journal of Negro Education, 80*(2), 149–162.

Smith, C. A., & Garrett-Scott, D. (2021). "We are not named": Black women and the politics of citation in anthropology. *Feminist Anthropology, 2*(1), 18–37. doi:10.1002/fea2.12038

Smith, C. A., Williams, E. L., Wadud, I. A., & Whitney, N. L. (2021). Cite Black Women: A Critical Praxis (A Statement). *Feminist Anthropology, 2*(1), 10–17. doi:10.1002/fea2.12040

Smith, W. A. (2004). Black faculty coping with racial battle fatigue: The campus racial climate in a post-civil rights era. *A long way to go: Conversations about race by African American faculty and graduate students, 14*(5), 171-190.

Smith, W. A. (2014). *Racial battle fatigue in higher education: Exposing the myth of post-racial America.* Rowman & Littlefield.

Sneed, R. S., Key, K., Bailey, S., & Johnson-Lawrence, V. (2020). Social and psychological consequences of the COVID-19 pandemic in African-American communities: Lessons from Michigan. *Psychological Trauma: Theory, Research, Practice, and Policy, 12*(5), 446–448. doi:10.1037/tra0000881 PMID:32525371

Sosoo, E. E., MacCormack, J. K., & Neblett, E. W. Jr. (2022). Psychophysiological and affective reactivity to vicarious police violence. *Psychophysiology, 59*(10), e14065. doi:10.1111/psyp.14065 PMID:35543565

Sparkman-Key, N., & Tarver, S. Z. (2022). Promoting Mental Wellness among Black Faculty: Strategies for Coping. *We're Not OK: Black Faculty Experiences and Higher Education Strategies*, 113-127.

Black Women Faculty Also Matter

Spates, K., Evans, N. M., Watts, B. C., Abubakar, N., & James, T. (2020). Keeping ourselves sane: A qualitative exploration of black women's coping strategies for gendered racism. *Sex Roles, 82*(9-10), 513–524. doi:10.100711199-019-01077-1

Stanfill, M., & Klean Zwilling, J. (2023). Critical Considerations for Safe Space in the College Classroom. *College Teaching, 71*(2), 85–91. doi:10.1080/87567555.2023.2179011

Stewart, J. T. (2022). Why are you talking white? Code-switching in academia. In A. M. Allen & J. T. Steward (Eds.), *We are not okay: Black faculty experiences and higher education strategies* (pp. 1–29). Cambridge University Press. doi:10.1017/9781009064668.002

Sue, D. W. (2010). *Microaggressions in everyday life: Race, gender, and sexual orientation* (1st ed.). John Wiley & Sons.

Sue, D. W., Rivera, D. P., Watkins, N. L., Kim, R. H., Kim, S., & Williams, C. D. (2011). Racial dialogues: Challenges faculty of color face in the classroom. *Cultural Diversity & Ethnic Minority Psychology, 17*(3), 331–340. doi:10.1037/a0024190 PMID:21787066

Sue, D. W., & Spanierman, L. (2020). *Microaggressions in everyday life*. John Wiley & Sons.

Sykes, B. L. (2021). Academic turning points: How microaggressions and macroaggressions inhibit diversity and inclusion in the academy. *Race and Justice, 11*(3), 288–300. doi:10.1177/21533687211001909

Tatum, B. D. (1994). Teaching White students about racism: The search for White allies and the restoration of hope. *Teachers College Record, 95*(4), 462–476. doi:10.1177/016146819409500412

Thomas, G. D., & Hollenshead, C. (2001). Resisting from the margins: The coping strategies of Black women and other women of color faculty members at a research university. *The Journal of Negro Education, 70*(3), 166–175. doi:10.2307/3211208

Thomas, V. (2020). "How Dare You!" African American Faculty and the Power Struggle With White Students. *Journal of Cases in Educational Leadership, 23*(4), 115–126. doi:10.1177/1555458920945762

Tisdell, E. J. (1998). Post-structural feminist pedagogies: The possibilities and limitations of feminist emancipatory adult learning theory and practice. *Adult Education Quarterly, 48*(3), 139–156. doi:10.1177/074171369804800302

Tong, R. (2018). *Feminist thought, student economy edition: A More Comprehensive Introduction*. Routledge.

Truong, K. A., Graves, D., & Keene, A. J. (2014). Faculty of color teaching critical race theory at a PWI: An autoethnography. *Journal of Critical Thought and Praxis, 3*(2), 1–30. doi:10.31274/jctp-180810-42

U.S. Department of Education, National Center for Education Statistics. (2020). *The Condition of Education 2020 (NCES 2020-144)*. USDoE.

Warren, P. Y. (2021). The room where it happens: Reflections on being a Black woman in the academy. *Race and Justice, 11*(3), 347–354. doi:10.1177/2153368720974744

Watson, N. N., & Hunter, C. D. (2016). "I had to be strong" tensions in the strong Black woman schema. *The Journal of Black Psychology, 42*(5), 424–452. doi:10.1177/0095798415597093

Watson-Singleton, N. N. (2017). Strong Black woman schema and psychological distress: The mediating role of perceived emotional support. *The Journal of Black Psychology, 43*(8), 778–788. doi:10.1177/0095798417732414

Weitz, R., & Gordon, L. (1993). Images of Black women among Anglo college students. *Sex Roles, 28*(1–2), 19–34. doi:10.1007/BF00289745

Wenger-Trayner, E., & Wenger-Trayner, B. (2015). *Communities of practice: A brief introduction.*

Wilson, B. L., Wolfer, T. A., Wooten, N. R., Pitner, R., Moore, S. E., & Anders, A. D. (2023). "Am I Next?": A qualitative study of Black college students' experiences of stress, trauma, and grief from exposures to police killings. *Journal of Human Behavior in the Social Environment*, 1–33. doi:10.1080/10911359.2023.2173353

Wong, B., Copsey-Blake, M., & Elmorally, R. (2022). Silent or silenced? Minority ethnic students and the battle against racism. *Cambridge Journal of Education, 52*(5), 651–666. doi:10.1080/0305764X.2022.2047889

Woods-Giscombé, C. L. (2010). Superwoman schema: African American women's views on stress, strength, and health. *Qualitative Health Research, 20*(5), 668–683. doi:10.1177/1049732310361892 PMID:20154298

Woods-Jaegar, B., Briggs, E. C., Gaylord-Harden, N., Cho, B., & Lemon, E. (2021). Translating cultural assets research into action to mitigate adverse childhood experience-related health disparities among African American youth. *The American Psychologist, 76*(2), 326–336. doi:10.1037/amp0000779 PMID:33734798

Yehia, B. R., Winegar, A., Fogel, R., Fakih, M., Ottenbacher, A., Jesser, C., Bufalino, A., Huang, R. H., & Cacchione, J. (2020). Association of race with mortality among patients hospitalized with coronavirus disease 2019 (COVID-19) at 92 US hospitals. *JAMA Network Open, 3*(8), e2018039–e2018039. doi:10.1001/jamanetworkopen.2020.18039 PMID:32809033

Young, A. A. Jr, Furhman, M., & Chesler, M. A. (2015). How race and gender shape perceived challenges to classroom authority and expertise. In *Faculty identities and the challenge of diversity* (pp. 57–76). Routledge.

Young, J. L., & Hines, D. E. (2018). Killing my spirit, renewing my soul: Black female professors' critical reflections on spirit killings while teaching. *Women, Gender, and Families of Color, 6*(1), 18–25. doi:10.5406/womgenfamcol.6.1.0018

Young, V. A., Barrett, R., Young-Rivera, Y., & Lovejoy, K. B. (2014). *Other people's English: Codemeshing, codeswitching, and African American Literacy.* Teachers College Press.

Zambrana, R. E., Ray, R., Espino, M. M., Castro, C., Douthirt Cohen, B., & Eliason, J. (2015). "Don't leave us behind" The importance of mentoring for underrepresented minority faculty. *American Educational Research Journal, 52*(1), 40–72. doi:10.3102/0002831214563063

Zidani, S. (2021). Whose pedagogy is it anyway? Decolonizing the syllabus through a critical embrace of difference. *Media Culture & Society, 43*(5), 970–978. doi:10.1177/0163443720980922

Chapter 8

Gendered Cultures, Under-Representation, and the Career Challenges of Women Academics in a South African University

Yaw Owusu-Agyeman
iD https://orcid.org/0000-0001-6730-5456
University of the Free State, South Africa

Reitumetse Mofana
University of the Free State, South Africa

ABSTRACT

The current study examines how gendered practices in a university in South Africa constrain the career progression of women academics. Drawing on feminist institutionalism, interview data were gathered and analysed from a sample of 20 men and women academics. The study revealed that gendered practices that constrain the career progression of women academics include weak academic nurturing culture, weak collegial relationships and networks among women academics, and preferences for men academics in leadership positions. The findings also revealed that while the women academics indicated that high academic workload, family responsibilities, and unfavourable promotion criteria constrain their career progression, some men participants believed that earmark scholarships and targeted mentoring arrangements for women could create a new class of elites. The study concludes by discussing the implications of the findings in relation to policy, practice, and future research.

DOI: 10.4018/978-1-6684-8597-2.ch008

Copyright © 2023, IGI Global. Copying or distributing in print or electronic forms without written permission of IGI Global is prohibited.

INTRODUCTION

In the face of many noteworthy efforts to address the causes of gender inequality in higher education (HE), women academics still experience forms of marginalization and inequality. Explanations often attribute such forms of marginalization and inequality to the lack of strong institutional policies and persistent gendered cultures that are antithetical to the career progression of women academics. For instance, gender discrepancies in power and the under-representation of women in senior management and professorial level persist (O'Connor, 2019). To ensure that female professionals including academics progress in their careers, there have been various charters, legislations and policy decisions at the international, national, and institutional levels. For instance, the United Nations' Sustainable Development Goal 5 (SDG5) highlights the importance of ensuring that women have equal opportunities for leadership at all levels of decision-making in political, economic, and public life (UN, 2021). Also, Aspiration 6, Goal 17 of the African Union Agenda 2063 emphasizes full gender equality in all spheres of life (AUC, 2021). While these international charters and conventions have been established to address the challenges countries face in promoting gender equality and women empowerment, studies from different countries reveal various forms of gender inequality (Hirsu et al., 2021; Macupe, 2020; Mergaert & Lombardo, 2014; Reynolds & Henderson, 2023).

To address the issues confronting the career progression of women academics in HE, the current study examines how gender inequalities in a university in South Africa constrain the career development of women academics. Secondly, this study seeks answers to how women academics in the university can advance their careers through institutional support and transformation that addresses all forms of gendered cultural practices. Barriers to the career progression of women academics have been challenged in prior studies on the bases of claims and counterclaims that men academics also experience perceived biases (Verge et al., 2018). In practice, prejudices against feminist policy, gendered professoriate networks, gender stereotypes, and the fallacy of equality (Verge et al., 2018) continue to hinder the career progression of women academics in HE. Beyond gendered practices in the HE sector are changes in the context of HE that have become highly competitive concerning value, competition for funding (Angervall, 2018) research output, teaching and learning delivery, and engaged scholarship which further impacts inequalities.

The importance of transforming institutional structure, culture, and policies to reflect evolving global trends that support the career advancement of women academics served as the current study's point of departure. Consequently, the following research questions were developed to guide the current study: (1) what gendered practices constrain the career progression of women academics in the university? and (2) what are the differences in the perceptions of men and women academics concerning gendered practices that constrain the career progression of women academics in the university? The current study commences by providing an overview of the South African HE context concerning gender and then proceeds to explain how feminist institutional theory (Chappell & Waylen, 2013; Clavero & Galligan, 2020) provides meaning to how perceived gender inequalities in the university constrain the career progression of female academics. Next, the study explains the empirical process used to gather interview data from the study participants regarding their opinion and experiences about how perceived gender inequalities constrain the career advancement of women academics. The study concludes by discussing the findings of the empirical study and provide recommendations on how perceived gender inequalities in the study setting could be addressed.

GENDER INEQUALITY IN SOUTH AFRICAN HE

Although progressive policies on gender equity have been introduced in South African Universities, women remain at the lower ranks of institutions (Herbst, 2020; Maphalala & Mpofu, 2017) with a few rising to occupy leadership positions (Moodly & Toni 2017). The culture of exclusion in HEIs in South Africa could be seen in the form of gendered processes such as male dominance, silencing of women's voices, and male patterns of networking that affects the advancement of women (Toni & Moodly, 2019). Again the underrepresentation of women in South African HE settings could be linked to patriarchal systems in Africa which include preserving and perpetuating sociocultural norms that recognize women as mothers, nurturers, and caregivers (Alabi et al., 2019) rather than individuals who could obtain educational qualifications and perform leadership roles. The different ethnic and racial groups in South Africa are deeply rooted in patriarchal systems with rigid stereotypical conditions that force women to accept the existing conditions which include the male superiority complex, privileges, and unequal share of power in education structures (Bodalina & Mestry, 2022). To address gender inequalities in South Africa, different legal frameworks (for example, the Employment Equity ACT of 1998, the Promotion of Equality and Prevention of Unfair Discrimination Amendment Act of 2000, and the Women's Empowerment and Gender Equality ACT of 2013) were established. Particularly, the Women's Empowerment and Gender Equality ACT of 2013 was established among other things to align all legal provisions relating to women's empowerment and to address the persistent discriminatory patriarchal attitudes and the lingering effects of apartheid faced by women in the education system (Republic of South Africa, 2013). Although these policy frameworks have been developed to address issues concerning gender equality in the country, there are persistent inequalities in institutions (Herbst, 2020; Maphalala & Mpofu, 2017).

Also, while the number of women in the academy in South Africa has increased over the years, they are mostly active in teaching whereas their men counterparts dominate the research field (Subbaye & Vithal, 2017). This is consistent with the 1997 White Paper on HE (Department of Education, 1997) that highlights the under-representation of women, especially in senior academic and management positions. In terms of statistics, the National Commission on Higher Education report of 1996 revealed that in 1993, women occupied 32% of the total research and teaching positions in South Africa (Mabokela, 2002). More worrying is the fact that the majority of these women academics were employed at the level of junior lecturer or lecturer positions, less than 3 percent of women held professorship positions, and about 8 percent held the position of associate professor (Mabokela, 2002). This compares to statistics from other geographical settings that show that in 2016 the percentage of female full-time professors (29% in Finland, 28% in Norway, 26% in Iceland, 25% in Sweden, and 21% in Denmark) was less than those of male professors (European Commission, 2019). Fast forward to 2021, not much has changed concerning the demographics of HE in South Africa and the representation of women academics. Black African women are the most under-represented group with about 16.10 percent representation in universities (DHET, 2019).

Although interventions at the state level through the Staffing South Africa University's Framework (SSAUF) which consist of four core programmes including the new Generation of Academics Programme (nGAP) have sought to address the imbalances in the representation of the previously marginalized group, there is still a lot to be achieved. Also, while the nGAP is a step towards addressing issues of under-representation in the university, there is a need for more interventions to address gendered practices that constrain the career progression of women academics. Prior study has shown that the continuous underrepresentation of women at the top echelon of universities in South Africa is in sharp contrast to the number of women who can be found in the lower levels (Toni & Moodly, 2019). To create an equitable academic profile, universities in South Africa have been urged to develop strategies and processes that aim at the transformation agenda initiated by the state (DHET, 2019). By developing strategies that aim at the creation of an equitable academic profiles of academics in universities, institutions could enhance the career progression of women academics and reduce perceived feelings of marginalization and discrimination that may be embodied in the culture of HEIs.

FEMINIST INSTITUTIONAL THEORY

Grounded on feminist institutionalism (Acker, 1992; Chappell & Waylen, 2013), this study examines how perceived gender inequalities in the university constrain the career progression of female academics in a university in South Africa. The scholarship of gender and institutions could be traced to Kanter's (1977) framework for conceptualizing the relationships between dominants and tokens in institutional settings and the work of Acker (1992) that examined how gender is conceptualized in the processes, practices, ideologies, and distribution of power in a social setting. The central idea of feminist institutionalism is that change is motivated by the internal structures and arrangements of institutions and not by societal forces (Clavero & Galligan, 2020). Consequent to the limitations of other forms of institutionalism (historical, sociological, and discursive institutionalism) and particularly because these forms of institutionalism did not adequately explain how institutional structures, rules, and practices influence gendered processes (Chappell & Waylen, 2013) feminist institutionalism was developed. Again, the seeming gender blindness of mainstream institutional theory also provided very little information concerning the relationship between gender dynamics and institutional structure, systems, and practices (Chappell & Waylen, 2013). Resultantly, feminist institutionalism was introduced as a new institutional theory that sought to provide a convincing explanation for institutional design and practices concerning gendered processes (Clavero & Galligan, 2020).

Gendered processes in institutions include explicit decisions and procedures that control, segregate, exclude, and build hierarchies based on race and class (Acker, 1992). This includes institutional structures that create unequal opportunities concerning leadership positions, unfair promotion policies, and the lack of transparency around promotion amongst other things could constrain the career advancement of women. Institutional structures and policies around sponsorship, collegial support, mentoring, and leadership are very important to the career progression of women academics. Beyond the hierarchies that are built in institutions, gendered processes include the construction of symbols, images, and ideologies that provide legitimacy to institutions such as universities (Acker, 1992). The images, symbols, arts, and ideologies are entrenched in the culture of universities. However, culture indirectly affects the careers of individuals through variances in human resource practices, and employment systems (Benson et al., 2020) within an institutional context. Prior study has shown that institutional context and culture directly influence resistance to gender equality initiatives in higher education institutions (Verge et al., 2018) especially, where the cultures and sub-cultures preserve male privilege and power as well as gendered norms, values, and practices (Mergaert & Lombardo, 2014). However, by altering the status quo that preserves informal and formal unequal norms, institutions could create spaces that support equality and break the culture of resistance to change (Mergaert & Lombardo, 2014).

Rules about gender which may be formal or informal shape how men and women behave in institutions. The informal rules include situations where female academics are nurtured to acknowledge the authority of men in the institution without question (Maphalala & Mpofu, 2017). However, overcoming the methodological challenges associated with examining how informal rules, norms, and practices constrain institutional transformation aimed at gender equality is a major issue because informal rules are disguised as accepted behaviour, often taken for granted, and are rooted in everyday gendered practices. While innovative behaviours, political knowledge and career initiative serve as some of the proactive career-building behaviours that enhance career advancement (Heslin et al., 2019), institutional policies, processes, and practices could either enhance or impede the career progression of women academics.

The current study refers to feminist institutionalism as a theory that seeks to explain the interplay between institutional structure, power, and culture that address the gaps related to gendered policies and practices in HE. While there are many advantages of feminist institutionalism, the theory has been critiqued based on its pluralistic approach, attention to formal and informal institutional environments, focus on gendered processes within and outside institutions, and its description of actors as having agency that is bounded by constraints (Mackay et al., 2010, p.584). Notwithstanding the weaknesses of feminist institutionalism, its use in explaining the interplay between institutional structure, culture, and power served as the main reason for its adoption as the theoretical underpinning of the current study. Furthermore, recognizing the presence of a gender structure in an institution is important because it provides fresh understanding of institutional power relations, how resources are distributed, and who distributed these resources (Chappell & Waylen, 2013). Also, individuals engage in internal processes while they construct their identity in the social setting (Acker, 1992).

METHODOLOGY

The context of the current study is a university in South Africa that was founded in 1904. There are currently, seven faculties with different academic programmes offered at the degree, honours, masters and doctoral levels. With a total staff population of 2,521, the university is located on three different campuses. A qualitative research approach was used to gather and analyze data from participants in the current study. Participants of the current study (20) were sampled from seven faculties spread over three campuses of the university – Bloemfontein, QwaQwa, and South Campuses all located in the Free State province. Purposive and snowball sampling techniques were used to select participants for the study. The participants were made up of 10 men and 10 women. The inclusion of men academics in the current study provided concurring and contrasting views about how institutional structure and gendered cultural practices constrain the career progression of women academics. The distribution of participants based on race were: Black Lecturers – 11; White Lecturers - 8 and an Indian Lecturer - 1. The academic ranks of participants were as follows: Professors (2); an Associate Professor (1); Senior Lecturers (6); Lecturers (8) and; Junior Lecturers (3). The researchers further de-identified the participants by allocating them pseudonyms.

A formal invitation by way of email was sent to all participants (men and women academic staff) in all three campuses of the university. Participants who consented to participate in the study were contacted by the researchers and the dates for the interviews were scheduled. Each participant was informed about the purpose of the study and afterward, requested to sign a consent form before the interview. The duration of the interview was between forty-five and sixty minutes and the interviews were held in meeting rooms or the offices of the participants. A semi-structured interview schedule was designed to gather data from the participants concerning their perceptions about how perceived gender inequalities in the university constrain the career progression of female academics. Also, by using a semi-structured interview schedule, the interviewers were able to probe and proceed with follow-up questions when necessary (Walker & Gleaves, 2016). Sample questions were: What are some of the gendered practices that constrain the career progression of women academics in the university? In your opinion, how do the current institutional culture and structures affect the promotion of women to leadership positions? As a male academic, what do you think are some of the gendered practices that negatively affect the career development of women academics?

The interview data were collected using voice recording devices that were subsequently transcribed and crosschecked with the voice recorded to ensure that the feedback of participants was correctly captured in the transcripts. To ensure the confidentiality of the information provided by participants, each participant was informed about the processes that would be used to safely process and store the data. Additionally, participants were informed not to provide any personal identifiers that could link them to the data. To increase the trustworthiness of the data collected, three major processes were followed. First, the methodical thoroughness of the research design (Rose & Johnson, 2020) was maintained by ensuring that the data collection process, the analysis of the data, and the discussion of the findings were consistent with the appropriate empirical procedure. Secondly, throughout the research, data credibility was maintained by following a repeated process of examining the data and codes from both male and female academics to ensure that their views were correctly captured and analyzed. Particularly, the codes were analyzed and discussed to reveal 1) the main ideas that emerged from the interviews regarding perceived gender inequalities in the university and 2) to describe the applicability of the research methods to future research (Rose & Johnson, 2020). The university's Research Ethics Committee approved this research. In line with the rules of ethical consideration, the rationale of the study, potential risks, and benefits as well as the right of participants were explained to all participants.

Data Analysis

The data were analyzed using thematic analysis that can be applied across different epistemologies and research questions (Nowell et al., 2017). Thematic analysis has been explained as a qualitative research method that is used for identifying, analyzing, organizing, describing, and reporting themes that emerge in a data set (Braun & Clarke, 2006; Nowell et al., 2017). Although various studies have explained the advantages of thematic analysis, its weakness includes a seeming lack of clear guidelines in its application (Nowell et al., 2017). To analyze the interview data, the first step was to read the transcripts to ensure that they were written with no language vagueness. The second step followed was to index the transcripts and to create respondent and cross-case memos based on the views of men and women participants. The third step involved the development of codes, categories, and themes. The basis for developing codes, categories and themes of the data gathered was to provide details about the characteristics of the dataset and the intended explanation of the study (Nowell et al., 2017).

In this study, the data were explored for important phrases and sentences from the participants that particularly addressed the issue of how perceived gender inequalities in the university constrain the career progression of female academics. To determine the best codes that characterize the views of participants, codes that appeared at least ten times or more were highlighted. Sample codes that emerged were: "there should be equal opportunities for men and women academics"; "the promotion policy does not discriminate between men and women academics"; and "promotion are based on merit". The fourth step involved collapsing the codes that were selected into categories. This involved grouping codes that

Gendered Cultures, Career Challenges of Women Academics

provided similar meanings. The fifth step involved identifying the themes based on the patterns developed from the codes and categories. Examples of the themes that emerged were: "weak collegial relationships and networks" and "weak academic nurturing culture." Therefore, by using the thematic framework, recurring patterns of meanings from the texts that emerged were grouped and analyzed according to the themes (Braun & Clarke, 2006).

FINDINGS

Six themes that emerged from the interview data analyzed are: gendered practices; promotion of women academics; earmark scholarships for women academics; gender inequalities and women's under-representation in leadership positions; academic nurturing culture; and collegial relationships and networks. The section also presents discussions on the differences and similarities between the perceptions of men and women academics concerning how gender inequalities constrain the career progression of women academics.

Women Academics

Gender inequalities and women's under-representation in leadership positions.

Gendered processes and practices consist of overt decisions and procedures that control, segregate, exclude, and build hierarchies in social settings grounded on race and class (Acker 1992). In HE settings, institutional cultures and gendered practices could affect the career progression of women academics in universities. This is because HE sectors continue to experience persistent forms of gender inequality (Hirsu et al. 2021; Macupe 2020) that are driven by institutional cultures, structure, and gendered practices. Some women participants shared their views about what they perceived as gendered practices in the university and how these practices constrain their professional practice and career progression. Excerpts below reflect the views of some women academics:

I have felt treated in specific ways because of my gender, age, and race. I have also felt treated as incompetent or as too young to be able to think. It emanates from the institutional culture. The authority of a man in a room is handled differently compared to the authority of a woman [Mia - early career academic].

Gendered practices are certainly an institutional culture issue. As a woman academic, you need to be assertive if you want your voice to be heard [Lethabo].

I believe that I would have been treated differently in my department if I was a man. The men in my department are advanced not because they are great teachers or have more research outputs, rather, I think that it is because they are men [Saartjie].

Some Participants also shared their opinion on how institutional structures and cultures influence women's academic leadership positions in the university. For instance, Palesa noted that more men could be found in leadership positions when compared to their women colleagues, "I see the top positions being filled by men than women. I want to see more women in the second tier of leadership and then after that, it would not matter too much" [Palesa].

The narrative of Mia suggests that other social identities such as age, race and social position shape the perceptions of women academics concerning how institutional culture affects their status and career. In the context of HEIs in South Africa, race, and gender represent some of the societal constructs that enhance or constrain women's participation in higher education (Maphalala and Mpofu 2017). Similarly, the views of Lethabo and Saartjie demonstrate some of the challenges some female academics face in their professional practice and work environment. In particular, the feedback from Saartjie shows that the privileges of men are sustained through institutional cultures and processes. A previous study has shown that while masculinity may be associated with power, strength, rationality, autonomy, control, and logic, femininity is associated with irrationality, passivity, care, nature, and emotion (Chappell & Waylen, 2013). The challenges shared by the participants are framed along formal and informal rules (Clavero & Galligan, 2020) as well as symbols, images, and ideologies that provide legitimacy to institutions (Acker, 1992).

Promotion of Women Academics

Promotion represents one of the important features of career development, and the objective career success of academics (Sutherland 2017). Some women participants shared their views concerning the relationship between gendered cultures and promotion in the university:

Although the promotion policy does not necessarily focus on the differences between men and women, we are not equal because some of us have other responsibilities that are overlooked [Saartjie].

As women academics, we are expected to run alongside our male colleagues at the same pace meanwhile, we have other responsibilities. Sadly, we do not get the expected support to be able to get promoted and build our careers [Mia].

Look, it is difficult for me to take leave and attend to my child when he is sick at home or take care of my son when the nanny is not well. Meanwhile I am expected to produce a certain number of articles to be promoted just like my men colleagues. We talk of being equal but, we are not all equal in terms of our additional responsibilities [Vivette].

The feedback from participants suggests that the promotion policy does not address the seeming challenges women academics face in combining different roles as well as the specific needs of women academics who have families in terms of their careers. Prior study has shown that women academics manage multiple roles that include teaching and research (Ramsey, 2021) and should be provided with support to develop their careers. This is also against the backdrop that teaching-heavy academic roles could adversely affect the capacity of women academics to produce research, and this has serious implications for their promotion because research enhances the chances of academics being promoted (Brabazon & Schulz, 2020).

Academic Nurturing Culture

The development of an academic nurturing culture for women academics especially through mentoring and coaching could enhance the career progression of female academics. Particularly, mentorship

Gendered Cultures, Career Challenges of Women Academics

for women academics is important in higher education because it serves to provide academics with the knowledge and skills needs for their professional practice (Oberhauser and Caretta 2019) through the support of established academics. The following are excerpts from the feedback of some participants:

We do not have adequate senior academics who can serve as mentors on this campus. I recently secured a funded programme on mentorship to help develop early career women academics. Unfortunately, I could not find mentors here. I was the only potential mentor [Elna].

I know that there are some good mentorship programmes currently running the university, but it is targeted and does not make provision for all academics. For an academic to be selected, she should be a high-flier and should have the attention of management to benefit from the targeted mentoring programmes. Remember that not everybody is going to be an A-rated scientist in the next five years [Rethabile].

I do not think that it is enough to only provide women academics with mentoring support if we intend to end inequity.......there are other important professional development programmes such as writing retreats and article writing training workshops that should be organized [Palesa].

The feedback from Elna revealed that the lack of mentors especially at the satellite campuses could adversely affect the career development of women academics. Similarly, the feedback from Rethabile suggests that the targeted mentoring arrangement only focused on a few academics. Although the narrative of Palesa represents some of the activities that could be implemented by the university to support the research and writing skills of women academics, such activities must be supported by institutional policy decisions. However, the feedback from all three participants reveals the importance of a nurturing academic culture in the university. A prior study by Brabazon and Schulz (2020) suggests that there should be more support for women academics especially through formal mentoring to tackle institutional gender equity challenges, increase their confidence in their professional practice and enhance their networking.

Collegial Relationships and Networks

Recent studies have shown that academics place significant value on their collegial relationships when making retention decisions (Miller & Youngs, 2021; Wijngaarden et al., 2020). Among women academics, collegial support is necessary for the development of women academics, particularly through group activities and discussions. For instance, Elna argued that "one of the challenges we currently have is the silos in which we operate not only as women academics but also as academics generally. I know that it is the culture of many universities, but we would have to address it properly." A similar opinion was shared by Mia who indicated that:

I think that the issue of networks and collegial relationships may be limited to academic groups or other groups. You need to first identify with the groups and so on…. There are also times I feel that there is a colleague who is doing excellently well and so I should approach that colleague to help me…you only get a no answer which suggests that the colleague is not ready to assist. We seem to be very busy and cannot create space for collaboration or what you may call collegial support and relationships.

While the feedback from Elna and Mia suggests some challenges in developing collegial relationships and networks, other participants such as Rethabile had different experiences:

There is a group of women black academics that meet to support each other in the area of research and career development. We support each other because the common thing in the group is that we all need support from each other [Rethabile].

Rethabile also explained that the objectives for the formation of the group include preparing black women academics to assume higher positions such as Deans and Deputy Deans. She added that "Everybody in the group is struggling in the positions that we find ourselves in, so it is important for us to share our experiences and learn from each other" [Rethabile]. The narratives of the participants revealed the importance of women groups to the career development of women academics. Another important finding is the clear objectives of the women groups that were highlighted by a participant. With these objectives, women participants can measure their success over a period.

Men Academics

Gendered Practices

There are perceived notions of male dominance and cultural influence on the career development of women academics. These include institutionalized cultures and sub-cultures that preserve male privilege, power, norms, values, and practices (Mergaert & Lombardo, 2014). Some male academics shared their opinion concerning gendered practices that adversely affect the career progression of female academics:

I do not think that our women colleagues have been marginalized or discriminated against. Remember that there are formal rules that govern the behaviour of students and staff in the university. To think that women academics are discriminated against by their male colleagues or excluded in decision-making processes is not accurate [Kamogelo].

A female colleague at one of our campuses had a bad experience with some young male students that bothered on intimidation. You know some of these young men think that they can take advantage of a woman. I took the case up at the faculty level as well as the institute [Johan].

I have not witnessed any form of discrimination against women academics at this university. Decisions that are made concerning our promotions, conditions of service, and others are for all academics [Bandile].

The responses from participants revealed mixed opinions. For instance, although intimidation as noted by Johan may not have a direct effect on the career progression of women academics, it could have a consequential effect on their psychological well-being and their ability to teach. However, while issues such as intimidation may not be common, it represents existing forms of gendered practices that could affect the ability of women to focus on their jobs and to deliver as expected. A prior study has shown that the culture of exclusion in HEIs includes silencing women's voices and male patterns of networking that affects the advancement of women (Toni & Moodly, 2019). Other narratives from some participants showed that women academics do not experience issues relating to discrimination or marginalization.

Gendered Cultures, Career Challenges of Women Academics

Promotion of Female Academics

The promotion of women academics in HE is important for their career development. Some participants challenged the assertion that women academics have been marginalized or discriminated against in terms of their promotion. The following narrative reflects the position of some participants:

I do not agree with the assertion that women academics in this university have been marginalized or discriminated against in terms of their promotion.....I am aware of the Emerging Scholar Accelerator Programme (ESAP) and the Future Generation Professoriate (FGP) programmes that have been designed to accelerate the promotion of Black Female academics to the professoriate [Sipho].

Speaking as a member of our department and faculty, I can testify that the promotion track is handled equally for males and females and that gender is no issue whatsoever in deciding who gets promoted. I think that the perception that men get promoted more easily than women and that overall, the career progression of women is not on the same track as males is false [Kamogelo].

The notion of meritocracy is flawed in a way. Sometimes the only way to achieve real transformation is through deliberate policy even if it sometimes means quotas; otherwise, the structural legacies of patriarchy will endure. I think that we can get enough capable women to fill positions throughout the strata of the university on merit. The university needs to be seen to be encouraging that as well [Adriaan].

The feedback from some participants suggests that the promotion of academics should be based on merit regardless of gender and that the university should create equal opportunities for men and women academics concerning promotion and career progression. However, other participants felt that the university should continue to support women academics to develop their careers and gain promotion. A prior study has revealed that progressive policies on gender equity have resulted in a few women academics rising to occupy leadership positions (Moodly & Toni, 2017).

Earmark Scholarships for Women Academics

Earmark scholarships for women academics in the university represent some of the institutional arrangements designed to support women to develop their careers. Some participants shared their views on how earmark scholarships for women academics could create new forms of inequality in the university while enhancing the career progression of female academics:

The majority of scholarships seem to be earmarked for women. I fear that this could create resentment amongst men academics [Lubanzi]

Historically black men have suffered the same way as women. It would be disadvantageous to get a new class of elite forced on us, regardless of our hard work.....that is unfair. Although I think that is very wrong, I do not dispute the fact that women academic staff should be supported. It must be done intelligently, without creating a new class. [Kamogelo].

Providing women academics with earmarked scholarships would be ushering them [women] in a certain direction...almost perceptively over their men counterparts [Thato]

The feedback from Lubanzi, Kamogelo, and Thato suggest were not in favour of targeted scholarships designed to support the career advancement of women academics. Contrastingly, other participants believed that the university should continuously support women academics through earmark scholarships and other targeted career development programmes. For instance, Johan argued that "I think that the special programmes designed to support the career development of women academics are very important. There should be awareness creation and open discussion...many of the times, we do not create the spaces for these conversations to happen in any meaningful way" [Johan]. However, while feedback from the majority of men participants pointed to the adverse effect of giving too much attention especially earmark scholarships to women academics at the expense of their male colleagues, it is important for the university to continuously support women academics through earmark scholarships.

Academic Nurturing Culture

While most universities in South Africa have developed policies on gender equity (Herbst, 2020; Maphalala & Mpofu, 2017), there is still a lot to be achieved in terms of developing an academic nurturing culture that could support the career development of women academics. For instance, Lubanzi noted that:

Some women academics do not have mentors. If there are no mentors for them, it means that they do not know where to go and from whom to get support. Therefore, we must have career progression programmes within the institution for our colleagues and ourselves [Lubanzi].

A similar view was shared by Johan who stated that "one of the challenges in many universities is the weak academic nurturing culture for young academics...not only women academics. As I indicated, there is the need for more conversations around this issue". One of the issues that could hinder women academics from achieving their full potential and taking advantage of special programmes to support them is their caregiving role. On his part, Sipho explained that "sometimes I think it is more difficult for women academics because they must raise children and fulfil their work obligations. Unfortunately, the university policies on promotion do not create special privileges for women academics". The views of Sipho reveal the multiple roles of women academics (Ramsey, 2021) and the need for the university to support their career progression. Also, the caregiving responsibilities of women in their families, low professional networks, weak mentoring structures and support, and challenges in producing research outputs (Maphalala & Mpofu, 2017) continue to affect the career progression of women academics.

DISCUSSION

The HE sector in South Africa is grappling with issues relating to gendered cultural practices, male dominance in academic leadership positions, the lack of policies that support the career advancement of women academics, and a lack of mentorship support for women academics. To address the issues related to the career progression of women academics, various interventions such as the provision of research grants, the creation of more opportunities in academic positions for women, and mentoring arrangements have been implemented (Maphalala & Mpofu, 2017; Naicker, 2013). While these interventions have focused on the features that confront women academics in their career progression, especially in the context of South Africa, very little was known about how perceived gender inequalities constrain the career progression of female academics from a feminist institutional theory approach. Again, by examining the six themes developed from the interview data, the current study sheds light on how the career progression of women academics is influenced by gendered cultures and inequalities.

The current study contributes to the literature on feminist institutional theory and gendered practices in HE by explaining four important features. First, institutional culture and structure are not only important to our understanding of how gendered processes and practices affect the career progression of women academics but also, they are directly linked to the transformation of institutions as spaces where gender equality could be enhanced. The findings of the current study revealed two major sources of perceived inequalities: a sub-culture of the university that recognizes the authority of men as important to the status quo and, a lack of strong interpersonal relationships. This is consistent with prior studies that suggest that gender equality and the career progression of women academics are embedded in the structure and culture of universities and are further shaped by individuals within the institution (Mergaert & Lombardo, 2014; O'Connor, 2020; Verge et al., 2018). Again, institutional features such as structure and culture explain how informal and formal rules and practices either enhance or constrain the career progression of women academics (O'Connor, 2020).

Secondly, the study revealed that other social identities such as age, race, and social position shape the perceptions of women academics concerning how institutional culture could affect their status and career progression. In the context of HEIs in South Africa, race and gender represent some of the societal constructs that enhance or constrain women's participation in higher education (Maphalala & Mpofu, 2017). Of cause the voices of the participants contribute to the increasing call for further research on gender inequalities in HE especially against the backdrop that the academic environment consists of intersecting systems of inequality (Breeze & Taylor, 2020) and gendered cultures that are preserved by men.

Thirdly, gender inequalities deepen institutionalized patriarchal system, constrain the career development of women academics, and limit the chances of women to occupy leadership positions. As mentioned in prior studies, an institutionalized patriarchal system elevates men to positions of leadership and status over women (Dlamini & Adams, 2014; Maphalala & Mpofu, 2017). Also, the slow pace of changes in the status quo, legitimating men-dominated structures and cultures, and the unwillingness of persons in authority to create structures that enhance women's representation in leadership positions (O'Connor, 2019) engender the under-representation of women academics in leadership positions. However, when women academics are offered the needed support to occupy leadership positions, it could shift the balance of institutional power from a predominantly men preserve to include women's representation in academic leadership positions. The current study argues that to reverse the current trend where male academics dominate leadership positions, especially at the department and faculty levels, there is the need for the university to first address the issues surrounding the informal rules and practices that elevates men to leadership positions over women. Secondly, women academics who aspire to take up leadership positions should be prepared through leadership training, mentoring, and institutional succession planning.

Lastly, the development of a strong academic nurturing culture and collegial relationships among women academics are essential to enhancing the career development of women academics. First, when the university focuses on supporting the career development of women academics through activities such as mentoring programmes, writing retreats, training programmes, and earmark scholarships, they could enhance their career progression. In essence, higher social resources by way of career support could lead to higher career success (Haenggli & Hirschi, 2020; Turban et al., 2017) among women academics. Secondly, there is the need for women academics to be encouraged to develop their careers through collegial relationships and women's career development groups. Through such collegial support which also serves as relational capital (Wijngaarden et al., 2020), women academics could develop networks and friendship that emerges from continuous interpersonal interaction among peers and different networks within and outside the university. Again, such collegial support will enable women academics to overcome gendered practices that are embedded in institutional cultures through the sharing of ideas and experiences.

LIMITATIONS AND FUTURE RESEARCH

The findings of the current study should be interpreted in light of two major limitations. First, the current study was conducted in a multicampus setting, which means that differences in the structure and subcultures of the different campuses and academic departments of the study setting may have influenced the responses given by some participants. The differences in the cultures of the multi campuses are also linked to the historical background of the university which is the outcome of a merger between a historically white university and a historically black university. Therefore, some responses of the participants could be based on the subculture of the campus and how staff make meaning of the link between the social setting and gender. Also, some of the findings may not apply to all departments in the university. Secondly, the use of feminist institutionalism as the theoretical underpinning of the current study limited our investigations to issues regarding institutional culture, structure, and practices within the university and how it constrains the career advancement of women academics. The use of other theories could provide additional insight into the different features that either enhance or constrain the career advancement of women academics. This study recommends that future studies should explore different theories to conduct a similar study.

CONCLUSION

The central issue explored in the current study has been how gender inequalities constrain the career progression of female academics in a South African university. The rationale for using feminist intuitionalism as the theoretical underpinning of the study yielded very important outcomes, especially by revealing how gendered practices constrain the career progression of women academics in the university. The findings of the current study revealed that gendered practices that are embedded in the structure and culture of the university constrain the career progression of women academics. These include: preferences for men academics in leadership positions at the department and faculty levels; social identities that shape the perceptions of women academics concerning how institutional culture could affect their status and career progression; weak academic nurturing culture; weak collegial relationships and networks among women academics and; the absence of the voices of women academics in the decision-making processes of some faculties.

The findings also include substantial differences between the perception of women and men academics concerning how gendered practices constrain the career progression of female academics in the university. While for both groups, weak academic nurturing culture in the university constrain the

Gendered Cultures, Career Challenges of Women Academics

career progression of female academics, some men participants raised concerns about how for instance, earmark scholarships, separate promotion tracks for women academics, and targeted mentoring arrangements could create a new class of elites and inequality. While both men and women academics decried the few women representations in academic leadership positions, the women academics attributed this development to preferences for male leadership positions based on culture and privileges as well as the lack of policies that address women's representation in leadership positions.

Although policies on gender equity have been introduced in South African Universities, what remains unchanged are the institutional cultures which include informal rules and norms that continue to constrain the career progression of women academics. To address these issues, universities must continuously support women academics to develop their careers through earmarked scholarships, continuous professional development programmes such as writing retreats and workshops, and targeted promotion of female academics to the professoriate. Also, the current study argues that universities must organize programmes not only for female academics but also for male academics to explain the importance of encouraging and supporting female academics to develop their careers in the universities. Lastly, continuous open conversations around the need to further support the career progression of female academics in the university will help to address the issues concerning gender inequalities.

REFERENCES

Acker, J. (1992). From sex roles to gendered institutions. *Contemporary Sociology*, *21*(5), 565–569. doi:10.2307/2075528

Alabi, O. J., Seedat-Khan, M., & Abdullahi, A. A. (2019). The lived experiences of postgraduate female students at the University of Kwazulu Natal, Durban, South Africa. *Heliyon*, *5*(11), e02731. doi:10.1016/j.heliyon.2019.e02731 PMID:31763469

Angervall, P. (2018). The academic career: A study of subjectivity, gender and movement among women university lecturers. *Gender and Education*, *30*(1), 105–118. doi:10.1080/09540253.2016.1184234

Bodalina, K. N., & Mestry, R. (2022). A case study of the experiences of women leaders in senior leadership positions in the education district offices. *Educational Management Administration & Leadership*, *50*(3), 452–468. doi:10.1177/1741143220940320

Brabazon, T., & Schulz, S. (2020). Braving the bull: Women, mentoring and leadership in higher education. *Gender and Education*, *32*(7), 873–890. doi:10.1080/09540253.2018.1544362

Braun, V., & Clarke, V. (2006). Using thematic analysis in psychology. *Qualitative Research in Psychology*, *3*(2), 77–101. doi:10.1191/1478088706qp063oa

Breeze, M., & Taylor, Y. (2020). Feminist collaborations in higher education: Stretched across career stages. *Gender and Education*, *32*(3), 412–428. doi:10.1080/09540253.2018.1471197

Chappell, L., & Waylen, G. (2013). Gender and the hidden life of institutions. *Public Administration*, *91*(3), 599–615. doi:10.1111/j.1467-9299.2012.02104.x

Clavero, S., & Galligan, Y. (2020). Analysing gender and institutional change in academia: Evaluating the utility of feminist institutionalist approaches. *Journal of Higher Education Policy and Management*, *42*(6), 650–666. doi:10.1080/1360080X.2020.1733736

Department of Education. (1997). *Education White Paper 3: A programme for the transformation of higher education (Notice 1196 of 1997)*. Pretoria: Department of Education, South Africa.

Department of Higher Education and Training. (2019). *Report of the Ministerial Task Team on the Recruitment, Retention and Progression of Black South African Academics*. DST. https://www.dst.gov.za/images/2020/02/Report_MTT_RRP_of_Black_Academics_web_final1.pdf

European Commission. (2019). *SHE Figures 2018. Directorate-General for Research and Innovation*. European Union.

Haenggli, M., & Hirschi, A. (2020). Career adaptability and career success in the context of a broader career resources framework. *Journal of Vocational Behavior*, *119*, 103414. doi:10.1016/j.jvb.2020.103414

Herbst, T. H. (2020). Gender differences in self-perception accuracy: The confidence gap and women leaders' underrepresentation in academia. *SA Journal of Industrial Psychology*, *46*(1), 1–8. https://hdl.handle.net/10520/EJC-1f3d5b9f20. doi:10.4102ajip.v46i0.1704

Heslin, P. A., Keating, L. A., & Minbashian, A. (2019). How situational cues and mindset dynamics shape personality effects on career outcomes. *Journal of Management*, *45*(5), 2101–2131. doi:10.1177/0149206318755302

Hirsu, L., Quezada-Reyes, Z., & Hashemi, L. (2021). Moving SDG5 forward: Women's public engagement activities in higher education. *Higher Education*, *81*(1), 51–67. doi:10.100710734-020-00597-0 PMID:34866648

Kanter, R. M. (1977). Some effects of proportions on group life: Skewed sex ratios and responses to token women. *American Journal of Sociology*, *82*(5), 965–990. doi:10.1086/226425

Mabokela, R. O. (2002). Reflections of black women faculty in South African universities. *Review of Higher Education*, *25*(2), 185–205. doi:10.1353/rhe.2002.0004

Mackay, F. (2011). Conclusion: Towards a feminist institutionalism? In M. L. Krook & F. Mackay (Eds.), *Gender, Politics and Institutions: Towards a Feminist Institutionalism* (pp. 181–196). Palgrave Macmillan. doi:10.1057/9780230303911_11

Mackay, F., Kenny, M., & Chappell, L. (2010). New institutionalism through a gender lens: Towards a feminist institutionalism? *International Political Science Review*, *31*(5), 573–588. doi:10.1177/0192512110388788

Macupe, B. (2020). Few women leaders in academia. *Mail & Guardian Online*. https://mg.co.za/education/2020-08-20-few-women-leaders-in-academia/

Maphalala, M. C., & Mpofu, N. (2017). Are we there yet? A literature study of the challenges of women academics in institutions of higher education. *Gender & Behaviour*, *15*(2), 9216–9224. https://hdl.handle.net/10520/EJC-b41b93666

Mergaert, L., & Lombardo, E. (2014). Resistance to implementing gender mainstreaming in EU research policy. *European Integration Online Papers, 18*(1), 1–21. http://eiop.or.at/eiop/texte/2014-005a.htm

Miller, J. M., & Youngs, P. (2021). Person-organization fit and first-year teacher retention in the United States. *Teaching and Teacher Education, 97*, 103226. doi:10.1016/j.tate.2020.103226

Moodly, A. L., & Toni, N. M. (2017). Gender equity in South African higher education leadership: Where are we twenty years after democracy? *Journal of Social Sciences, 31*(3), 138–153. doi:10.20853/31-3-917

Naicker, L. (2013). The journey of South African women academics with a particular focus on women academics in theological education. *Studia Historiae Ecclesiasticae, 39*, 325–336.

Nowell, L. S., Norris, J. M., White, D. E., & Moules, N. J. (2017). Thematic analysis: Striving to meet the trustworthiness criteria. *International Journal of Qualitative Methods, 16*(1), 1–13. doi:10.1177/1609406917733847

O'Connor, P. (2019). Gender imbalance in senior positions in higher education: What is the problem? What can be done? *Policy Reviews in Higher Education, 3*(1), 28–50. doi:10.1080/23322969.2018.1552084

O'Connor, P. (2020). Why is it so difficult to reduce gender inequality in male-dominated higher educational organizations? A feminist institutional perspective. *Interdisciplinary Science Reviews, 45*(2), 207–228. doi:10.1080/03080188.2020.1737903

Oberhauser, A. M., & Caretta, M. A. (2019). Mentoring early career women geographers in the neoliberal academy: Dialogue, reflexivity, and ethics of care. *Geografiska Annaler. Series B, Human Geography, 101*(1), 56–67. doi:10.1080/04353684.2018.1556566

Ramsey, L. R. (2021). A Strong Teacher Identity May Buffer Woman-Scientist Identity Interference: Preliminary Evidence from a Teaching-Intensive University. *Gender Issues, 38*(1), 65–78. doi:10.100712147-020-09254-3

Republic of South Africa. (1998). *Employment Equity Act, 1998*. Republic of South Africa. https://www.gov.za/sites/default/files/gcis_document/201409/a55-980.pdf. Accessed on 1/7/2021

Republic of South Africa. (2003). *Promotion of Equality and Prevention of Unfair Discrimination Amendment Act of 2000*. Republic of South Africa. https://www.justice.gov.za/legislation/acts/2000-004.pdf

Republic of South Africa. (2013). *Women's Empowerment and Gender Equality Bill*. Republic of South Africa. https://www.gov.za/sites/default/files/gcis_document/201409/b50-2013womenempowerment-genderequality06nov2013.pdf. Accessed on 1/7/2021

Reynolds, P. J., & Henderson, E. F. (2023). Gender and the symbolic power of academic conferences in fictional texts. *Higher Education Research & Development, 42*(3), 728–741. doi:10.1080/07294360.2022.2089097

Rose, J., & Johnson, C. W. (2020). Contextualizing reliability and validity in qualitative research: Toward more rigorous and trustworthy qualitative social science in leisure research. *Journal of Leisure Research, 51*(4), 432–451. doi:10.1080/00222216.2020.1722042

Subbaye, R., & Vithal, R. (2017). Gender, teaching and academic promotions in higher education. *Gender and Education*, *29*(7), 926–951. doi:10.1080/09540253.2016.1184237

Sutherland, K. A. (2017). Constructions of success in academia: An early career perspective. *Studies in Higher Education*, *42*(4), 743–759. doi:10.1080/03075079.2015.1072150

The African Union Commission. (2021). *Goals & Priority Areas of Agenda 2063*. The African Union Commission. https://au.int/agenda2063/goals. Accessed on 1/07/2021

Toni, N. M., & Moodly, A. L. (2019). Do institutional cultures serve as impediments for women's advancement towards leadership in South African higher education? *South African Journal of Higher Education*, *33*(3), 176–191. doi:10.20853/33-3-3137

Turban, D. B., Moake, T. R., Wu, S. Y. H., & Cheung, Y. H. (2017). Linking extroversion and proactive personality to career success: The role of mentoring received and knowledge. *Journal of Career Development*, *44*(1), 20–33. doi:10.1177/0894845316633788

United Nations. (2021). *Department of Economic and Social Affairs Sustainable Development*. UN. https://sdgs.un.org/goals/goal5

Verge, T., Ferrer-Fons, M., & González, M. J. (2018). Resistance to mainstreaming gender into the higher education curriculum. *European Journal of Women's Studies*, *25*(1), 86–101. doi:10.1177/1350506816688237

Walker, C., & Gleaves, A. (2016). Constructing the caring higher education teacher: A theoretical framework. *Teaching and Teacher Education*, *54*, 65–76. doi:10.1016/j.tate.2015.11.013

Wijngaarden, Y., Hitters, E., & Bhansing, P. V. (2020). Cultivating fertile learning grounds: Collegiality, tacit knowledge and innovation in creative co-working spaces. *Geoforum*, *109*, 86–94. doi:10.1016/j.geoforum.2020.01.005

Chapter 9

Nurturing and Empowering of Women in Leadership Positions:
A Study With Special Reference to the Indian Subcontinent

Oindrila Chakraborty

J.D. Birla Institute, India

ABSTRACT

The philosophical dimensions of women's empowerment and nurture in all spheres of life will be addressed in this chapter. Additionally, there will be an effort to look at the problems and obstacles those women's empowerment faces both globally and on the Indian subcontinent. Another endeavor would be launched to examine the situation in the Indian Subcontinent with a small survey of women in senior roles across several industries. The chapter also provided instances of empowered women from the Indian subcontinent.

INTRODUCTION

In global scenario, women's roles are changing dramatically. In practicality, every profession today, whether it is in the kitchen or in the armed forces, women and men share the same podium with equal rights. Working women are no longer an anomaly and are increasingly seen as essential workers. The proportion of women in managerial positions has steadily increased in Indian businesses and educational institutions just like many other neighbouring countries, and this trend is likely to sustain into the future. The women in educational administration are no exception. It has not been without significant personal sacrifice for the Indian ladies to evolve from the enigmatic figures, draped in metres of cloth, called Saree to the educated, prosperous, and accomplished professional that they are today. This picture is as vivid and lively as the difficult journey they had to get where they have reached. These are women who have broken free from manacles that date back thousands of years, who have travelled in the uncharted territory, who have the guts to start over, and who are willing to bear the consequences of their decisions. Although there have been some minor gains because of this sea-change in the positions and proportions,

DOI: 10.4018/978-1-6684-8597-2.ch009

Copyright © 2023, IGI Global. Copying or distributing in print or electronic forms without written permission of IGI Global is prohibited.

Nurturing and Empowering of Women in Leadership Positions

there are still very few women holding high-quality leadership and managerial positions in higher education and other significant areas, and this is a major concern from an equity standpoint (HESA, 2010). In order to understand the leadership abilities and traits that women bring to top leadership roles, it is crucial to study those who have already been successful in doing so. The qualities of encouraging academic settings, where women's ability for academic, corporate and political leadership is acknowledged and celebrated, must also be emphasised (Airini et al., 2011). In order to identify leadership styles and significant aspects of organisational contexts and cultures, as well as factors that encouraged and supported women in leadership roles or hindered and dissuaded them from taking on such roles, the research sought to examine the nature of women's leadership for the type of work undertaken, and relationships with co-workers and senior management in academia and other essential zones (Griffiths, 2009).

Nowadays, most of the institutions across the world are going through a pressing need for the deliberate preparation of future leaders for higher education and other related fields, especially women leaders. Due to the dearth of women in leadership roles, a lot of schools & universities and corporate positions are currently attempting to build programmes those enhance the gender-based leadership abilities of faculty, staff, and administrators. Special attention must be paid to the advancement of women in these programmes. However, in order to do so properly and efficiently, different support programmes are also being designed.

MAIN FOCUS OF THE CHAPTER

This chapter would seek answers for the conceptual facets of women empowerment and nurturing. Also, it would like to explore different theoretical and practical aspects of women empowerment in academia and other essential arenas. Also, there would be an endeavour to investigate the issues and challenges related to women's empowerment globally as well as in Indian subcontinents. There would be another initiative to check the scenario in Indian subcontinents with a minuscule survey with women in leadership positions from various fields like academia and research (Higher Education), medical, law, entrepreneurial ventures, media (including social media), and journalism. The main purpose of the chapter is to explore the journey of these successful women (the representing sample) aka leaders through their own eyes, unveiling the practical scenario in the developing countries. Figure 1 is portraying the purpose of the chapter in a concise manner.

The sample profile of the respondents has been given in Table 1, showing the sample distribution across the countries, while Table 2, Table 3 and Table 4 are showing their age, education and profession, respectively. Figure 2 and Figure 3 showcase the profile of the respondents. This chapter primarily deals with following research questions:

1. What are the conceptual and theoretical facets of women empowerment?
2. What are the determinants of women empowerment globally?
3. Are the determinants same or different in Indian Subcontinents?
4. How the women are dealing with the problems and challenges in the Indian subcontinent?
5. What are the initiatives taken in these countries to deal with the problems of women empowerment?

Nurturing and Empowering of Women in Leadership Positions

Figure 1. Showing the purpose of the chapter

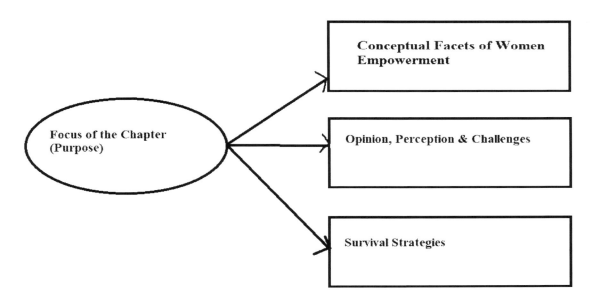

Figure 2. Showing the professional categories of the respondents

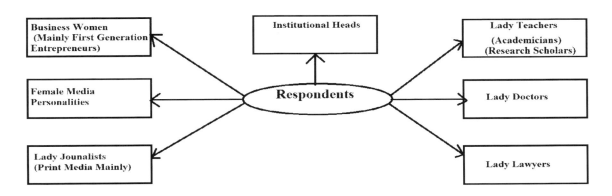

Table 1. Showing the sample distribution over the countries

Country	Number of Respondents
India	84
Pakistan	23
Bangladesh	45
Nepal	62
Bhutan	12
Total	226

Nurturing and Empowering of Women in Leadership Positions

Table 2. Showing the age distribution of the respondents

Age	Number of Respondents
25-35	102
36-45	68
46-55	50
56 and above	6
Total	226

Table 3. Showing the educational qualifications of the respondents

Education	Number of Respondents
Under Graduate	36
Post Graduate	112
Doctorate	78
Total	226

Table 4. Showing the profession of the respondents

Profession	Number of Respondents
Academia and Research	96
Medical	35
Law	20
Entrepreneurial Venture	35
Media	15
Journalism	25
Total	226

Figure 3. Showing the profession of the respondents

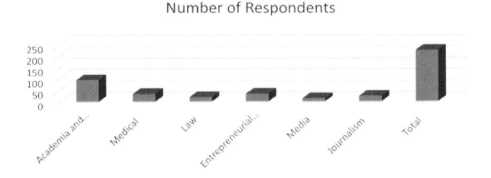

BACKGROUND OF WOMEN EMPOWERMENT AND LEADERSHIP IN GLOBAL SCENARIO

Women empowerment and leadership in various fields including academia, have gained significant attention and thrust in recent years since, more and more individuals and organizations recognize the need to address gender inequality and promote the full participation and representation of women in various sectors due to the global pressure for gender equality. There is also a need to identify the unique problems and challenges of the gender under question. Historically, women have faced significant barriers in accessing education and leadership roles, but various intrinsic and extrinsic efforts have been made to address these issues over the years.

Historical Context

In the past, women were often excluded from educational opportunities, and their access to leadership roles in academia and several related fields was severely limited. The societal structure in ancient India and surrounding countries was predominantly patriarchal, where women's roles were often confined to domestic duties and child-rearing. Women were involved in religious rituals and were respected as custodians of culture and knowledge within the purview of their households. However, some ancient texts like the Rigveda did recognize the importance of women and their contributions to society (Ghosh, 2017). But medieval period in the Indian subcontinent saw a further subsequent and vivid decline in women's status due to the influence of certain religious and cultural practices. Purdah (seclusion) and sati (widow self-immolation) were some of those practices, which severely restricted women's autonomy and agency (Sen, 2006). The Bhakti movement, on the other hand, provided a platform for some women to challenge societal norms and contribute to spiritual and literary spheres (SarDesai, 2013). The British colonial rule in the Indian Subcontinent suddenly brought both positive and negative impacts on women's empowerment and acted as an impetus for upliftment of the society. On one hand, the spread of western education and exposure to feminist idealism inspired some Indian women to advocate for women's rights and on the other hand, the oriental women started blindly emulating the western ones without any profound contemplation (Chaudhuri, 1990). Raja Ram Mohan Roy and Ishwar Chandra Vidyasagar were some of the prominent figures who championed women's education and social reforms during this phase. With this, the situation gradually began to change as societies moved towards the recognition of the importance of women's education and active contributions to various fields. The gradual and steady progress of women empowerment started rolling with a slow pace in 19th century, opening the doors of education to the women of different spectrums of the society. Though the actual opportunity of highest level of education was only available to a handful of elite class women (Chaudhuri, 1990).

Women's Education and Access to Leadership Positions

Efforts to promote women's education and enhancement in their participation in academia gained a rapid momentum in the 20th century. This included campaigns for girls' education, the establishment of women's colleges and universities, and the inclusion of women in mainstream educational institutions. The struggle for independence in India and surrounding countries in the early 20th century provided a platform for women to participate in the nationalist movement actively. Women like Sarojini Naidu, Annie Besant, and Kamala Nehru played pivotal roles in the fight for freedom and contributed to raising awareness about women's rights and empowerment in India and neighbouring countries (Das,1993). Globally, the first wave of feminism emerged in the late 19th and early 20th centuries, focusing on securing the basic civil and political rights for women, such as the right to vote and access to education. Women's suffrage movements in countries like the United States, the United Kingdom, and New Zealand achieved significant milestones during this period as well (Offen, 1988). The second wave of feminism, starting in the 1960s, brought attention to broader issues such as reproductive rights, workplace discrimination, and gender roles in society. The publication of Betty Friedan's "The Feminine Mystique" in 1963 ignited discussions about women's dissatisfaction with traditional domestic roles and their aspirations for greater autonomy and opportunities (Friedan, 1963). The global women's movement gained further momentum in the 1990s with the United Nations' Fourth World Conference on Women held in Beijing in 1995. The conference led to the adoption of the Beijing Declaration and Platform for Action, which outlined a comprehensive framework for promoting gender equality and women's empowerment worldwide (United Nations, 1995). As a result, the number of women pursuing higher education and academic careers started growing steadily over time (Sekhar, 2014). But in Indian subcontinents the picture was not that rosy, as women were still confronting cultural and societal norms, which discouraged their pursuit of higher education and leadership roles due to religious or social belief (Malhotra et al., 2007). Not only norms and beliefs, stereotypes about women's abilities and traditional gender roles often were hindering their progress in academia along other fields. However, with the rise of women's movements and increasing awareness about gender equality, these barriers have been challenged. Though the leadership positions have been still evasive for the women, while progress has been made in increasing the representation of women in academia and other significant sectors (United Nations Development Programme, 2019). There is still a substantial gender gap, especially at the highest leadership levels. This is owing to women's consistent under-representation in senior administrative and leadership positions such as university or business presidents, deans, department heads, and team leader positions. Despite tremendous improvements in education and the labour market in recent decades, the scenario did not change much. In the United States, for example, women occupy only 26.4% of college and university presidency (Cook, 2011). The reason lies in the fact that, women are less likely than men to be perceived as leaders, even when they demonstrate the same leadership behaviours (Eagly and Karau, 1991). This is because of the role congruity theory, which suggests that people have stereotypes about what it means to be a leader, and these stereotypes are often inconsistent with the female gender role (Eagly and Karau, 2002). However,

Nurturing and Empowering of Women in Leadership Positions

efforts are going on to promote gender diversity in leadership roles. To encourage women empowerment and leadership in specific sectors including academia, many institutions have implemented gender equity initiatives (UNICEF, 2007). These initiatives may include policies to support work-life balance, targeted recruitment and retention efforts for women faculty and staffs, mentoring programmes, and measures to address unconscious bias in the macro level (United Nations, 2015). Global initiatives and movements to promote women's empowerment and leadership, including the Beijing Declaration, Millennium Development Goals, and Sustainable Development Goals aim to advance women's rights in education, healthcare, political participation, and economic empowerment as large scale initiatives at macro level (United Nations, 2015 and 2019). Academic research on women and their roles plays a crucial role in shaping changes and driving attention towards leadership roles in micro level as well (Tong, 1998; Eagly and Carli, 2007). Encouraging women scholars to publish their work and participate in research projects has become essential in increasing their visibility and impact (Brescoll, 2015). Along with academic progress in micro level, several small inclusive progresses like Supportive networks and organizations, focusing on empowering women, providing mentors, network opportunities, and resources to help women navigate challenges and advance in their academic careers through empathetic hand holding are taking places (Dworkin, and Allen, 2006; Bhattacharjee and Pal, 2008). These platforms also bring together prominent women leaders to inspire the next generation and frame an inclusive leadership practice to pursue their ambitions fearlessly (UN Women, 2023). In addition to this, Political leadership for women empowerment has seen significant progress, with notable figures like Kamala Harris becoming the first female Vice President of the US and Ursula von der Leyen becoming the first female President of the European Commission. Countries like Rwanda and Bolivia have implemented gender quotas to increase women's participation in politics (United Nations, 2019). In the business world, women's leadership skills, communication skills, and emotional intelligence have been recognized (Kulkarni and Mishra, 2022). Companies with diverse and gender-neutral leadership teams are performing better, increasing productivity, collaboration, organizational dedication, and fairness (Athal, 2019; Eagly, 2023). However, significant challenges remain, such as discrimination and inequality in education, including politics, and science, technology, engineering, and mathematics (STEM) fields, healthcare, and economic opportunities (National Academies of Sciences, Engineering, and Medicine, 2018; National Center for Women & Information Technology, 2020). Despite efforts to promote gender equality and women's leadership in academia, women still face discrimination and inequality in various aspects of their lives. Efforts to increase women's representation in senior leadership roles, address gender bias and discrimination, and support women in humanities and social sciences are crucial for building a diverse and inclusive community (American Association of University Professors- AAUP, 2018).

THEORETICAL CONCEPTS AND LITERATURE REVIEW RELATED TO WOMEN EMPOWERMENT

Women empowerment is a multidimensional concept that refers to the process of providing women with the necessary tools, resources, and opportunities to enable them to participate fully in economic, social, and political spheres of society. The concept of women empowerment has gained significant attention in recent years due to its potential to improve the lives of women and their families, and its positive impact on economic development and social well-being.

Several studies have examined the concept of women empowerment from different perspectives. For instance, Kabeer (1999) identified three interrelated components of women empowerment, including *agency*, *resources*, and *achievements*. Agency refers to the ability of women to make decisions and take actions that affect their lives. Resources refer to the economic and social resources that women need to exercise their agency effectively. Achievements refer to the outcomes of women's actions, such as improved economic status and social well-being. Another important aspect of women empowerment is gender equality. According to the United Nations (2015), gender equality is the key to women empowerment, and it refers to the equal rights, opportunities, and treatment of women and men in all aspects of life. Gender inequality is a pervasive problem in many countries, and it affects women's access to education, healthcare, employment, and political participation. Women's economic empowerment is also a critical aspect of women empowerment. Women's economic empowerment refers to the process of enabling women to participate fully in the economy by providing them with access to resources, markets, and economic opportunities. Women's economic empowerment has the potential to reduce poverty, promote economic growth, and enhance women's overall well-being (World Bank, 2016). Women's empowerment has become a critical issue globally, as evidenced by the adoption of the United Nations Sustainable Development Goal (SDG) 5, which aims to achieve gender equality and empower all women and girls by 2030. Scholars have emphasized the importance of women's empowerment for promoting economic growth, reducing poverty, and improving social well-being. Several studies have examined the factors that influence women's empowerment in order to find a suitable solution. For instance, Mahmud et al. (2012) found that women's access to education, employment, and healthcare were critical determinants of women's empowerment. Similarly, Nave and Persson (2019) found that women's participation in decision-making processes, access to resources, and social support were key factors in promoting women's empowerment. Women's access to resources, especially economic resources has colossal impact on some of the studies. According to Kabeer (2015), women's economic empowerment involves not only increasing women's access to income-generating activities but also addressing the structural barriers that limit women's participation in economic activities. Kabeer suggested that policies and programmes that focus on improving women's access to markets, credit, and training can be effective in promoting women's economic empowerment. But economic empowerment is not only the solution for liberating women from their years of figurative confinement. One of the significant aspects of women's empowerment, which could liberate them, is political participation. Several studies have shown that women's participation in political processes can promote gender equality and women's empowerment. For instance, Feres and Gomes (2019) found that women's participation in local politics increased women's access to healthcare, education, and other public services. The sustainable development demands for women's empowerment, as it would reduce poverty, and promote gender equality. Along with economic empowerment and political empowerment another significant aspect of women's empowerment is education. Several studies have shown that women's education is positively associated with women's empowerment. For instance, Rahman et al. (2021) found that women's education was a key predictor of women's empowerment in rural Bangladesh. Similarly, Durrani et al. (2021) found that women's education was positively associated with women's economic empowerment. Similarly, another key element to strengthen women's empowerment is women's participation in the labour force. Women's participation in labour force has enhanced magnificently in global scenario in recent decades, but women still face significant challenges in accessing quality jobs and earning equal pay for equal work. Chaudhary et al. (2021) found that women's participation in the informal sector was positively

Nurturing and Empowering of Women in Leadership Positions

associated with women's economic empowerment. Similarly, Guo and Tsai (2021) found that women's participation in the labour force was positively associated with women's political empowerment.

Women's empowerment is also closely related to gender-based violence. Gender-based violence is a pervasive problem globally, and it limits women's access to education, employment, and other resources. Several studies have shown that interventions which address gender-based violence can promote women's empowerment. For instance, García-Moreno et al. (2015) found that a community-based intervention in Uganda that addressed gender-based violence and women's empowerment improved women's economic status and reduced their experience of intimate partner violence. The extent of covert politics with the successful women leaders is also insufficiently investigated barring a few. There is enough literature support for unnecessary burden on women leaders to perform unrealistically during crises, pressurizing them to a failing proposition because of gender bias, discrimination and stereotyping. They are likely to be replaced frequently than their male counterparts with less scope given to them to justify their worth (Jiang and Luo, 2021; Ovadia and Brawer, 2021). Though they have been proven to be better leaders with improved firm performance in long run, in case they have been able to sustain their professional positions, especially with superior record of employee job satisfaction, financial performance and organizational outcomes (Bechmann et al., 2020; Salgado et al. 2021). They are assisting in increasing women's representation in corporate world in top leadership positions (Huang and Kisgen, 2021). This is due to the transformational leadership style of the women leaders associated with their work-related outcomes such as job satisfaction and organizational commitment (Karakas et al., 2021). Not only transformational leadership style, women leaders are also found to be better in certain traits than the male counterparts. Baldissarri and Piccoli (2021) found that women leaders were rated higher than men on communal leadership competencies (such as team-building and communication skills) hinting towards their continuous success stories. But the predicaments are also equally challenging than their male counterparts, if not more. In the article "The Glass Cliff: Evidence that Women are Over-Represented in Precarious Leadership Positions" by Ryan and Haslam (2005), the authors investigated the phenomenon of the "glass cliff," which refers to the tendency for women to be appointed to the leadership positions that are precarious and have a high risk of failure. The study indicates to the trend of women being more likely to be appointed to the leadership positions during times of crisis or when organizations are facing challenges. The concept of the glass cliff is a counterpart to the well-known "glass-ceiling," which refers to the invisible barriers that prevent women from reaching higher-level positions in the corporate world. The glass cliff hypothesis suggests that women are often promoted to leadership roles in difficult and risky situations, which may have a higher likelihood of failure and increased chances of criticism. The research involved analysing historical data on company performance and leadership appointments and also conducting experiments to gauge people's perceptions and attitudes toward leadership appointments in different contexts. The research raised questions about the role of unconscious biases and gender stereotypes in the selection of leaders and some Key issues like over-representation of women in risky situations, stereotyping women to be more skilled in difficult situation with feminine attributes like empathy, collaboration, and nurturing traits and being subjected to harsher criticism in case of failure. As a whole, women's empowerment is a process with improving women's access to education, employment, and other resources, addressing gender-based violence, and promoting women's participation in political, social, labour force and other spheres of society and thus promoting sustainable development. Figure 4 and 5 depict the literature-based determinants and challenges in a global scenario.

Figure 4. Showing the determinants of women empowerment as per the literature

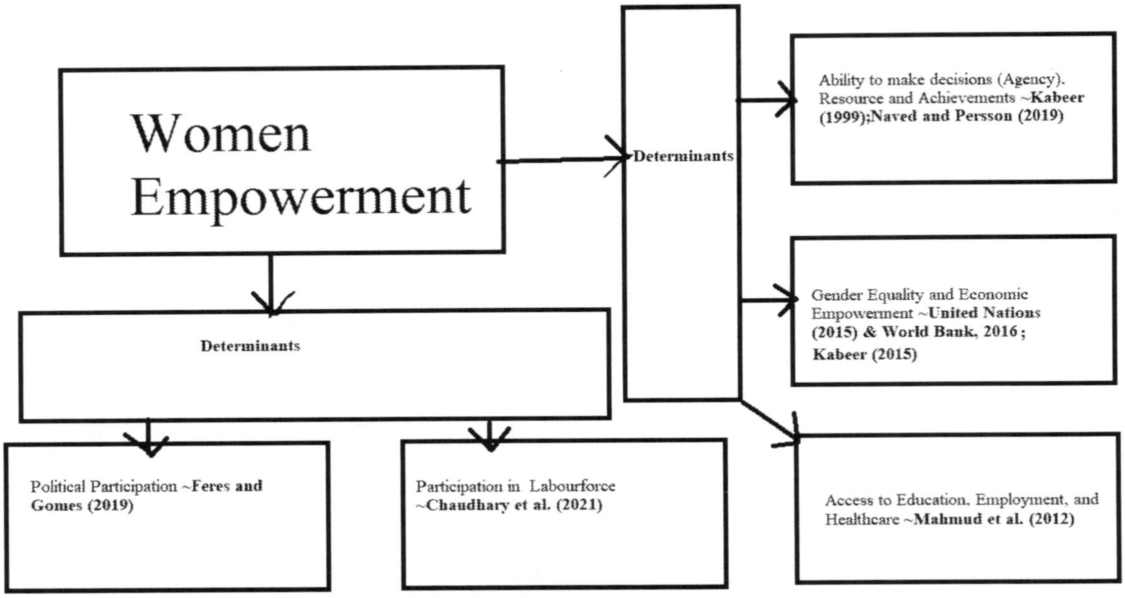

Figure 5. Showing the challenges of women empowerment as per the literature

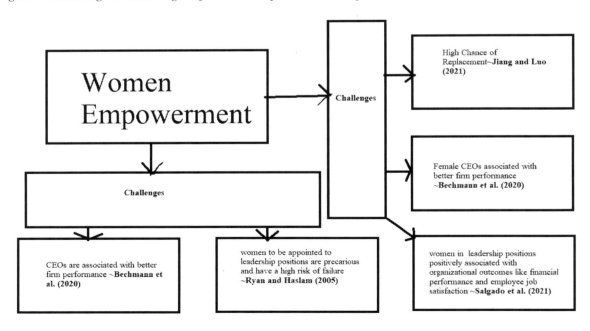

ISSUES, PROBLEMS, AND CHALLENGES IN WOMEN EMPOWERMENT

While significant progress has been made in women's empowerment in recent years, many challenges still exist. Some issues, problems, and challenges like gender-based violence, gender-based discrimination, limited access to healthcare for women, less economic empowerment, lack of political representation by women leaders, restrictive cultural and social norms, challenging gender roles, lack of Inclusion etc. still persisting in Indian subcontinents. These areas are often being matter of interest to the academicians:

Gender-Based Violence

Gender-based violence remains to be one of the most significant challenges faced by women globally. Women are at a higher risk of experiencing physical and sexual violence than men, not only at home but also at workplace. This issue is particularly prevalent in developing countries where women's rights are often violated, especially in Islamic countries and lower economic strata of the society. The condition is a bit hashed up in comparatively higher economic strata and secular countries but still reported to exist. Though quite comparatively less reported or unreported, domestic violence is not uncommon in fast worlds. There are enough literature supports for this issue. A study by Heise et al. (2019) found that one in three women worldwide have experienced physical or sexual violence at some point in their lives. As per another study, the issue is particularly prevalent in developing countries, where women's rights are often not respected (Krug et al., 2002).

Discrimination

Discrimination against women is still prevalent in many societies, and this can take many forms, including pay inequality, limited access to education, and job opportunities, among others. A study by the World Bank (2020) found that women globally earn 16% less than men for the same work. This inequality can limit women's economic opportunities and hinder their ability to participate fully in society and it is a proof that discrimination against women is still prevalent in many societies.

Lack of Access to Education

Women in many parts of the world still face significant barriers to access education. These barriers include cultural practices, poverty, and inadequate educational infrastructure. A study by UNESCO (2015) found that 31 million girls of primary school age were out of school worldwide. Access to education is the most essential aspect for women's empowerment and growth. However, many barriers to education exist for women, particularly in developing countries.

Limited Access to Healthcare

Women in many countries face significant challenges accessing healthcare services. These challenges can include cultural barriers, inadequate health infrastructure, and a lack of trained healthcare professionals. Rural areas are more prone to such kind of problems due to lack of awareness and facilities (UN Women, 2020).

Economic Empowerment

Women continue to face significant challenges in the economic arena, including limited access to credit, unequal pay, and limited job opportunities. (Kabeer, 2019).

Lack of Political Representation

Women are still underrepresented in political leadership positions globally. This lack of representation hinders progress towards gender equality and can result in policies that do not reflect women's interests. According to the Inter-Parliamentary Union (2021), women hold only 25.5% of parliamentary seats worldwide, which are unfortunate scenarios to represent women' position globally.

Cultural and Social Norms

Cultural and social norms can significantly impact women's empowerment. Practices like early marriage, female genital mutilation, and other harmful practices can prevent women from reaching their full potential (UNICEF, 2020).

Challenging Gender Roles

There are some difficult gender roles, stereotypically excepted from women because of gender bias in patriarchal society. A study by Benschop and Brouns (2021) found that women leaders in academia continue to face challenges related to gender bias, including gender stereotyping and discrimination. The study suggests that these challenges can be mitigated through the implementation of diversity and inclusion policies and practices.

Lack of Inclusion

Chatterjee (2017) found that empowering women in leadership positions is important in the Indian context to increase the horizon of inclusivity. According to Chatterjee (2017), cultural and societal norms are significant barriers to empowering women in leadership positions in India. Mukherjee and Majumdar (2020) conducted a literature review on women in leadership roles in Indian organizations and highlighted the need for organizations to create gender-sensitive policies and practices to empower women in leadership roles. Ahuja and Chawla (2021) examined the context of women in leadership positions in India. They emphasize the importance of creating a supportive work environment for women in leadership positions in India.

Glass-Ceiling, Non-Acceptance, and Work-Life Balance

According to Kumar (2018), women in leadership positions in India face significant issues and challenges because of glass-ceiling and non-acceptance both at home and workplace. Kumar (2018) argued that women in leadership positions face challenges related to work-life balance in India. Smith et al. (2021) found that women leaders in academia face unique challenges related to work-life balance and

Nurturing and Empowering of Women in Leadership Positions

the intersection of gender and race. The study suggests that institutions need to implement policies that support the work-life balance of all faculty members, including women leaders.

Mentorship Challenges

A study by Huang and Tien (2021) examined the impact of mentoring on the career development of women leaders in academia. The study found that mentoring can be an effective strategy for women leaders in academia to overcome gender-related challenges and advance their careers. Mahmood and Iqbal (2019) conducted a study on nurturing women leaders in Pakistan's corporate sector and found that mentoring and coaching programmes can help to nurture women leaders in Pakistan.

The survey revealed some of the issues and challenges like gender inequality, glass- ceiling, payment disparity, stereotypical gender roles, etc. which have been furnished in concise manner through Table.5 and Figure 6. Many women expressed that, initially some of the male co-workers and subordinates felt embarrassed and occasionally tried to dominate them, but those behaviours eventually stopped. They also felt that the work ecosystem had implicitly promoted incompetence by holding them to higher standards than their male counterparts and also subtly passed on a perception of incompetence. But everything was smoother with times and ultimately, they came out victoriously. Most of them admitted that their family was extremely supportive and encouraging along the organization, to make them successful. It has been quite evident that unless it is a concerted effort, it is not possible to break free the barriers. Many respondents mentioned of stereotypical gender role but that also faded with time once they started working towards it.

Table 5. Showing the issues and challenges faced by women leaders in their respective fields

Issues and Challenges for Female Leaders	Number of Respondents	Percentage (%)
Glass-ceiling	29	13
Gender Inequality	60	27
Insubordination from Male Subordinates	100	44
Payment Disparity	5	2
Perception of Incompetence	78	35
More Efforts than Male Colleagues	85	38
Gender Stereotype	95	42
Family Support	204	90

Figure 6. Showing the issues and challenges faced by women leaders in their respective fields in Indian subcontinents

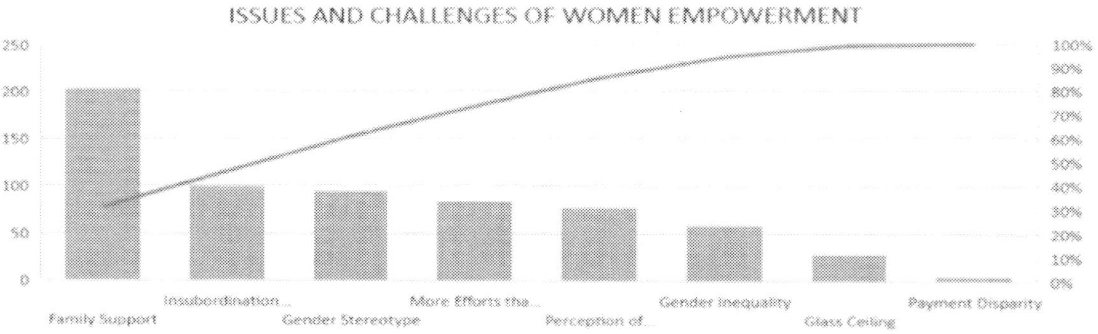

RESEARCH DESIGN

The survey was conducted in India, Bangladesh, Pakistan, Nepal, and Bhutan, focusing on women who are financially and socially established. The interaction was recorded through structured telephonic interviews, mailed questionnaires, face-to-face interactions, and WhatsApp messages. The research used purposive sampling techniques and referencing (snowball technique) along the promise to maintain anonymity and ensure respondents felt secure and safe about freedom of expression. The author contacted most respondents through their known references to maintain parity and authenticity. The research was primarily exploratory, using four types of questions: dichotomous closed-ended questions with options of nominal responses (mostly Yes/No) [The dichotomous close ended questions have been set based on pilot survey and literature review, where many of the predicaments for the women empowerment, surfaced to exist in the global context], open-ended contingency-based questions, independent open-ended questions, and close-ended multiple choice questions. The data was categorized into categories based on similarity matrix and coded for summarization and discussion. The semi-structured questionnaire was used for qualitative exploratory research, with category coding or pattern coding being helpful for in-depth analysis of open-ended responses. The process of category coding is illustrated in a flowchart under Figure 7d. The research design has been depicted in the flowchart under the heading of Figure 7a. Figure 7b highlights the nature of questions. The facets of the questionnaire have been depicted under Figure 7c. Some of the categorized responses with common theme have been exhibited as Appendix B & Appendix C while the questionnaire with total 40 questions has been furnished as Appendix A under 'Appendix section'. Refer to Appendix A, B and C to check the questionnaire, and category coding sample-tables respectively.

Figure 7a. Showing the basic research design construct

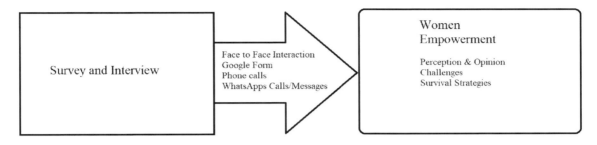

Figure 7b. Showing the nature of questions used in questionnaire

Figure 7c. Showing the basic research facets to explore in Indian subcontinent

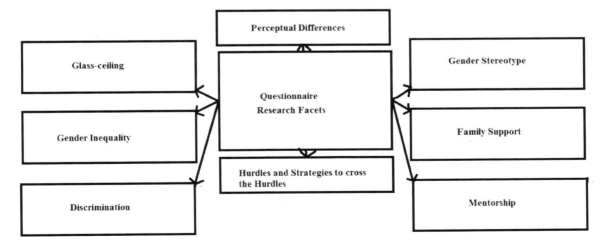

Figure 7d. Showing the process of category coding

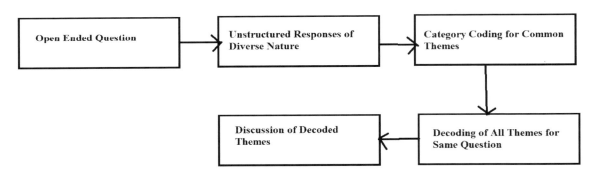

DISCUSSION

Women in higher education and other significant areas, face several challenges that can hinder their academic and professional progress. While progress has been made in recent decades, there are still areas where gender inequality persists. Based on the survey, some of the challenges faced by women in higher education and other prominent fields have revealed several significant insightful aspects, described below:

Gender Bias and Stereotypes: Women are frequently encountering gender bias and stereotypes that are affecting their opportunities and advancement in academia and other fields like media & journalism. These biases are manifesting in various ways, such as assumptions about women's abilities, limited expectations, stereotypes about the suitable academic, technical and other qualifications along the disciplines. Many of the respondents lamented regarding the underestimation of their qualifications and abilities in the respective fields, which they could overcome with persistent efforts. The hard work and endless innovative exertion were the strategies to deal with the situation in most of the cases. Most of the respondents admitted about herculean task to break the barrier, since they have been taken too lightly by authorities. This portion has been overlapped with stereotypical gender roles and glass-ceiling effect, all indicative of gender-based discrimination, sometimes with limited professional growth, doubting abilities to the extent of murky politics and subtle workplace bullying.

Underrepresentation in Leadership Roles: Underrepresentation of women in leadership positions within higher education and other institutions is quite a relevant issue. This lack of representation is impacting decision-making processes and hinder the implementation of policies and initiatives that address gender disparities. Many women claimed, though they are in leadership positions but they have felt a certain degree of disparity in the percentage of representation of the different genders, triggering favouritism towards patriarchy.

Unequal Access to Resources and Funding: Women are facing challenges in accessing research grants, scholarships, and other financial resources necessary for their academic pursuits. This is limiting their ability to engage in research, attend conferences, and access opportunities for professional development. Though this predicament is not supported by a statistically significant data but has often surfaced during discussions with the women leaders.

Work-life Balance: Balancing official responsibilities along with family and personal commitments are becoming particularly challenging for women. Traditional gender roles and societal expectations often placing a greater burden on the women, making it difficult to navigate the demands of professional

Nurturing and Empowering of Women in Leadership Positions

call of duties while managing family responsibilities perfectly. Work-life balance recognizes the need for women to have time and energy for their personal lives and interests outside of work. It acknowledges that women have diverse roles and responsibilities, such as pursuing a career, managing household chores, raising children, caring for family members, and engaging in social and community activities. Achieving work-life balance is about finding a meaningful integration of these various aspects of life, allowing women to excel in both their professional and personal domains.

Some of the respondents admitted the fact that though their families have been extremely supportive yet the levels of expectation from them were always higher compared to the male members in the families. Some of them cited a few examples like the main meals, evening tea and snacks were mostly expected to be cooked and served by the female members, in case the married couple is staying with the families; as in the Indian subcontinents there is a common system of joint families, which means staying with the old parents and siblings of the male member, even if he is married and independents. Also, if any guest was expected to come, the female members were expected to be present at home, albeit professional responsibility and call of the duty. The primary responsibilities of the children' well-being is also reflecting upon the mother, most of the time. Though the majority of the respondents also admitted the fact that their families gradually accepted the nature of their duties, reducing the burden of expectation from them. It could be achieved only through a palatable open discussion with the family members in most of the cases. Some of them also admitted to stretch themselves to a dangerously higher level, with a self-inflicted burden on themselves with guilt trip in heart, when they do not find a suitable strategy to balance both personal and professional life. The unmarried ones complained less about the stereotypical gender roles.

Most of the respondents admitted a balanced approach to work and personal life helps women avoid excessive stress, burnout, and the negative impacts of long-term overwork. Most of them acknowledged that women have unique challenges, including societal expectations, gender roles, and the potential for conflicting demands between work and personal responsibilities and recognized the importance of flexibility, support systems, and effective time management to help women effectively juggle their multiple roles and find fulfilment in all aspects of life.

As per the survey, work-life balance for women should encompass strategies and practices that enable them to set boundaries, prioritize self-care, nurture relationships, pursue personal goals, and maintain a healthy and fulfilling lifestyle.

Discrimination and Harassment: Many of the women in higher education and other considered industries, have faced discrimination and harassment. Some of them experienced it to the extent of sexual harassment sometimes subtly like using abusive language or passing unnecessary vulgar comments, using lewd language, which have created hostile work or study environments, unless fought back with immense courage. Such experiences initially undermined their confidence, impeded their progress, and negatively impacted their mental health, but gradually they could come out of it. For instance, many of the respondents admitted professional harrowing is not rare in any of the industries, but over times, the system accepts the talent and prospects of the women, else the women change the organisation or the circumstance to triumph the situation.

Lack of Mentorship and Networking Opportunities: Limited access to mentors and professional networks hinders women's career advancement. Establishing meaningful connections and receiving guidance from experienced individuals is essential for career development, but women could have faced barriers in accessing these opportunities. All the respondents accepted the fact that they got their mentors within the organisations or in vicinity. For the business women, they accepted to have people in their lives for professional hand holding, either within the family or from the surrounding ecosystem.

Gender Pay Gap: Women in academia and media, globally often face a gender pay gap, where they are paid less than their male counterparts for similar roles and achievements. This pay disparity can have long-term implications for financial security and contribute to the underrepresentation of women in higher-ranking positions. Though, fortunately in the developing countries the gender based pay gap is not directly evident in the organised sectors like academia and related fields, but indirectly reflected through limited promotional scopes, appraisal outcomes and rapid recognition of the talents & efforts.

Intersectionality: It is important to recognize that the experiences of women in higher education and other significant sectors are influenced by intersecting factors such as race, ethnicity, socioeconomic status, and sexual orientation. Women from marginalized groups often faced compounded challenges, of both gender and race-based discrimination.

Addressing these challenges requires intensive determinations from individuals, institutions, and society as a whole. Strategies such as implementing gender-equitable policies, promoting diversity and inclusion, providing mentorship and networking opportunities, and raising awareness about the issues faced by women in higher education can help create more supportive environments and enable equal opportunities for all. Some of the respondents expressed some of the probable individual and organisational roles, which could support the women empowerment, given in figure 8.

Figure 8. Showing individual and organisational roles in the women empowerment

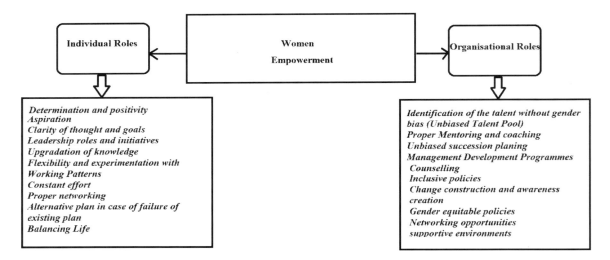

NURTURING WOMEN'S EMPOWERMENT IN INDIAN SUBCONTINENT: PROBABLE SOLUTIONS AND STRATEGIES TO DEAL WITH THE OPPRESSION

The Indian subcontinent is home to a large number of women who face social, economic, and political challenges, across the borders both in home front and workplaces, which have been already highlighted in the discussion section. Despite efforts to promote women's empowerment, gender inequalities persist in the region, nourishing the poison of suppression of the women along with marginalizing and oppress-

Nurturing and Empowering of Women in Leadership Positions

ing them for centuries. However, there are several possible ways to promote women's empowerment in the region through individualistic development, Institutional development and with government initiatives. The following section discusses a few possible developments adapted by government and could be adapted by organizations and women for self-development:

Education

Education is the key to women's empowerment which can help them to acquire the knowledge along the skills, necessary to participate fully in society, pursuing their career goals, with some informed and worthy decisions about their own lives. As per literature, education is one of the most important factors that contribute to women's empowerment in the Indian subcontinent. Several studies have shown that women's education is positively associated with women's empowerment. For instance, Mahapatro and Bhattacharya (2021) found that women's education was a significant predictor of women's empowerment in rural India. Similarly, Ullah et al. (2020) found that women's education was positively associated with their participation in decision-making.

Though in upper and middle income group, education is not an extremely evident crisis, but in lower income group this a choice to be made, in case of more than one child in the family. To sort this problem, several initiatives have been adapted by the governments. Beti Bachao, Beti Padhao (Save the Girl Child, Educate the Girl Child) Campaign launched in 2015 in India, is such an initiative aiming to address gender imbalance and promote the education and welfare of girls. National Women Development Policy, introduced in 2011 in Bangladesh, is another initiative, aiming to promote gender equality, women's empowerment, and the elimination of discrimination against women in all spheres of life. Also, the Female Secondary School Stipend Programme in Bangladesh provides financial incentives to girls from low-income families to encourage their secondary school enrolment and completion. Primary Education Stipend Programme in Bangladesh is another such initiative that provides stipends to encourage primary education and reduce dropout rates among disadvantaged children. Ehsaas Programme in Pakistan is a comprehensive poverty alleviation initiative that includes various components such as interest-free loans, education scholarships, and health insurance to promote education of girl child. Waseela-e-Taleem Programme in Pakistan is an additional initiative offering cash transfers to encourage school enrolment and attendance among children from disadvantaged backgrounds. Women's Literacy Programme in Nepal focuses on increasing women's literacy rates and improving their access to education, aiming to empower them socially and economically. National Education Loan Programme in Nepal offers subsidized loans to students from economically marginalized backgrounds to pursue higher education, as well.

Economic Empowerment

In addition to education, women's participation in the labour force is also crucial for their empowerment in the region. However, women face significant challenges in accessing quality jobs and earning equal pay for equal work. Rahman et al. (2020) found that women's participation in the labour force was positively associated with their empowerment. Similarly, Kibria et al. (2020) found that women's participation in non-agricultural wage employment was positively associated with their empowerment. Women's economic empowerment is also essential for their overall development. Providing women with access to credit, training, and other resources can help them start businesses and become financially independent. Self-help groups (SHGs) and such kind of other initiatives may accelerate the progress.

Self-Employed Women's Association (SEWA),National Rural Livelihoods Mission (NRLM), Mahila Arthik Vikas Mahamandal (MAVIM) in India; Grameen Bank, BRAC (NGO),Bangladesh Women's Health Coalition (BWHC) in Bangladesh; Kashf Foundation, Aurat Foundation, Thardeep Rural Development Program (TRDP) in Pakistan; Women's Foundation Nepal,Women Development Advocacy Centre (WDAC), Rural Women's Development and Unity Centre (RUWDUC)in Nepal; Bhutan Network for Empowering Women (BNEW),RENEW (Respect, Educate, Nurture, and Empower Women) in Bhutan are just a few initiatives of the numerous self-help groups and organizations working towards women's empowerment in the Indian subcontinent. Many more initiatives exist at the grassroots level, driven by local communities and NGOs, which are making significant contributions to women's empowerment. The governments of these countries also taking inclusive policies to include women power in every possible way. Mahila e-Haat is one of those initiatives, with an online Indian platform providing a space for women entrepreneurs to showcase and sell their products, promoting economic empowerment. Mahatma Gandhi National Rural Employment Guarantee Act (MGNREGA) in India Provides a 100-day employment guarantee per household in rural areas and includes women empowerment. Pradhan Mantri Jan Dhan Yojana (PMJDY) in India is a financial inclusion programme that aims to provide banking services to the unbanked population. VGD (Vulnerable Group Development) Programme in Bangladesh targets extremely poor women in rural areas, providing them with cash and food support to reduce their vulnerability and enhance their well-being. Safety Net Programme includes various initiatives in Bangladesh such as the Vulnerable Group Development (VGD) programme to support economically suppressed women in the country. Test Relief Programme offers temporary employment and cash transfers to women in Bangladesh during times of natural disasters or emergencies. Benazir Income Support Programme (BISP) in Pakistan provides financial assistance to low-income women across Pakistan, aiming to alleviate poverty and promote social empowerment. Women on Wheels Programme in Pakistan is another initiative facilitating women's mobility by providing them with subsidized motorbike training and ownership opportunities.

Legal and Political Empowerment

Ensuring women's rights and representation in the legal and political system is crucial. This includes addressing issues such as domestic violence, gender discrimination, and political representation. This can be achieved through Workshops and abatement of rigid gender biased laws through amendments. Protection against Harassment of Women at the Workplace Act in Pakistan enacted in 2010, addresses workplace harassment and establishes mechanisms for reporting and redressal. Maternity Benefit Act under Indian legislation provides right for maternity leave and other benefits to ensure the well-being of women in the workforce during pregnancy and after childbirth. Gender Equality Act passed in 2006 in Nepal, promotes gender equality and prohibits gender-based discrimination in various aspects of life, including education, employment, and access to resources. Safe Motherhood Programme is another initiative in Nepal providing maternal health services, including prenatal and postnatal care, to improve the health and well-being of women during and after pregnancy. Gender-responsive Budgeting in Bhutan incorporates gender considerations into its national budgetary process to allocate resources that address gender inequalities and promote women's empowerment.

Awareness-Raising

Raising awareness about women's issues and the importance of women's empowerment can help change social attitudes and behaviours. This can be done through Media Campaigns, Public Events, Girls' Education Initiatives, Women's Health Camps, Anti-Domestic Violence Campaigns, Microfinance & Entrepreneurship Workshops, Legal Rights Awareness Workshops, Women's Leadership Training Workshops, Social Media Campaigns, Gender Sensitization in Schools and Colleges, Sports, Media and Celebrity Endorsements, Engaging Men in Gender Equality, Community Theatre & Street Plays and Community Outreach Programmes.

Gender-Sensitive Policies

Governments and organizations should implement gender-sensitive policies that promote women's empowerment and address issues such as gender-based violence, access to healthcare, and education. National Commission for Women and Children (NCWC) in Bhutan established in 2004, works to ensure gender equality and the protection of women's and children's rights through policy advocacy and implementation.

Reservation

The government can take initiatives for reservation for women to certain extent, the way it is done for certain castes and communities.

Social Welfare Schemes

There can be enormous social welfare schemes to empower women. Social Security Allowance Programme in Nepal provides monthly cash transfers to elderly citizens, single women, and people with disabilities. Kidu Programme in Bhutan is a social welfare programme that offers support to vulnerable individuals and families in the form of financial assistance, healthcare services, and education.

It is quite evident that promoting women empowerment requires a multi-faceted approach that addresses holistically social, economic, and political factors. In the Indian subcontinent, gender-based violence and women's empowerment are intimately related. Women's access to resources such as education, employment, and other opportunities is hampered by the widespread issue of gender-based violence in the area. Numerous researches have demonstrated how gender-based violence prevention strategies can support women's empowerment. For instance, Bhatia et al. (2021) discovered that women's social and economic empowerment in rural India was enhanced by a community-based intervention that addressed gender-based violence and women's empowerment. On summary, advancing women's educational opportunities, helping them enter the workforce, and combating gender-based violence are essential for achieving women's empowerment on the Indian subcontinent. Policy initiatives that concentrate on these issues can aid in reducing gender disparities and advancing sustainable development in the area.

FUTURE RESEARCH DIRECTIONS

Since, the study incorporates the feedback and response profiling of the socially established women mostly, it does not fathom the problems of cross economic strata, especially lower economic class of women; therefore, a more comprehensive study across all economic strata would be more useful with significant data analysis. The study primarily focuses on exploratory research without high degree of descriptive and any causal research to establish any hypotheses-based relationship of attributes. Therefore, any further research with more hypotheses-oriented direction can open up many other horizons, unfolding underlying reasons and relationships. The open-ended questions, though shed lights on the occurrence of many peculiar scenarios, but have been avoided by many respondents, in case of written responses. The interviews unfolded many dimensions, which were missing in the written responses. Solely dedicated and open-ended face to face interview with each and every respondent could have unveiled many more controversial angles and solved this limitation. The length of the questionnaire could have been another limitation though has been initially designed to capture the robustness of the framework. The open-ended questions brought much insightful information, but convergence of the responses towards a point of commonality was a difficult task and could have been pointed out as a major limitation of the process. In the future research endeavours, these angles should be considered for the further research scope in the same direction.

CONCLUSION

Empowering women has significant multifarious impact, including promoting gender equality, reducing poverty, increasing economic growth, enhancing social development, improved health outcomes, better education, and stronger families. Basically, empowered women are the quintessential biomarker for a healthy and progressive society. However, achieving women's empowerment requires concerted efforts from individuals, communities, governments, organisations and international organizations for global uplift. It entails dispelling gender stereotypes, advancing women's education and employment prospects, providing access to healthcare and legal services, and avoiding systemic barriers to encourage women's full participation in the economy and society. In order to achieve women's empowerment, it is essential to recognize and address the structural inequalities that underpin gender-based discrimination and violence. This includes addressing patriarchal norms and practices, promoting women's representation in decision-making roles. Moreover, women's empowerment is not a one-time achievement but an ongoing process that requires sustained efforts and commitment. It is essential to continue investing in women's education, health, and economic opportunities, promoting gender-sensitive policies and programmes, and ensuring that women's voices and perspectives are heard and valued in all spheres of life. It is also important to recognize that women's empowerment is not a one-size-fits-all approach. Different women may face unique challenges and barriers to empowerment based on their socioeconomic status, ethnicity, race, religion, and other factors and these have been shown as the hurdles of women's empowerment under Figure 9. Recognizing and addressing the systemic injustces and hurdles which support gender-based discrimination and violence is crucial, if women are to be empowered. Therefore, it is essential to adopt a holistic and intersectional approach to women's empowerment that takes into account the diverse experiences and needs of women from different backgrounds. Finally, women's empowerment is not just a women's issue, but a societal issue that affects everyone in the society- from a child to an adult of any gender, race or religion. We all have a role to play in promoting gender equality, challenging gender stereotypes, and creating a more inclusive and equitable society. By working together, we can create a world where women and girls can fully realize their potential and contribute to a better future for all.

Figure 9. Showing the compendious diagrammatic representation of the hurdles of women empowerment

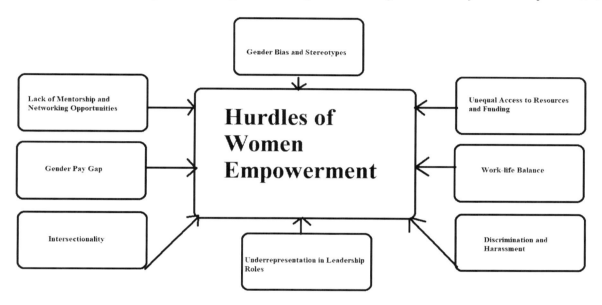

APPENDIX A. FURNISHING THE QUESTIONNAIRE FOR THE SURVEY

Women Empowerment in Professional Field

Please respond to the following questions, keeping in mind your professional growth pattern in your Native place along with your family support from women empowerment point of view. Your responses will not be exposed for any commercial purpose and will be treated as completely discrete information, maintaining anonymity and confidentiality to the fullest. The questionnaire has many contingent and conditional questions, in case those are irrelevant and uncomfortable, you can always skip the question to answer the next one. Thank you for your cooperation and support:

*Country:
*Age group: Below 25/ 25-35/36-46/ above 4/Do not prefer to disclose
*Educational Qualification: Undergraduate / Postgraduate/ doctorate/ Do not prefer to disclose
*Profession: Academia & Research/ Medical/ Law/ Entrepreneurial Venture/ Journalist/Do not prefer to disclose
*Marital Status: Married/ Unmarried /Do not prefer to disclose
*Income group/ capita/Month: Below700 USD/ 700 USD-1000 USD/1001 USD-2000 USD/ More than 2000 USD /Do not prefer to disclose

Nurturing and Empowering of Women in Leadership Positions

1. *Did you feel at any point of time, your female gender has been an obstruction in your professional growth (glass-ceiling)? Yes/ No*
2. *In case of Yes, please let us know briefly how it affected your professional growth (if possible with example) …*
3. *Have you got your immediate family support for your professional growth? Yes/No*
4. *Is the hindrance more from your maiden family/ in-laws? Maiden/ In laws/ No hindrance*
5. *Does the hindrance in your family still persist? Yes/No*
6. *In case of No, please let us know briefly how you managed to get the support from your family…*
7. *Have you been treated differently from the male colleagues in your professional arena (gender inequality in the workplace)? Yes/ No*
8. *Have you ever evidenced a different Behaviour approach for the male counterpart in your immediate family (gender inequality at home)? Yes/ No*
9. *In case of Yes, please let us know briefly where it happened, with example without naming anybody (Workplace or home-based gender inequality) …*
10. *Do you face insubordination from your male colleagues/ subordinates? Yes/ No*
11. *Please let us know about the experience of insubordination briefly, in case of it is Yes…*
12. *Did you face payment disparity based on gender in any of your organizations, where you worked (direct)? Yes/ No*
13. *Did you face payment disparity based on gender in any of your organizations, where you worked (indirect)? Yes/ No*
14. *Please let us know briefly what kind of payment disparity happened, (if possible, with example) without naming anybody or the organization (even if it is indirectly showcasing Gender-based pay gap) …*
15. *Did you face 'gender based Perceptual differentials' from your higher authority in any of the organizations, where you worked? Yes/ No*
16. *In case of Yes, how did you manage to smoothen the Perceptual Differences, please tell us briefly?...*
17. *Was there any perception of incompetence from higher authority in any of the organization, where you worked? Yes/ No*
18. *Do you feel it's due to gender based preconceived notion? Yes/ No*
19. *How did you manage to overcome the perception of incompetence?...*
20. *Do you have to give more efforts than the male colleagues at your workplace? Yes/ No*
21. *Do you face stereotypical gender roles at your workplace or at your home (any role that you are supposed to perform just because you are a woman)? Yes/ No*
22. *In case of Yes, briefly tell us a few instances please …*
23. *Is it easy to maintain a work life balance being a woman? Yes/ No*
24. *In case of Yes, let us know how do you balance your work life?...*
25. *What are the roles expected from you at home and workplace?...*
26. *If you cannot manage to maintain a work life balance what could happen?...*
27. *Do you stretch yourself too much with the apprehension of negative social perception (Self Inflicted Burden)? Yes/ No*
28. *How do you manage to maintain a work life balance? Please let us know a few of your strategies…*
29. *Have you ever faced discrimination and harassment in your work place? Yes/ No*
30. *In case of Yes, please tell us briefly about your experience and the nature of discrimination and harassment (without naming anybody or the organization) …*

Nurturing and Empowering of Women in Leadership Positions

31. *Do you think women are fairly represented in leadership position in your country? Yes/ No*
32. *What is your take on overall women in leadership position?...*
33. *Have you been affected by any of the following factors in your workplace? Race/Ethnicity/ Socioeconomic status/Sexual orientation/ Part of any marginalized group*
34. *Did you feel any mentorship/ hand holding experience helped in your professional growth? Yes/ No*
35. *In case of Yes, let us know about your mentorship/ hand holding experience...*
36. *Was the mentor available in your professional surrounding? Yes/ No*
37. *Let us know about a few personal roles which helped you to grow as a professional...*
38. *Let us know about a few Institutional roles which helped you to grow as a professional...*
39. *Let us know about some unique hurdles, made your professional growth, as a woman leader, a difficult one (which are not discussed already) ...*
40. *Let us know about any unique strategy/ strategies that helped you to grow, as woman leader (which are not discussed already) .....*

APPENDIX B. FURNISHING THE CODING OF QUESTION IN THE QUESTIONNAIRE

Coding

Categorization to bridge the gap- Gender Bias	Coding
Innovative Technique	A
Persistent efforts	B
Hard work	C
Herculean task	D

APPENDIX C. FURNISHING THE CODING OF QUESTION IN THE QUESTIONNAIRE

Coding

Categorization- Underrepresentation in Leadership Positions	Coding
Patriarchal Mentality	A
Disparity in the percentage of representation	B
Favouritism towards male gender	C

REFERENCES

Airini, S. C., Conner, L., McPherson, K., Midson, B., & Wilson, C. (2011). Learning to be Leaders in Higher Education: What Helps or Hinders Women's Advancement as Leaders in Universities. *Educational Management Administration & Leadership*, *39*(1), 4462. doi:10.1177/1741143210383896

American Association of University Professors. (2018). *The Impact of Gender Bias on Hiring and Promotion Decisions in Academia*. Author.

Athal, K. (2019). The Rise of Women Leaders in The Corporate World. *The Times of India*. https://timesofindia.indiatimes.com/blogs/krishna-athal/the-rise-of-women-leaders-in-the-corporate-world/

Baldissarri, C., & Piccoli, V. (2021). Gender Differences in the Evaluation of Leadership Competence: A Meta-Analysis. *Frontiers in Psychology*, *12*, 653525.

Bechmann, K., Jenewein, S., & Ruenzi, S. (2020). Women CEOs and Firm Performance: Evidence from Europe. *Journal of Corporate Finance*, *65*, 101785.

Benschop, Y., & Brouns, M. (2021). Women Leaders in Academia: Progress, Challenges, And Strategies. *Current Opinion in Psychology*, *42*, 34–39.

Nurturing and Empowering of Women in Leadership Positions

Bhatia, J. C., Cleland, J., Bhagavan, M., & Singh, K. K. (2021). Addressing Gender-Based Violence to Promote Women's Empowerment in Rural India: Findings from a Cluster-Randomised Controlled Trial. *The Lancet. Global Health*, *9*(1), 69–78.

Bhattacharjee, A., & Pal, J. (2008). The Impact of Support Networks on Women's Empowerment. *Gender & Society*, *22*(2), 165–187.

Brescoll, V. L. (2015). Women and Leadership: A Review of Recent Literature. *The Leadership Quarterly*, *26*(1), 6–32.

Chatterjee, A. (2017). Empowering Women in Leadership: A Study of Indian Scenario. *Asian Journal of Management Research*, *8*(2), 239–249.

Chaudhary, A., Shrestha, R. P., & Karki, S. (2021). Women's Participation in Informal Sector and their Economic Empowerment: Evidence from Nepal. *The Journal of Development Studies*, *57*(6), 940–957.

Chaudhuri, M. (1990). Feminism in India: Two Histories of Women's Movements. *The Indian Historical Review*, *17*(1), 97–112.

Cook, M. (2011). *Women Presidents of Colleges and Universities: A Status Report*. American Council on Education.

Das, N. (1993). Women's Participation in the Indian Freedom Movement: A Historical Perspective. *Social Action*, *43*(1), 59–68.

Doe, J. (2020). Women's Empowerment in the Indian Subcontinent: A Historical Perspective. *Journal of Gender Studies*, *25*(3), 145–165.

Durrani, A. M., Farooqi, A. N., & Mubarik, M. S. (2021). Women's Education and Economic Empowerment in Pakistan. *Journal of Asian and African Studies*, *56*(1), 73–89.

Dworkin, S. L., & Allen, A. (2006). The Role of Support Groups in Women's Empowerment: A Review of the Literature. *Social Science & Medicine*, *62*(1), 115–127.

Eagly, A. H. (2023). The Impact of Women Leaders on Organizational Outcomes: A Review of the Research. *The Academy of Management Annals*, *17*(1), 1–58.

Eagly, A. H., & Carli, L. L. (2007). *Through the Labyrinth: Women and Leadership*. Harvard Business Press.

Eagly, A. H., & Karau, S. J. (1991). Gender and the Emergence of Leaders: A Meta-analysis. *Psychological Bulletin*, *108*(2), 233–256. doi:10.1037/0033-2909.108.2.233

Eagly, A. H., & Karau, S. J. (2002). Role Congruity Theory of Prejudice toward Female Leaders. *Psychological Review*, *109*(3), 573–598. doi:10.1037/0033-295X.109.3.573 PMID:12088246

Feres, J. G., & Gomes, C. (2019). Women's Political Participation and Public Policies: Evidence from Brazil. *World Development*, *120*, 24–37.

Friedan, B. (1963). *The Feminine Mystique*. W. W. Norton & Company.

García-Moreno, C., Jansen, H. A., Ellsberg, M., Heise, L., & Watts, C. H. (2015). Prevalence of Intimate Partner Violence: Findings from The WHO Multi-Country Study On Women's Health and Domestic Violence. *Lancet*, *368*(9543), 1260–1269. doi:10.1016/S0140-6736(06)69523-8 PMID:17027732

Ghosh, P. (2017). Women in Ancient India: A Historical and Socio-Cultural Perspective. *Asian Journal of Social Science Studies*, *2*(2), 32–42.

Griffiths, V. (2009). Women Managers in Higher Education: Experiences from the UK. *International Journal of Learning*, *16*(10), 397405. doi:10.18848/1447-9494/CGP/v16i10/46648

Guo, Y., & Tsai, M. (2021). Women's Labour Force Participation and Political Empowerment in China. *Journal of Women, Politics & Policy*, *42*(1), 1–23.

Gupta, S., & Khan, F. (2021). Breaking Barriers: Women Leaders in the Indian Subcontinent. *Gender & Society*, *38*(1), 23–42.

Heise, L., Kotsadam, A., & Ellsberg, M. (2019). Ending Gender-Based Violence. *Lancet*, *393*(10189), 398–399. PMID:31155275

Higher Education Statistics Agency-HESA. (2010). *Staff at Higher Education Institutions in the UK 200910. Statistical First Release,154.* HESA.

Huang, Q., & Kisgen, D. J. (2021). Female Board Representation and Firm Performance: Evidence from the UK. *Journal of Financial Economics*, *140*(2), 349–371.

Huang, Y., & Tien, C. (2021). Mentoring and Career Development of Women Leaders in Academia: A Review of the Literature. *Educational Research Review*, *35*, 100361.

Inter-Parliamentary Union. (2021). *Women in National Parliaments*. Inter-Parliamentary Union.

Jiang, L., & Luo, Y. (2021). Exploring Gender Differences in CEO Turnover: Evidence from the US. *Journal of Business Research*, *131*, 29–38.

Kabeer, N. (1999). Resources, Agency, Achievements: Reflections on the Measurement of Women's Empowerment. *Development and Change*, *30*(3), 435–464. doi:10.1111/1467-7660.00125

Kabeer, N. (2015). Gender Equality, Economic Growth, and Women's Agency: The "Endless Variety" and "Monolithic Presumptions" of Neoclassical Economics. *Feminist Economics*, *21*(3), 1–28. doi:10. 1080/13545701.2014.926558

Kabeer, N. (2019). *Women's Economic Empowerment and Inclusive Growth: Labour Markets and Enterprise Development*. Overseas Development Institute.

Karakas, F., Bingol, D., & Mutlu, H. (2021). The Relationship between Perceived Leadership Style and Work-Related Outcomes: The Role of Gender. *Journal of Business Research*, *132*, 615–625.

Kibria, S. M. G., Oishi, M., & Rahman, M. H. (2020). Women's Participation in Non-Agricultural Wage Employment and Empowerment in Rural Bangladesh. *Women's Studies International Forum*, *79*, 102317.

Krug, E. G., Dahlberg, L. L., Mercy, J. A., Zwi, A. B., & Lozano, R. (2002). *World Report on Violence and Health*. World Health Organization. doi:10.1016/S0140-6736(02)11133-0

Nurturing and Empowering of Women in Leadership Positions

Kulkarni, A., & Mishra, M. (2022). *Aspects of Women's Leadership in the Organisation: Systematic Literature Review*. Sage Journals.

Kumar, R. (2018). Women in Leadership Positions in India: Issues and Challenges. *Journal of Management Research and Analysis*, *5*(3), 176–179.

Kumar, R. (2019). Women's Empowerment Initiatives in South Asia: A Comparative Analysis. *Development Studies Research*, *30*(4), 345–362.

Mahapatro, M., & Bhattacharya, S. (2021). Women's Empowerment in Rural India: Role of Education, Economic, and Social Resources. *Journal of Developing Areas*, *55*(2), 137–151.

Mahmood, S., & Iqbal, N. (2019). Nurturing Women Leaders: A Study of Pakistan's Corporate Sector. *South Asian Journal of Management*, *26*(2), 95–110.

Mahmud, S., Shah, N., & Becker, S. (2012). Measurement of Women's Empowerment in Rural Bangladesh. *World Development*, *40*(3), 610–619. doi:10.1016/j.worlddev.2011.08.003 PMID:23637468

Malhotra, A., & Mather, S. (2007). *Women's Education in Developing countries: Learning for Life*. World Bank.

Mukherjee, S., & Majumdar, S. (2020). Women in Leadership Roles in Indian Organizations: A Review of the Literature. *Journal of Social and Political Sciences*, *3*(4), 545–554.

National Academies of Sciences, Engineering, and Medicine. (2018). *The Science of Sex Differences in Science, Technology, Engineering, and Mathematics*. Washington, DC: The National Academies Press.

National Center for Women & Information Technology. (2020). *Why are Women still Underrepresented in STEM?* National Center for Women & Information Technology.

National Girls Collaborative Council. (2019). *The Gender Gap in STEM: Where We Stand and Where We Need to Go*. National Girls Collaborative Council.

Naved, R. T., & Persson, L. Å. (2019). Factors associated with Women's Empowerment in Rural Bangladesh. *Development in Practice*, *29*(3), 257–266.

Offen, K. (1988). Defining Feminism: A Comparative Historical Approach. *Signs (Chicago, Ill.)*, *14*(1), 119–157. doi:10.1086/494494

Ovadia, S., & Brawer, M. (2021). Women Leaders in Israeli Academia: Challenges and Opportunities. *Gender in Management*, *36*(3), 318–334.

Pahuja, P., & Chawla, D. (2021). Women in Leadership: A Study of Indian Context. *Indian Journal of Human Resource Development*, *21*(1), 47–59.

Rahman, M. S., Akter, S., & Hoque, N. (2020). Women's Empowerment and Labour Force Participation in Bangladesh: Evidence from a Nationally Representative Survey. *Women's Studies International Forum*, *80*, 102364.

Rahman, M. S., Rahman, M. E., & Sultana, P. (2021). Women's Education and Empowerment in Rural Bangladesh. *Social Indicators Research*, *154*(1), 233–255.

Ryan, M. K., & Haslam, S. A. (2005). The glass Cliff: Evidence that women are overrepresented in precarious leadership positions. *British Journal of Management, 16*(2), 81–90. doi:10.1111/j.1467-8551.2005.00433.x

Salgado, S. R., Perez, S. S., & Mosquera, J. C. R. (2021). Women's Representation in Top Leadership and its Relationship with Organizational Outcomes: A Meta-Analysis. *Frontiers in Psychology, 12*, 630036.

SarDesai, D. R. (2013). The Bhakti Movement: An Indian Response to the Challenge of Islam and Christianity. *World History Connected, 10*(3), 1–19.

Sekhar, K. C. (2014). Impact of Education on Women's Empowerment: A study in Madhurai district, Tamil Nadu. *Journal of the Indian Anthropological Society, 49*(1), 1–16.

Sen, S. (2006). Women and Social Reform in Colonial India. *Economic and Political Weekly, 41*(17), 1667–1672.

Smith, A., Robinson, J., & Lowry, D. (2021). Women Leaders in Higher Education: Balancing Work and Life. *Journal of Women and Gender in Higher Education, 14*(1), 1–18.

Smith, A. B. (2018). Women in Leadership: Challenges and Opportunities in the Indian Subcontinent. *International Journal of Management and Leadership, 12*(2), 87–105.

Tong, R. (1998). *Feminist Thought: A Comprehensive Introduction* (3rd ed.). Westview Press.

Ullah, S., Ullah, R., & Haque, M. A. (2020). Women's Empowerment Through Education and Decision-Making Power: A Case Study of Pakistan. *Gender, Technology and Development, 24*(3), 267–287.

UNESCO. (2015). *Education for all 2000-2015: Achievements and challenges*. UNESCO.

UNICEF. (2007). *Girls' Education: Achieving Gender Equality and Empowering Girls for Development*. UNICEF.

UNICEF. (2020). *Female Genital Mutilation/ Cutting*. UNICEF.

United Nations. (1995). *Beijing Declaration and Platform for Action*. UN. https://www.un.org/womenwatch/daw/beijing/platform/

United Nations. (2015). *Gender Equality and Women's Empowerment*. UN. https://www.un.org/sustainabledevelopment/gender-equality/

United Nations. (2015). *Transforming Our World: The 2030 Agenda for Sustainable Development*. United Nations.

United Nations. (2019). *Progress towards the Sustainable Development Goals: Report of the Secretary-General*. United Nations.

United Nations Development Programme. (2019). *The Gender Gap Report 2019*. United Nations.

Women, U. N. (2020). *The Impact of COVID-19 on Women*. UN Women.

Women, U. N. (2023). *About UN Women*. UN Women. https://www.unwomen.org/en/about-us

Women Deliver. (2020). *The state of women's rights: A progress report. Washington*. Women Deliver.

Nurturing and Empowering of Women in Leadership Positions

World Bank. (2016). *Women's Economic Empowerment*. World Bank. https://www.worldbank.org/en/topic/gender/brief/womens-economic-empowerment

World Bank. (2020). *Gender Equality and Development. Washington*. World Bank.

ADDITIONAL READING

Babcock, L., & Laschever, S. (2003). *Women don't ask: Negotiation and the Gender Divide*. Princeton University Press. doi:10.1515/9780691212845

Brown, B. (2012). *Daring greatly: How the Courage to be Vulnerable Transforms the way we live, love, parent, and lead*. Avery.

Feldt, G. (2010). *No Excuses: 9 Ways Women Can Change How We Think About Power*. Seal Press.

Frankel, L. P. (2014). *Nice girls don't get the corner office: Unconscious mistakes women make that sabotage their careers*. Business Plus.

Gates, M. (2019). *The Moment of Lift: How Empowering Women Changes the World*. Flatiron Books.

Gillard, J., & Okonjo Iweala, N. (2020). *Women and Leadership: Real Lives, Real Lessons*. MIT Press.

Helgesen, S., & Goldsmith, M. (2018). *How Women Rise: Break the 12 Habits Holding You Back from Your Next Raise, Promotion, Or Job*. Hachette Books.

Kay, K., & Shipman, C. (2014). *The confidence code: The Science and Art of Self-assurance---What Women should know*. Harper Business.

Sandberg, S. (2013). *Lean in: Women, work, and the will to lead*. Knopf.

Wojcicki, S. (2019). *The Power of Women at Work: Secrets to Unlocking Your Potential*. Houghton Mifflin Harcourt.

KEY TERMS AND DEFINITIONS

Gender Inequality: Gender inequality refers to the unequal treatment or opportunities provided to individuals based on their gender, often resulting in a disproportionate distribution of power, resources, and benefits between men and women. It can manifest in various forms, such as unequal access to education, employment, healthcare, political representation, and wages, as well as gender-based violence, discrimination, and stereotypes. Gender inequality is considered a social, economic, and political issue that hinders the progress and well-being of individuals and societies, and it is a fundamental violation of human rights.

Women's Empowerment: Women empowerment refers to the process of enabling women to take control of their lives, both socially and economically. Women empowerment is a quintessential concept that encompasses various dimensions such as economic, social, political, and cultural aspects, enabling women to exercise their rights, access opportunities, and participate fully in all aspects of society.

Nurturing and Empowering of Women in Leadership Positions

Work-life Balance for Women: Work-life balance for women refers to the equilibrium and harmony between a woman's professional or work-related responsibilities and her personal life, including family, relationships, self-care, and leisure activities. It involves creating a sustainable and fulfilling lifestyle that allows women to meet their career aspirations while also maintaining their overall well-being and quality of life.

Chapter 10

Women and Universities:
Determining Factors and Profiles of University Systems According to Gender Composition

Teodoro Luque-Martínez
University of Granada, Spain

Nina Faraoni
https://orcid.org/0000-0003-1582-5104
University of Granada, Spain

Luis Doña-Toledo
University of Granada, Spain

ABSTRACT

Nowadays, the presence of women in the university is the majority. The question is whether indicators of university results used in university rankings are linked to this presence. The aim of the article is to identify indicators considering different dimensions like teaching or volume of scientific production, analysing in what way the presence of women can be explained. The study involves six international academic rankings. The results showed that certain indicators, such as internationalization or industry income, were those that helped most to discriminate the unequal presence of women among university students. Universities should establish measures for the international recruitment of students and teaching staff, as well as designing measures that favour international collaboration. Likewise, the higher the income, the lower the presence of women, which highlights the scant presence of women following technical and technological courses, which are precisely those sorts of qualifications that capture more resources from industry.

DOI: 10.4018/978-1-6684-8597-2.ch010

Copyright © 2023, IGI Global. Copying or distributing in print or electronic forms without written permission of IGI Global is prohibited.

INTRODUCTION

At the beginning of the 20th c., women at university represented even less than 1% of all enrolments (Giménez-Salinas, 2005). Today, although the proportion of female students at university is in the majority in many cases (53% between Bachelor and Master according to UNESCO, 2021), the issue of gender inequality in Higher Education (HE) remains a matter of global concern. According to UNESCO report, higher levels of education correspond to lower proportions of women, as reaffirmed by Khan et al. (2019). Despite this, the factors that have made this increase possible may be summarized in the 'liberation' of the workforce from domestic service (Martínez-García, 2007; Carmona-Valdés, 2015); in the expansion of the services sector of the economy (Shavit & Blossfeld, 1996); and in the growing need for a second income to sustain a family (Alba, 2000).

In the field of higher education and research, little attention has been devoted to the issue of gender inequality, which has characterised most societies over the centuries (August & Waltman, 2004; Odhiambo, 2011).

Although there are signs of an increased presence of women in higher education (UNESCO, 2021), investigation is needed to better understand and to verify whether that is so, and were it so, what the causes and what the consequences might be.

This context leads to the question of whether the gender composition of the student body at universities anything has to do with, or is associated with, certain HE-related indicators such as the volume of scientific output, quality indicators (citations, awards, number of top publications), university reputation or level of internationalisation of universities. If this is the case, it is worth asking which of these indicators help to discriminate the presence of female students in universities and to identify types of universities according to their gender composition. No research has been detected in the literature that directly addresses this task, which is why this research is of a seminal nature. Specifically, the objectives of this study are:

- In relation to the presence of female students at university, the decisive indicators are identified, in order to understand the differences associated with the presence or not of female students at universities, considering different dimensions (teaching, volume and quality of scientific production, degree of internationalisation, massification of the university and relations with industry).
- Analysis and characterisation of the types of university systems/countries, in particular, segmentation of the world's universities according to the presence of women in the student body with special reference to GDP per capita, population and region.

Answering these questions helps to identify university systems characterised by a higher presence of female students, apart from the results they present, i.e., the performance of the different university systems.

Finally, the impact of the socio-economic context on the presence of female students is revealed, so that recommendations can be formulated to advance the goal of desirable equity. All this should be approached from a social marketing perspective.

Women and Universities

THEORETICAL FRAMEWORK

Women and University

Analysing HE management and the balance between female and male students, Fogelberg et. al. (1999) make it clear that efforts to balance and promote the presence of female students at university have become more frequent since the 1980s. These efforts were accompanied by preliminary research on gender balance among students, which was rather descriptive in nature. For this reason, a need was identified for more articulate studies on the intrinsic reasons for gender imbalance in higher education that effectively address its structural barriers (Acker, 1990; Ely & Meyerson, 2000). David (2012) pointed out some gaps in the literature on universities and gender, stating that mainstream research in education does not consider perspectives and issues dealing with gender balance or female presence in universities. However, in other fields of study, there is a growing body of work on gender inequality. As a result, researchers began to take an interest in the subject and, according to the results obtained in their research, to call for greater balance between female and male students in the university institution (Cama et al., 2016). On the other hand, in the last decade, a greater number of studies have begun to be published, analysing the presence of women among the teaching staff or in management positions within the academic structure, although there is need for further research, especially at the student body level.

The tendencies detected in the study of teaching staff, for example, are summarized in four large groups (Cama et al., 2016):

- Studies under the perspective of gender differences that try to give responses to the unequal rates of tenured professorships and promotion among teaching staff.
- Studies that examine the presence of women in leadership positions and administration in higher education.
- Studies centred on the promotion of gender equality.
- Studies on the salary gap between men and women as faculty members.

On the last point, pay inequality in favour of men has been noted in many universities around the world. Research by Currie and Hill (2013) highlights the different situations in different countries. Canada and Sweden, for example, monitor university accounts by requiring pay reviews to ensure that there is no inequality and equal pay for equal work. If we look at managerial positions and higher positions, gender inequality in HE becomes even clearer (Appleby & Bathmaker, 2006), in access to senior positions there are significant differences between men and women (Tzanakou & Pearce, 2019). In this line of research, it is possible to go deeper by country considering, in addition to nominal salary, dedication, responsibility or management positions held.

However, having a balanced composition in academic leadership positions not only decreases gender inequality within the institution, but also increases productivity and human capital development (Cama et. al., 2016). In addition to greater equality, this also generates benefits for the economy and society at large, both at national (Blackwell & Glover, 2008), European (European Commission, 2005), and global (UNESCO, 2007) levels. In short, the balance between women and men in higher education has an impact on greater scientific production and, therefore, a better position of universities in international rankings (Luque-Martínez et al., 2020). Especially in those rankings that are based on bibliometric indicators related to the scientific production of universities.

From the perspective of student studies, a frequent topic in research is the analysis of differences in career choice according to gender (Gámez & Marrero, 2003; Papadópulos & Radakovich, 2003; Sáinz et al., 2004; Friedmann, 2018; Roemer et al., 2020). The trend of female students' choice is towards humanities, health sciences and education, while technical careers are chosen to a greater extent by male students (Zeegers, 2004). In the choice of STEM (Science, Technology, Engineering and Mathematics) careers, there is an important difference between women and men, as they are chosen to a greater extent by men (Çelik & Watson, 2021).

There are numerous studies that attempt to understand or explain why there are differences in career choice (Correll, 2001; Navarro-Guzmán & Casero-Martínez, 2012; Carmona-Valdés, 2015; Trotter, 2017; Friedmann, 2018) and how it could be managed (Çelik & Watson, 2021). On the one hand, some have argued that the difference in choice and male predisposition for certain careers can be explained by biological differences (Muñoz & Mullet, 1990). Some authors believe that women choose by seeking the satisfaction of their interests or personal preference and men, by their nature, are guided by the professional opportunities that the chosen option will offer them or the salary (Friedmann, 2018). On the other hand, Cubillo and Brown (2003) consider 'socio-political' the cultural barriers and distorted beliefs that are formed in situations of gender imbalance in society and, as a result, at university.

For Nguyen (2013), it is cultural traditions, rooted in each country or society, that determine the attitudes of a set of people towards different subjects. Women maintain a stronger sense of family duty than men perceive, which is an obstacle to their academic progress, since they feel a greater sense of responsibility towards fathers, sons, and husbands (Kulis & Sicotte, 2002; Sax et al., 2002; Morrison et al., 2011). Wolfinger et al. (2008) stated that some women opt for less complicated careers that involve less time and dedication, which in turn translates into seeking less demanding or part-time employment. This means fewer years of experience, fewer opportunities for promotion and career advancement, and therefore, lower earnings (Kulis & Sicotte, 2002).

It is well established that, in most countries, women constitute most of both undergraduates and graduates (UNESCO, 2021). However, men are in the majority at universities in Eastern Europe, Sub-Saharan Africa, and Asia. Despite efforts to combat gender imbalance from early childhood (Timmers et al., 2010; Teelken & Deem, 2013; Tzanakou & Pearce, 2019), the so-called 'think male' gender rule still exists (Powell et al., 2002).

From all the above points, three key issues can be inferred:

(1) the existence of gender inequality in leadership positions in the HE system and in technical and technological degrees (Roemer et al., 2020).
(2) the invisible barriers that complicate women's academic and professional career development.
(3) the need for research to identify policies and strategies to achieve balance.

Having identified these three circumstances, we will focus on the factors with the greatest explanatory power for the presence of female students at university.

University Rankings

Since the turn of the century, the presence and influence of university rankings has grown enormously, affecting university reputation and management. At the same time, there has been increasing research on the role of rankings, for example on how particular programmes or policies have influenced the improve-

Women and Universities

ment of rankings positions or their usefulness in improving and promoting university activity (Vernon et al., 2018). Existing literature has questioned their usefulness (Johnes, 2018) and has extensively analysed the methodologies used for their preparation (Çakır et al., 2015). It has also been concerned with the influence they have on students when selecting a university (Ordorika & Lloyd, 2015). Other aspects analysed are the factors that influence the position of universities in these rankings, such as the size of the university and the number of professors (Docampo & Cram, 2015).

Currently, the use of rankings as a tool for researching gender equity issues in universities is arousing the interest of academics (Khan et al., 2019; Luque-Martínez et al., 2020; Xiao et al., 2020; Reverter-Bañon, 2021). This is the framework of the present study, which aims to identify segments and groups of universities according to gender composition. To this end, we use the indicators of the universities included in the selected global academic rankings. In addition, the relationship between the presence of female students and country-specific indicators, such as population and income level, is analysed to define profiles of national university systems and understand their characteristics.

METHODOLOGY

Step 1: Selection of Rankings

For the analysis, six synthetic and global university rankings with their respective indicators were chosen. A global ranking is understood as one that considers all the universities in the world; and a synthetic ranking is understood as one that provides a summary score of the different indicators with which it is elaborated, although a single final score will always be open to criticism (Docampo, 2008; Docampo, 2010; Hazelkorn, 2012; Luque-Martínez & Del Barrio-García, 2016). This score determines the position of the university, an outcome that affects the visibility, prestige, and reputation of universities (Safón, 2019). Because of this, the main point to be considered when analysing international rankings is to know what they measure, while recognising their advantages and disadvantages, due to the selection process, method of data collection and weightings of the indicators. Considering these aspects, rankings can be a useful tool for analysing trends in the performance of university institutions. The academic rankings chosen for the analysis are:

- Academic Ranking of World Universities (ARWU): http://www.shanghairanking.com
- Center for World University Rankings (CWUR): https://cwur.org/
- National Taiwan University (NTU): http://nturanking.csti.tw/
- Quacquarelli Symonds-QS ranking (QS): https://www.topuniversities.com/university-rankings
- Times Higher Education (THE): https://www.timeshighereducation.com/world-university-rankings
- University Ranking by Academic Performance (URAP): http://www.urapcenter.org

These rankings are the most widely recognised and used globally. The aim of this number of different academic rankings is to have diversity in the indicators used.

Step 2: Data Preparation

The data were downloaded from the websites of each ranking. Table 1 shows the rankings, the number of universities in each ranking and the respective indicators. The explanation of the indicators can be found in the tables in the appendices.

Table 1. University rankings selected for the analysis

Ranking	N. of universities	Criteria
A: ARWU	500	Alumni, Award, HiCi, N&S, PUB., PCP
C: CWUR	1000	Quality Education, Alumni Employment, Quality of Faculty, Publications, Influence, Citations, Broad Impact, Patents
N: NTU	500	11 Years of Articles, Current Articles, 11 Years of Citations, Current Citations, Average Citations, H-Index, HiCi Papers, Hi-Impact Journal Articles
Q: QS	936	Academic Reputation, Employer Reputation, Faculty Student, Citation per Faculty, International
T: THE	980	Teaching, Research, Citation, Internationalization, Industry Income
U: URAP	2000	Article, Citation, Total Document, AIT, CIT, Collaboration

Source: Own elaboration, based on the websites of the rankings.

A joint database was created with all the data available on the websites of each ranking. This required a process of homogenisation of the names of the institutions appearing in the rankings, which were not always identical.

The population data were obtained from official UN statistics and the source for the GDP data was the International Monetary Fund (IMF).

Step 3: Dependent Variable and Criterion Variables

The dependent variable, or variable to be explained, is the gender composition of the university student body. The indicator used is the percentage of women in the student body of the universities, data provided by the THE ranking. A total of 924 institutions were considered for which data was available. This variable, initially expressed as a percentage, was recoded to be used as an ordinal variable to check for differences according to country characteristics (such as population or GDP per capita), identifying three categories with similar frequency:

- Category 1: lowest percentage of female students (47% of the student body or less).
- Category 2: the most balanced, representing those universities where the percentage of female students is between more than 47% and less than 55%.

Women and Universities

- Category 3: universities where the percentage of female students equals or exceeds 55% of the total.

Step 4: Segment Identification

The purpose of the data analysis is to identify the indicators of the rankings that most contribute to discriminating or explaining the gender composition of the universities and to identify segments or subsets of universities with similar profiles. For this purpose, segmentation trees, ANOVA, and non-parametric tests (Kruskal-Wallis) are used, using SPSS Statistics v20 software.

The different typologies of universities are obtained through a segmentation tree, or hierarchical segmentation (Luque-Martínez, 2012), where the dependent variable is the presence of women in the university student body, which is measured as a percentage. The independent variables considered are the 42 indicators of the six rankings used: ARWU, CWUR, NTU, QS, THE and URAP (see appendices).

DATA ANALYSIS AND RESULTS

Segmentation of University

Given the number of universities, having completed different tests with different specifications, and with the intention of obtaining sub-sets of a reasonable size, specifications were established so that the tree would have four levels, with a minimum number of cases of 40 for the division of a parent node, and 10 for the node resulting from the decision. The CHAID (CHi-square Automatic Interaction Detection) option from the IBM SPSS software package was used.

This procedure selects the independent variable with the highest interaction with the dependent variable as a predictor. If there are no significant differences, the categories of the predictor variable appear fused.

In the solution, the independent variables that appear as predictor variables, and which are therefore those with greater discriminatory power than the dependent variable, are those linked to internationalization, income from industry, citations in absolute values, by teacher and by impact, massification of the university, and the quality of employment of graduates. The validity of the classification is acceptable, as shown by the measure of risk. The variance between the node is low (0.009), as well as the estimation of the crossed validation (0.013).

Figures 1 and 2 show the detail of the segmentation. The first predictor variable is shown in greater detail in figure 1. The presence of women students at university is the variable related with internationalization, according to the ranking indicator. So, a higher ratio of international students and teachers and international collaboration with projects is equatable with a higher presence of women students.

The category with the lowest level of internationalization, the least numerous with 10.5% of the total, is divided into two groups, based on citations by teacher, according to QS ranking. The group of universities with most citations by teacher is the one that has the lowest presence of women. It is a very small group of universities, only 11.

The group that presents an intermediate level of internationalization (20% of the total) is divided into three groups, according to the income raised from industry for the university. The association is clear: a higher level of income, a lower presence of women students at university.

In particular:

Women and Universities

- The category with the lowest income from industry and with the highest presence of female students (68 in all) was divided into two groups, according to the total impact of the articles produced at the university, (*AIT* indicator from URAP). At that low-income level, the universities with a higher impact had a higher female students' presence than those with a lower impact.
- The intermediate category of income from industry (70 universities) was also divided into two groups, according to the number of highly cited articles (indicator of the CWUR ranking). The group of universities with more highly cited articles corresponded to those with the lowest presence of women students.
- The group with most income raised from industry, also with a lower percentage of women students (45 universities), was likewise divided by number of citations (indicator of the URAP ranking). The group with a higher presence of female students had the higher number of citations.

Figure 1. Summary of the segmentation tree: Part 1

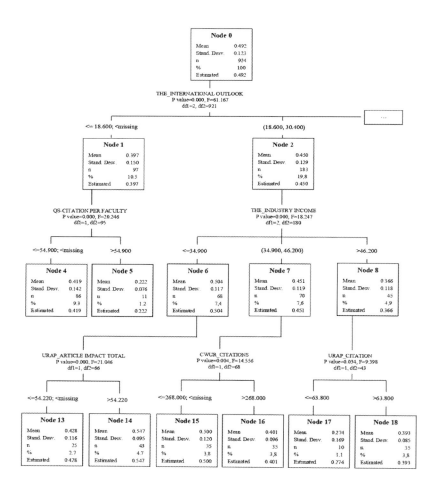

Women and Universities

The group that presented the highest level of internationalization and the highest presence of women students is much larger (644 universities, 70% in all). It was also divided by the level of income raised from industry, this time into four groups in the same way. There was a lower women presence among the students at higher levels of income, as shown in figure 2:

- The group with the lowest level of income raised from industry was not divided, although it was a numerous group composed of 237 universities (25% in all) with a majority presence of 56% of female students.

- The second group was distributed according to the quality indicator of 'number of articles that appear in highly influential journals' from the CWUR ranking (CWUR_INFLUENCE). The universities with the lowest scores for this indicator were those with higher percentages of female students. In turn, the group with the lowest score for *CWUR_INFLUENCE* was divided according to the student/teacher ratio. It was precisely the higher ratios that corresponded to the higher presence of women at university.

- The third group by level of income from the category of highest score for internationalization was divided into two groups, according to the number of full-time students: the higher the number of students, the higher the percentage of female students. The group with the highest number of full-time students was divided in accordance with the indicator of citations from the THE ranking. The group with the least citations was the one with the highest presence of female students.

- Finally, the group with the highest level of income among those of greater internationalization was also divided according to the citations. In this case, the group with most citations also had a higher percentage of female students. The group with the lowest number of citations was divided into two groups, according to the quality of the employment achieved by their graduates, the universities with the highest scores were the ones in this group that had the highest presence of women among students.

Figure 2. Summary of the segmentation tree: Part 2

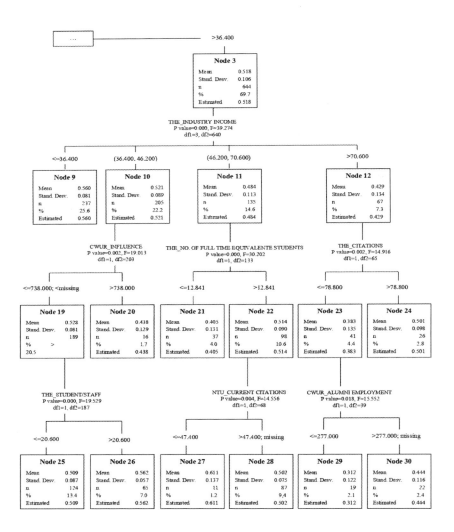

From higher to lower presence, one third of universities with a higher percentage of women students, over 56% of the total, as is shown in table 2, are concentrated in 3 segments (table 2):

- Node 27 is a small segment with only 11 universities that has an average percentage of female students over 60%. These universities have a high level of internationalization, and a medium-high level regarding income raised from industry. In addition, they are universities with many students and with lower levels of citations in recent years. Australia and Canada are the countries that have more universities in this group, each one with two universities.

Women and Universities

- Node 26 is more numerous, grouping together 65 universities. In this segment, women among students represent 56.2% of the total in average terms, and these universities have high levels of internationalization, medium-low levels of income raised from industry, lower levels of influence over their publications, and they are massified, that is they have high student/teacher ratios. In this group, 13 Italian, 11 Australian, and 6 Canadian and US universities stand out, as well 5 from Greece, 4 from Germany, and 3 from both Ireland and France.
- Finally, node 9 is the most numerous of all with 237 universities, which means one out of every four. The average presence of women among students reaches 56%, and the group is composed of universities with high levels of internationalization and low levels of income raised from industry. The countries with most universities in this group are the United Kingdom (61), USA (29), Spain (14), France (11), Australia (10), Italy (9), and Egypt (8).

Table 2. Detail of the groups formed with CHAID, dependent variable % of women at university

Node	Node by node			Accumulated		
	N	Percentage	Average	N	Percentage	Average
27	11	1.2%	61.09	11	1.2%	61.09
26	65	7.0%	56.20	76	8.2%	56.91
9	237	25.6%	56.02	313	33.9%	56.24
14	43	4.7%	54.72	356	38.5%	56.05
25	124	13.4%	50.94	480	51.9%	54.73
28	87	9.4%	50.17	567	61.4%	54.03
24	26	2.8%	50.08	593	64.2%	53.86
15	35	3.8%	50.03	628	68.0%	53.65
30	22	2.4%	44.36	650	70.3%	53.33
20	16	1.7%	43.81	666	72.1%	53.10
13	25	2.7%	42.84	691	74.8%	52.73
4	86	9.3%	41.92	777	84.1%	51.54
21	37	4.0%	40.51	814	88.1%	51.03
16	35	3.8%	40.11	849	91.9%	50.58
18	35	3.8%	39.29	884	95.7%	50.14
29	19	2.1%	31.21	903	97.7%	49.74
17	10	1.1%	27.40	913	98.8%	49.49
5	11	1.2%	22.18	924	100.0%	49.17

Source: Own elaboration.

The second third of universities corresponds to those universities that have a more balanced gender distribution (see table 2). There is greater uniformity than in the former group, given that there are five segments (see figure 1 and appendices 7):

- The three segments of this third that present the highest women presence from among all students are:
  - Node 14 (with 43 universities): universities with medium level of internationalisation, low level of income from industry and high impact of their publications.
  - Node 28 (87 universities): high level of internationalisation, medium-high level of income from industry, many students and higher level of citations.
  - Node 25 (124 universities): high level of internationalisation, medium-low level of income from industry and lower influence of their publications. In absolute terms, the countries with the most universities in this segment are the USA (75), the UK (29) and the UK (29). (75), UK (29), Canada (11), Germany (15), Australia (9), and Italy (10). Also noteworthy in relative terms, with respect to the total university system, is the number of universities in Spain (8).
- The other two segments consist of universities that have a high level of internationalization, with high income levels raised from industry and a high citations impact (node 24, with 26 universities), or with medium levels of income raised from industry and low levels of citations, according to CWUR ranking (node 15, with 35 universities). The countries where most universities were found in these groups were USA (13), Germany, and Taiwan with six universities, and Holland and Russia with four in each country.

The last third corresponds to the universities with a lower women presence among the students and is even more heterogenous, given that it is divided into 10 nodes (of the 18 identified). Along general lines, these universities have lower levels of internationalization and higher levels of income raised from industry. The countries with most universities present in this third are from Asia: China (34), Japan (56), India (28), Taiwan (19), South Korea (13), and Iran (11), although they are also from the USA (18, which is not much in comparison with the total for the country), Brazil (14), and Russia (10).

Differences by Population and GDP

On the basis of the division into three tertiaries according to the composition of the students, an ANOVA analysis of the difference in means was performed, in order to confirm whether there were differences between those groups with respect to the *population* and the *Gross Domestic Product (per capita GDP)* of the countries in which universities are located according to World Bank data.

With respect to the *population*, statistically significant differences (F Snedecor = 29,656; p-value = 0.00) were found, and likewise with respect to the *per capita GDP* (F Snedecor = 13,596; p-value = 0.00). The universities with the highest presence of male students are found in countries with much higher populations, which surpass the general average population of the countries under consideration by 55.5%. In addition, they are poorer, given that their GDP per capita is around 87.4% of the average of the countries under consideration. The group of universities with a higher presence of women among the students is found in countries with very much smaller populations, and with GDP per capita practically equal to the general average.

Finally, the group of universities with a balanced gender profile of students is found in countries with population sizes in-between the two former groups, but with higher income, because their GDP per capita is over 11% higher than the general average.

Women and Universities

There are 25 countries that has at least 9 universities for which the gender distribution is known. Those countries can be divided into three groups, according to whether most of their universities have a majority, a minority, or a balanced presence of students.

The group of countries with a higher percentage of universities with most female students is headed by the United Kingdom, followed by Australia, Italy and Canada. In descending order of percentages, Spain, France, Thailand, Finland, and Chile also belong that same group. Among all three groups, it occupies the intermediate position, in terms of both population and GDP per capita.

The group of countries in which the universities with a balanced presence of women and male students predominated was composed of 7 countries. At its head is Holland, followed by Switzerland and the USA. In addition, Poland, Germany, Czech Republic, and Sweden appear in descending order.

The group of countries in which the universities with a higher presence of men are in a majority are concentrated in Asia, and are led by India (93.33%), China (89.47%), Japan (85.58%), Iran (86.62%), Taiwan (73.08%), and other countries such as South Korea and Turkey, as well as Russia and Brazil. Among these three groups there are statistically significative differences, both for *population* (Chi-square Kruskal-Wallis = 7.755; p-value = 0.021), and *per capita GDP* (Chi-square Kruskal-Wallis = 9.898; p-value = 0.007).

CONCLUSION

The purpose of this study is to identify profiles of university systems in accordance with the presence of women among the students of the institutions and it has sought to measure the performance of those universities with regard to the indicators present in the international academic rankings.

First, the variable with most discriminatory power to explain the presence of women at universities is internationalization, measured as the presence among students and teaching staff of people from other countries to which international collaboration in university publications must be added. A higher level of internationalization implies a higher presence of women at university. The international openness of universities favours the presence of female students. Universities should, therefore, establish measures for the international recruitment of students and teaching staff, for the presence of women among the students to progress, as well as designing measures that favour international collaboration, especially in publications. This argument is more in favour of the internationalisation of universities as a factor for the advancement of equality and social development.

Second, the negative relation between income raised from industry by universities and the presence of female students at those universities: the higher the income, the lower the presence of women among the students. An observation that coincides with the current literature, that highlights the scant presence of women following technical and technological courses (such as engineering). It is precisely those sorts of qualifications that capture more resources from industry through the different forms of collaboration that exist, whether research projects or contracts. The explanation behind that observation is due to what has previously been mentioned in the literature; women usually choose less technical, less technological careers (Zeegers, 2004; Roemer et al., 2020).

Third, by grouping the segments identified into three categories of greater or lesser female presence, uniformity is greater in the group of universities with a greater presence of female students. The third of universities with the highest presence of women responded to two simple characteristics: a high level of internationalization and low or intermediate levels of income raised from industry. The most balanced third, due to a similar presence of male and female students, was somewhat more diverse and basically consisted of universities with a medium level of internationalization and with a low level of income or a high level of internationalization with a medium/high level of income, as well as a high level of impact of the citations or number of citations. Finally, the third part with the smallest presence of women among the students was much more diverse. It has a common characteristic: less internationalization and more income from industry, but afterwards there were many sub-groups because of the differences between the different indicators with which the rankings were prepared that have been considered. The highest presence of female students was found at universities with greater similarities between each other, while the lowest presence of women among the students at university was associated with common causes but nuanced by different indicators. This result highlights even more that, to increase the presence of female students, the principal measures must be taken on specific aspects relating to internationalization and relations with industry.

Fourth, the results on the presence of women students at university by country underlines what had previously been found in the literature. In other words, it is the countries of the western world where women have a higher presence, particularly Australia, Canada, Italy, USA, France, Germany, Spain, United Kingdom, Greece, and Ireland. In general terms, the universities of those countries, as well as having higher proportions of women students, were also the most internationalized, but they showed different levels of income raised from industry.

Fifth, from the analysis of the relation between population or GDP per capita of the territories where the universities were found and their gender composition it was concluded that: the universities with a higher male students' presence were found in very much more highly populated countries. On the other hand, those countries were also the poorest, with a per capita GDP that was less than the average of the other countries. The countries that presented a per capita GDP that was line with the general average, and the least populated countries, were those with universities that had a higher presence of women students. The countries with higher-than-average income presented a balanced percentage of men and women at university. The explanation for this situation might reside in cultural aspects, as the activities of the poorest countries continue under social structures where the role of women is still relegated to caring for the family and for the house (Morrison et al., 2011).

The average income of the countries with higher percentages of universities where female students are in a majority, i.e., with more women than men, such as the United Kingdom, Australia, Italy, and Canada, double the average incomes of the group of those countries with universities where male students are in a majority, such as India, China, Japan, Iran, Taiwan, and other Asian countries. In general terms, the presence of women at university acts as an indicator of the social development of the country in question. For that reason, it is expected that the development of the knowledge society will also have the potential to change the nature of gender relations, with implications for work and organization as a whole (Walby, 2011).

In view of the results, it is concluded that progress with university internationalization go hand in hand with a higher presence of women among the students, while greater financing, due to the relation with the business world among universities is associated with a lower presence of women. This situation is due to that university-business relation that is linked to the technological offer of the universities in which there are still far fewer women. Internationalization of the university and the inclusion of women in technical careers are therefore factors to be strengthened, in order to advance towards equality. The result shows that equality in university composition is a feature of more developed countries, although there are exceptions, of which Japan may be the best example.

An important implication for university management is to establish measures for the international recruitment of students and teaching staff, as well as to design measures that favour international collaboration, particularly in publications. The internationalisation of universities is a factor in the advancement of equality, balance and social development. A composition of the structure of the student body, including the teaching staff, more in line with the gender composition of the population implies a social change, in many countries a major social change, which necessarily involves becoming aware of and implementing social marketing strategies as pedagogy (Kennedy et al., 2022) for the different stakeholders.

The result achieved makes it possible to identify the systems where there is most room for improvement in gender equity, and therefore for action, both from a geographical perspective and in terms of internal policies in institutional management. For example, by promoting internationalisation and through international collaboration which, among other benefits, are also a source of cultural enrichment. This study empirically confirms the link between development and balance in the student composition of universities. This should also be taken into account by those responsible for management and university systems in different countries.

The limitations of the work have to do with the limitations of the rankings whose indicators have been used for the study. In particular, the selection of the indicators themselves, as well as the weighting of each one. Also, regarding the nature of their indicators (bibliometric or using surveys).

REFERENCES

Acker, J. (1990). Hierarchies, jobs, bodies: A theory of gendered organizations. *Gender & Society*, *4*(2), 139–158. doi:10.1177/089124390004002002

Alba, A. (2000). La riqueza de las familias: Mujer y mercado de trabajo en la España democrática. *Ariel*.

Appleby, Y., & Bathmaker, A. M. (2006). The new skills agenda: Increased lifelong learning or new sites of inequality. *British Educational Research Journal*, *32*(5), 703–717. doi:10.1080/01411920600895742

August, L., & Waltman, J. (2004). Culture, climate, and contribution: career satisfaction among female faculty. *Research in Higher Education, 45*, 177e192. doi:10.1023/B:RIHE.0000015694.14358.ed

Blackwell, L., & Glover, J. (2008). Women's scientific employment and family formation: A longitudinal perspective. *Gender, Work and Organization*, *15*(6), 579–599. doi:10.1111/j.1468-0432.2007.00385.x

Çakır, M. P., Acartürk, C., Alaşehir, O., & Çilingir, C. (2015). A comparative analysis of global and national university ranking systems. *Scientometrics*, *103*(3), 813–848. doi:10.100711192-015-1586-6

Cama, M. G., Jorge, M. L., & Peña, F. J. A. (2016). Gender differences between faculty members in higher education: A literature review of selected higher education journals. *Educational Research Review*, *18*, 58–69. doi:10.1016/j.edurev.2016.03.001

Carmona-Valdés, S. E. (2015). Hacia una educación con equidad. *Praxis (Bern)*, *11*(1), 8–18. doi:10.21676/23897856.1549

Çelik, H., & Watson, F. (2021). Understanding the leaky pipeline system: Behavioural ecological approach to the social marketing of women thriving in STEM careers. *Journal of Social Marketing*, *11*(4), 616–632. doi:10.1108/JSOCM-03-2021-0051

Correll, S. J. (2001). Gender and the career choice process: The role of biased self-assessments. *American Journal of Sociology*, *106*(6), 1691–1730. doi:10.1086/321299

Cubillo, L., & Brown, M. (2003). Women into educational leadership and management: international differences? *Journal of Educational Administration, 41*, 278e291. doi:10.1108/09578230310474421

Currie, J., & Hill, B. (2013). Gendered universities and the wage gap: Case study of a pay equity audit in an Australian university. *Higher Education Policy*, *26*(1), 65–82. doi:10.1057/hep.2012.19

David, M. E. (2012). Feminism, gender and global higher education: women's learning lives. *Higher Education Research & Development, 31*, 679e687. doi:10.1080/07294360.2012.691465

Docampo, D. (2008). Rankings internacionales y calidad de los sistemas universitarios. *Review of Education, 1*, 149–176.

Docampo, D. (2010). On using the Shanghai ranking to assess the investigation performance of university systems. *Scientometrics*, *86*(1), 77–92. doi:10.100711192-010-0280-y

Docampo, D., & Cram, L. (2015). On the effects of institutional size in university classifications: The case of the Shanghai ranking. *Scientometrics*, *102*(2), 1325–1346. doi:10.100711192-014-1488-z

Ely, R. J., & Meyerson, D. E. (2000). Theories of gender in organizations: A new approach to organizational analysis and change. *Research in Organizational Behavior*, *22*, 103–151. doi:10.1016/S0191-3085(00)22004-2

European Commission. (2005). *Communication to the Spring European Council: Working together for growth and jobs: integrated guidelines for growth and jobs (2005-2008)*. EC. https://ec.europa.eu/economy_finance/publications/pages/publication6410_en.pdf

Fogelberg, P., Hearn, J., Husu, L., & Mankkinen, T. (Eds.). (1999). *Hard work in the academy: Research and interventions on gender inequalities in higher education*. Helsinki University Press.

Friedmann, E. (2018). Increasing women's participation in the STEM industry: A first step for developing a social marketing strategy. *Journal of Social Marketing*, *8*(4), 442–460. doi:10.1108/JSOCM-12-2017-0086

Gámez, E., & Marrero, H. (2003). Metas y motivos en la elección de la carrera universitaria: Un estudio comparativo entre psicología, derecho y biología. *Anales de Psicología*, *19*(1), 121–131.

Giménez-Salinas Colomer, E. (2005). Mujeres en la Universidad: Cien años de prohibiciones. In E. Giménez-Salinas Colomer (Ed.), *Doctas, Doctoras y Catedráticas. Cien años de acceso libre de la mujer a la universidad* (pp. 57–72)., Available at https://mujeresconciencia.com/app/uploads/2015/02/Doctas_doctoras_Castellano_Completo.pdf

Hazelkorn, E. (2012). The Effects of Rankings on Student Choices and Institutional Selection. In B. Jongbloed & H. Vossensteyn (Eds.), *Access and expansion post- massification: Opportunities and barriers to further growth in higher education participation*. Routledge.

Johnes, J. (2018). University rankings: What do they really show? *Scientometrics*, *115*(1), 585–606. doi:10.100711192-018-2666-1

Kennedy, A. M., Veer, E., & Kemper, J. A. (2022). Social marketing AS pedagogy. *Journal of Social Marketing*. doi:10.1108/JSOCM-08-2021-0192

Khan, M. S., Lakha, F., Tan, M. M. J., Singh, S. R., Quek, R. Y. C., Han, E., Tan, S. M., Haldane, V., Gea-Sánchez, M., & Legido-Quigley, H. (2019). More talk than action: Gender and ethnic diversity in leading public health universities. *Lancet, 393*(10171), 594–600. doi:10.1016/S0140-6736(18)32609-6 PMID:30739695

Kulis, S., & Sicotte, D. (2002). Women scientists in academia: geographically constrained to big cities, college clusters, or the coasts? *Research in Higher Education, 43*, 1e30 doi:10.1023/A:1013097716317

Luque-Martínez, T. (2012). *Técnicas de análisis de datos en investigación de mercados*. Pirámide.

Luque-Martínez, T., & Del Barrio-García, S. (2016). Constructing a synthetic indicator of research activity. *Scientometrics, 108*(3), 1049–1064. doi:10.100711192-016-2037-8

Luque-Martínez, T., Faraoni, N., & Doña-Toledo, L. (2020). Los rankings académicos y la distribución por género de las universidades. *Revista Española de Documentación Científica, 43*(2), e261. doi:10.3989/redc.2020.2.1663

Martínez García, J. S. (2007). Clase social, género y desigualdad de oportunidades educativas. *Review of Education, 342*, 287–306.

Morrison, E., Rudd, E., & Nerad, M. (2011). Onto, up, off the academic faculty ladder: The gendered effects of family on career transitions for a cohort of social science Ph.D.s. *Review of Higher Education, 34*(4), 525–553. doi:10.1353/rhe.2011.0017

Muñoz, M. T., & Mullet, E. (1990). Los determinantes de las preferencias profesionales de los adolescentes. *Evaluación Psicológica, 6*, 155–170.

Navarro Guzmán, C., & Casero Martínez, A. (2012). Análisis de las diferencias de género en la elección de estudios universitarios. *ESE. Estudios sobre Educación, 22*, 115–132. doi:10.15581/004.22.2075

Nguyen, T. L. H. (2013). Barriers to and facilitators of female Deans' career advancement in higher education: An exploratory study in Vietnam. *Higher Education, 66*(1), 123–138. doi:10.100710734-012-9594-4

Odhiambo, G. (2011). Women and higher education leadership in Kenya: a critical analysis. *Journal of Higher Education Policy and Management, 33*, 667e678. doi:10.1080/1360080X.2011.621192

Ordorika, I., & Lloyd, M. (2015). International rankings and the contest for university hegemony. *Journal of Education Policy, 30*(3), 385–405. doi:10.1080/02680939.2014.979247

Papadópulos, J., & Radakovich, R. (2003). *Estudio Comparado de Educación Superior y Género en América Latina y el Caribe*. IESALC-Unión de Universidades de América Latina. https://www.ses.unam.mx/curso2007/pdf/genero_es.pdf

Powell, G. N., Butterfield, D. A., & Parent, J. D. (2002). Gender and managerial stereotypes: Have the times changed? *Journal of Management, 28*(2), 177–193. doi:10.1177/014920630202800203

Reverter-Bañon, S. (2021). La igualdad de género en la universidad. Capitalismo académico y rankings globales. *Investigaciones Feministas, 12*(2), 271–281. doi:10.5209/infe.72331

Roemer, C., Rundle-Thiele, S., Pang, B., David, P., Kim, J., Durl, J., Dietrich, T., & Carins, J. (2020). Rewiring the STEM pipeline - a C-B-E framework to female retention. *Journal of Social Marketing, 10*(4), 427–446. doi:10.1108/JSOCM-10-2019-0152

Safón, V. (2019). Inter-ranking reputational effects: An analysis of the Academic Ranking of World Universities (ARWU) and the Times Higher Education World University Rankings (THE) reputational relationship. *Scientometrics, 121*(2), 897–915. doi:10.100711192-019-03214-9

Sáinz, M., López-Sáez, M., & Lisbona, A. (2004). Expectativas de rol profesional de mujeres estudiantes de carreras típicamente femeninas o masculinas. *Acción Psicológica, 3*, 111–123.

Sax, J. J., Hagedorn, L. S., Arredondo, M., & Dicrisi, F. A. (2002). Faculty research productivity: Exploring the role of gender and family-related factors. *Research in Higher Education, 43*, 423e446. doi:10.1023/A:1015575616285

Shavit, Y., & Blossfeld, H. P. (1996). Equalizing educational opportunity: Do gender and class compete? In R. Erikson & O. J. Jonsson (Eds.), *Can education be equalized? The Swedish Case in Comparative Perspective* (pp. 233–254). Westview Press.

Teelken, C., & Deem, R. (2013). All are equal, but some are more equal than others: Managerialism and gender equality in higher education in comparative perspective. *Comparative Education, 49*(4), 520–535. doi:10.1080/03050068.2013.807642

Timmers, T. M., Willemsen, T. M., & Tijdens, K. G. (2010). Gender diversity policies in universities: A multi-perspective framework of policy measures. *Higher Education, 59*(6), 719–735. doi:10.100710734-009-9276-z

Trotter, L. J. (2017). Making a career: Reproducing gender within a predominately female profession. *Gender & Society, 31*(4), 503–525. doi:10.1177/0891243217716115

Tzanakou, C., & Pearce, R. (2019). Moderate feminism within or against the neoliberal university? The example of Athena SWAN. *Gender, Work and Organization, 26*(8), 1–21. doi:10.1111/gwao.12336

UNESCO. (2007). *Science, Technology and Gender: An International Report*. UNESCO.

UNESCO. (2021). Instituto Internacional de la UNESCO para la Educación Superior en América Latina y el Caribe. *Women in higher education: has the female advantage put an end to gender inequalities?* Organización de las Naciones Unidas para la Educación, la Ciencia y la Cultura. París, Francia. https://unesdoc.unesco.org/ark:/48223/pf0000377183

Vernon, M. M., Balas, E. A., & Momani, S. (2018). Are university rankings useful to improve research? A systematic review. *PLoS One, 13*(3), e0193762. doi:10.1371/journal.pone.0193762 PMID:29513762

Walby, S. (2011). Is the knowledge society gendered? *Gender, Work and Organization, 18*(1), 1–29. doi:10.1111/j.1468-0432.2010.00532.x

Wolfinger, N., Mason, M., & Goulden, M. (2008). Problems in the pipeline: Gender, marriage, and fertility in the Ivory Tower. *The Journal of Higher Education, 79*(4), 388–405. doi:10.1080/00221546.2008.11772108

Xiao, Y., Pinkney, E., Au, T. K. F., & Yip, P. S. F. (2020). Athena Swan and gender diversity: A UK-based retrospective cohort study. *BMJ Open, 10*(2), e032915. doi:10.1136/bmjopen-2019-032915 PMID:32051310

Zeegers, P. (2004). Student learning in higher education: A path analysis of academic achievement in science. *Higher Education Research & Development, 23*(1), 35–56. doi:10.1080/0729436032000168487

APPENDICES

Appendices 1: Academic ranking of world universities, ARWU

Criteria	Indicator	Weight
Quality of Education	Alumni of an institution winning Nobel Prizes and Field Medals (Alumni)	10%
Quality of Faculty	Staff of an institution winning Nobel Prizes and Field Medals (Award)	20%
	Highly cited researchers in 21 broad subject categories (HiCi)	20%
Research Output	Papers published in Nature and Science* (N&S)	20%
	Papers indexed in Science Citation Index-expanded and Social Science Citation Index (PUB)	20%
Per Capita Performance	Per capita academic performance of an institution (PCP)	10%

Appendices 2: CWUR world university rankings, CWUR

Criteria	Indicator	Weight
Quality of Education	Measured by the number of a university's alumni who have won major international awards, prizes, and medals relative to the university's size.	25%
Alumni Employment	Measured by the number of a university's alumni who have held CEO positions at the world's top companies relative to the university's size.	25%
Quality of Faculty	Measured by the number of academics who have won major international awards, prizes, and medals.	10%
Research Performance (Research Output, High-Quality Publications, Influence, Citations)	i) Research Output, measured by the total number of research papers. ii) High-Quality Publications, measured by the number of research papers appearing in top-tier journals. iii) Influence, measured by the number of research papers appearing in highly influential journals. iv) Citations, measured by the number of highly cited research papers.	40%

Appendices 3: National Taiwan university ranking, NTU

Criteria	Indicator	Weight
Research productivity	Number of articles in the last 11 years Number of articles in the current year	25%
Research impact (Current citations)	Number of citations in the last 11 years Number of citations in the last 2 years Average number of citations in the last 11 years	35%
Research Excellence	H-index of the last 2 years Number of Highly Cited Papers Number of articles in the current year in high-impact journals	40%

Women and Universities

Appendices 4: QS World university rankings, QS

Criteria	Indicator	Weight
Academic reputation	It is measured using a global survey in which academics have to identify the institutions where they believe the best work is taking place within their own field of expertise.	40%
Employer reputation	Based on a global survey that asks employers to identify the universities that, according to them, are educating the best graduates.	10%
Faculty/Student ratio	Ratio between teachers and number of students.	20%
Citations per faculty	An attempt is made to evaluate the impact of university research by measuring the number of citations per teacher.	20%
International faculty ratio/International student ratio	These indicators assess the institution's ability to attract foreign students and teachers.	5% + 5%

Appendices 5: Times higher education world university rankings, THE*

Criteria	Indicator	Weight
Citations	Citation's impact (normalized average citations per paper) (Database: Thomson Reuter's Web of Science)	30%
Teaching	1 - Income per academic 2 - Reputational survey – teaching 3 - PhD awards per academic 4 - PhD awards / bachelor's awards 5 - Undergraduates admitted per academic	30%
Research	1 - Papers academic and research staff 2 - Research income (scaled) 3 - Reputation survey – research	30%
International outlook	1 - Ratio of international to domestic students 2 - Ratio of international to domestic staff 3 - Proportion of internationally co-authored research papers	7.5%
Industry income	1 - Research income from industry (per academic staff).	2.5%

* The indicators of No. of FTE students, No. of students per staff, Percentage of international students, and Female: Male ratio are not shown in the table.

Appendices 6: University ranking by academic performance, URAP

Criteria	Indicator	Weight
Article	A measure of current scientific productivity which includes articles published in journals that are listed within the first, second and third quartiles in terms of their Journal Impact Factor.	21%
Citation	A measure of research impact and scored according to the total number of citations received in 2013-2017 for the articles published in journals that are listed within the first, second and third quartiles in terms of their Journal Impact Factor.	21%
Total Document	The measure of sustainability and continuity of scientific productivity and presented by the total document count which covers all scholarly output of the institutions, including conference papers, reviews, letters, discussions, and scripts, in addition to journal articles published during the period 2013-2017.	10%
Article Impact Total (AIT)	A measure of scientific productivity in 23 subject areas between 2013 and 2017. The data indicate whether the institution is performing above or below the world average in that field. This indicator aims to balance the institution's scientific productivity with the field normalized impact generated by those publications in each field.	18%
Citation Impact Total (CIT)	A measure of research impact in 23 subject areas between 2013 and 2017. The data indicate whether the institution is performing above or below the global average in that field. This indicator aims to balance the institution's scientific impact with the field normalized impact generated by the publications in each field.	15%
International Collaboration	A measure of global acceptance of a university. International collaboration data is obtained from InCites for the years 2013-2017.	15%

Women and Universities

Appendices 7: Segmentation tree of the universities of the world: General diagram

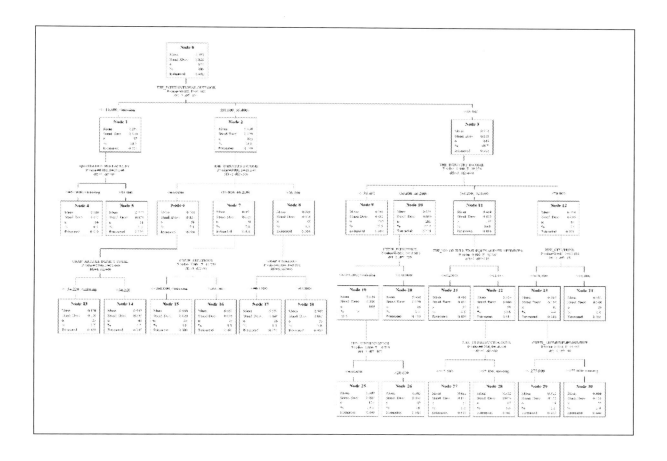

215

Chapter 11
Nobody Wants to Work Under These Conditions

Ivania Delgado

https://orcid.org/0009-0002-2604-0863

Social Work Core Faculty, Pacific Oaks College, USA

Nafiza Spirko

MSW Graduate Student, USA

Saudia Rahamat

Community Project Manager/DEI Consultant, Canada

ABSTRACT

This book chapter explores the history of capitalism in the United States and its roots in slavery. It reviews business organizational theories born under the exploitation and dehumanization of enslaved people. The chapter attempts to make the legacies of these systems visible in today's working conditions that have led to the great resignation exacerbated by COVID-19. The chapter, per the authors, uses the context of the education and training of helpers to highlight how these systems impact students in their academic journeys, career opportunities, and financial stability from an intersectional lens. Lastly, as a call to action for readers, it explores the Caremongering movement, a bottom-up mutual aid network that can teach industry management and decision-makers lessons on creating equitable, inclusive conditions that meet the needs of the people.

NOBODY WANTS TO WORK UNDER THESE CONDITIONS

As part of their education, social workers and psychologists (helpers) must complete training to apply what they have learned in their courses during internship and practicum across different settings that serve multiple populations for various reasons. Students are asked to provide services at hospitals, mental health clinics, schools, and more. The populations they serve include those seeking services for mental health reasons such as post-traumatic stress disorder and depression. Clients may exist at multiple intersections of oppression (intersectionality) because they are part of the under-resourced and

DOI: 10.4018/978-1-6684-8597-2.ch011

Copyright © 2023, IGI Global. Copying or distributing in print or electronic forms without written permission of IGI Global is prohibited.

Nobody Wants to Work Under These Conditions

marginalized by-design communities experiencing houselessness, lack of health care, and economic instability because of income inequality. Students are placed in high-stress and high-demand learning environments where they witness human suffering while navigating intrapersonal spheres of suffering across the privilege spectrum. Students and employees may be vicariously traumatized, burned out, and experience stress-related physical, psychological, and spiritual consequences; potentially leading helpers to seek the services they provide. Responsibilities include providing direct services to clients, meeting with their supervisors, participating in internal and multi-disciplinary meetings, and driving to and from multiple locations, mostly done under unpaid terms. On top of being unpaid, it is an additional expense for students because they pay to be enrolled in courses and practicums as part of their training. Helpers could benefit from examining organizational theories and interrogating how they shape the learning and working conditions of the front-line helping professions. It is also important to consider the intersections of gender, race, class, and ability. According to *The Social Work Profession: Findings from Three Years of Surveys of New Social Workers* with data from 2017-2019, most people who become social workers are women from different racial and ethnic backgrounds. Around 90% of those with a Master of Social Work degree between 2017 and 2019 were women. More than 22% of new social workers were Black American, and 14% were Hispanic/Latino- these figures are considered high when compared to other healthcare occupations. Many social workers are the first in their families to attend college and become first-generation graduates. In 2019, more than 46% of the people who got their MSW degree were the first ones in their families to graduate college. This was especially true for Black/African American individuals, where 57% were the first in their families, and for Hispanic/Latino individuals, where it was 73%. Take into consideration that these graduates may be incurring student loans. If we look at what the American Psychological Association reported, in 2021-2022, approximately 83% of students enrolled in clinical psychology degree programs were women. According to a Washington Post article by Danielle Douglas-Gabriel, women are responsible for two-thirds of the education debt. Institutional racism makes it so that among women, Black women carry the highest average debt one year after graduating. On average, Black women owe $41,466 for their undergraduate studies and $75,085 for graduate school. (Douglas-Gabriel, 2022) An ongoing reflection and conversation of how helpers in leadership, management, and administrative positions contribute to employee satisfaction, team building, and collaboration, addressing employee motivation, supporting employee goals, and supporting self-care for everyone in the organization is ethically required. For example, social workers are guided by a guided by a code of ethics, as well as trained in a set of educational competencies that explicitly asks social workers to address social, racial, economic, and environmental justice utilizing anti-oppressive frameworks such as intersectionality. Social workers must ensure that working conditions, including policies, practices, and material resources, promote self-care at the workplace. Social workers are expected to connect historic oppression and racism that have contributed to the uneven distribution of material capital today. Social workers are tasked with remaining vigilant of practices that rob people of their dignity and create barriers to comprehensive wellness (CSWE, 2022), foundational pieces that aspire to establish and nourish intergenerational success. The authors will include a historical analysis of slavery and colonization as it relates to the development of the current American capitalist economic system and their connection to organizational theories. Historical research will be reviewed, and a lens of decolonial criticality will be implemented to connect these histories to current-day organizational-macro-level practices that create dehumanizing and exploitative working conditions. The authors aim to respond to the dominant, liberal, and deficit-based idea that has permeated industry via mainstream news that states, "Nobody Wants to Work Anymore," and people are "quiet quitting." As discussed in the media, quiet quitting is described as people doing the "minimum" in their current positions. It is part of the nobody wants to work cultural messaging that people are being exposed to within the context of the great resignation. The great resignation is what the ongoing corporate agility - active autonomous agility of the worker within the corporate system- that the COVID-19 pandemic has brought is called. People are changing jobs and quitting in droves, and this has been highlighted throughout the pandemic in the face of equitable working resources being proven viable and actionable. Despite the prevailing social narrative that says individuals are reluctant to work, using shaming tactics like labeling behaviors as quiet quitting, increasingly, many are rejecting these narratives. Instead, they challenge the narratives by highlighting normalized ableist, racist, and oppressive conditions within organizations that increase exposure to COVID-19, physical and psychological health issues, particularly when we take gender, race, and class into account. The authors use organizational theory to frame the discussion and include author testimony to discuss the tension and conflict that presents itself when you consider what is being taught in the classrooms versus what is happening when helpers find themselves in organizations that reduce human beings to tasks, deadlines, productivity, and center profit. Helpers also question how these training sites and jobs ask them to contribute to systems of oppression. The authors will discuss how white supremacist systems continue to exploit the labors of Native American, Black, Brown, Latinx, and Indigenous Peoples in workspaces and higher education. Authors aim to uncover these connections made invisible in the helping profession's curriculum and hidden under the guise of professionalism. The authors seek to interrogate the material conditions through a lens of criticality that considers the historical and dialectics that critical theories focus on. The main objective is to critique managerial styles and organizational structures and visualize equitable working conditions that embrace the helpers' full humanity so they can better see and serve the full humanity of the communities they are entering or may even come from. Working conditions that do not ask people to work through the pain, exhaustion, vicarious trauma, and burnout and do not ask people to lose agency over their own psychological, physical, and spiritual health. The COVID-19 pandemic has amplified the proletariat experience of burnout of body and mind (Cotel et al., 2021). According to recent studies, lower socio-economic groups have been disproportionately affected by the negative economic consequences and have also experienced higher fatality rates (Stevano et al., 2021).This level of exhaustion has turned workers' and students' attention towards pushing back on capitalist institutional designs, suggesting abolitionist theory as a guide to dismantling individualist systems and imagining systems that could be built on collectivist culture (Peña, 2022). The authors want helpers to ask questions about social, economic, and political power within organizations rooted in colonization and enslavement to make the systems visible and transparent to all who engage with them. Visibility allows for closer examination and interrogation that can lead to changes resulting in the transparency needed to ensure systems do not repeat the same mistakes. We can make these changes at all levels, including students, faculty, supervisors, and administrators; changes that, when actioned across all levels, establish healthier interwoven foundational systems accessible by all. The call to action is to intervene by changing the curriculum, providing training and education to current leaders and managers, and empowering helpers to resist oppressive conditions and transform their relationships with work and self-care. As students graduate and move beyond entry-level positions, many will hold management and leadership positions in their professions. Helpers must self-examine and reflect on what they have been taught in their courses about managing people and leadership in many situations. They must examine their intersectional practices as they join organizations and take on intern supervisors, program coordinators, managers, and directors' roles. The authors' connections in this chapter may benefit multiple academic disciplines and industries seeking to transform

Nobody Wants to Work Under These Conditions

their work environments by reducing oppressive and unfair working conditions. After all, the great resignation is a window of opportunity and reclamation to reject the call to go back to normal, since going back to normal means normalizing inequitable access to mental health resources and quality of life satisfaction for many people. We expect students in the helping professions to gain knowledge and skills through classroom instruction and practicum hours. In addition, they must meet the competencies outlined by the program's accrediting bodies. According to the program's accrediting organization, the students must prioritize the well-being of the people they interface with. They accomplish this by learning and applying theory, using a systems-based approach, engaging in policy action, and using and implementing anti-oppressive frameworks. Courses focusing on the macro-environment include lessons on organizational theories derived from business and management literature (Kirst-Ashman & Hull, 2019, p.149). Uncovering the historical contexts of these theories is crucial and done by teaching beyond the textbook. "Historians are currently working to integrate the South more fully into the story of American capitalism. New research describes a vigorous, violent system where innovation and brutality go hand in hand (Rosenthal, 2016, p. 63)." For example, we usually discuss the following theories in a way that erases the origins of slavery.

CLASSICAL ORGANIZATIONAL THEORIES

These theories are described as being rigid and highly standardized. Workers are expected to do as they are told, and their input is not desired. They are provided instructions and directives that should be completed in a standardized way, and this does not include or welcome the thoughts and feelings of the workers. Helpers learn about Frederick W. Taylor's Scientific Management in class within the context of macro-level management and supervision. They learn that Scientific Management requires observation and assessment that encourages standardization. These standards are then used to dictate what they expected of the worker. Each worker has a set of tasks (standardized) that the worker must complete. As such, employee selection processes include gathering information on the trainability of the worker in connection to the level of productivity needed by the organization. Classical organizational theories have hierarchal structures. Managers decide, and workers carry out the standardized tasks that the managers request. Students do not learn that these practices have roots in slavery and come from dehumanization and exploitation and are practiced and developed with people held in bondage. Enslavers measured how much enslaved people would produce in terms of labor, knowledge, and skills. They developed ways to document patterns of labor of the enslaved and would use these to manage, predict, and create incentives to increase productivity. Enslavers would capitalize on the dehumanizing conditions of the enslaved to experiment with new ways of increasing the profit of their plantations. Rosenthal (2016) explains that Thomas Affleck created, reproduced, and sold one of the most well-known accounting books, but these types of plantation accounting documents had existed as early as the 1780s in Jamaica, British West Indies, and other places. Furthermore, Rosenthal explains that these calculations are complex and that part of what made this type of commoditization and innovation profitable was its roots in dehumanization. If you do not see the people enslaved as fully human, it justifies the conditions in which they are laboring. Their (2020) explains that getting people to work more in less time is a process Marx called condensation of labor. This process of intensifying labor is exploitative but brings about profit.

Thier (2020) explains that this process was dubbed Taylorism after Frederick Taylor. However, Baptist (2016, p.51) describes this process in the enslaved laboring on plantations, "We know from enslavers' cotton-picking books that the average amount picked per day by enslaved picker rose by 400 percent from 1800 to 1860, in a steady curve." Baptist discusses personal narratives from enslaved people, abolitionists, and historians, and all include variations of similar processes. The enslaved people were assigned a quota. Whether or not they met the quota, they did not end early; when everyone was brought back in from the fields, the overseer would use a scale, a lamp, and a whip. The plantation overseer was called "the first salaried manager in the country" by Alfred Chandler (Rosenthal, 2016, p.63). The overseer would measure the weight of the baskets, and if quotas were not met, they would violently torture the enslaved through whippings and label them simultaneously as lazy or good for nothing. If enslaved people exceeded their quota, this would become their new quota. They also developed incentives to increase productivity, such as providing extra food, clothing, and money. Baptist (2016) cautions readers to avoid thinking that incentives are only about increasing production. Incentives were also used to inform the entire system about what enslaved people could produce or accomplish that would result in a profit for all involved.

The whip made cotton. And whip- made increases in the efficiency of picking had global significance. They pushed down the real price of cotton, which by 1860 had fallen to one quarter of its 1800 price, even as demand had increased many times over. U.S. cotton producers effectively set the world price for this all-important commodity. So efficiency gains in picking created a pie from which many could take a slice. (Baptist, 2016, p. 51)

Another classical theory that we can still see in the present-day concerns from workers regarding power, decision-making, and the placing of profit over worker concerns is the Administrative Theory of Management developed by Henri Fayol. He focused on what administrators should accomplish. He outlined six principles administrators should follow when planning, organizing, commanding, coordinating, and controlling (Kirst-Ashman & Hull, 2019, p.151). Fayol advocated for specialized tasks to be given to workers to increase productivity. He encouraged having a manager in command at every level to dictate to workers their responsibilities, supervise them, and increase compliance. He supported centralized power wherever productivity was the most affected. Fayol also stated that administrators at the top of the hierarchy delegated job tasks and duties to the workers. However, workers should have only one supervisor so the work is consistent and each specialized group focuses on its goal. The point is to reduce confusion and always maximize productivity. Marx would talk about this as one cause of alienation. They robbed workers of their full humanity by working on repetitive, tiring tasks that did not make space for creativity, imagination, or community. Everyone works on a single piece of the puzzle at a distance from one another, with no power. Thier (2020), describing alienation through a Marxist lens, writes:

Along with collectivization of labor, the exploited workforce has to be supervised for maximum efficiency. There's no greater danger to efficiency than a large alienated group of workers laboring together. Their interests naturally lead to sabotage, slowdowns, or— heaven forbid— organizing efforts! The market treats workers as individuals —necessary inputs for production— and, as was discussed in the previous chapter, reduces our mental and physical capabilities to their barest and most alienated forms. (p. 123)

Blassingame (1977) contains a narrative of James Curry, born in North Carolina, who names his enslaver Moses Chambers. In this narrative, Curry describes some of what Baptist (2016) mentioned.

Nobody Wants to Work Under These Conditions

"When arranging the slaves for hoeing in the field, the overseer takes them, one at a time, and tries their speed, and places them accordingly in the row, the swiftest first, and so on. Then they commence, and all must keep up with the foremost" (Blassingame, 1977, p.135). You may wonder what happened to James Curry. He broke the law and fled, went through even more life and death situations, but eventually found himself in New York and then Massachusetts, where abolitionists and other freed Black folks supported each other. At the end of his narrative, he dreamed of going to Canada and lived in Canada for 27 years. However, in a horrific display of white supremacist violence, when James Curry returned to the United States to reconnect and recover his family, a group of White men beat him.

"Capitalism was created on plantations. The roots of it are violence and theft." (Hersey, 2022)

CAPITALISM AND HIGHER EDUCATION: TESTIMONIO

In this section, we will explore how academia gives precedence to the needs of capitalist industry by utilizing the method of *testimonios* as a means of analysis. "Testimonios a tool for inscribing our own struggles and understandings, by which we control the authorial process and in which we become subject and object of inquiry, create new knowledge, and affirm our epistemology." (Delgado Bernal et al., 2012) Our aim is not to be objective. Our aim is to include our personal, educational, and professional knowledge utilizing concepts from critical theory, such as including power structures and historical material conditions that shape our educational and occupational experiences. Our current training and education in higher education institutions frequently center on the industry's needs. As a result, students complete internships without pay, incur massive student loan debt, and face barriers when looking for work. This debt load is concerning because helping professionals are not producing goods for wages. Instead, helpers provide services that promote sustainable human health outcomes.

Cultural gaslighting is inherent in capitalism, a foundational pillar, promising workers that hard work will lead to economic stability, a sense of dignity, and freedom (Freire, 1978; Ruíz, 2020). The lived experience of helpers and those we help increasingly prove to be the opposite of this promise. The American mantra of pulling yourself up by the bootstraps is not health-promoting, not for mental health outcomes or economically. In *Poverty, By America* by Matthew Desmond (2023, pg 17) he writes that Black and Latinx people are twice as likely to be poor compared to their white counterparts and that the wealth gap has been this way since the 1960's. This wealth gap is a complex issue with deep historical roots, including differences in access to education and employment opportunities between racial and ethnic groups. Helpers are becoming burned out from oppressive institutions, low wages, and cultural gaslighting as white supremacist ableist systems continue exploiting the labors of Black, Latinx, and Indigenous people in workspaces and higher education.

According to Schraedley et al. (2021), what students and faculty in higher education feel are the effects of neoliberalism seeping into higher education over the last 30 to 40 years.:

Reagan's neoliberal administration promoted educational reform through market-driven strategies of deregulation, privatization, high-stakes test-based evaluations, and weakened teacher tenure and seniority rights, among other things. In subsequent decades, the United States higher education system became plagued by an ever-declining revenue stream from municipal, state, and federal governments. (Schraedley et al., 2021, p. 3)

Privatization of Universities has been shifting the focus of academia from public interest- including imagining possibilities of improving social systems- to private interest, which is product-focused, a shift that has created the academic-industrial complex. Students are treated as customers who further University funding by paying exorbitant tuition fees, filling physical attendance quotas that lead to more departmental funding, and they are given a choice of majors which are predominantly geared towards the production of more skilled workers to be funneled into the capitalist economy (Poe et al., n.d.). This academic-industrial complex creates more entrepreneurial students who choose majors with the largest job markets, such as engineering, computer science, and business. In contrast, humanities subjects such as social studies, multicultural studies, and gender studies receive much poorer attendance and less funding. Capitalism is reinforced by this subject selection. We continue to move away from subjects that allow us to take an inventory of human history and think of new possibilities and systems of coexisting in a community with one another. Corporatization of higher education directly affects the working conditions of helpers who are, again, not working to create a product but to improve health outcomes. We are slipping down on the priority list in the trajectory of this capitalist economy.

Becoming a social worker is taxing emotionally and financially as chronically under-funded social systems exploit our labor while we are in school. Before qualifying for the licensing exam, social work higher education requires students to gain professional training via practicums (internships). It is one of many fields in the helping professions to require student practicums. (Fields continues to be a word that connotes exploitative labor conditions.) The Council on Social Work Education (CSWE) requires Bachelor of social work students to work at least 400 practicum hours and Master of social work students at least 900 (Petra et al., 2020), all with no guaranteed form of financial compensation. The COVID-19 pandemic has heightened burnout in students who need 40-hour jobs to afford housing that is often worth more than half their salaries.

Stacked on that, students in higher education pay an average of $19,680 of yearly state tuition fees, all while taking care of their personal and often their family's health (Lederer et al., 2021; Research.com, 2021). In these practicums, students are matched with a social work agency, not always working with the population of their choice. Most students must afford their own transportation, some might receive mileage reimbursement, and few receive a stipend. None of this, however, accounts for maintenance costs, wear-and-tear, and depreciation of the value of our vehicles with increased mileage. In practicums, we expect students to complete organizational tasks as employees and clinical students provide mental health counseling to clients without financial supplementation for their intellectual property, time, and effort. Many students are sole providers for themselves, are single parents, or have other dependents with various needs while they attend school to better their financial situation. They must adjust work schedules for an average of 18 to 24 practicum hours per week. Most social work agencies are open during regular business hours, which clashes with students' regular 9 to 5 job hours. Thus, in pursuit of a degree, students often have no choice but to cut down their income hours, work on weekends, tap into savings, borrow money, or sometimes transfer to another school that offers more after-hours agency options. For these reasons, students continue to petition for wages in field practicums, which cost each student an average of $6,800 (Pay The Interns, 2022).

An unpaid student intern is held to the same expectations and worth as a paid employee. Upon entering a probably understaffed community agency, interns assume various roles and tasks. In mental and behavioral health agencies, interns work with clients experiencing trauma, abuse, neglect, and sometimes self-injurious behaviors, both suicidal and non-suicidal. We can expect them to complete secretarial tasks, billing tasks, cleaning tasks, sometimes soothe dysregulated children, pool multiple

Nobody Wants to Work Under These Conditions

client resources by contacting other agencies, advocate for client rights, facilitate group counseling, and much more. Sometimes not being able to secure resources can mean a client has nowhere to sleep that night (if a student is working with the houseless population or a displaced family). Interns complete high-stress tasks while navigating workplace staff dynamics, sometimes assuming various roles when an agency is understaffed. The impact of not navigating these working conditions as required of the student worker is the risk of losing the practicum position, failing an internship course, and ultimately not graduating from the program.

Students across the helping professions are placed in different settings. Some of these settings are challenging for interns due to systemic inequalities embedded in them, and one of those settings is child welfare. The child welfare system in the United States is known for its racial disparities in child removals due to abuse reports that may have been rooted in implicit bias. The intern's willingness to comply with these inequitable processes is required of all helping professionals, for example, mandated reporting policy. When helpers initiate mandated reporting, surveillance of a family is initiated, potentially leading to child removals, and incarceration for parents and their children entering the foster care system. If we are unwilling to participate in the system as it exists today, we risk losing our licensure, credentials, and ability to earn a livable wage.

Dorothy Roberts explains that there is a stark parallel between prison and foster care systems (Roberts, 2022). The rates of children taken into the foster care system are roughly the same as adults incarcerated per capita. 576 per 100,000 foster children are taken into the child welfare system, as 580 per 100,000 adults are incarcerated. Parents are sent to prisons, increasing prison capital and profit with each body count, causing substantial caregiver fatigue for social workers who continually see Black and brown people suffering disproportionately (Copeland, 2022). Angela Davis underscores that slavery was never completely eradicated from social systems rooted in racism. We feel its effects today in repressive, for-profit carceral institutions that continue to evolve into exploitative iterations of themselves (Davis et al., 2022). Mandated reporting frequently stops the social work process of assessing a family's resource deficits and providing services that have proven to reduce rates of domestic abuse, such as supplementing the family's income, providing parenting coaching, and affordable, safe housing- all a result of racial capitalism. The mental toll of being unable to help families with resources instead of leading them towards incarceration and separation creates enormous emotional fatigue across the helping professions.

As a result, many students consider alternative practices to carceral systems, such as an abolitionist framework. Taking a critical social work perspective is to see how oppression exists and is maintained in our systems. Yet, students are often thwarted in their efforts to do so through their cultural lenses, especially non-white students (Yearwood et al., 2022). Seldomly are alternatives amplified. For example, certain strategies, such as resource pooling in extended-kin networks, have been shown to have increased family stability in Black neighborhoods with concentrated poverty and a lack of institutional resources (Jarrett et al., 2010). In another example, elderly Alaskan Natives have abstained from alcohol and maintained recovery through spirituality and defining their roles and desires to engage in grounding cultural practices while role modeling for younger generations (Lewis & Allen, 2017). Alternate practices could look like helpers providing services rooted in community building and collectivist healing instead of showing a willingness to report families to the Department of Children and Families (DCF) or filing a police report for a client in crisis.

Lastly, another example of high stress in the student's journey, where the needs of the industry are centered over the needs of the community, is the licensure process. Passing or not passing the licensing exam directly affects a social worker's ability to earn higher wages as well as our ability to assume positions with more decision-making power to help our clients. In 2022, the licensing exam to become a clinical social worker came under scrutiny. The Association of Social Work Boards (ASWB) released a 2022 report on the licensing exam pass rates. It showed a disproportionate number of white students passing over Black, what they deem as Hispanic, and Indigenous students (Nienow et al., 2022).

As we try to understand the meaning behind these results, we can see that for at least the last ten years, White people have scored significantly higher on the licensing exam than people of color (Nienow et al., 2022). These pass rates directly affect the ability of a social worker to earn higher wages, which begs the question of why non-white social work students are not reaching a higher earning potential at the same rates as their white peers. These results may shed some light on occupational advancements and income disparities. A popular interpretation of this new data is that white ideologies of how communities should function are more heavily focused upon in the licensing exam, and then all who take the exam are asked to understand and report on the white definitions of ethical, social work practice (Yearwood et al., 2022). As a result, Black and Indigenous ethical, social work practice definitions may be excluded from licensure.

These are examples of how capitalism is embedded in our systems that place profit over people, individualism over collectivity, and industry over the critical inquiry, pushing for social justice transformation in our disciplines. As we navigate capitalist systems in the classroom and at our internships, we look to our professors, advisors, and internship supervisors for guidance and support. This author recognizes that these conditions may get worse before they get better because of current social, economic, and political circumstances that have arisen during this writing. Even though there have been wins, like the halting of the Stop WOKE Act in Florida, the fear-inducing effects experienced by faculty, staff, and students in higher education are still there as new bills continue to be introduced (such as HB 999), and we wait with caution for what censorship may be passed into law. Censorship of EDI (equity, diversity, and inclusion) is censorship of historical and current experiences of discrimination. Students' learning and sense of belonging suffer when professors have to think about what content they teach and how they teach it. At this time, students are taking risks to protest threats to EDI in schools through the first amendment rights of protesting, walkouts, teach-ins, and signing petitions. Part of what we would maintain with these proposed bills is the centering of whiteness in our social systems. Centering whiteness creates feelings of invisibility, invalidation, and frustration in students and a sense of being constantly threatened by oppression and violence. It can also lead to internalized oppression, where Black and Indigenous students begin to believe in the harmful stereotypes and biases perpetuated by the dominant culture of white supremacy. In the profoundly insightful writings of Dr.Gayatri Sethi, she eloquently expresses how"[m]any folks of color refer to university campuses as modern-day plantations. In the mouths of whiteness, sending us back to the plantation is a weaponized reality" (Sethi, 2021, p.144).

Dr. Sethi writes about the state of "unbelonging" in a country where whiteness is the standard for human behavior. She expresses that unbelonging is a commitment to the discomfort of being villainized, removed, and disdained and, simultaneously, a refusal to cower and comfort those in power. Dr. Sethi asks, importantly, could the path to being free from unbelonging be to root ourselves in community and our heritage as we dismantle oppressive systems?

WE HAVE ALWAYS DONE IT THIS WAY SUPPORTS THE STATUS QUO

One of the most significant barriers that colonialism and its legacy of capitalist pipelining today is the belief that a new way is impossible. This idea is perpetuated through cultural messaging that frowns upon challenging the status quo and dis-encourages critical analysis that may bring forward new alternatives. The cultural messaging controls the narrative that anything worth doing has been done, and if it is not still around, then it must have failed.

As we reflect on these three pandemic years, we cannot deny the impact that COVID-19 has had on our lives and society. The pandemic brought many challenges that tested our resilience, adaptability, and collective ability to care for one another. However, one of the most significant effects of COVID-19 has been on workers and working conditions, as workplaces were scrambling to strategize new ways to navigate the uncertainties and complexities of a rapidly changing world while also attempting to mitigate mass burnout.

The pandemic highlighted how our current systems of work, ideologies, and change management frameworks have been negligent in preparing and being equipped to handle crises of this potential scale. On the other hand, we have experts who know enough to forecast the necessity to be proactive rather than reactive, to audit gaps and fill them before they widen, and to innovate in mindful, intersectional applications that work with the most and not the few in mind. As we continue to navigate this new labor landscape, we must ask ourselves: What did we learn from this pandemic experience, and how can we use this knowledge today to create a better future for workers across generational identities? We need to realize the reality of working conditions and build a normalized ideology of sustainable solution-based frameworks and systems that will grow and scale to serve all when we prioritize and collaborate.

The primary way to act on this collaboration today is to imagine a new way of working is possible and can be seen in action in our lifetime, prioritizing worker well-being, dignity, and agency. To act on achieving this requires a shift away from the traditional models of work that have long dominated our society through colonial introductions and enablement. It requires rethinking our systems, structures, ideologies, policies, and practices around worker protection, compensation, and representation. These changes require a willingness to listen to and learn from workers themselves. Employers and supervisors need to move towards more equitable and inclusive models that center on the needs and experiences of the diverse socioeconomic working class, especially now in this new emerging reality of living in a post-pandemic restructure.

When employees' voices are not valued in conversations that directly affect them, their job satisfaction decreases, and they become disengaged from their work, resulting in reduced productivity and potential turnover, as we have seen reported over the years we have been in the pandemic. Regardless of industry, whether it is evident to the administration or not, if they are in toxic work environments and feel like their needs are being ignored, it can lead to high stress and depression (BetterHelp, 2021), creating an atmosphere for burnout. Burnout can manifest in many ways, including increased cynicism, decreased productivity, and withdrawal from work (TeamBuilding.com, n.d.). Employees feel valued and appreciated when they feel like they are seen, their voices heard, and we account for their needs. It creates a sense of belonging, increasing job satisfaction and engagement (Investors in People, n.d.). It is important to remember that workers are the backbone of any company. It is essential that the voices and viewpoints over many industries, particularly the helping professions comprising frontline/essential workers, should be taken into account when devising sustainable supports, with their input prioritized within the decision-making process.

Discussion: Lessons from the Bottom

The pressing need for liberation within helping professions like social work and psychology is evident in multiple aspects of higher education, encompassing curriculum design, teaching practices, student internships, and even post-graduation job conditions. Addressing this imperative requires a focus on designing strategies that effectively expose and challenge the enduring impacts of imperialism, colonialism, and racism that have influenced the development and practice across these disciplines. These professions have become entangled in systems of oppression, perpetuating harm across institutions such as the ones mentioned in this chapter, including but not limited to higher education, child welfare, and clinical mental health services. For example, in this chapter we utilize concepts that have roots in decolonial efforts and critical theory. An essential starting point, though not the sole one, is to reassess whose voices hold sway in shaping these disciplines across time- including whose voices were named as founders and part of the origins of these disciplines to who gets to be considered a knowledge producer today. "The list of critical intellectuals who have contributed to liberation theory is long, with many remaining anonymous. Historically, intellectuals from subordinated groups whose critical theoretical work sustains direct ties to subordinated populations have been overlooked and often maligned within European and North Ameican social theory." (Collins, 2019) This reevaluation demands a profound consideration of race, class, gender, and ability, both domestically and internationally. By acknowledging the existing power dynamics and hierarchies entrenched within academia, we can unlock the potential for meaningful research, wisdom, and lived experiences to emerge from marginalized and under-resourced perspectives. One strategy would be to listen to, study with, and learn about social movements on the ground. Examples of folks that have organized and mobilized around the pressing issues of the people include the Dream Defenders, Miami Workers Center, and organizations that promote political education through popular education methodologies that enhance one's analysis of the material conditions of local and international communities like The People's Forum located in New York. The idea, as Ignacio Martin Baro, a liberation psychologist who practiced in El Salvador- is to answer the pressing questions of the community and act on these by creating solutions by the people and for the people. Here we explore the structure of the Caremongering movement, which has many lessons that we can learn from. The prioritized concerns are about the needs of working-class students who aspire to engage in purposeful work that includes financial and social opportunities that will address the material conditions arising from the effects of micro to macro of a history of institutional racism, imperialist wars, and classism. It does not need to be perfect, but it needs to start today. So, the question now becomes, as we look towards the future, what structures can we look to for inspiration to build just, equitable, and resilient work systems that prioritize the well-being of all workers, particularly those historically marginalized and disenfranchised? Again, we do not have to look far. At the height of the instability brought upon by the lockdowns that shifted everything we knew to be our normal day-to-day, when fear seemed to be the only emotion of the masses, the Caremongering movement became the solution to the voice of need presented in the wake of systemic gaps, the voice of needs from the most disenfranchised to those who never thought they would be in a situation where they were now the ones needing help.

Caremongering is a grassroots movement that emerged in response to the COVID-19 pandemic and a counter-narrative to fear-mongering in the wake of this collective trauma we were all surviving. Starting in Toronto, Canada, the movement spread like wildfire globally, with over 100 groups in Canada alone. The movement is based on the principles of care, compassion, and solidarity, and it aims to create a community of people who care for each other in times of crisis and build with thriving in mind. A

Nobody Wants to Work Under These Conditions

network of community members from diverse backgrounds united, with equal access to voice concerns, to support each other and local communities by providing mutual aid, emotional support, and resources that most did not know how to advocate for (Liveworkwell, 2021).

A considerable part of its success is how the foundational structure of Caremongering is based and built on a participatory model that enables and empowers individuals within the community to take ownership of their collective well-being, voice the noticed concerns and brainstorm or offer potential solutions. The movement operates on a decentralized basis, with groups organizing themselves to respond to the immediate needs of their communities and how to structure those solutions on an equitable and sustainable scale. They created the foundational structure by tackling three pressure points - buy-in (a sense of community), auditing gaps (recognizing the intersectional variables effect on inclusion), and autonomy/advocacy (ownership).

These lessons include insights about psychological safety because of its mutual aid roots in addressing basic needs in high-stress situations, which are scalable and not tied up by the time cost of hierarchical decisions. As this grassroots movement was taking shape, individuals had a range of critical needs that preoccupied people: food, safety equipment and supplies, legal representation, and resources and money. People sought financial assistance for many necessities, including housing, paying bills, feeding their families, medical care, transportation, and pet care. What Caremongering exemplifies is that emotional intelligence and empathy can become the foundation building blocks of cultures that aim to see the individual, help them see themselves, and provide a space to be vulnerable without repercussions. These building blocks are class-conscious and unveil the material realities of people that need changing. Caremongering created a culture where members who joined Caremongering could lean into nonjudgmental and inclusive support. Caremongering allowed folks to navigate the new social landscape during re-opening initiatives and promoted rebuilding in the aftermath.

First, it creates an inclusive sense of community and belonging, which is often lacking in traditional workplaces. A study of 300 leaders over two years found that teams with better psychologically safe work cultures report higher levels of performance and reduced levels of interpersonal conflict (Center for Creative Leadership, 2022). By providing emotional support by engaging in levels of emotional intelligence and resources rooted in intersectionality, Caremongering groups are helping reduce the stress and anxiety that workers often experience, particularly during times of crisis, by being safe to which workers can turn. A considerable way this can be exemplified is in the access to babysitting for working parents, mainly working moms (CBC News, 2020), considering the data states that 58% of mothers found childcare responsibilities difficult during the pandemic (Parker, 2022). This issue is something that industries, companies, teams, management, whomever, wherever, whenever, can integrate into work culture standards in things like how needs are collected and then actioned quarterly. The way workers' voices are respected and attended to and the emphasis on the mental and emotional well-being of each person and the collective unit shows a commitment to fostering a conducive atmosphere.

The second main pivot point that Caremongering groups prioritize and what is needed in the workforce to recognize working conditions is the lens of those marginalized and vulnerable workers, including those who may be facing intersections of discrimination, poverty, or other forms of social injustice, into how the solution is built and best actioned on to ensure those specific needs are foundational to the suggested solutions, and how by extension, serve all. An example of such solutions in the group is how the community organization delivered goods like groceries, medicine, and PPE to those most in danger of being harmed by COVID-19 and those working as frontline/essential workers, resulting in an eventual network anyone could access once the routine and sustainability of the solution were recognized and invested in (CBC News, 2020).

The last pillar of the triad participatory structure of Caremongering is how the participatory model promotes, enables, and advocates for a sense of empowerment and agency. We see this already in the workforce where workers, individually and as a collective, are empowering equity in work cultures without full participation in collaboration with their industries. We can see this in ERGs committees comprising employees taking on additional emotional labor without changing management budgets or alternative compensation (CultureAlly, 2022). If adequately met halfway, collaboration would be more inclusive and proactive in mitigating potential burnout that can lead to quiet quitting.

By giving workers the space and access to a voice in decision-making processes and empowering them to take ownership of their collective well-being, a structure like the Caremongering groups could help to create a more democratic and participatory workplace culture, something that can mend and improve relationships departmentally and managerially. Given the well-established reputation of participatory management approach as 'Industrial democracy,' corporations can consider Caremongering as a model for versatility and cooperative organization. Such a pivot to worker-centric systems would favorably impact their return on investment (ROI) and streamline cross-functional communications.

As a whole, sustainable network, Caremongering represents a new model of community-based care, parallel to work culture ideology, that has the potential to transform the way we think about work, work-life balance, care, equity and inclusion, and social justice. Its participatory structure and focus on collective well-being offer a powerful alternative to traditional workplace hierarchies and individualistic models of care.

If we do not see the humanity in the worker, we do not build work cultures with the human in mind. The Caremongering model gives us insight into what people can build together, their priorities, and how much corporations contribute to the inequities people experience. Focusing on collective well-being and participatory design by integrating emotional intelligence, intersectionality, and marginalized workers' perspectives, Caremongering groups promote inclusivity, psychological safety, and empowerment. This promotion is a bottom-up movement that industries can study and use to redesign work cultures.

The bottom line and the call to action to make a new way possible is clear: it is imperative that we act and transition to the new way of working. The pandemic has highlighted placing workers (including student interns, graduates, and seasoned helpers) at the center of our efforts to scale and build with the collective voice of workers, works. Because what we know at this point is that nobody should have to work under these oppressive conditions.

REFERENCES

The People's Forum. (2018, August 28). *About*. The People's Forum. https://peoplesforum.org/about/#mission

BetterHelp. (2021, March 19). *How can a toxic work environment impact your mental health?* BetterHelp. https://www.betterhelp.com/advice/current-events/how-can-a-toxic-work-environment-impact-your-mental-health/

Blassingame, J. W. (1977). *Slave Testimony: Two Centuries of Letters, Speeches, Interviews, and Autobiographies*. LSU Press.

Nobody Wants to Work Under These Conditions

Board of Governors of the Federal Reserve System. (2020). *Report on the economic well-being of U.S. households in 2019* (Publication No. R-2019-7). Federal Reserve. https://www.federalreserve.gov/publications/2019-economic-well-being-of-us-households-in-2019-bull-etin.htm

CBC News. (2020, April 2). *'Caremongering' groups spreading kindness and support amid COVID-19 outbreak*. CBC News. https://www.cbc.ca/news/canada/toronto/COVID-19-caremongering-1.5518092

Center for Creative Leadership. (2022). *Creating a psychologically safe workplace: Guidelines for organizational leaders*. CCL. https://cclinnovation.org/wp-content/uploads/2022/05/psychologicallysafe.pdf

Collins, P. H. (2019). *Intersectionality as Critical Social Theory*. Duke University Press.

Copeland, V. (2022). *Dismantling the carceral ecosystem: Investigating the role of "child protection" and family policing in Los Angeles* [Doctoral dissertation, UCLA]. https://escholarship.org/uc/item/3rc7z257

Cotel, A., Golu, F., Pantea Stoian, A., Dimitriu, M., Socea, B., Cirstoveanu, C., Davitoiu, A. M., Jacota Alexe, F., & Oprea, B. (2021). Predictors of burnout in healthcare workers during the COVID-19 Pandemic. *Health Care*, *9*(3), 3. doi:10.3390/healthcare9030304 PMID:33803286

Davis, A. Y., Dent, G., Meiners, E. R., & Richie, B. E. (2022). *Abolition. Feminism. Now*. Haymarket Books.

Delgado Bernal, D., Burciaga, R., & Flores Carmona, J. (2012). Chicana/Latina*testimonios*: Mapping the methodological, pedagogical, and political. *Equity &amp. Equity & Excellence in Education*, *45*(3), 363–372. doi:10.1080/10665684.2012.698149

Desmond, M. (2023b). *Poverty, by America*. Crown.

Douglas-Gabriel, D. (2022, April 6). What the student loan payment pause has meant to black women. *The Washington Post*. https://www.washingtonpost.com/education/2022/04/03/black-women-student-loan-freeze/

Freire, P. (1978). Pedagogy of the Oppressed. In J. Beck, C. Jenks, N. Keddie, & M. F. D. Young (Eds.), *Toward a sociology of education*. Routledge.

Hersey, T. (2022). *Rest is resistance: A Manifesto*. Little, Brown Spark.

Investors in People. (n.d.). *Feeling valued: The dimensions organisations must deliver on*. Investors in People. https://www.investorsinpeople.com/knowledge/feeling-valued-the-dimensions-organisations-must-deliver-on/

Jarrett, R. L., Jefferson, S. R., & Kelly, J. N. (2010). Finding community in family: Neighborhood effects and African American kin networks. *Journal of Comparative Family Studies*, *41*(3), 299–328. doi:10.3138/jcfs.41.3.299

Kelly, A. (2023, March 24). *Should you compensate your erg leaders?* CultureAlly. https://www.culture-ally.com/blog/shouldyoucompensateyourergleaders

Kirst-Ashman, K. K., & Hull, G. H. (2019). *Human behavior in the Macro Social Environment: An Empowerment Approach to understanding communities, organizations, and groups*. Cengage.

Lederer, A. M., Hoban, M. T., Lipson, S. K., Zhou, S., & Eisenberg, D. (2021). More than inconvenienced: The unique needs of U.S. college students during the COVID-19 pandemic. *Health Education & Behavior*, *48*(1), 14–19. doi:10.1177/1090198120969372 PMID:33131325

Lewis, J. P., & Allen, J. (2017). Alaska native elders in recovery: Linkages between indigenous cultural generativity and sobriety to promote successful aging. *Journal of Cross-Cultural Gerontology*, *32*(2), 209–222. doi:10.100710823-017-9314-8 PMID:28478599

Liveworkwell. (2021). *Caremongering: A guide to citizen-led action during a pandemic*. https://liveworkwell.ca/sites/default/files/pageuploads/CareMongering%20Report%20-%20Final%20-%20January%2018.pdf

Megan, M. P. (n.d.). How many hours is enough? the effects of changes in field practicum hours on student preparedness for Social Work: The field educator. *Field Educator Journal*. https://fieldeducator.simmons.edu/article/how-many-hours-is-enough-the-effects-of-changes-in-field-practicum-hours-on-student-preparedness-for-social-work/

Nienow, M., Sogabe, E., & Husain, A. (2022). Racial disparity in social work licensure exam pass rates. *Research on Social Work Practice*, *10497315221125884*. doi:10.1177/10497315221125885

Pay The Interns. (2022). *Pay The Interns*. PtI. https://paytheinterns.com

Peña, L. G. (2022). *Community as rebellion: A syllabus for surviving academia as a woman of color.* Haymarket Books.

Poe, M., Polster, C., Kaag, J., & Traphaga, J. W. (n.d.). *New books in critical theory*. Apple Podcasts. https://podcasts.apple.com/us/podcast/new-books-in-critical-theory/id593872749

Research.Com. (2021, July 5). *Social work degree guide: 2022 Costs, requirements & job opportunities.* Research.com. https://research.com/degrees/social-work-degree

Roberts, D. (2022). *Torn apart: How the child welfare system destroys black families—and how abolition can build a safer world*. Basic Books.

Robinson, P. A., & Aldana, J. J. H. (2020). Making lemonade from the lemon of cultural taxation: Developing global citizens who think critically and who promote diversity and social justice. In J. Keengwe (Ed.), *Handbook of Research on Diversity and Social Justice in Higher Education* (pp. 1–18). IGI Global. doi:10.4018/978-1-7998-5268-1.ch001

Rosenthal, C. (2016). Slavery's scientific management: Masters and managers. In S. Beckert & S. Rockman (Eds.), *Slavery's capitalism: A new history of American Economic Development* (pp. 62–86). University of Pennsylvania Press., doi:10.9783/9780812293098-003

Ruíz, E. (2020). Cultural Gaslighting. *Hypatia*, *35*(4), 687–713. doi:10.1017/hyp.2020.33

Schaeffer, K. (2022, May 10). *Working Moms in the U.S. have faced challenges on multiple fronts during the pandemic*. Pew Research Center. https://www.pewresearch.org/fact-tank/2022/05/06/working-moms-in-the-u-s-have-faced-challenges-on-multiple-fronts-during-the-pandemic/

Nobody Wants to Work Under These Conditions

Schraedley, M. K., Jenkins, J. J., Irelan, M., & Umana, M. (2021). The Neoliberalization of higher education: Paradoxing students' basic needs at a hispanic-serving institution. *Frontiers in Sustainable Food Systems*, *5*, 689499. doi:10.3389/fsufs.2021.689499

Sethi, G. (2021). *Unbelonging*. Mango and Marigold Press.

Stevano, S., Franz, T., Dafermos, Y., & Van Waeyenberge, E. (2021). COVID-19 and crises of capitalism: Intensifying inequalities and global responses. *Canadian Journal of Development Studies*, *42*(1–2), 1–17. doi:10.1080/02255189.2021.1892606

TeamBuilding.com. (n.d.). *Workplace toxicity: Everything you need to know*. Team Building. https://teambuilding.com/blog/workplace-toxicity

The social work profession findings from three years of surveys of new social workers. (n.d.). CSWE. https://www.cswe.org/CSWE/media/Workforce-Study/The-Social-Work-Profession-Findings-from-Three-Years-of-Surveys-of-New-Social-Workers-Dec-2020.pdf

Thier, H. (2020). *A people's guide to capitalism: An introduction to Marxist economics.* Haymarket Books.

Yearwood, C., Walker, C., Dettlaff, A., & Cohen, S. (2022). *Addressing Racism in Social Work Licensing #StopASWB - Charla Yearwood, LCSW; Cassandra Walker, LCSW, CCTP; Alan Dettlaff, PhD, MSW.* Doin' the work podcast, episode 56. https://dointhework.podbean.com/e/addressing-racism-in-social-work-licensing-stopaswb-charla-yearwood-lcsw-cassandra-walker-lcsw-cctp-alan-dettlaff-phd-msw/

ADDITIONAL READING

Adnan, M., Rathore, F. A., Javaid, M., & Farooq, F. (2021). Understanding Teacher Burnout Following COVID-19: A Tipping Point. *Teaching and Teacher Education*, *105*, 103440. doi:10.1016/j.tate.2021.103440

Centers for Disease Control and Prevention. (2021). *COVID-19 and mental health of food retail, food service, and hospitality workers.* CDC. https://stacks.cdc.gov/view/cdc/114238/cdc_114238_DS1.pdf

Chand, S. (n.d.). *Participative Management.* Management Study Guide. https://www.managementstudyguide.com/participative-management.htm

Culpeper #7058. (n.d.). *Writing about "slavery"? this might help.* NAACP Culpeper #7058. https://naacpculpeper.org/resources/writing-about-slavery-this-might-help/

Edmondson, A. (2019, April 29). *What is psychological safety at work?* Ideas.TED.com. https://ideas.ted.com/what-is-psychological-safety-and-why-is-it-the-key-to-great-team-performance/

El-Sabawi, T., & Fields, M. (2021, June 21). *The discounted labor of BIPOC students & faculty.* California Law Review. https://californialawreview.org/the-discounted-labor-of-bipoc-students-faculty/

Flaherty, C. (2022, May 9). *Mixed Message.* Inside Higher Ed. https://www.insidehighered.com/news/2022/05/09/uf-seems-endorse-new-state-anti-crt-law

Geggis, A. (2023, January 13). *Paul Renner requests emails about faculty hiring, discipline and curriculum at state's higher ed institutions.* Florida Politics - Campaigns & Elections. Lobbying & Government. https://floridapolitics.com/archives/581137-paul-renner-requests-emails-about-faculty-hiring-discipline-and-curriculum-at-states-higher-ed-institutions/

Het-IMO. (n.d.). *Circular Leadership.* Het-IMO. https://www.het-imo.net/circular-leadership/

Mishel, L., Schmitt, J., & Shierholz, H. (2020). *Why unions are good for workers—especially in a crisis like COVID-19: 12 policies that would boost worker rights, safety, and wages.* Economic Policy Institute. https://www.epi.org/publication/why-unions-are-good-for-workers-especially-in-a-crisis-like-COVID-19-12-policies-that-would-boost-worker-rights-safety-and-wages/

Professional Development. (n.d.). *Home.* Retrieved January 6, 2023, from https://naswmn.socialworkers.org/Professional-Development/Professional-Resources/Code-of-Ethics

Rabin, R. C. (2020, March 5). 'I want to be safe': Health workers demand measures to combat Coronavirus. *The New York Times.* https://www.nytimes.com/2020/03/05/us/coronavirus

Reinicke, C. (2022). *Past financial crises have made millennials "more cautious, more proactive" in how they manage money, survey finds.* CNBC. https://www.cnbc.com/2022/06/21/past-financial-crises-have-affected-how-millennials-manage-money.html

Wolff, R. D. (2018). *Understanding Marxism.* Lulu.com.

KEY TERMS AND DEFINITIONS

BIPOC: Black, Indigenous, and People of Color, used to center the position of BIPOC folks in relation to others and in relation to structural levels of oppression and racism.

Bottom-Up Processes: grassroots level organizing, power from the people that shapes social change and policies that will benefit the majority of people and not just those at the top.

Capitalism: private ownership of property and means of production, profit-making through market competition that depends on the exploitation of people and their labor, and the accumulation/hoarding of wealth and capital by the elite.

Critical Theory: It is an umbrella term with different theories that analyze power structures that contribute to social inequalities, and interrogate and critique dominant ideologies to disrupt and create change.

Decolonizing: In its most honest and transformational meaning, it means land back with reparations. There is no decolonizing without this. However, disrupting and destabilizing the status quo includes interrogation and naming colonialism and imperialism at multiple levels and that includes cultural impositions and knowledge systems that aim to erase and oppress and perpetuate colonial ways of being and knowing.

Dialectical: From Marxist writings, it considers the contradictions and tensions within one issue that could also lead to change.

Great Resignation: When there is a large number of people leaving their jobs due to inequitable working conditions, dehumanizing managerial styles, lack of benefits that compromise the worker's health, and exposure to psychological and physiological illness.

Intersectionality: A term coined by Kimberly Crenshaw, but historically discussed by many Black feminist scholars and thinkers such as Ida B. Wells, bell hooks, Patricia Hill Collings and more. It is the consideration of multiple identities that compound the experience of oppression for one person. It is an analysis of systems of oppression across structures, identities, and time and geography.

Material Conditions: The material aspects of people's lives, such as their economic stability, housing conditions, access to healthcare and nutrition, and other material resources that ultimately determines their quality of life and how long they may live.

Profit Over Life: A core value of capitalism which consists of prioritizing the bottom line, productivity, and financial gain and profit-making over human life-which includes the quality-of-life people lead, climate and environment, and more.

Chapter 12
The Trials and Triumphs of a Solo Mother–Academic

Maureen E. Squires
SUNY Plattsburgh, USA

ABSTRACT

It is well documented in the literature that mothers in academia often work a "second shift," performing a majority of the uncompensated labor at home in addition to the compensated labor in the workforce. Further, this second shift is compounded by a "child tax," where mothers are penalized by the academy for caregiving responsibilities. Yet, much of the existing literature on gender disparity among faculty in higher education pertains to two-parent, heterogenous family structures. This results in a significant void and underrepresentation of other groups. The focus of this chapter is "solo parents," specifically solo-mother-academics. A solo parent is one who has no co-parent with whom to share caregiving responsibilities. In this chapter, the author presents a literature review, highlights of the author's experiences as a solo-mother in the academy, and ways to navigate both worlds. This work is influenced by qualitative research methods.

THE CHALLENGES AND THE VOID

Women are expected to "work as if they do not have family responsibilities and raise children as if they don't have work obligations" (Zappala-Piemme & Squires, 2021, p. 143). While not a new phenomenon, the COVID-19 pandemic highlighted society's and the workforce's unrealistic expectations of working mothers. It also exacerbated the disproportionality in domestic labor between employed mothers and employed fathers. Tasks like ensuring the health and safety of family members, supporting the academic needs of children, and maintaining household chores have been - and continue to be - split unequally among men and women (Boesch & Hamm, 2020; Carlson, Petts, & Pepin, 2021; Cohen & Hsu, 2020; Frederickson, 2020; Ibarra, 2020; Krivkovich et al., 2022; Perelman, 2020; Pineault & Rouzer, 2020).

Mothers in academia are not spared from this experience. They work a "second shift," performing much of the uncompensated labor at home in addition to the compensated labor in the workforce (Hochschild, 1989). This second shift is often compounded by a "child tax" where mothers are penalized by

DOI: 10.4018/978-1-6684-8597-2.ch012

Copyright © 2023, IGI Global. Copying or distributing in print or electronic forms without written permission of IGI Global is prohibited.

The Trials and Triumphs of a Solo Mother-Academic

the academy for caregiving responsibilities (Cardel et al., 2020). Concerningly, much of the existing literature on gender disparity among faculty in higher education pertains to two-parent, heterogenous family structures. This results in a significant void and underrepresentation of other groups.

The focus of this chapter is "solo parents," specifically solo mother-academics. A solo parent is one who has no co-parent with whom to share caregiving responsibilities. My writing is both personal and professional as I reflect on my own experience and explore extant research. I intertwine academic and creative writing to tell this story. What follows is a literature review, highlights of my experiences as a solo mother-academic, and ways to navigate both worlds as a caregiver and college professor.

LITERATURE REVIEW

Representation of Women-Academics in Higher Education

Women-academics are underrepresented in the academy. The American Association of University Women (AAUW), the College and University professional Association for Human Resources (CUPA-HR), and the National Center for Education Statistics (NCES) illustrate that such gender inequality occurs on multiple levels. According to the *Characteristics of Postsecondary Faculty* published by NCES (2022), 51 percent of college faculty are women. This marks an increase over the past decade, which appears positive on the surface. But increased women presence in the academy has occurred at the lowest and least compensated ranks.

For instance, women comprise the majority of non-tenure track positions. Such positions typically include part-time adjuncts or annual lecturers who are not eligible for the same benefits as full-time faculty (NCES, 2022). Nor are they eligible to shift to tenure-track positions, which can lead to higher ranks. These "contingent positions are the least secure and worst remunerated teaching positions in higher education" (Colby & Fowler, 2020, p. 4). Women also hold fewer tenure-track and full-professor positions than their male counterparts (Colby & Fowler, 2020). In fact, only 27 percent of tenured faculty are women and 32.5 percent of full professors are women (Colby & Fowler, 2020). It has also been found that women make up merely one-third of top-level positions in the academy (Bichsel & McChesney, 2017). Men are more than twice as likely to serve as college presidents or chief executive officers than women and more than four times likely to serve as chief information officers or chief athletics administrators than their female counterparts (Bichsel & McChesney, 2017). Conversely, women are more likely to fill positions of department chair, administrative officer, or assistant dean (Bichsel & McChesney, 2017). Some people falsely and unfairly assume that mother-academics will "prioritize family over work and [be] unable to hold more time-intensive and demanding leadership positions" (Schnackenberg, 2020, p. 6-7). Such lower-level administrative positions carry less prestige and lower salaries (Alcalde & Subramaniam, 2020).

This gender disparity is problematic for several reasons. First, it can stifle productivity at the institution. One could argue that a homogeneous faculty body limits innovation whereas a diverse faculty body leads to varied intellectual contributions. Moreover, it excludes the experiences and voices of women-academics: a significant proportion of employees and students on college campuses. Some even claim that underrepresentation of women-faculty "affects not only those seeking careers in academia but also the success of the students they serve" (Colby & Fowler, 2020, p. 12). This diminishes the student experience.

Second, this inequity reduces the earning potential for women-academics. Salary typically is connected to rank and position. If women-academics hold lower academic ranks or attain junior-level administrative positions, they also earn less money than men-academics. The financial gender gap is exacerbated by another form of salary inequality. Of faculty employed full-time, women earn an average of 81.2 percent of every dollar that men earn (Colby & Fowler, 2020). These factors negatively affect current and future financial security for women-academics.

In sum, studies have shown that compared to men, women in the academy often take longer to attain promotion, are less likely to achieve tenure, attrit at higher rates, experience a publication slump, and hold lower leadership positions (Cardel et al., 2020; AAUW, n.d.; Flaherty, 2020; Hamlin, 2021; Segeral, 2021; Windsor, Crawford, & Breuning, 2021). Such advancement (or lack thereof) often coincides with women's childbearing years. Women's "under-performance" or "under-achievement" in the academy has been partly attributed to motherhood, which is often perceived as (or exists as) a barrier to women-academics reaching their full potential. Women-academics are disadvantaged by both societal expectations and institutional systems.

The Academy's (Unrealistic) Expectations

Colleges and universities greedily demand faculty time. Institutions are "attention-needy" (Schnackenberg, 2020, p. 9).and expect faculty to have a "constant 'campus' presence" (Schanckenberg, 2018). At some institutions, "the ideal worker in academia devotes most of their lives to scholarly pursuits" (Lekchiri et al., 2022, p. 41). Beyond teaching, scholarship, and service, faculty are expected to advise majors, grade student work, sponsor student clubs/organizations, promote programs and charm prospective students, revise curriculum, assist with accreditation efforts, collaborate on college-wide initiatives, give talks, submit mounds of paperwork, and the list goes on. Stated another way, "structurally, academia requires an evolving division of activities that tend to demand attention beyond a typical 'work day'" (CohenMiller, 2016). Moreover, numerous researchers have documented that women in the academy perform significantly more service than men. Time spent on committees and boards is less time devoted to scholarship, which is central to promotion.

Add to this the responsibilities of motherhood: 24 hours per day, seven days per week, 365 days per year. It is no surprise that many mother-academics are conflicted by loyalties to family and to work (Blithe & Elliott, 2020; Kiburz et al., 2017; Lekchiri et al., 2022; Schnackenberg, 2020). In the literature, this has been described as *interrole conflict* (Kiburz et al., 2017) where "different life identities produce unique sets of responsibilities and pressures, many of which are oftentimes incompatible" (Schnackenberg, 2020, p. 8) or *work-life conflict* (Blithe & Elliott, 2020). At times, such discord coincides with *role overloading* (Bornstein, 2009), where boundaries blur as working mothers try to concurrently juggle multiple responsibilities of distinct parts of their lives. As some purport, these identity dilemmas are amplified by "the incompatibility of current expectations to prioritize work above all else" (Pineault & Rouzer, 2020).

Institutional policies also present obstacles to mother-academics. These range from biases in hiring and promotion, to insufficient onboarding models, to lack of adequate family leave, to name a few (Colby & Fowler, 2020; Kelly, 2019; LeBlanc et al., 2022; Lekchiri et al., 2022; Schanckenberg, 2018; Schnackenberg, 2020). The problem is exacerbated when women experience a *sticky floor* (Iverson, 2011) or *glass ceiling* (Mason & Goulden, 2002). In the academy, women's lack of advancement has been referred to as the "leaky pipeline" (Cardel et al., 2020; Schnackenberg, 2018) because many women are filtered out by a flawed channel. Others describe this phenomenon as "chutes and ladders" (Windsor

The Trials and Triumphs of a Solo Mother-Academic

& Crawford, 2021; Windsor et al., 2021). Chutes are the "circumstances that derail career trajectories -- including pregnancy; struggles with infertility; bias in hiring decisions; daily parenthood challenges; gender-based harassment or the culmination of microaggressions; and precarious employment in short-term contingent, or adjunct faculty positions" (Windsor et al., 2021, p. 510). Regardless of metaphor, such gender-biased barriers make it challenging for women, especially mothers, to climb the career ladder as instructor, scholar, steward, or leader.

MotherScholars/MotherLeaders

Relatively recently, scholars in this area have problematized the typical notion of mother-academics. Rather than having split and compartmentalized identities, academics like Matias (2011) and Lapayese (2012) discuss the interlaced elements of being a mother in the academy. "The role of the mother and the role of the scholar each inform and improve the other, making them intertwined in the best way" (Schnackenberg, 2020, p. 2). As such, the concept of MotherScholar describes the experience as synergistic. Yet this synchronicity may be more of a fallacy and less of a reality. (Previously discussed literature illustrates the numerous struggles of mothers in academia.) Schnakenberg (2021) expands on the concept, introducing the term MotherLeader. MotherLeaders are academic mothers "who accepted administrative and/or leadership positions in higher education" (p. 5). Like MotherScholars, MotherLeaders are often "left in the ethical double-bind of no-win solutions and choices" (Schnackenberg, 2020, p. 3) as they try to sufficiently allocate time and attention to children and the academy. Often, this results in "sacrificing one commitment for another and constantly feeling guilty and neglectful for doing so" (Schnackenberg, 2020, p. 3).

In most cases, the decision to pursue a position of leadership in the academy is optional. Admittedly, some women-academics may feel obligated to serve in a leadership position when no other viable candidate exists. Regardless, leadership positions often carry more responsibility and stress than a typical faculty position. This complicates the already complex life of mother-academics. Leadership in higher education "can be and often is the very antithesis of the calm and pleasant existence envisioned for the ideal motherscholar" (Schnackenberg, 2020, p. 2-3). This is because "the leader is expected to be ever-present, always available to listen, to problem solve, and to represent those whom she leads" (Schnackenberg, 2020, p. 3) -- much like her responsibilities as a mother. So, to be a MotherLeader is to "be all things to all people all the time," or so it seems (Schnackenberg, 2020, p. 3).

Solo Parents

A person can be a solo parent by choice (through pregnancy/birth, surrogacy, or adoption) or circumstance (the death of a spouse or an estranged partner). A solo parent is distinct from a single parent who shares caregiving responsibilities with another person. It is "altogether different...whether by choice or by design or by just damn bad luck" (Grinwald, 2017). A solo parent acts alone to make decisions about, and act on, the welfare of his/her child(ren). In the words of one solo parent, "It means the full mental, emotional financial weight of raising children is on my shoulders alone...It means I am the only person standing between me and my children and whatever storm threatens to batter us...It means I have to give them [my children] twice as much, even I if feel half as capable" (Roth, 2020). That is not to say solo parenting is harder than single parenting. Single parenting is accompanied by its own set of challenges, like balancing family values, caregiving responsibilities, and competing schedules. I am simply addressing my lived experience as a solo parent.

According to a recent study supported by the National Center for Family & Marriage Research, nearly 30% of mothers in the United States are single (Wiborg, 2022). Of that group, 9% are solo mothers. The majority of these solo mothers have never been married. A greater proportion of solo mothers are Black, Indigenous, or People of Color (BIPOC) compared to white solo mothers (Wiborg, 2022). Additionally, solo mothers have higher educational attainment than non-solo mothers. For example, 63% of solo mothers have attained some college compared to 50% of non-solo mothers (Wiborg, 2022). That places me in an extraordinarily small group of women who are solo mothers, never married, with doctorates, working as college faculty.

Framework

This chapter is descriptive, personal, and reflexive. It draws from narrative research based on the assumption that "people live and/or understand their lives in storied forms...[and that] these stories are played out in the context of other stories" (Josselson, 2011, p. 224). As such, narratives are both personal (rooted in one's own experience) and public (embedded in social, cultural, familial, religious, etc. experiences). Moreover, narrative inquiry gives space for the messiness and fluidity of meaning-making. Such messiness corresponds with SoloMotherScholarhood. Narrative inquiry gives space for storytellers to depict "how they connect and integrate the chaos of internal and momentary experience...how they link bits of their experience...[and] how they structure the flow of experience and understand their lives" (Josselson, 2011, p. 224). Here, I provide the narrative of one solo mother-academic who is walking in two worlds: motherhood and academia.

Additionally, this chapter is both academic and creative. I integrate findings from current literature with my own poetry. Meaning-making involves a myriad of methods. One such approach is art-based research, which uses "the expressive qualities of form to convey meaning" (Barone & Eisner, 2012, p. xii). This qualitative research design can be used to collect, analyze, and/or represent data. It encompasses multiple genres like literary techniques, visual art, performance art, and new media (Knowles & Cole, 2008). At times, I use poetry to distill my thoughts and express my emotions. These "creative and innovative forms of knowledge production and translation hold the potential of revealing subtle, yet powerful insights on particular phenomena" (K. McCoy-Coleman, personal communication, June 7, 2023). This combination of narrative and arts-based framework provides shape for this chapter.

Further, I have chosen to use the term solo mother-academic to name my existence. While this may change in the future, presently, it captures my lived and comprehensive experience. I am the sole caregiver for my son. Additionally, I am an academic in a broad sense. I am neither MotherScholar nor MotherLeader: I am both and more. I am also MotherSteward: a mother who is a college faculty member and devotes substantial time and energy to service at the department, college, and community levels. These are my salient identities.

The Trials and Triumphs of a Solo Mother-Academic

MY STORY AND IDENTITY AS A SOLO MOTHER-ACADEMIC

I am a solo mother who is employed as a college professor - a full professor. Specifically, I am the foster-adoptive mother of a preschooler; I parent without the assistance of a partner; and I work as a department chair at a four-year public institution. As I write this piece, I have replayed "our story" many times in my head, from the moment the Department of Social Services called me asking if I would take an 8-week-old infant, to today - as I scramble to craft this chapter at the end of the semester, before I pick up my son from daycare, while I confirm his doctor appointments and respond to countless work emails, and fulfill other chair responsibilities that mount over the summer. Until now, I had not penned our story. This chapter is both personal and professional. It serves as a catharsis for my arduous journey as a solo mother-academic and adds to the scant literature on solo parenting in the academy. I begin this section with a personal poem.

Frenetic Solo Mothering-Professing

A life in snippets.

That's all that I recall from those first years as a solo mother-academic.

Those first years - during the pandemic - essential for bonding with a tiny human being

AND

financial security for this new family

AND

professional identity, intellectual and emotional well-being, for this new mother.

~

Changing my son's diaper.

Sending an email response to a student.

Microwaving dinner.

(Because there's no time to make a home-cooked meal.)

Responding to a colleague's text message.

Reading a book to my son

while glancing at the screen of my laptop -

monitoring my online course from the corner of my eye.

~

There is no "me time" or "self-care time" or "mindfulness" or "reflection."

There is barely time for a bathroom break.

It simply is.

~

It is demanding.

It is exhausting.

It is herculean.

It can be soul-shattering.

It can be unnerving.

It can be lonely.

It is fantastical.

It is miraculous.

It is awesome.

When I Arrived

When I arrived on campus, I was greeted by warm colleagues. My faculty mentor happened to be one of the longest standing members of the department. As such, he held institutional knowledge and knowledge of the community. To this day, two comments he made stand out. First, he described this area as a "great place to raise a family but not a good place to make a family." I did not fully understand this quip until I lived here for a while. Taking up residence in a remote small college town five hours away from family and friends meant that I did not know many people here. Yet once the semester started, colleagues turned into acquaintances and some into close friends. This was the foundation of *my* community. Dating was a whole other story. I tried dating in-person and online. Living in a conservative town where I was sometimes perceived as unapproachable simply because I had a doctorate made finding a partner challenging. It did not help matters that I started searching for Mr. Right in my mid- and late-30s. Though intelligent in many ways, I held foolish assumptions about what my life *should* look like.

The Trials and Triumphs of a Solo Mother-Academic

Second, my faculty mentor recommended that I postpone "having a family" until I obtained tenure. He explained that having a child now would jeopardize my pursuit of tenure. At first, the Type A, first-born, middle class, Catholic in me thought that made sense. Reflecting on the women faculty and peers in my doctoral program, I realized that there were no mother-academic role models. The women faculty members at the R1 institution I attended as a doctoral student were either unmarried or divorced and childless. This is not uncommon. According to the *2004 National Study of Postsecondary Faculty* which "collects data regarding the characteristics, workload, and career paths of full- and part-time postsecondary faculty and instructional staff at public and private not-for-profit 2- and 4-year institutions in the United States," women-academics are less likely than men-academics to be married or have children (NCES, 2004). While 2004 is the most recent iteration of this study, other literature (Fothergill & Felty, 2003; Lapayese, 2012; Schnackenberg, 2018) highlights similar concerns. These data show that high-achieving or successful women in the academy are likely to be unmarried and childless, whereas the reverse is true for men in the academy. Was it impossible (unrealistic) for motherhood and professorhood to co-exist, especially as an unmarried woman?

Maybe I should focus on securing my career, getting married, and buying a house before becoming a parent. Once I lived the life of an academic for several years, I began to question the linear path of what I ought to do. I was unmarried and working long hours. Even though I worked at a teaching institution, I still felt the pressure to publish and serve on multiple committees. Those were important elements of the performance review process. Many nights and weekends it was just the custodian and me in the office. I struggled to find balance between my obligations as a junior faculty member and to have a life outside of academia.

Being Driven and Feeling Burned Out

I consider myself a highly driven person - someone who likes to excel, craves productivity, and is in constant pursuit of improvement. By 29, I earned a Certificate of Advanced Study in Educational Leadership; by 31, I obtained my doctorate; by 32, I was employed in a tenure-track position. Some would consider this the career trajectory of the "ideal worker" (Drago & Colbeck, 2003). I had solely focused on becoming a successful academic, temporarily ignoring the call to become a mother. I was on my way to earning tenure and promotion, serving as department chair in my late 30's and achieving full professorship in my early 40's.

During my early years in academia, I was not convinced that I could be both: an academic and a mother. I made numerous sacrifices in my doctoral studies; most doctoral students do. I took a leave of absence from teaching high school (which resulted in no income or contributions to my retirement fund for several years), relocated to a new city, declined social outings with friends, and postponed starting a family. Would climbing the career ladder require more sacrifices? And who would suffer as a result of those sacrifices?

Career advancement came at a cost: the cost of denying my authentic self. As years passed, I became acutely aware that I had not nurtured the other parts of my identity that made me a whole person. I had earned the praise of colleagues and nominations for awards, but such accolades no longer brought me joy. I was burned out and felt unfulfilled after giving my entire adulthood to education, mostly higher education. It took a series of serendipitous events (and examination of my insecurities and genuine hopes) for me to acknowledge that I needed to make a change. What I really wanted was to become a mother.

Nearing 40, I realized that I had to stop waiting for "the right" time or circumstances to have a family. I already had tenure and was financially stable. If I were going to do this, it was now or never. Weighing my options, I decided to pursue adoption. I became a licensed foster-adopt parent in January 2018, cared for and helped to reunify my first foster child that spring/summer, and welcomed my (now) son in October 2018.

Ironically, both of my foster children arrived during academic advising: one of the busiest and most chaotic times for a professor. Further, during the COVID-19 pandemic I was essentially a solo *new* mother. My son and I were confined to the four walls of our house while I cared for him, taught online, led as chair, served on committees, supported numerous students and faculty through the sudden transition to virtual learning and the emotional turmoil of the pandemic, tried to work on scholarship, and do housework. I remember thinking, "I didn't sign up for this." I did not expect to be raising a toddler during a pandemic while isolated and working full-time. But no one did.

Mommy's Here and There

"Beautiful, beautiful, beautiful, beautiful boy."

Lyrics wash over me and I cannot help but smile - awestruck by your beauty.

I gaze at you sleeping in my arms (laptop balanced on my legs).

You, my son, are my greatest gift.

And like a cherished gift, I want to protect and nurture you.

Motherhood is also a source of pain -

Pain from striving to be enough for you, to give enough to you.

~

You're with me for such a short time,

Yet my attention is divided.

I'm focused on gaining a promotion in the academy

(which will better our lives).

I'm preoccupied with

Teaching,

creating scholarship,

The Trials and Triumphs of a Solo Mother-Academic

serving on committees,

attending professional development,

personnel problems,

student concerns,

revitalizing a shrinking program.

~

"Every day, in every way, it's getting better and better."

Is it?

Is it, really?

I feel more pressure to produce, more pressure to succeed, more pressure to excel.

And am I doing the same for you?

Am I becoming a better mother?

Am I engaged enough?

Am I growing more patient, empathic, loving?

Am I doing this solo mothering thing in the best way possible?

~

"Life is what happens to you while you're busy making other plans."

Life is quickly passing bye.

Where has my attention and energy been spent?

It's been divided between you and academia.

It's been sucked out by the academy -

by a system that depletes me.

~

"...Have no fear. The monster's gone, he's on the run, and your [mommy's] here."

I'm here cradling you, tickling you, kissing your boo-boos, nursing you through illnesses, watching and listening as you hit milestones.

I'm here holding your hand as we cross the street, cheering you on as you ride your bike, beaming as you embrace a ladybug.

You exude beauty,

genuine curiosity,

and pure joy.

I worry that the academy has left me tattered, too drained to enjoy these fleeting moments with you, too fractured to be fully present for you.

~

"It's a hard row to hoe. Yes, it's a long way to go."

This is not an easy path.

There is no balance as a solo mother-academic.

There is an enduring sense of being here, there, everywhere, and nowhere - simultaneously -

And a perpetual wondering if my presence - if I - am enough for you and the institution.

Struggles and Joys of Being a Solo Mother-Academic

Consciously Unaware

I did not make the decision to become a solo foster-adoptive parent lightly. The Model Approach to Partnership in Parenting (MAPP) training for foster parents is comprehensive and intense. The MAPP curriculum "integrates four cornerstone principles to ensure foster and adoptive parent readiness" (CAK, n.d.). These include partnership, healing, mutual selection, and integrated learning. Throughout the entire process, prospective foster-adoptive parents are expected to reflect on their own experiences, knowledge, skills, and goals critically and candidly. They must enter the role willingly and be found capable of performing the responsibilities of foster-adoptive parents (CAK, n.d.).

Essential elements of mutual selection include knowing one's own family, building strengths, and building connections (CAK, n.d.). Reflecting on what my faculty mentor said when I first arrived on

The Trials and Triumphs of a Solo Mother-Academic

campus, this is a "great place to raise a family..." I realized that I could raise a child here. Though my biological family lived 300 miles away, I had a work family. These administrative assistants, colleagues, and administrators supported my decision to become a solo mother-academic. They helped my son and me move from an apartment to a house; brought us meals during numerous COVID-19 quarantines; and swapped infant/child hand-me-downs.

I realized that I was entering an unpredictable (and uncontrollable) state. But I really had no idea how challenging life would be (regardless of the MAPP training and my professional training) as a solo mother-academic. There are so many unknowns as a foster-parent. You never know when you will get the call to welcome a child into your home or how long you will have a child in your care. Sometimes, you are given little information about the level or types of trauma the child has been exposed to or the exceptionalities he may have. Initially, it is often unclear the number of appointments (medical, court, visitations, etc.) the child will have and the complexity of the systems (foster care, Medicaid, family court, federally funded services, etc.) in which you will function can be overwhelming. I also didn't realize how -- somehow -- things would work out and that planning for every potential obstacle was not a good use of my time.

My Village

Identifying (or creating) my family was essential. Building on strengths was equally important: my own strengths, the strengths of my foster children, and the professional relationships I had built on and off campus. This allowed me to nurture more connections with local individuals and agencies to support my foster children, me as a foster-adoptive parent, and me as a working-mother.

For instance, I stayed in touch with members from my MAPP class. We served as confidential sounding boards for each other. We supported each other through countless court hearings, shared trauma-informed parenting tips, and celebrated adoptions together. I joined the Child Care Coordinating Council of the North Country (CCCCNC). This non-profit agency offers "high quality, responsive and dynamic programs and services...to support and strengthen families and childcare professionals" (CCCCNC, n.d.). Specifically, the organization serves as a Family Resource Center (providing parent-child playgroups, parenting support groups, and parent education classes); a Child Care Resource and Referral Center; a Family and Community Engagement Center (providing technical assistance on the special education process); and a Permanency Resource Center (offering support, education, and respite, for post-adoptive families). The CCCCNC provides holistic services and resources that benefit children and families, thereby improving the community overall.

While the campus did not have codified family-friendly policies (beyond the standard family leave), support came from the local level. Before I even pursued motherhood, a colleague invited me to join her research. She introduced me to other writers and publishers, helping me establish my reputation as a scholar. My dean nominated me as the featured scholar at the college's Celebration of Scholarship one year. She also supported my application to pursue a fellowship at the college's Institute for Ethics in Public Life and a state-level Drescher Fellowship. Such opportunities showcased my scholarship and even granted course-release time so that I could advance my research. Experiences like these provided me the time and resources to compile a robust portfolio for performance review and promotion. Sometimes I would bring my son to college events.

Before I could send my son to daycare, I wore him in a baby carrier when I met with students during office hours. (Some officemates greeted us warmly; others "looked the other way.") My son attended his first college lecture at six months old and his first matriculation ceremony at 13 months old. He was riding through campus on his Strider bicycle at two. He has even been lovingly called "the mayor of Sibley Hall" because he is so well known. I was allowed to temporarily switch to remote meetings during the summer when my backup-backup babysitter was diagnosed with COVID-19 and I had no child care for my son. (His typical daycare was closed that week.) Maybe that is a privilege of working in a human services field or parenting after COVID-19: colleagues cared about my child and my life as a mother-academic. Faculty and staff had each other's backs and acted with empathy even though codified family-friendly policies did not exist. Not all academic departments or campus office spaces are this receptive of children in the workplace.

Other times, especially when serving as the department chair, I needed to keenly focus on work. Once again, colleagues were significant members of my community. Amy entertained my son while I gave a keynote address; Emily watched him while I helped new students register for courses at orientation; and Yong babysit him so I could attend commencement. I also hired many babysitters to fulfill my job responsibilities. That is right, I paid to work. Open Houses, orientations, accepted student days, webinars, student organization/athletic/music/theater events, and committee meetings often occur in the evenings or during the weekends. This is prime "family time" and time when most childcare facilities are not open.

Though many people consider it idyllic to have the flexible schedule of a college professor, it was both a blessing and a curse. I could plan courses, grade assignments, respond to email, and draft manuscripts late at night or early in the morning (providing my son was still asleep). But I could not be a mother 24-7 and be an academic 24-7. There was a financial, physical, mental, and emotional cost. Yet I consider myself fortunate. Just before my son's first birthday, a spot opened at the premier daycare center in the area. The childcare center happened to be located on campus -- in my office building. (The process of finding childcare started months earlier with 35 phone calls to local centers and home providers and lengthy waiting lists.) Not all families are as lucky as I am to have excellent childcare -- and just down the hallway. In fact, affordable and accessible childcare is often an obstacle for mother-academics (Cardel et al., 2020; Doherty, 2021; Fonseca-Chavez et al., 2019; Schnackenberg, 2018; Schnackenberg, 2020; Schnackenberg, 2021).

I worked with other women across campus to shed light on the experiences of mother-academics and those in care-giving roles. Networking opportunities did not exist, so we created our own. We surveyed campus members, identified obstacles to career advancement, brainstormed potential solutions, and presented ideas to college administration. We organized campus talks about caregiving, started a Facebook networking campaign, and hosted a Bring Your Child to Campus Day. We advocated for changes to childcare legislation, additional resources for local childcare providers, and prestige for the childcare profession. We are now in the nascent stages of forming a MotherScholar group on campus. This will serve two general roles. First, it will be a caregiving network where mother-academics can share stories and support each other through the various phases of mothering and professing. Second, it will be a repository for MotherScholar resources (publications, pedagogy, and policy) where members can easily access information to support their scholarship and advocacy work.

Worth the Wait

It was my choice to postpone motherhood, though influenced by some social-cultural norms. That decision had benefits and challenges. Entering the academy as a single woman, I had the opportunity to devote as much time to my career as I wanted. I could polish courses, join numerous committees, serve

The Trials and Triumphs of a Solo Mother-Academic

as a department chair, and devote time to scholarship. I launched my reputation at the College and in the field, thereby improving my opportunities for career advancement. I could go "all in." I felt less anxious, as one gigantic part of my life was becoming secure. Being a single academic, I also had the time to teach overloads and accept contract work. This helped to establish my financial base, beneficial immediately and once I became a mother.

Waiting on motherhood also provided me the opportunities to gain confidence in myself and authentically assess my personal and professional goals. Though I will always question my abilities as a mother and professor, I gathered enough resolve to go "all in" as a mother. I had to allow myself to be vulnerable, to sit in messiness, and to trust that things would work out in the end. None of this was easy for me, but I made the commitment to myself to move forward.

Perhaps I would have more energy as a younger mother. Maybe I would run around more or stay up later. (I take my son hiking, swimming, and bike riding, but I am ready for bed the moment he falls asleep.) But I would also have more self-doubt. In a way, I think that proving myself -- to myself -- in the academy helped me believe that I could be a solo mother-academic. I had the skills, knowledge, and drive to establish a strong teaching, service, and scholarship record. I could use those same dispositions to be an attuned and loving mother.

Your Story - Your Song

The books are closed,

the boards erased

You laid the cornerstone.

The bell has rung.

Class is over.

Look how much you've grown

~.

Your roots are gaining traction.

Your eyes, fixed on the sky.

You're open to new spaces

And bounding up staircases

And granting yourself graces

Through a kinder, gentler eye.

The Trials and Triumphs of a Solo Mother-Academic

~

It may feel cold and lonely

But you are not the only,

The only person here,

Other mothers will draw near

~

Your voice will fill the lecture hall,

The corridor, the quad

Your presence will be felt by all

And they will soon applaud

~

You managed to get up again

To profess another day

To laugh and cry and ponder life

As these fleeting moments stray

~

You wonder how you did it

With a little one in tow.

You're grateful that you did it

That you'll always know.

~

Balance is impossible

The Trials and Triumphs of a Solo Mother-Academic

You'll never find that spot

Where all the tension melts away

That's just not life - it's not.

~

But you will find a rhythm

To working and caregiving

And embrace the murkiness

Of the life that you are living.

~

You are mother. You are teacher.

You are woman standing strong.

Like a phoenix you will rise.

This will be your song.

SURVIVAL STRATEGIES FOR A SOLO MOTHER-ACADEMIC

The following points are gathered from reflecting on my own experience, learning about the experiences of other mother-academics, and reviewing evidence-based research in extant literature. These recommendations are not exclusive to solo mother-academics. Other mothers in academe could benefit from these as well as we strive for parity and advancement in higher education.

Build Your Village

Many of the strategies I used to advance my career as a solo mother-academic were informal, some serendipitous. The following practices are not institutionalized and rely on individuals taking ownership of their career success. While problematic, this highlights the power of grass-roots efforts.

Once I accepted my teaching position, I had no control over who my colleagues or immediate supervisor would be. As luck would have it, colleagues were willing to become co-researchers and were understanding when a toddler commandeered our Zoom meeting or became ill, requiring a meeting to be rescheduled. And I reciprocated when similar situations arose for them. My dean, also a mother-academic, encouraged me to pursue fellowships and leadership positions. This support existed simply because I was in the right place at the right time. What about other solo mother-academics who work outside the human services field, in programs traditionally filled by men, or who are unfamiliar with the *hidden curriculum* of higher education? Are they as lucky as I? If such a village doesn't automatically exist: build one.

Relationships are an essential part of personal and professional growth. Connecting with people in similar situations provides social support and helps to manage shifting, or newly constructed, identities (Segeral, 2021; Spradley et al., 2020). Such support systems are a way for mother-academics to check on each other and can be used as a tool to motivate each other to reach scholarship goals (Lekchiri et al., 2022; Spradley et al., 2020). A longitudinal study following women on the tenure track found that relationships significantly matter. The women-academics who thrived were those who "sought out making meaningful connections with co-researchers, students, faculty, and administrators" (Kelly, 2019).

I believe that building your village can start when you are job hunting. Explore the community resources available to working mothers. Ask the Human Resources office about family-friendly practices on campus. Gather information from the faculty members you meet during the interview process. While I did not collect data in this way, recent tenure-track hires did. They were open about their desire to be both a scholar and a mother, explaining how the intersection of their identities made them a better academic and parent. In post-hiring conversations, they shared that the discussions they had about parenting and working in academia during their interviews greatly influenced their decision to accept positions at this institution.

Once hired, formalize relationships with co-researchers and fellow mother-academics. Consider joining community organizations, non-profit agencies, religious establishments, etc. to expand your social network. As a newly hired junior faculty member, request mentoring, particularly from a senior faculty member who has had implicit bias training and understands the existing, sometimes unacknowledged, inequities in the academy (Windsor & Crawford, 2021; Windsor et al., 2021). A recently tenured MotherScholar could be a particularly strong mentor (Schnackenberg, 2018). Such mentors can make explicit higher education's hidden-curriculum, empathize with junior faculty, advocate for change, and serve as a "ladder" rather than a "chute" for women-academics.

Systemic Changes Required

Success for mother-academics should not be left up to chance or rely solely on the individual. Systemic policy change is needed. What follows is an inventory of potential solutions that can surmount the *mommy penalty*. Cardel et al. (2020) serves as a foundation. Their work provides a comprehensive review of barriers that prevent women academics from rising in the academy and feasible recommendations to address these equity issues. Such actions are supported by others in the field. Numerous factors can ameliorate the impracticable position of mother-academic. Here, workload, tenure and promotion, and childcare will be discussed.

Create Sustainable and Equitable Workload

Higher education holds the notion that faculty members should be "working all of the time" (Lekchiri et al., 2020, p. 48). Moreover, the academy regards itself above all else and promotes a culture where faculty are expected to give more of themselves than is humanly possible. Since the COVID-19 pandemic, and coupled with decreasing resources for higher education, faculty plates are now overflowing. Their

The Trials and Triumphs of a Solo Mother-Academic

jobs are not sustainable. As powerfully stated, "we must move away from the expectation that academic work can and should continue without interruption from inconvenient factors such as health concerns or pregnancy, disruptions in childcare schedules, family crises, and the daily mental load of working while managing household and caregiver work" (Windsor et al., 2020, p. 511). Family life should not be considered a hindrance in academia. Additionally, higher education must acknowledge the multiplicity and fluidity of faculty identities. Faculty are more than scholars.

There are numerous ways to create a sustainable workload for mother-academics. Campuses could schedule events during a typical workday as much as possible (Doherty, 2021; Cardel et al., 2020; Fonseca-Chavez et al., 2019; Schnackenberg, 2018; Schnackenberg, 2021). This includes teaching, meeting times, office hours, and networking events, to name a few examples. Such intentional scheduling is aligned with typical childcare offerings. Institutions should avoid last-minute deadlines, meetings, or emails (LeBlanc et al., 2022). Late requests can be challenging to accommodate when childcare needs to be arranged. Additionally, universities could allow virtual work, if appropriate, to address unanticipated family issues that arise (Schnackenberg, 2021).

Additionally, equitable workload can be achieved in several ways. Universities can gather and reflect on institutional data, using that to set gender-equity goals specific to the university (Bartel, 2018; Bichsel & McChesney, 2017; Schnackenberg, 2018). This requires candid conversations and purposeful policymaking. Institutions should limit uncredited service (Bartel, 2018; Schnackenberg, 2018). It is well documented that women perform a disproportionate amount of service in higher education (Cardel et al., 2020). Further, women are more likely to engage in internal service rather than external service (Cardel et al., 2020). Internal committees often lack prestige or decision-making power. Campuses should nominate women to lead important initiatives and increase women's presence on university-wide committees (LeBlanc et al., 2022; Schnackenberg, 2018). Institutions can also create mother-academic pipelines, programs that support women through recruitment, retention, promotion, and leadership (Cardel, et al., 2020; Schnackenberg, 2018). This could be supported by intentional mentoring programs (Cardel et al., 2020; Schnackenberg, 2018). Mentoring programs comprised of members who promote diversity, equity, and inclusion and other mother-academics are preferred. Lastly, institutions should establish salary parity between men and women professors and administrators (Schnackenberg, 2018).

Revise Tenure and Promotion Policies

Expectations and policies around tenure and promotion require adjustment. One such change is to extend the tenure clock, though this is financially disadvantageous as it delays promotion and a raise (Fonseca-Chavez et al., 2019; Lekchiri et al., 2022; Schnackenberg, 2018; Schnackenberg, 2020; Schnackenberg, 2021). Another option is to establish part-time tenure-track positions (Schnackenberg, 2018; Schnackenberg, 2020). A reduced load (with expectations for promotion drawn across a longer span of time) allows mother-academics to better engage in multiple aspects of their lives. Additionally, institutions could offer course releases, funding for research or teaching assistants, lower service requirements (Lekchiri et al., 2022), training, and networking support (Cardel et al., 2020). These interventions can make it possible for mother-academics to reach tenure and pursue career advancement.

Address Child Care Needs

Childcare needs must be addressed holistically and in creative ways. Faculty members have unique schedules. They teach in the evenings, advise college-events on the weekends, and present at conferences (which often requires travel). Such job responsibilities fall outside of the typical 9am to 5pm workday, when most childcare facilities are open.

Adequate paid parental leave is one component (Cardel et al., 2020; Doherty, 2021; Schnackenberg, 2018; Schnackenberg, 2020; Schnackenberg, 2021). This allows caregivers to bond with their new child and continue to earn a salary. Equitable leave policies may also need to be adjusted or written. Such policies should be grounded in evidence-based research, destigmatized, and openly communicated.

Another factor is access (or lack thereof) to affordable childcare. Childcare is expensive. According to a 2020 report published by the U.S. Department of Labor, "childcare data shows prices are untenable for families" (Landivar, 2023). Families across the country are paying up to $17,000 per child, per year for childcare expenses. This represents nearly 20% of median family income per child (Landivar, 2023). Additionally, more than 50-percent of Americans live in childcare deserts, where they have few options or little access to child care (Sciamanna, n.d.). To address this, institutions could provide childcare subsidies (Doherty, 2021; Fonseca-Chavez et al., 2019) or support the creation of on-campus childcare centers (Schnackenberg, 2018; Schnackenberg, 2020; Schnackenberg, 2021). Also, many childcare centers will not accept infants (Doherty, 2021; Fonseca-Chavez et al., 2019), care for sick children, or provide coverage during snow days, on evenings, or weekends (Fonseca-Chavez et al., 2019). Childcare options could be more flexible. Childcare could be offered at conferences so that solo mother-academics can network and share their research with border audiences (Doherty, 2021; Fonseca-Chavez et al., 2019). Lastly, institutions could adopt family-friendly practices like collaborative scheduling, where the university and local school districts plan calendars together, and family programming, where children are welcomed on campus to attend university events (Fonseca-Chavez et al., 2019). These are concrete steps that institutions can take to address child care needs of women-academics and improve the overall work environment.

Steps Forward

There is work to be done. While the COVID-19 pandemic brought to light the struggles of working mothers, these challenges are not new -- nor have they been adequately addressed. Women-academics are still disproportionately represented in academic ranks, less likely to serve in prestigious leadership roles, underpaid, and more likely to perform domestic responsibilities than men-academics. Solo mother-academics are in a particularly precarious position as the well-being of their family and the health of their career lie solely on their shoulders. In many cases, "villages" do not already exist; therefore, solo mother-academics are building their own "communities." Institutions of higher education can do much to build systems of support. Such interventions include, but are not limited to, creating sustainable and equitable workload, revising tenure and promotion policies, and addressing childcare needs.

Moreover, the topic of solo mothers, and specifically solo mother-academics, still remains virtually invisible in the literature. To complicate matters, seemingly no research exists regarding solo mother-academics who foster children or care for children with exceptionalities. (Research on solo father-academics is absent as well.) We need to hear these voices, understand their stories, and create communities -- both on and off campus -- that address the distinct needs of these parent-academics. Research, advocacy, and

The Trials and Triumphs of a Solo Mother-Academic

policy change is necessary. Nuanced conceptualizations of motherhood and academic-career success can help to illustrate the complex and fluctuating nature of solo motherhood in the academy.

My story is unfinished. I am the mother of a soon-to-be-kindergartener and a mid-career women-academic. Recently, after six years as a department chair, I decided to resign this position. Is this best for me professionally? Time will tell. Is this best for my son? Maybe. Is this best for me? Yes and no. Having less leadership responsibilities means having more flexibility with my schedule. This is good. But settling on my new identity without that leadership component will be difficult. I hope to resume leadership roles at the university in the future, but I do worry that a blip, however long, in my CV may imply to some that I am not committed to my career. Yet I cannot dwell on that. Perseverating on the numerous career obstacles in the future will not help me in the present. I have to believe that I, like all mother-academics, am doing my best to raise a loved and loving child while supporting the growth of my students, the institution, and the greater community.

REFERENCES

Alcalde, C., & Subramaniam, M. (2020, July 17). Women in leadership: Challenges and recommendations. *Inside Higher Ed*. https://www.insidehighered.com/views/2020/07/17/women-leadership-academe-still-face-challenges-structures-systems-and-mind-sets

American Association of University Women (AAUW). (n.d.). *Fast facts: Women working in academia*. AAUW. https://www.aauw.org/resources/article/fast-facts-academia/

Barone, T., & Eisner, E. W. (2012). *Arts based research*. SAGE Publications. doi:10.4135/9781452230627

Bartel, S. (2018, December 19). *Leadership barriers for women in higher education*. AACSB. https://www.aacsb.edu/insights/articles/2018/12/leadership-barriers-for-women-in-higher-education

Bichsel, J., & McChesney, J. (2017, February). *The gender pay gap and the representation of women in higher education administrative positions: The century so far*. College and University Professionals Association for Human Resources (CUPA-HR). www.cupahr.org/surveys/briefs.aspx

Blithe, S. J., & Elliott, M. (2020). Gender inequality in the academy: Microaggressions, work-life conflict, and academic rank. *Journal of Gender Studies*, *29*(7), 751–764. doi:10.1080/09589236.2019.1657004

Boesch, D., & Hamm, K. (2020, June 3). *Valuing women's caregiving during and after the coronavirus crisis*. American Progress. https://www.americanprogress.org/issues/women/reports/2020/06/03/485855/valuing-w mens-caregiving-coronavirus-crisis/

Bornstein, R. (2009). Women and the quest for presidential legitimacy. In Allen, J. K., Bracken, S. J., & Dean, D. R. (Eds.), Women in academic leadership: Professional strategies, personal choices, pp. 208-237. Sterling, VA: Stylus Publishing.

Cardel, M. I., Dhurandhar, E., Yarar-Fisher, C., Foster, M., Hidalgo, B., McClure, L. A., Pagoto, S., Brown, N., Pekmezi, D., Sharafeldin, N., Willig, A. L., & Angelini, C. (2020). Turning chutes into ladders for women faculty: A review and roadmap for equity in academia. *Journal of Women's Health*, *0*(0), 1–13. https://www.liebertpub.com/doi/full/10.1089/jwh.2019.8027. doi:10.1089/jwh.2019.8027 PMID:32043918

Carlson, D. L., Petts, R., & Pepin, J. (2021). Changes in US parents' domestic labor during the early days of the COVID-19 pandemic. *Sociological Inquiry*. Advance online publication. doi:10.1111oin.12459 PMID:34908600

Child Care Coordinating Council of the North Country (CCCCNC). (n.d.). *Family resource centers*. CCCCNC. https://www.ccccnc.org/

Children's Alliance of Kansas (CAK). (n.d.). *The MAPP institute*. CAK. https://www.childally.org/mapp

Cohen, P., & Hsu, T. (2020, June 3). Pandemic could scar a generation of working mothers. *New York Times*. https://www.nytimes.com/2020/06/03/business/economy/coronavirus-working-women

Cohen Miller, A. (2018). Creating a participatory arts-based online focus group: Highlighting the transition from DocMama to Motherscholar. *Qualitative Report*, 23(7), 1720–1735.

Colby, G., & Fowler, C. (2020). *Data snapshot: IPEDS data on full-time women faculty and faculty of color*. American Association of University Professors (AAUP). https://www.aaup.org/sites/default/files/Dec-2020_Data_Snapshot_Women_and_Facult _of_Color.pdf

Doherty, M. (2021, September 20). The quiet crisis of parents on the tenure track. *The Chronicle of Higher Education*. https://www.chronicle.com/article/the-quiet-crisis-of-parents-on-the-tenure-track

Flaherty, C. (2020, April 21). No room of one's own. *Inside Higher Ed*. https://www.insidehighered.com/news/2020/04/21/early-journal-submission-data-suggest-covid-19-tanking-womens-research-productivity

Fonseca-Chavez, V., Martinez, T., Doris, J., & Wilson, C. S. (2019). In their own words: Single mothers in academia on what really works and what we need to know. *Medium*. https://medium.com/national-center-for-institutional-diversity/in-their-own-words-fa940d9b98a

Fothergill, A., & Felty, K. (2003). 'I've worked very hard and slept very little': Mothers on the tenure track in academia. *Journal for Research on Mothering*, 5(2), 7–19.

Frederickson, M. (2020, May). *COVID-19's gendered impact on academic productivity*. Github. https://github.com/drfreder/pandemic-pub-bias

Grinwald, F. (2017). Why solo parenting is nothing like single parenting. *Huffington Post*. https://www.huffpost.com/entry/why-solo-parenting-is-nothing-like-single-parenting_b_5a9174be4b026a89a7a2c49

Hamlin, K. A. (2021, March 30). Why are there so few women full professors? *Chronicle*. https://www.chronicle.com/article/why-we-need-more-women-full-professors

Hochschild, A. (2012). *The second shift: Working families and the revolution at home*. Penguin Group.

Ibarra, H. (2020, September). *Why WFH isn't necessarily good for women*. Herminiaibarra. https://herminiaibarra.com/why-wfh-isnt-necessarily-good-for-women/

Iverson, S. V. (2011). Glass ceilings and sticky floors: Women and advancement in higher education. In J. L. Martin (Ed.), *Women as leaders in education: Succeeding despite inequity, discrimination, and other challenges*. Praeger.

Josselson, R. (2011). Narrative research: Constructing, deconstructing, and reconstructing story. In Wertz, F. J., Charmaz, K., McMullen, L. M., Josselson, R., Anderson, & McSpadden (Eds.) *Five ways of doing qualitative analysis: Phenomenological psychology, grounded theory, discourse analysis, narrative research, and intuitive inquiry*. New York, NY: Guilford Press.

Kelly, B. T. (2019). *Though more women are on college campuses, climbing he professor ladder remains a challenge*. Brookings. https://www.brookings.edu/blog/brown-center-chalkboard/2019/03/29/though-more-women-are-on-college-campuses-climbing-the-professor-ladder-remains-a-challenge/

Kiburz, K. M., Allen, T. D., & French, K. A. (2017). Work-family conflict and mindfulness: Investigating the effectiveness of a brief training intervention. *Journal of Organizational Behavior, 38*(7), 1016–1037. doi:10.1002/job.2181

Knowles, G., & Cole, A. L. (2012). *Handbook of the arts in qualitative research: Perspectives, methodologies, examples, and issues*. SAGE Publications.

Krivkovich, A., Liu, W. W., Nguyen, H., Rambachan, I., Robinson, N., Williams, M., & Yee, L. (2022). *Women in the Workplace*. McKinsey. https://www.mckinsey.com/featured-insights/diversity-and-inclusion/women-in-the-workplace

Landivar, C. (2023, January 24). *New Childcare data shows prices are untenable for families*. U.S. Department of Labor. https://blog.dol.gov/2023/01/24/new-childcare-data-shows-prices-are-untenable-for-famies

Lapayese, Y. V. (2012). *Mother-Scholar: (Re)imagining K-12 education*. Sense. doi:10.1007/978-94-6091-891-9

LeBlanc, S. S., Spardley, E., Beal, H. O., Burrow, L., & Cross, C. (2022). *Being Dr*. Mom and/or.

Lekchiri, S., Chuang, S., Crowder, C. L., & Eversole, B. A. W. (2022). The disappearing research agendas of mother-scholars in academia during the COVID-19 pandemic: Autoethnographic studies. *New Horizons in Adult Education and Human Resource Development, 34*(3), 40–53. doi:10.1002/nha3.20357

Mason, M. A., & Goulden, M. (2002). Do babies matter? The effect of family formation on the lifelong careers of academic men and women. *Academe, 88*(6), 21–27. doi:10.2307/40252436

National Center for Education Statistics (NCES). (2004). *2004 National study of postsecondary faculty (NSOPF:04) technical report*. U.S. Department of Education, Institute of Education Statistics. https://nces.ed.gov/pubs2006/2006179.pdf

National Center for Education Statistics (NCES). (2022). Characteristics of postsecondary faculty. *Condition of Education*. U.S. Department of Education, Institute of Education Statistics. https://nces.ed.gov/programs/coe/indicator/csc

Perelman, D. (2020, July 2). In the Covid-19 economy, you can have a kid or a job. You can't have both. *New York Times*. https://www.nytimes.com/2020/07/02/business/covid-economy-parents-kids-career-homeschooling.html

Pineault, L., & Rouzer, S. (2020, October). Even ivory towers can't protect women from "bearing the brunt" of the COVID-19 pandemic. *Impact of COVID-19 on gender equity in academia*. APA. https://www.apa.org/science/leadership/students/gender-equity-academia

Publishers.

Roth, E. (2020). I'm a solo parent, not a single parent. *Scary Mommy.* https://www.scarymommy.com/solo-parent-not-single-parent

Schnackenberg, H. L. (2018). motherscholar:MotherLeader. In Schnackenberg, H. L. & Simard, D. A. (Eds.), Challenges and opportunities for women in higher education leadership (pp.29-43). IGI Global.

Schnackenberg, H. L. (2020). Motherscholar:Motherleader and the ethical double-bind. InSquires, M.E. & Yu, Y., & Schnackenberg, H. L. (Eds), Ethics in higher education (pp.127-141). Nova Science Publishers.

Schnackenberg, H. L. (2021). Motherscholar:MotherLeader & the pandemic. In H. L.

Schnackenberg & D. A. Simard (Ed.), *Women and Leadership in Higher Education During Global Crises* (pp. 116–146). IGI Global.

Sciamanna, J. (n.d.). *Center on American progress: Child care desserts.* Child Welfare League of America. https://www.cwla.org/center-on-american-progress-child-care-deserts/

Segeral, N. (2021). Academic single mothering during a pandemic. *Journal of Motherhood Initiative,* *12*(1).

Spradley, E., LeBlanc, S. S., Olson-Beal, H., Burrow, L., & Cross, C. (2020). Proving our maternal and scholarly worth: A collaborative autoethnographic textural and visual storying of MotherScholar identity work during the COVID-19 pandemic. *Journal of Motherhood Initiative, 11*(2), 189–209.

Wiborg, C. E. (2022). *"Solo" and "nonsolo" single-parent households in the U.S., 2021. Family Profiles.* National Center for Family & Marriage Research., doi:10.25035/ncfmr/fp-22-17

Windsor, L. C., & Crawford, K. F. (2021, August 23). Academia isn't a leaky pipeline: It's a game of chutes and ladders -- and we can even the odds. *The Chronicle of Education.* https://www.chronicle.com/article/academe-isnt-a-leaky-pipeline

Windsor, L. C., Crawford, K. F., & Breuning, M. (2021). *Not a leaky pipeline! Academic success is a game of chutes and ladders.* Cambridge. doi:10.1017/S1049096521000081

Zappala-Piemme, K. E., & Squires, M. E. (2021). Leading in the new normal: The experiences of women leaders in P-20 education during the COVID-19 pandemic. In H. L.

Chapter 13
A Tale of Two Universities:
Primary Carers Working in Australian Universities

Helen Hodgson

https://orcid.org/0000-0003-4135-2769

Curtin University, Australia

Dorothea Bowyer

Western Sydney University, Australia

ABSTRACT

Returning to work after a career break can be challenging, accordingly employers implement a range of policies, practices, and strategies to support and retain working parents. This chapter analyses the work-family policies at two universities in the Australian university sector, through the eyes of academic parents. Grounding the discussion in the Australian industrial relations system, the authors examine the lived experience of academic parents drawing on two separate qualitative studies at two different Australian Universities. Initiatives in place to enhance career progression for academic parents are tested against lived experience. The authors find that policies and strategies need to be overhauled and suggest more feasible ones that universities can implement to enable the academic parent, who is juggling an academic career with parenting, to succeed in the post COVID uncertainty faced by the higher education sector.

INTRODUCTION

Returning to work after a career break in any occupation, including academia, can be challenging. Employers implement a range of policies, practices, and strategies to support and retain working parents. The question however remains as to how employers can facilitate the transition and mitigate the impact that a career break has on their employees. Our research examines the institutional framework in place at two separate Australian universities to support academic parents to identify whether these policies effectively assist university staff to achieve a work-life balance.

DOI: 10.4018/978-1-6684-8597-2.ch013

Copyright © 2023, IGI Global. Copying or distributing in print or electronic forms without written permission of IGI Global is prohibited.

Australian universities are at the forefront of implementing gender equity policies and supports, including parental leave, phased-return-to-work, on-campus childcare facilities, flexible working practices, and family leave (Marchant and Wallace 2016; WGEA 2018). These policies and supports apply both to mothers and fathers, and are designed to keep careers on track while parents make time for new children or other family obligations (Roberat and Erskine, 2005); work-related resources enable work-to-family enrichment and improve quality of life and functioning in the home domain. Providing an enriching and supportive work environment may be an important strategy for minimizing work-family conflict (WFC), burnout, and subsequent reduced career development in academia.

Although universities are leaders in implementing policies to support academic parents, there is evidence that formalized institutional support (re)creates gender inequities (Marsh, 2015), and is sometimes ineffective or not accessed (Roberat and Erskine, 2005; Armenti, 2004). The COVID pandemic has already impacted career cycles, progression, and work practice in Higher Education globally, and there is a need for the Sector to fully acknowledge that it has also intensified gender inequities (Malisch et al. 2020; Willey 2020).

This paper sets out to examine the work-family policies implemented in Australian universities through an analysis of the policies of two universities, through the eyes of academic parents. After summarising the literature and the industrial relations framework that applies to Australian universities we will examine the lived experience of academic parents as identified in two separate research projects at two different Australian Universities. The initiatives at these universities to enhance career progression for academic parents, who are predominantly mothers, are examined against lived experience as reported by participants in the study. We will suggest how policies could be adapted to the post-pandemic era so that universities can proactively engage in and navigate the pandemic consequences to sustain their future competitiveness and retain their workforce. We identify policies and strategies that need to be reviewed and more feasible ones implemented so that the academic parent who is juggling an academic career with parenting can succeed in the uncertain times that the Higher Education sector faces post-COVID.

BACKGROUND

There is a substantial body of literature regarding the effect of the "motherhood penalty" on careers (Pepping and Maniam, 2020), particularly relative to child-free women (Baker, 2010, Budig et al. 2012). The effects range from the application process (Correll et al, 2017) to retirement (Austen et al, 2015). This includes the effect of career interruptions for childbirth but continues after the mother returns to work, with reduced workforce participation through part-time work and carer responsibilities. Lost wages from motherhood tend to be highest for high-earning women, regardless of whether their work record is more continuous than less highly-paid women (England et al 2016). The phenomenon is observed in developed economies where women are participating in the paid labor market, although cultural norms and policies contribute to the extent of family wage gaps in different countries (Cukrowska-Torzewska and Lovasz, 2020).

Within this body of literature, there is a stream that addresses the challenges of balancing an academic career with parenthood, concluding that the primary caregivers in academia have lower publication rates and are less likely to get promoted (Kennelly and Spalter-Roth, 2006, Huopalainen 2019, Cohen 2020). The academic primary carer is typically a woman who struggles post-parental leave to meet performance expectations of self, supervisors, colleagues, and other stakeholders (McDermott, 2020) and to safe-

A Tale of Two Universities

guard their professional identity (Van Engen, 2019). Nikunen (2012, p.713) observes that the tertiary education sector's impression of "being an egalitarian and family-friendly workplace" becomes "one of a competitive meritocracy with demands that are not easy to meet and which are unequal in terms of gender when the talk turn to careers".

Academic mothers have concerns about the consequences of accessing institutional support, such as being considered less serious about their work (Drago and Walliams, 2000; Heijstra et al, 2017) while male academics are reluctant to take parental or family leave, or use such leave to engage in writing and research (Marsh, 2015; Armenti 2004).

Pandemic experiences reported to date call for an examination of existing policies that focus on support to parents in organizations. The pandemic has impacted career cycles, progression, and work practice throughout the global knowledge industries, and has had a particular impact on Higher Education. It has spotlighted the importance of workplace gender policies in academia and the Higher Education sector needs to fully acknowledge gender inequities as they are being intensified by the pandemic (Malisch et al. 2020; Willey 2020).

Teaching academics were required to transform their teaching strategies to remote learning, in a very short period (Casacchia et al, 2021; Watermeyer et al 2020) and researchers had to change focus, and methods, or defer projects. Early research has shown a reduction in research outputs by women compared with men, largely because women disproportionately shouldered the responsibility for home learning of children and other care responsibilities (Wright et al, 2020; Bowyer et al, 2021; Statti et al, 2021; Guy & Arthur 2021).

Inequalities in women's and men's academic careers existed well before COVID-19 (Monroe et al, 2008; Valian 2005). In normal times women in academia publish less, are subject to interrupted careers, and achieve higher positions less frequently than men (Oleschuk, 2020). Under the emotional stress of the pandemic, it has been documented that female academics submitted fewer manuscripts for publication and tweeted fewer work-related messages than men (Dolan and Lawless 2020; Amano-Patiño et al, 2020K; Kim and Patterson, 2020). Mothers of young children were forced to reorganize their job priorities during the global pandemic while women's care responsibilities for their families also increased and took precedence (Chemaly, 2020; Faherty 2020; Alon et al. 2020; Boncori 2020; Costa 2020; Crook, 2020; Minello 2020; Pettit 2020; Staniscuaski et al. 2020; Willey 2020).

Universities have increasingly adopted flexible work practices in work organization and enabling parents in the workplace (Anderson, 2008; Knights and Clarke, 2014; Nikunen, 2014). Perversely, enhanced access to flexible work conditions and parental leave can negatively affect career progression. This dilemma is not unique to academic parents: it is experienced by parents in many professions and is being noted in the post-COVID workplace (Deloitte, 2020). The particular challenge for academics and researchers is how a career break affects the pipelines that govern academic and research careers. Research projects take time to establish, complete and publish; taking time out of the academic workforce can reduce outputs when the academic parent is under pressure to show their merit relative to their peers.

Universities can reinforce ambition in working parents (post-pandemic more than ever), encouraging the visibility of *academic parenting* and minimizing the gender inequity gap by creating the right culture for staff impacted by a career break.

This paper adds to the literature by exploring the effects of caring obligations, the "motherhood penalty" and resulting career breaks on academic parents, the majority of whom are women, through the lived experience of parents employed at two different universities. We specifically interrogate the effects of the institutional settings and relevant policies adopted by universities in the Australian Higher

Education sector for staff returning to work after a career break. The aim is to showcase, compare and contrast the implemented policies and lived-experience pre-pandemic at two Australian institutions.

Industrial Relations Framework

The Australian industrial relations framework allows organizations to enter into employment agreements with employees, subject to overarching legislation and compliance with specified minimum National Employment Standards (NES). Each university in Australia operates under an Enterprise Agreement specific to that university, reflecting local and strategic differences.

The NES require that all employers in Australia allow 12 months unpaid leave concerning the birth or adoption of a child to an employee with more than 12 months service and the employee is entitled to return to the same, or an equivalent, position. The parent of a child under school age also has the right to request flexible working hours, which can only be refused on "reasonable business grounds". An employer may exceed the standard, often by providing paid leave within the prescribed 12-month period or extending the unpaid leave entitlement.

The Higher Education sector exceeds the minimum parental leave requirements under the Act although the conditions for leave above the NES vary between institutions. The average duration of paid parental leave entitlement across the higher education sector is 16.1 weeks, compared to 10.9 weeks of paid leave across all industries (WGEA n.d.).

Regardless of any entitlement to leave under an employment agreement, an eligible employee who earns less than $150,000 pa may be entitled to a Federal Government income support payment (Paid Parental Leave Act, (Cth) 2010) that is equivalent to the minimum wage for up to 18 weeks in respect of a primary carer, and two weeks for a secondary carer. This leave can be taken flexibly: the first 12 weeks must be taken in a block during the first 12 months, with the balance able to be taken flexibly within 24 months of birth or adoption of a child. In contrast, not all university Enterprise Agreements allow flexibility in paid leave entitlements.

However, the availability of longer parental leave has highlighted risks for parents who find that when they take a significant break from their workplace their career trajectory can stall (Oleschuk, 2020). For an academic, the career interruption can result in a year or more of limited outputs while their contemporaries are building their academic and research portfolio.

The NES allow "Keeping in Touch Days" allowing an employee to work for up to ten days a year during their parental leave period, to "keep in touch with his or her employment to facilitate a return to that employment after the end of the period of leave" (*Fair Work Act* 2009, s.79A). For an academic parent, these "keeping in touch days" could be used to maintain research or specialized teaching activities, however, some university Enterprise Agreements do not acknowledge the right to access keeping in touch days, and the right is not well known or understood by parents or their line managers.

Progress in respect of gender equality in Australian workplaces is monitored by the Workplace Gender Equality Agency (WGEA) with the principal objects of the organization being to promote gender equality and remove barriers to equal participation in employment and the workforce, including family and caring responsibilities.

Employers with more than 100 employees, including universities, are required to report to WGEA on a range of gender equality indicators, with the data then published by WGEA. Data extracted from WGEA in respect of the Higher Education sector shows that, as a class, the Higher Education sector

A Tale of Two Universities

has appropriate policies and procedures in place to provide and evaluate flexible working and parental leave (WGEA n.d.).

Career Progression in the Higher Education Sector

Universities have recognized that women in non-traditional fields of research (STEM or STEMM[1]) face particular challenges. The data, set out in Figure 1, show that across the university sector the proportion of women employed at each level of academic achievement reduces significantly as the academic level increases[2]. The proportion of male academics increases above Level C whereas the proportion of female academics decreases.

Figure 1. Proportion of female to male academic staff, Australia, 2019 to 2021

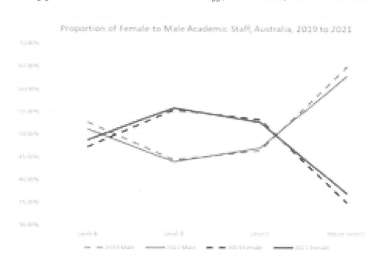

Source: Author calculations from Department of Education, Skills and Employment: Selected Higher Education Statistics – 2021 Staff data

Women are also more likely than men to be employed on a fractional full-time or a part-time basis. Table 1 shows that although 58% of employees are female, in 2021, nearly three times as many women as men were employed on a fractional full-time basis.

Table 1. Higher education sector employees by gender and full/part-time employment

Full-time (by headcount)			Fractional Full-time (by headcount)			Total #		
Males	Females	Persons	Males	Females	Persons	Males	Females	Persons
42,990	49,742	96,506	7,440	21,064	28,552	50,430	70,806	121364
35.4%	41%	76.7%	6.1%	17.4%	23.5%	41.6%	58.3%	100.0%

\# The data exclude casual staff, however, estimates of casual staff employed during the 2021 year show a reduction of 15.2% between 2020 and 2021 compared to a reduction of 7.0% for full-time staff and 6.2% for fractional full-time staff, presumably as a result of the COVID pandemic.

Source: Department of Education, Skills and Employment: 2021 Staff full-time equivalence, Table 1.1 Accessed 19/05/2022.

Athena Swan

The Athena Swan accreditation framework is a gender equity and diversity framework launched in the UK in 2005. The Australian program commenced with a pilot in 2015, and the first Bronze level accreditations were awarded in 2018. In order to achieve accreditation, each university was required to develop a Gender and Diversity Action Plan from an audit of the institution against the SAGE framework for gender equity, diversity, and inclusion. To progress to Silver status each subscriber must be able to show progress and impact against five Key Priority Areas that the subscriber has identified (SAGE, 2020). However, there is concern emerging that the Athena Swan project may not be considered a priority by universities at a time of constrained budgets, resulting in a lack of action in implementing policy changes (de Aguiar et al, 2022).

Research Grant Success

Data collected by the Australian Research Council (ARC) shows a significant difference in the outcomes for male and female researchers. Data collected about the research workforce as part of the Excellence in Research for Australia (ERA) evaluation in 2015 and 2018 included a gender analysis (ARC 2019, ARC 2016). These data show that although in 2018 women made up 44% of the research workforce, the distribution across disciplines is uneven. Women made up fewer than half of the researchers in the STEMM disciplines. Although 52% of researchers in Medical and Health Sciences are female, when disaggregated, female researchers only predominate in Public Health and Health Sciences, Nursing, and Paediatrics and Reproductive Medicine (ARC, 2019).

The report also shows that female researchers were significantly underrepresented at senior levels, with only 36% of researchers at level D and 25% of researchers at level E being female. Even in those Fields of Research where there are more female than male researchers, at level E there are more male (58%) than female (42%) researchers (ARC, 2019).

Both the Australian Research Council (ARC) and the National Health and Medical Research Council (NHMRC) have adopted the Research Opportunity and Performance Evidence (ROPE) principles (ARC 2020)and the "Eligibility and Career Interruptions Statement" (ARC 2019) (NHMRC 2020) to support researchers resuming a career after an interruption when they apply for grants or fellowships. The career interruptions identified in the policies include parental leave and carer responsibilities. In addition, if a researcher takes a career break while they hold a fellowship or Early Career Researcher Award the grant will be extended for the duration of parental leave.

However, universities are increasingly engaging in demand-driven research governed by a commercial contract which may include timelines that cannot be deferred as a consequence of a researcher taking parental leave. In such cases, another researcher may need to be allocated to the project and the original researcher may find their role in the project redundant. In addition to reduced research outputs when excluded from the project, pipeline effects are multiplied if relationships with research partners are not maintained.

Researchers on fixed-term contracts are at a particular disadvantage. If tied to funding for a particular project they are likely to lose their role on that project if they take parental leave, and if their contract expires while on leave the university does not have any obligation to find them another position.

A Tale of Two Universities

THE CASE STUDIES

Research Design

This empirically designed scoping study used a case study methodology to investigate the phenomenon (Yazan, 2015; Yin 2003) of workplace support, culture, and return to work policies at two Australian tertiary institutions, University A and University B. The collaboration arose after the researchers, examining institutional policies around academics returning to work after career breaks within their own universities, identified the overlap of their respective projects on different sides of the country and decided to compare results.

Both researchers examined the parental leave and workplace flexibility policies for their universities via document analysis and combined it with empirical evidence to inform the lived experiences of parents before, during, and on returning to work post parental leave. The overarching research question aiming to explore the lived experiences of post-career break of academic and professional staff at both institutions was similar enough to combine the data sets and report on the findings.

The data collection at both institutions focused on employees' work history and career breaks, the support received during their career breaks, their experiences on returning to work, and their familiarity and access to policy documentation. Each researcher aimed to identify career breaks' effects on staff and examine their University's policies and practices, and the similarity in their investigative approach led to this collaborative study. The combined findings inform this paper to make appropriate policy recommendations to address the negative effects of career breaks while encouraging Academic career progression.

The chosen investigative lens of academic parenthood experiences reflects Rubin (2012) as "qualitative research is not simply learning about a topic, but also learning what is important to those being studied" (p. 15). Triangulating and comparing the data sources used in each case study provided the researchers with sufficient compelling evidence to ensure the robustness of the narrative to tell the *tale of the two universities*.

Case Context: Introducing the Two Universities

The two universities that are the focus of this study are based on the opposite sides of Australia on the West and East Coast respectively. Both Universities have Bronze level membership of Athena Swan and report data on workplace gender equality to WGEA. Females outnumber males at both universities as they do in the High Education sector overall. The gender composition at both universities is very similar, with an approximate 60 to 40 female ratio. Table 2 compares some of the key features of the respective universities:

A Tale of Two Universities

Table 2. Characteristics of the two universities

	University A:	University B:
Location	West Coast	East Coast
Multi-Campus	Yes	Yes
Gender ratios	60.4% female and 39.6% male	62.3% female and 37.7% male
Parental Leave	A primary caregiver is entitled to 26 weeks of paid parental leave on the birth or adoption of a child that may be taken at half pay with a further 26 weeks of unpaid leave (52 weeks total). This may be extended to up to two years without pay, Leave must be taken in a continuous block. Any unused leave is lost when the parent returns to work. A non-primary carer is entitled to 15 days of paid leave. The Enterprise Agreement allows staff to purchase extra leave days.	Paid maternity leave is 20 weeks or it can be taken at half the base rate of pay for up to 40 weeks. An employee (including a casual employee) who becomes pregnant is entitled to up to 52 weeks of maternity leave. The agreement allows staff to apply for leave without pay and other leave entitlements for a total of 104 weeks. This leave may be taken in several separate periods during the total leave period.
Academic Roles	Research only; Teaching only Teaching and Research	Teaching and Research only

Source: WGEA report and Enterprise Agreements for each university

Data Collection

Data were collected at each university before the disruption caused in the Australian academic sector by COVID-19 in 2020/21. The two data sets, Policy data and Experience data were analyzed separately using the Leximancer 4.51 qualitative data mining software to map the individual data sets to assist with the central themes and concepts extraction process (Smith and Humphreys, 2006, Angus et al., 2013). Excel was used to tabulate the Qualtrics survey and the reported facts from the WGEA report section. This approach facilitated a multi-source cross-institutional comparative consideration of meaningful insights into workplace gender policies at both institutions. Leximancer 4.51, a Computer-Assisted Qualitative Data Analysis Software (CAQDAS), does not operate as a substitute for the researcher's immersion in, or interpretation of the data but enriches the research process (Crofts and Bisman; 2010 p.197) and enhances credibility (Lemon et al, 2020). In this study, semantic and relational analysis through Leximancer identified and provided a visual representation of word occurrences, patterns, and the key concepts that made up the themes assisting our chosen interpretative paradigm. Following the Leximancer analysis of the combined qualitative data sets and documents, the researchers reengaged directly with the data to explore and interpret its meanings.

The first stage of the research for both researchers was to review the policy data (Policy) obtained from their institutions' Enterprise Agreements and the policies and practices established to regulate parental leave. Policy data establishes the priorities of each university in respect of their public commitment to removing barriers experienced by academic parents and facilitated cross-institutional comparison. This stage of the investigation aimed to evaluate and review the workplace gender policy details of flexible work arrangements, leave provision (length and accessibility), return to work arrangements, childminding facilities, and other work-to-family enrichment support offered to parents.

A Tale of Two Universities

The selected three documents for in-depth textual content analysis, using Leximancer 4.51 qualitative data mining software for each of the two universities were as follows:

1) the clauses within each institution's Enterprise agreement that address parental leave and flexible work arrangement policies;
2) the submitted and publicly available WGEA compliance reports (2018/19), specifically Gender Work/Life Balance (indicator 4) and workforce gender composition; and
3) Athena Bronze SWAN Institution Application documentation: "Supporting and Advancing Women's Careers", section 5, Career Development.

Experience data consisted of staff perceptions at each university on the topic of career breaks. At University A ethics approval[3] was obtained for a mixed-method methodology. A Qualtrics survey was disseminated among university staff through internal communications inviting responses from staff who had taken at least one career break of at least one month, asking them about their experience before, during, and after the leave. Over three months 65 complete responses were received; 86% female. Twenty-six percent were professional staff and 74% were academic staff. Participants in the survey were invited to self-nominate to participate in a series of focus groups and meetings to discuss in detail the themes raised in the survey. A total of twenty staff members participated in this stage through three focus groups and eight individual interviews.

More than half of the responses identified parental leave as the reason for the career break. Other reasons included personal illness; caring for another person; secondments outside academia, and utilising accrued leave however the numbers in each category were insufficient to allow useful analysis.

At University B, a purely qualitative methodology was followed. In accordance with ethics approval[4] the themes for discussion were developed through round table discussions and an in-house seminar session centering around the policies, provisions, and lived experiences of carers returning to work. This informed the follow-up data collection by way of interviews and focus groups. An overall participant recruitment email was sent out through the university's Engaged Parent Network with an open invitation to join the study by participating in focus groups or individual interviews. The selection criteria required the participants to: (1) be either professional staff or academics holding teaching or research active roles (2) be employed by the university full-time or part-time, (3) have returned to work post parental career break within the past 48 months.

The data extracted to inform the findings for this study was derived predominantly from the focus groups and interviews across both universities. The interview protocol at both institutions comprised semi-structured questions focussing on a) reflections on parental leave experiences before, during, and upon return to work and b) their level of awareness, uptake, and hindrances regarding institutional support strategies available to retain working parents.

Hence, the combined data that tells the *'tale of the two universities'* consists of the responses of n=40 participants (21 at University A and 19 at University B) (see Table 3). The participant sample at University A consisted of nineteen academic and two professional staff members, including two males. At University B ten were professional staff and nine were academic staff, including three males. Academic staff at University A were evenly split between research-only and combined teaching and research (T&R) roles. All academic staff at University B hold teaching and research positions.

Table 3. Participant profile

Type of Interview	University A	University B
Focus Groups participants	13	15
Individual interview	8	4
Gender:		
Female	19	16
Male	2	3
Employment Type		
Professional	2	10
Teaching & Research	9	9
Research Only	8	N/A. All academic positions are classified as Teaching and Research
Teaching Only	2	

The focus groups and interviews were recorded, transcribed, and examined thematically using Leximancer software package 4.51.

Data Analysis

Findings: The People Experience and Workplace Support

Consistent with the evidence discussed in the literature, findings from the Experience data set confirm that in Australia, academic women undertake a larger share of parenting responsibilities than their male colleagues, even where the criteria for accessing workplace support are not gendered. The Leximancer conceptual map identifies 'female' and 'women's role as the caregiver' as key themes in this study. Additional themes relating to the effects of career breaks were the management of work, research progression, and identity. Notable concepts pointed towards the 'struggle', the 'career', the 'workload', and the 'progression'; linked to the 'role' of a woman in providing care whilst aspiring to return to work.

A Tale of Two Universities

Figure 2. Conceptual map of themes that emerged in focus group discussion

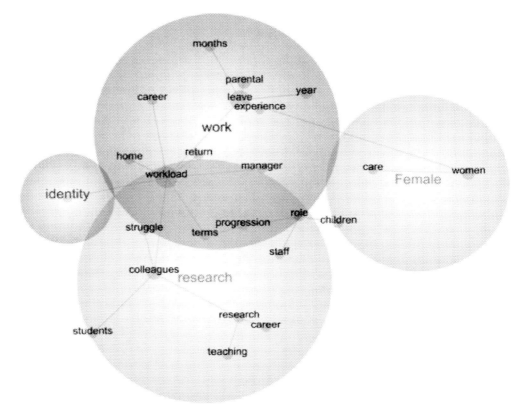

Alongside the recognition of participants about various struggles and challenges in their experiences of returning to work, the majority also held positive reflections on their experiences. The lived experiences conferred in our *tale of two universities*, assist us in rethinking the available policies essential for a post-pandemic cultural shift to balance work and family/caring commitments, standardize the lived experience of the progressive, family-friendly policies of the universities, and assist parents to resume career and professional identity in light of the teaching, research and professional duties in modern universities.

Work Culture and Carer Responsibilities

Participants acknowledged the flexibility and available parental support schemes at both institutions; nevertheless, they admitted that parents, especially women, make constant trade-offs juggling their work-life balance.

I had six months' leave in a teaching and research role. And yes, the kind of dynamic in terms of returning and trying to get momentum up is so hard to achieve. Since I am back, it's been really hard. The caring responsibilities never stop. I kind of also take care of my mother and my grandfather. So it is just a never-ending role. (A1)

Many participants identified a lack of clarity around the details of parental leave and the options available. Difficulties were reported in the interpretation of parental leave entitlements and flexible work agreements due to the language used.

It was always me looking up all the information, looking up the workplace agreements, and telling my supervisor and also HR, this is what I'm going to do. This is what my rights are. No one actually said to me that these are your options, which would suit you best Or none wanted to sit down and discuss it with me. (B4)

A preference for broader communication and simpler terminology used in parental leave and return to work policies at both institutions would assist with consistency in interpretation.

The wording is so technical. It is all very legal language. I had to read it like three times, and I had to confirm it with somebody else. (A6)

Policy implementation is inconsistent and dependent on whether senior colleagues and supervisors understand the complexity of carers' responsibilities.

I don't have any brothers or sisters or family around here or anyone to be able to draw on. So I can empathize about not having people around you, some sort of community to do that. (A7)

Driven by financial and career considerations, staff sometimes cannot afford to remain on a career break, and the lack of appropriate childminding options is a further limitation.

I really wanted to extend my leave because I didn't feel ready to come back and I was not sure what I come back to. However, we had no choice because of our financial situation. We made the choice that I had to come back and then we were confronted with the lack of childcare availability (A2)

I brought my children in - probably I should not have - but I brought them in for the first two weeks because I had no options. Like I had to be here to meet students and meet people, and the daycare hadn't started yet. (A 3)

Hence, the participants referred to a need for increased visibility of the universities to become more family-friendly work environments.

I was told you can't bring children into the workplace. I said, well, the day care's not open, I don't know what you want me to do. I was told I had to take the day as leave or find someone to look after the children. This was completely unsympathetic, and I was so stressed from trying to do it, I was trying to juggle a baby while I was on a telephone, and I gave myself a neck strain that was so bad that I couldn't move my arm, or my neck for about a week. The physio said, this isn't a strain, you're just incredibly stressed. It was really terrible. (A12)

Finally, participants stated that supervisors ought to recognize and understand the need for flexibility for parents.

A Tale of Two Universities

My kids are five and seven now, and I remember those years, ...I think the further I get away from it, the less you kind of remember really how difficult it was. And that is what makes it hard for me to relate to my staff. (A2)

At both institutions, participants appreciated that as employers the universities have policies allowing flexible work opportunities and supporting career progression, and this does reduce the stress of balancing work and caring commitments. Nevertheless, the interviews showed that participants, predominantly women, need more support at an institutional level to deal with childcare issues, caring responsibilities, and a more structured return to work post-career break to achieve a work-life balance and experience greater job satisfaction.

Findings indicate that having an existing support network in place for women at various levels of their careers such as the University B 'Engaged Parent Network' to provide personal support could be beneficial for resuming work post-career break more positively.

Career Progression Implications

Interviewees at both universities agreed that initiatives for return post-career break and employee engagement are provided to retain personnel. Nevertheless, most academic staff rated the effect of the career break on their career progression as unfavorable, with staff engaged in both teaching and research (T&R) staff reporting the most negative outcomes.

The survey at University A showed that universities' policies to support researchers seemed to be moderately effective, with research staff consistently being more satisfied with keeping-in-touch measures, coverage of usual duties, ongoing engagement with long-term projects, and return to work measures. Conversely, teaching and research (T&R) staff were dissatisfied across all these areas. Participants voiced a call for a more structured phased return back.

I suppose initially when you're away for a year- it's a long time. When you come back I was apprehensive, is it going to be the same dynamic, is it going to be the same? What have I missed? What do I need to catch up with so that I can resume where I left off? Is it even possible to do so? (B6)

A review of the duration of parental leave reported in the University A survey showed that academic staff take significantly shorter periods of parental leave than professional staff and are less likely to take unpaid parental leave.

I returned much sooner than I wanted to. I had no choice as my replacement was leaving, and I had to resume my teaching and research responsibilities. In hindsight, I should have stayed away longer. But here I thought the longer I am away the harder it will be to resume where I left off. (B5)

The female academic participants justified the earlier return to work as necessary to maintain career progression and not lose what they referred to as their professional identity. They also reported completing projects while on parental leave.

My field moves pretty fast, I was right in the middle of a really major science project when I went on maternity leave, and I had to come back and finish that, there was no question of coming back part-

time. …. I had to make a conscious decision - I had to set up a lot of things myself to make sure that it wouldn't be too hard later on. (B3)

I did have a grant during my first maternity leave. It went completely pear-shaped when I was on maternity leave, so I was very conscious not to apply for another one, I wanted to have another child. So my publications are really good, but it's my grants and my HDR (Higher Degree(Research)) completions that suffered. (A4)

Both researchers heard women voice the anxiety arising from the struggle of keeping a mentally and physically sound work-life balance and wanting to enjoy their time away from the workplace. They could not relax in their carer roles due to constant qualms and worries about their academic future and career progression. Participants sought increased transparency and consistency in policies to reduce worrying, allowing them to appreciate their career break and experience a better return to work.

I struggled and almost had an identity crisis- I am now a new Mum and I am also a researcher. So what does this mean? I quite liked having that dual identity, that I'm more than one thing. I felt that the university expected more from me than I could immediately give back, but I tried my hardest to get back into it. Having this new dual role was far more difficult than doing what was expected before I had children. (B14)

Jakubiec (2015) acknowledges this anxiety in individual female research-active staff to hurry back to academic work, stating that "some women, even while on maternity leave, felt pressure to be engaged and remain active in faculty life and academic tasks (p.46)." Gaio Santos and Cabral-Cardoso (2008) found that women felt "pressured" to return to work soon after childbirth…and having children is regarded as a lack of commitment to academic work and ultimately could be detrimental to the career. Thus, the organizational culture seems to implicitly "condemn…having children" (p.452).

In our tale of lived experiences, the respondents, primarily women, noted that they cannot focus on resuming and maintaining their professional identity while feeling that they must continually choose between career and family and even family formation, accompanied by feelings of anxiety and guilt associated with those decisions. Women reported delaying having a family in the hope of achieving a permanent appointment first or giving up on the possibility of a permanent position to have children.

I'm kind of going through a certain stage in my life where I tell myself, do it now and have kids or never. It's more for my partner because he really wants to have kids. But we're in a situation where we can't manage that. I've always been the breadwinner. The one with the highest income. (A17)

The findings support Wolf-Wendel and Ward (2006) that while the gendered split of academic work exists at both universities; women in higher education experience a happier sense of professional identity when the value of the more 'feminine' teaching duties is recognized. The commercialization of institutions and the pressure to publish, adopting more 'masculine' academic work patterns to re-immerse themselves in research, create stress amongst academic mothers struggling to maintain a work-life balance. To embrace a return to work post-career break a more rewarding and positive experience is needed for women. Support schemes need to reflect an institutional understanding of the female role and compart-

A Tale of Two Universities

mentalized struggles of being a carer. After all, the role of the mother continues past infancy and still has a central role post-childbirth in balancing caring and work obligations.

I still have my phasing back to work day off. My smallest one is so attached to me that after the weekend she doesn't like me leaving. ...to switch on and off from the child screaming at home and getting to sit down and to think about my students, do everything, doing lectures, teaching, research – let me tell you, it's really hard. (B7)

Our 'tale' thus reinforces the criticisms of the neoliberal agenda of contemporary institutions and the masculine model of the 'ideal worker'. The female's role as a carer requires more recognition. Furthermore, the findings highlight the need for institutions to change policy and cultural attitudes to assist women with maintaining their professional identity and drive; in particular, we call for such change and address this in the next section and recommendations in a post-COVID environment.

Policy: Rhetoric vs. Reality

Findings: University Commitments to Academic Parents

Now that we have set out how academic parents experience their job, we examine whether the policies that the universities are putting in place are working. The analysis of the Enterprise Agreements and the WGEA reports that were included in the Policy Data set (Figure 3A) showed that these documents were more concerned with the structure of formal leave entitlements in respect of parental leave that staff members were entitled to take, with a lesser of focus on flexible work arrangements that would be facilitated under the policy. Notably, these documents tended to be gender blind, with female and gender not appearing in the conceptual map generated by Leximancer.

In contrast the conceptual map for the Athena Swan documentation (Figure 4) identified work and family balance as an issue experienced predominantly by females, and the processes that need to be in place to support work-family balance.

Figure 3a. Parental Leave and Flexibility Clauses in Enterprise Agreements: University A and B

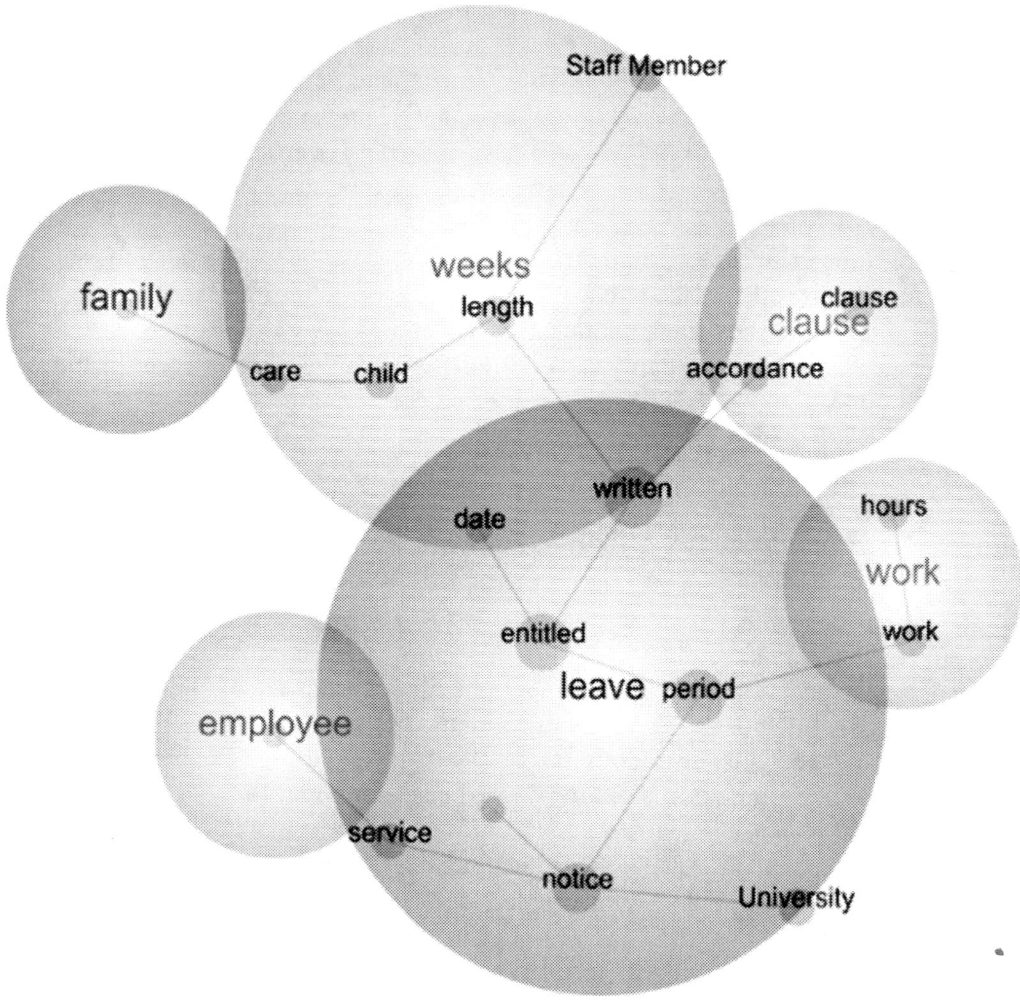

A Tale of Two Universities

Figure 3b. Conceptual Maps of Policy Documents (Policies)

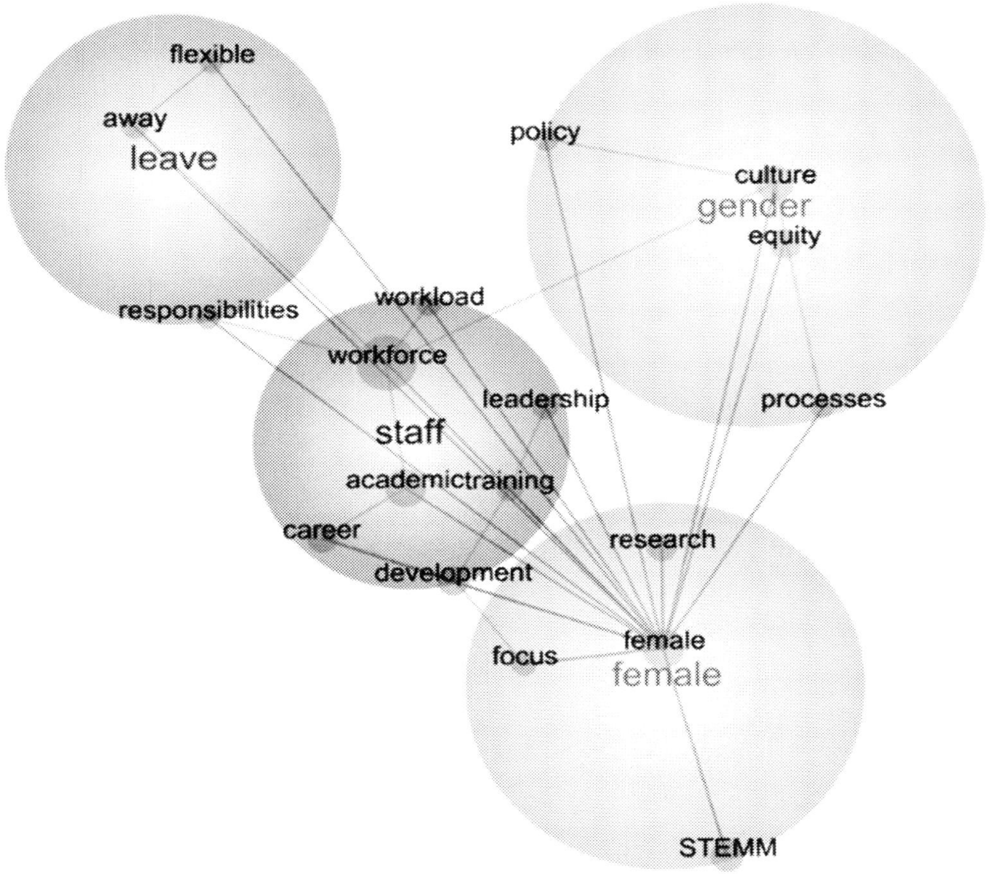

Challenges of Flexible Work

Universities, including those in this study, score very highly in the WGEA data set (WGEA n.d.) in respect of flexible work, and having a formal policy to support carers. They have relatively generous paid parental leave provisions and are more likely than not to have childcare services available on campus.

This support was recognised by the parents who participated in this research although parents do face challenges in relation to how these policies are applied in practice. They told us that flexible work arrangements were not being observed with parents working during their parental leave as well as on days that they were not scheduled to work. Researchers who were supervising research students tended to maintain that supervision during periods of leave, largely from a sense of obligation to the student; but also to ensure that they were the supervisor of record when the student completed.

*I had my work performance and planning review straight after I got back because of the timing. So I got in, and I said, I'm very proud of what I accomplished last year, here are all the things that I did while I was **not** on leave, and here are all the things I did while I was **on** leave. So my manager said, oh, you can't talk about any of the stuff you did on leave. We don't want you to put that in anything written down because it would imply that the university is making you work. (B5)*

Psychologically it was really frustrating to be minimizing those accomplishments, which I was very proud of. I did a conference talk a week after giving birth, the second child. I was proud of that, and they're like, no, no, you can't say that. Well, I'm still here, aren't I? I'm proud of it. (A9)

Administrative duties were frequently dealt with on a non-working day. Deadlines for information and student concerns would need to be attended to regardless of the agreed working schedule:

I'm the type of person that if you get an email, and if I check it, if it's a quick thing, I can do it quickly, and I'd prefer to do that than to come in on a Monday morning and have 20, 30 things to respond to. (B2)

The administrative issues around demand and the operational requirements of the child care service, including the Commonwealth Funding model, can make it difficult to access the campus-based childcare service.

Yeah, I'm not at (campus-based childcare service), because I found it very inflexible ... I choose to have one closer to home...(B3)

(M University) one I'm told basically goes, student or staff member? When you say, staff member, they go, oh sorry, we're prioritizing students with kids, which - okay, fair enough, but surely that just means you need more capacity because you can't just sort of offer half a service, really. (A5)

Policies around flexible work can be incompatible with timetabling requirements. Timetabling all classes across a university is a major logistical undertaking, and there is an expectation that academics are available during core teaching hours for example from 8 am to 6 pm. The right to flexible hours conflicts with the timetabling processes of the university, particularly where childcare centers have strict policies around drop-off and pick-up times:

So my wife and I just put our days in that we wanted the kids in daycare and crossed our fingers and hoped that the two days off we were having did not align exactly with the dates that I would be required to teach; ...had that not happened, I would have had to either make the decision to not take that time off or somehow swap my teaching with someone else at the last minute. (B12)

Timetabling challenges can be difficult to resolve where an academic parent is a leader in an area of particular expertise, making it more difficult to substitute a colleague as the teacher of that class.

The policies in place around flexible hours and timetabling work most effectively where there is a champion who was prepared to advocate for the parent, or where there is a substitution that could be arranged internally:

A Tale of Two Universities

…it expected that there are particular days that you know are unavailable ahead of time. We get to communicate that to the head of school and then he advocates if there's a scheduling conflict. So I feel that that the support is there and that's genuine. (A6)

The higher rate of dissatisfaction among teaching and research (T&R) staff shown in the survey at University A suggests that the juggle of career and family becomes even more challenging when juggling the already disparate requirements of classroom teaching and research outputs with family.

Participants from University B positively referred to the 'Engaged Parent Network (EPN)' which operates as a staff networking platform to support a positive, collaborative, inclusive, and family-friendly culture within the university. Over the years with the support of the research leadership, the EPN has provided coaching and collaborative activities to support parents and carers, as well as providing opportunities for staff to connect around shared experiences.

The EPN has established itself as an inclusive network in terms of what can be done to better assist parents upon their return from maternity and parental leave and is open to the wider university community of academics, professional staff, students (Research, Undergraduate, and Postgraduate) and overall Mothers, Fathers, and Carers. (B5)

The EPN has become a proactive hub for several important interdisciplinary gender equity research projects and has facilitated the establishment of the Student Parents Network (SPU) to provide student-parents with a similar effective and safe space for social support, career and educational mentoring, and academic pathway advice. Through COVID-19, both the SPU and the EPN led discussions on gender equity and the way forward, organizing multiple coaching sessions to support staff working from home; and providing support to students to continue their studies in such difficult uncertain times.

Recognising Career Interruptions in a Research Trajectory

Much of the work to date on the challenges faced by academic parents prioritized research over teaching challenges. Many researchers delay having a family until after completing a PhD and juggling postdoctoral positions with family formation.

The ROPE policy discussed earlier is supposed to address this hurdle by ensuring that career breaks are taken into account. Those participants who had engaged with the ARC on ROPE guidelines generally found that university support was forthcoming.

I took my Future Fellowship from the beginning as point 8 (FTE). So it was five years instead of four years, and I was on that, probably the same as you, trying to extend it as long as you can because you didn't have a continuing position at the end. The ARC was great for that in that's a standard thing that the ARC does, and so no universities can say, no, you can't do that. (A9)

I think, well, both of my children were on my DECRA[5]. The DECRA, like any ARC grant, any fellowship from the ARC, they're very clear saying, you can take it part-time - so the DECRA was three years - or up to six years part-time. So I had a plan in my head, okay, I'm going to take six months off, then I'm going to go part-time, then hopefully, have another child, six more months off. And I kind of planned, for me, it worked in a good place, that I managed to do a five-year DECRA instead of a three-year. (A4)

However in respect of the assessment of grant applications, there is still a degree of skepticism that the ROPE principles are being applied, and there are still misunderstandings as to how the ROPE principles apply for promotion within each University:

So you go to a conference or something, and you meet someone who is on the College of Experts, or who's in your field, a very important person, and basically said to me, oh, yeah, you can write that you've had six months off, but at the end of the day, we look at how many papers you've got, how many citations you've got and all of that, and if you're not as good as somebody else, it doesn't matter that you've worked part-time and they've worked full-time, they'll give the grant to this person. (A8)

As I said, when I went for a promotion this year, and I had my meeting with my PVC, he misdefined the relative-to-opportunity policy. He said that I still had to achieve the same as everybody else, even though I was part-time and had two career breaks, and only had 20 percent research, was expected to have six-figure grant, have a research team running underneath me, and have had multiple HDR completions. I challenged him on that, and he wasn't backing down. He commended me on what I had achieved, said it was quite amazing given that I've had two career breaks and had been part-time, but it wasn't sufficient for him to support me for associate professor. (A10)

A career interruption has a long-term effect on a researcher's output. ROPE principles alone do not address career interruptions, and research careers are becoming more precarious as universities rely more heavily on industry-funded research partnerships.

THE COVID PANDEMIC

The data from the two projects described in this article was collected before the COVID pandemic. While the effect of the pandemic is not a theme of this research, the evidence emerging from the higher education sector is that remote working has exacerbated the issues raised in our research.

Although academics have traditionally had more autonomy over their working conditions than other workers the evidence and narratives of academics that emerged from the pandemic have highlighted the challenges, as they detail some of their experiences balancing care and work (Boncori, 2020; Statti et al, 2021; Abdellatif, 2020). Teachers were forced to rapidly adapt to new technologies and teaching systems (Casacchia et al, 2021; Watermeyer et al 2020) while home-schooling children (Guy and Arthur, 2021).

Researchers faced similar challenges: research plans and agendas that could not be adapted to the remote work environment faced delays or cancellations. There is now a solid evidence base showing a reduction in research outputs by women compared with men, largely because the responsibility for home learning of children and other care responsibilities was disproportionately shouldered by women (Wright et al, 2020; Viglione 2020; Bowyer et al, 2021; Statti et al, 2021). Notably, women could not devote time to writing up the results of their research (Peetz et al, 2022).

During the pandemic, Australian universities cut staff (Universities Australia 2020), were less flexible in respect of leave, and provided less information on balancing care responsibilities with remote work than their international counterparts (Nash and Churchill, 2020). This may have been because universities focussed on the remote learning experience for international and domestic students without adequate appreciation of the pressure this placed on staff.

A Tale of Two Universities

CONCLUSION AND RECOMMENDATIONS

In the studies discussed in this paper initiatives currently in place at two Australian universities to enhance career progression were tested against the lived experience of academic parents, who are predominantly mothers.

Our analysis of the policies that universities are implementing shows that the higher education sector is well aware of the challenges that academic parents face. Although universities have a high proportion of female employees they are more likely to be working part-time and in non-managerial positions than their male counterparts (DESE, 2022).

The results point toward Higher Education Institutions needing to do more to embed a culture of care within their organizational culture. Ambition is influenced by the daily trade-offs of being a working parent and whether these are made easier or harder by an employing organization, not by parenthood itself, (Abouzahr et al, 2017). Thus, culture plays a major role in preserving and fostering ambition and promotion of leadership after parental leave.

While the university sector has adopted policies to support gender equity, the lived experience of academic parents, predominantly female, shows that implementation of these policies can be patchy. Universities are complex organizations where expectations and cultures differ across faculties and disciplines. The needs of an academic parent may not be easily accommodated within the localized culture, even if within university policies.

This is the strength of programs like Athena Swan and the ROPE principles, in identifying where work is needed to address areas of concern and developing specific responses. However, these programs are regarded with skepticism if not implemented consistently. Managers must understand the policies that are available to provide support; which must be applied consistently across the university.

Communication and access to resources is essential. We strongly recommend that the relevant policies and procedures are made readily available, in plain English, to all staff including applicants and line managers. Human resource specialists should be available to mediate and work out a plan that suits the needs of the staff member. Where a plan has been developed for leave, return to work, flexible work, or teaching availability there must be mechanisms for the staff member to ensure that the plan is followed by all parties, without the line manager placing pressure on the staff member to work outside the agreed parameters.

This study recommends that universities provide support to parenting networks that can facilitate access to information as well as sharing experiences, providing personal support and well-being and resilience programs for those parents who choose this assistance. The EPN experience shows that an in-house parent support group is worth the investment of time and resources as it does improve working conditions for parents. It has become an outlet for parents to voice their views about work policies or concerns over incidents, and share parenting advice as they juggle work-life commitments. Such networks provide visibility of parenthood in the workplace and can assist with a needed cultural shift of making care within academic institutions more visible.

The natural experiment in working flexibly that was forced on the global community by COVID has also exposed the challenges that accompany flexible working (Deloitte, 2020 Peetz et al, 2022). Although working parents have the flexibility to shape their working hours to accommodate work-family balance, the worker may feel unable to disconnect from the workplace. True flexibility recognizes when a person is not expected to be working and recognizes the right to switch off.

Parenting is not the only reason for career interruptions. It is known that women take on a significant burden of care for other family members, and older women are frequently the primary carer. In 2018 data showed that more than twice as many women as men aged 55 to 64 are the primary carer for a person with a disability (ABS, 2018). These carers are less visible in the workplace although many juggle the carer role with employment. This needs to be explored further: is the lack of visibility because there are few policies to assist this cohort, or are there few policies because of their lack of visibility?

Ultimately, although universities are implementing policies and strategies to support academic and professional parents, it is clear that academic parents still experience challenges in managing the demands of work and family at a time when they need to build their careers. These policies and strategies must be made fit for purpose in the post-COVID workplace so that the academic parent who is juggling an academic career with parenting has an equal opportunity to succeed.

Women are the majority of staff at universities and they still carry the highest parenting load. They also are a visible example to undergraduate and postgraduate students. Until universities develop policies that reflect the needs of academic parents, women will continue to be underrepresented at senior academic levels.

ACKNOWLEDGEMENTS

This research was supported by the universities that were the subject of the research. University A funded a Provost Fellowship. University B provided seed funding from the Deputy Vice Chancellor's office.

REFERENCES

Abdellatif, A., & Gatto, M. (2020). It's OK not to be OK: Shared reflections from two PhD parents in a time of pandemic. *Gender, Work and Organization*, 27(5), 723–733. doi:10.1111/gwao.12465 PMID:32837005

Abouzahr, K. (2017). *Dispelling the Myths of the Gender "Ambition Gap."* Report issued by The Boston Consulting Group (BCG). https://on.bcg.com/2nIa6GC

Amano-Patiño, N., Faraglia, E., Giannitsarou, C., & Hasna, Z. (2020). Who is doing new research in the time of COVID-19? Not the female economists. *Publishing and Measuring Success in Economics, 13*.

Anderson, G. (2008). Mapping academic resistance in the managerial university. *Organization, 15*(2), 251–270. doi:10.1177/1350508407086583

Angus, D., Rintel, S., & Wiles, J. (2013). Making sense of big text: A visual-first approach for analysing text data using Leximancer and Discursis. *International Journal of Social Research Methodology, 16*(3), 261–267. doi:10.1080/13645579.2013.774186

Armenti, C. (2004). May babies and posttenure babies: Maternal decisions of women professors. *Review of Higher Education, 27*(2), 211–231. doi:10.1353/rhe.2003.0046

Austen, S., Sharp, R., & Hodgson, H. (2015, January). Gender impact analysis and the taxation of retirement savings in Australia. In *Australian Tax Forum, 30* (4), 763-781.

A Tale of Two Universities

Australian Bureau of Statistics. (2019). *Disability, Ageing and Carers, Australia: Summary of Findings Reference period 2018* (Cat 4430.0). ABS.

Australian Research Council. (2016). State of Australian University Research 2015-16: Volume 2 Institutional Insights. Australian Research Council, Canberra.

Australian Research Council. (2019). *Gender and the Research Workforce. Excellence in Research for Australia (ERA) 2018.* Australian Research Council.

Australian Research Council. (2019b). *ARC Policy Statement: Eligibility and Career Interruptions.* ARC. https://www.arc.gov.au/policies-strategies/policy/arc-policy-statement-eligibility-and-career-interruptions (last modified 12/12/2019)

Australian Research Council. (2020). *ARC Research Opportunity and Performance Evidence (ROPE) Statement.* ARC. https://www.arc.gov.au/policies-strategies/policy/arc-research-opportunity-and-performance-evidence-rope-statement

Baker, M. (2010). Motherhood, employment and the "child penalty". *Women's Studies International Forum, 33*(3), 215–224. doi:10.1016/j.wsif.2010.01.004

Boncori, I. (2020). The Never-ending Shift: A feminist reflection on living and organizing academic lives during the coronavirus pandemic. *Gender, Work and Organization, 27*(5), 677–682. doi:10.1111/gwao.12451 PMID:32836999

Bowyer, D., Deitz, M., Jamison, A., Taylor, C. E., Gyengesi, E., Ross, J., Hammond, H., Ogbeide, A. E., & Dune, T. (2022). Academic mothers, professional identity and COVID-19: Feminist reflections on career cycles, progression and practice. *Gender, Work and Organization, 29*(1), 309–341. doi:10.1111/gwao.12750 PMID:34898865

Budig, M. J., Misra, J., & Boeckmann, I. (2012). The motherhood penalty in cross-national perspective: The importance of work-family policies and cultural attitudes. *Social Politics, 19*(2), 163–193. doi:10.1093p/jxs006

Casacchia, M., Cifone, M. G., Giusti, L., Fabiani, L., Gatto, R., Lancia, L., Cinque, B., Petrucci, C., Giannoni, M., Ippoliti, R., Frattaroli, A. R., Macchiarelli, G., & Roncone, R. (2021). Distance education during COVID 19: An Italian survey on the university teachers' perspectives and their emotional conditions. *BMC Medical Education, 21*(1), 1–17. doi:10.118612909-021-02780-y PMID:34107926

Chemaly, S. (2020). Coronavirus could hurt women the most. Here's how to prevent a patriarchal pandemic. *Institute for Women's Policy Research. NBC News.*

Cohen, S., Hanna, P., Higham, J., Hopkins, D., & Orchiston, C. (2020). Gender discourses in academic mobility. *Gender, Work and Organization, 27*(2), 149–165. doi:10.1111/gwao.12413

Correll, S. J., Benard, S., & Paik, I. (2007). Getting a job: Is there a motherhood penalty? *American Journal of Sociology, 112*(5), 1297–1338. doi:10.1086/511799

Crofts, K., & Bisman, J. (2010). Interrogating accountability: An illustration of the use of Leximancer software for qualitative data analysis. *Qualitative Research in Accounting & Management.*

Crook, S. (2020). Parenting during the Covid-19 pandemic of 2020: Academia, labour and care work. *Women's History Review, 29*(7), 1–13. doi:10.1080/09612025.2020.1807690

Cukrowska-Torzewska, E., & Lovasz, A. (2020). The role of parenthood in shaping the gender wage gap– A comparative analysis of 26 European countries. *Social Science Research, 85,* 102355. doi:10.1016/j. ssresearch.2019.102355 PMID:31789194

de Aguiar, T. R. S., Haque, S., & Bender, K. A. (2022). Athena SWAN gender equality plans and the gendered impact of COVID-19. *Gender, Work & Organization, 29*(2), 591-608. https://doi.org/ AGUIAR etAl.608 doi:10.1111/gwao.12784de

Deloitte. (2020). *Understanding the pandemic's impact on working women.* Deloitte. https://www2. deloitte.com/content/dam/Deloitte/global/Documents/About-Deloitte/gx-about-deloitte-understanding-the-pandemic-s-impact-on-working-women.pdf

Department of Education, Skills and Employment (DESE). (2022). *Higher Education Staff Numbers for 2021, Table 2.5.* DESE. https://www.dese.gov.au/higher-education-statistics/resources/2021-staff-numbers

Drago, R., & Williams, J. (2000). A half-time tenure track proposal. *Change, 32*(6), 46–51. doi:10.1080/00091380009601767

England, P., Bearak, J., Budig, M. J., & Hodges, M. J. (2016). Do highly paid, highly skilled women experience the largest motherhood penalty? *American Sociological Review, 81*(6), 1161–1189. doi:10.1177/0003122416673598

Gaio Santos, G., & Cabral-Cardoso, C. (2008). 'Work-Family Culture in Academia: A Gendered View of Work-Family Conflict and Coping Strategies'. *Gender in Management, 23*(6), 442–457. doi:10.1108/17542410810897553

Guy, B., & Arthur, B. (2020). Academic motherhood during COVID-19: Navigating our dual roles as educators and mothers. *Gender, Work and Organization, 27*(5), 887–899. doi:10.1111/gwao.12493 PMID:32837022

Heijstra, T. M., Steinthorsdóttir, F. S., & Einarsdóttir, T. (2017). Academic career making and the double-edged role of academic housework. *Gender and Education, 29*(6), 764–780. doi:10.1080/0954 0253.2016.1171825

Huopalainen, A. S., & Satama, S. T. (2019). Mothers and researchers in the making: Negotiating 'new' motherhood within the 'new' academia. *Human Relations, 72*(1), 98–121. doi:10.1177/0018726718764571

Kennelly, I., & Spalter-Roth, R. M. (2006). Parents on the job market: Resources and strategies that help sociologists attain tenure-track jobs. *The American Sociologist, 37*(4), 29–49. doi:10.1007/BF02915066

Knights, D., & Clarke, C. A. (2014). It's a bittersweet symphony, this life: Fragile academic selves and insecure identities at work. *Organization Studies, 35*(3), 335–357. doi:10.1177/0170840613508396

Lemon, L. L., & Hayes, J. (2020). Enhancing trustworthiness of qualitative findings: Using Leximancer for qualitative data analysis triangulation. *Qualitative Report, 25*(3), 604–614. doi:10.46743/2160-3715/2020.4222

A Tale of Two Universities

Malisch, J. L., Harris, B. N., Sherrer, S. M., Lewis, K. A., Shepherd, S. L., McCarthy, P. C., & Deitloff, J. (2020). In the wake of COVID-19, academia needs new solutions to ensure gender equity. *Proceedings of the National Academy of Sciences of the United States of America, 117*(27), 15378–15381. doi:10.1073/pnas.2010636117 PMID:32554503

Marchant, T., & Wallace, M. (2016). Gender balance in teaching awards: Evidence from 18 years of national data. *Journal of Higher Education Policy and Management, 38*(4), 393–405. doi:10.1080/136 0080X.2016.1181885

Marsh, K. (2015). Motherhood in US Academe: How the Presence of Women Disrupts the Ideal Worker Model in Colleges and Universities. *Journal of the Motherhood Initiative for Research and Community Involvement.*

McDermott, M. (2020). Becoming a Mother in the Academy: A Letter to My Children. In *Women Negotiating Life in the Academy* (pp. 161–173). Springer. doi:10.1007/978-981-15-3114-9_13

Monroe, K., Ozyurt, S., Wrigley, T., & Alexander, A. (2008). Gender equality in academia: Bad news from the trenches, and some possible solutions. *Perspectives on Politics, 6*(2), 215–233. doi:10.1017/S1537592708080572

Nash, M., & Churchill, B. (2020). Caring during COVID-19: A gendered analysis of Australian university responses to managing remote working and caring responsibilities. *Gender, Work and Organization, 27*(5), 833–846. doi:10.1111/gwao.12484 PMID:32837013

National Health and Medical Research Council. (2020). *Eligibility Fact Sheet - Investigator Grants 2020: Appendix A.* National Health and Medical Research Council. https://www.nhmrc.gov.au/sites/default/files/documents/attachments/Investigator-Grants-Eligibility-Fact-Sheet-2020.pdf

Nikunen, M. (2012). Changing university work, freedom, flexibility and family. *Studies in Higher Education, 37*(6), 713–729. doi:10.1080/03075079.2010.542453

Nikunen, M. (2014). The 'entrepreneurial university', family and gender: Changes and demands faced by fixed-term workers. *Gender and Education, 26*(2), 119–134. doi:10.1080/09540253.2014.888402

Oleschuk, M. (2020). Gender equity considerations for tenure and promotion during COVID-19. *Canadian review of sociology.*

Peetz, D., Baird, M., Banerjee, R., Bartkiw, T., Campbell, S., Charlesworth, S., Coles, A., Cooper, R., Foster, J., Galea, N., de la Harpe, B., Leighton, C., Lynch, B., Pike, K., Pyman, A., Ramia, I., Ressia, S., Samani, M. N., Southey, K., & Weststar, J. (2022). Sustained knowledge work and thinking time amongst academics: Gender and working from home during the COVID-19 pandemic. *Labour & Industry, 32*(1), 72–92. doi:10.1080/10301763.2022.2034092

Pepping, A., & Maniam, B. (2020). The Motherhood Penalty. *Journal of Business and Behavioral Sciences, 32*(2), 110–125.

Roberat, S. R., & Erskine, W. (2005). Beyond the fear factor: Work/family policies in academia-resources or rewards? *Change, 37*(6), 19–25. doi:10.3200/CHNG.37.6.19-25

SAGE. (2020). *Pathway from Athena SWAN Bronze to Silver Award: Design Elements.* SAGE. https://www.sciencegenderequity.org.au/wp-content/uploads/2020/08/SAGE-Pathways-Bronze-to-Silver-Award-Design-Elements.pdf accessed 19 March 2021

Statti, A., Evans, J., Torres, K. M., & Torres, I. (2021). Balancing Career and Caregiving Roles in the Midst of a Global Pandemic: The Narratives of Four Females in Higher Education. In H. Schnackenberg & D. Simard (Eds.), *Women and Leadership in Higher Education During Global Crises* (pp. 159–174). IGI Global. doi:10.4018/978-1-7998-6491-2.ch010

Valian, V. (2005). Beyond gender schemas: Improving the advancement of women in academia. *Hypatia, 20*(3), 198–213. doi:10.1111/j.1527-2001.2005.tb00495.x

Van Engen, M. L., Bleijenbergh, I. L., & Beijer, S. E. (2021). Conforming, accommodating, or resisting? How parents in academia negotiate their professional identity. *Studies in Higher Education, 46*(8), 1493–1505. doi:10.1080/03075079.2019.1691161

Viglione, G. (2020). Are women publishing less during the pandemic? Here's what the data say. *Nature, 581*(7809), 365–367. doi:10.1038/d41586-020-01294-9 PMID:32433639

Watermeyer, R., Crick, T., Knight, C., & Goodall, J. (2021). COVID-19 and digital disruption in UK universities: Afflictions and affordances of emergency online migration. *Higher Education, 81*(3), 623–641. doi:10.100710734-020-00561-y PMID:32836334

Willey, N. L. (2020). Parenting policies and culture in academia and beyond: Making it while mothering (and fathering) in the academy, and what COVID-19 has to do with it. *Journal of the Motherhood Initiative for Research and Community Involvement.*

Wolf-Wendel, L. E., & Ward, K. (2006). 'Academic Life and Motherhood: Variations by Institutional Type'. *Higher Education, 52*(3), 487–521. doi:10.100710734-005-0364-4

Workplace Gender Equality Agency (WGEA). (2018). *Insight Guide: Towards gender-balanced parental leave.* Commonwealth Government of Australia.

Workplace Gender Equality Agency (WGEA). (n.d.). *Data Explorer.* WGEA.

Wright, K. A., Haastrup, T., & Guerrina, R. (2021). Equalities in freefall? Ontological insecurity and the long-term impact of COVID-19 in the academy. *Gender, Work and Organization, 28*(S1), 163–167. doi:10.1111/gwao.12518

Yazan, B. (2015). Three Approaches to Case Study Methods in Education: Yin, Merriam, and Stake. *Qualitative Report, 20*(2), 134–152. doi:10.46743/2160-3715/2015.2102

Yin, R. K. (2003). Case study research: Design and methods (3rd ed.).

KEY TERMS AND DEFINITIONS

Athena Swan: The Athena Swan is an accreditation framework for gender equity and diversity and recognizes the advancement of gender equality in higher education. It was launched in the UK in 2005.

A Tale of Two Universities

Conceptual Map: A Leximancer concept map illustrated the 'Theme', a group or cluster of related concepts. It assists in the thematic and relational analysis of qualitative data.

Leximancer: A computer software developed in Australia in 2006 at the University of Queensland by Dr Andrew Smith, that allows the conduct of quantitative content analysis using a machine learning technique.

ROPE: Research Opportunity and Performance Evidence. A Statement that researchers write as part of a funding or promotion application. This statement includes additional information about a researcher's achievements to date in the context of part-time work and career breaks.

STEMM: Science, Technology, Engineering, Mathematics, and Medicine are disciplines where women are underrepresented.

ENDNOTES

[1] STEM includes Science, Technology, Engineering, and Mathematics; STEMM includes Medicine.

[2] In the Australian academic structure Level A (associate lecturer) is the lowest level and Level E (Professor) is the highest level.

[3] HRE2019-0596 Exploring Strategies to Support Career Progression During and After Career Breaks

[4] HREA approval H13283 Project on the Impact of Parenting on Careers

[5] Discovery Early Career Research Award sponsored by the Australian Research Council

Chapter 14

Motherscholar and MotherLeader:
The More Things Change, the More They Stay the Same

Heidi L. Schnackenberg
SUNY Plattsburgh, USA

ABSTRACT

For students in higher education, the pandemic brought about some lasting educational changes. There are more online courses and program options, more social-emotional support services, and increased resources to support student learning. Conversely, faculty lives are very similar to what they were before the pandemic, with some notable work-creep. In addition to traditional responsibilities, professors are doing more virtual meetings and online teaching, and devising ways to support students as they find their new normal. For motherscholars, this back-to-normal-plus-extras environment can be devastating. While the refrain to "get back to normal" gave many people comfort, "normal" wasn't such a great space for academic mothers in the first place. Has anything changed for motherscholars and MotherLeaders in higher education post-pandemic? If things haven't changed, then what does that say, about academic mothers and their value in higher education? This chapter will explore this issue and call for an implementation of much-needed practice and policy changes in the academy.

INTRODUCTION

Now that the pandemic is almost over, have the lives of faculty in higher education dramatically changed? For students in higher education, the pandemic brought about some lasting educational changes. There are more online courses and program options (Pokhrel & Chhetri, 2021), more social-emotional support services, and more faculty support for students. Conversely, faculty lives are very similar to what they were before the pandemic, with some notable work-creep. In addition to all of the previous and traditional faculty responsibilities, professors are doing more Zoom conferences and online teaching, engaging in professional development to learn how to better teach online, and devising ways to creatively support

DOI: 10.4018/978-1-6684-8597-2.ch014

Copyright © 2023, IGI Global. Copying or distributing in print or electronic forms without written permission of IGI Global is prohibited.

Motherscholar and MotherLeader

students as they find their new normal. For women in higher education, this back-to-normal-plus-extras environment can be devastating.

Almost endlessly during the pandemic, many individuals vocalized/wrote/posted how they wanted things to go "back to the way that they were," but what if "the way they were" wasn't so great for some people in the first place? Women in higher education have traditionally faced challenges in the academy that their non-female counterparts have not. Individuals identifying as female participate in more service work than males (Guarino & Borden, 2017). While a necessary component of professor work, it is essentially considered "academic housekeeping" (Kalm, 2019), often invisible, and not the kind of work that builds a vitae. The vitae-building, promotable, work in higher education generally comes in the form of grants, research and publication. Aiston and Jung (2015) found that internationally, women academics produce less scholarly work than men, therefore positioning them poorly for pay increases, recognition, and promotion. While women achieve more, or the same, excellence in teaching as men (Subbaye & Vikthal 2017), that is often not weighted as heavily as scholarly productivity when it comes to tenure and promotion decisions. Thus, female academics face obstacles to professional advancement and security that are not present for male professors.

BACKGROUND

Being an academic mother in higher education compounds professional challenges in numerous ways. Academic mothers, termed *motherscholars* (Matias & Nishi, 2018), illustrates the interconnectedness between a woman's life as a professional in higher education, and their life as a mother. Each role informs the other, and elevates both lived experiences, thus making motherscholars desirable workers in the academy. While this idea sounds good in theory, the actual work lives of motherscholars does not provide evidence of that mutually beneficial relationship. The literature reveals challenges for academic mothers, including overt or subtle lack of support for women pursuing tenure and motherhood at the same time, work policies that interfere with family responsibilities, limited or no childcare centers on college campuses, lack of systematized maternity/parental leave and/or the misperception that any leave taken for childbirth or childcare is a "break" and an opportunity to "catch up" on scholarship, and the overall lack of support for systemic policy changes that include stopping the tenure clock, part-time tenure-track positions, and extended time to tenure (Anderson, 2012; Baker, 2012; Birken & Borelli, 2015; Castendeda & Isgro, 2013; Harris, 2015; Hodge, 2017; Hunt, 2015; Isgro & Casteneda, 2015; Jaschik, 2012; Jaschik, 2017; Laypayese, 2012; Lapayese, 2017; Leonard, 2013; Lubrano, 2012; Newman, 2014; Nora, Rochelle, Lopez & Williams, 2017; Rhoads & Rhoads, 2012; Rivera, 2017; Rodino-Colocino, Niesen, Noble & Quail, 2017; Slaughter, 2013; Turban, Freeman & Waber, 2017; Ward & Wolf-Wendel, 2012; White, 2016; Williams & Jessica, 2015; Young, 2015). Though these challenges may appear to only be detrimental to academic mothers, they also negatively impact institutions of higher education in general (Sabat, Lindsey, King, Jones, 2016). Just as unbiased employment policies enable organizations to reach their full potential (Bailyn, 2016), inequitable employment practices have a detrimental effect on both employees and workplace productivity and environment.

MAIN FOCUS OF THE CHAPTER

Issues, Controversies, Problems

While the typical professional life of motherscholars is fraught with obstacles, their lives during the COVID-19 pandemic became, in many ways, untenable (CohenMiller, 2020). Crook (2020) reflected that academics with caregiving responsibilities during the pandemic were suddenly put in the impossible position of working a full-time job, while also caring for children, parents, spouses, family, etc. on a full-time basis. Being thrown into such a no-win situation resulted in detrimental effects on the mental health of motherscholars (Fulweiler, Davies, Biddle, Burgin, Cooperdock, Hanley, Kenkel, Marcarelli, Matass, Mayo, Santiago-Vazquex, Traylor-Kowles, & Ziegler, 2021). The results of research by Bastain, et al. (2022) reveal that the degree and amount of pandemic-related life changes positively correspond to traumatic stress in mothers from diverse backgrounds. Pascale, Ehrlich, and Hicks-Roof (2022) state that the pandemic dismantled motherscholars coping mechanisms over the role strain that they experience in the duality of their lives. So while role strain increased during COVID-19, motherscholars ability to navigate the complexities of these roles decreased. Additionally (and unsurprisingly), both Deryugina, Shurchkov, and Stearns (2021), and Petit (2021), found that academic women with children suffered an enormous loss of time and productivity on their research and scholarship. Kim and Patterson (2021) even go so far as to conclude that women with familial obligations became less professionally visible during the pandemic. It's likely not much of a stretch to assume that if academic mothers were invisible to the world, they were likely lost to themselves as well (Spradley, LeBlanc, Olson Beal, Burrow, & Cross, 2020). In her work, Reister (2022), identified the need for motherscholars to have determination, resiliency, and management skills over the complexity of roles in their lives in order to approach a satisfactory work-life balance during the COVID-19 pandemic. Unfortunately, consistently expending such extraordinary effort to maintain a manageable day-to-day can lead to physical and emotional distress, eroding one's dignity and sense of well-being (Heath, Darkwah, Beoku-Betts, Purkayastha, 2022). While possession of these skills is admirable, it is unfair to expect such superhuman qualities from academic mothers, the majority of whom are trying to achieve something as simple as a reasonable personal and work life.

Given that motherscholars faced deep, almost insurmountable, professional and personal challenges during the COVID-19 crisis, it stands to reason that MotherLeaders suffered as well (Schnackenberg, 2021). Put simply, MotherLeaders are academic mothers who hold leadership positions in colleges and universities (Schnackenberg, 2018; Schnackenberg, 2020; Schnackenberg, 2022). In general, the large preponderance of women, parents or single, who hold leadership positions in higher education are at the middle-management levels, i.e. Department Chairs (Schnackenberg & Simard, 2016). As most Department Chairs will attest, this position is filled with a lot of paper-processing, scheduling, problem-solving, recruitment, retention, and general student and faculty social and emotional support. This last aspect, the *emotional labor* (Hartley, 2018) of the institution, became ever more prominent during the pandemic (Costa, 2020). While Department Chair and other academic middle-management positions often come with some amount of course-release or stipend, the compensation rarely equates to the extra time required to do the job well. Therefore, these positions are often as much service work, as they are paid administrative positions. (Though upper administration would likely disagree with this characterization.) Given that a fair amount of service is equated with academic middle-management positions, which are often held by women in the academy (many of them caregivers), it is important to know how service work is viewed in institutions of higher education. Flaherty (2014) situates service in what and who institutions of

Motherscholar and MotherLeader

higher education value: colleges and universities tend to value scholarly productivity more than service. Since women do more service than men in the academy (Guarino & Borden, 2017), and men produce more scholarship, in particular throughout the pandemic (Fazackerley, 2020), it is clear that the work more often accomplished by men is valued more than the work more often done by women. Yet female academics hold more middle-management and MotherLeader positions than their male counterparts, thus doing more necessary, yet unrecognized and unrewarded work. This situation was exacerbated by the extra labor created by the pivot to virtual work during the pandemic. Thus, MotherLeaders were left with an incredible sense of fatigue and burn-out during the pandemic (Gewin, 2021). One would think that this implosion would lead to extensive systemic change in higher education to improve the lives of both motherscholars and MotherLeaders, but it has not.

As the pandemic clearly demonstrated, the support systems and structures that motherscholars and MotherLeaders rely on to fulfill the many responsibilities that they have are fragile at best (Pratt, Goates-Jones, Cutri, Wheeler, & Walden, 2022). Lim, Cerdeña, Azim, and Wagner (2022) assert that structural issues have been (perhaps intentionally) mischaracterized as individual challenges for motherschol-arscholars, thereby discrediting academic mother's struggles and disempowering any collective ability to make change and improvements. In their research, The Motherscholar Collective (Myles-Baltzly, Ho, Richardson, Greene-Rooks, Azim, Frazier, Campbell-Obaid, Eilert, & Lim, 2021) charges institutions of higher education with the transformational empowerment of motherscholars. Bowyer et al. (2022) argue for an overall demasculinization of the systems and norms in the academy, and endorse a culture of care, collaboration, and collegiality, and Lantsoght, Tse Crepaldi, Tavares, Leemans, and Paig-Tran (2021) suggest that policies that attend to individual circumstances assist in creating a more positive workplace culture which leads to increased productivity. While it's clear that sweeping changes to institutions, organizations, and overall academic culture need to be made, there are also specific policy changes that can be implemented to better the work lives of motherscholars and MotherLeaders.

SOLUTIONS AND RECOMMENDATIONS

CohenMiller and Loveto (2022) recommend a normalization of caregiving and its challenges in colleges and universities by providing flexibility in teaching modality, tenure clock options, paid leave, and on-site childcare. McDermott (2020) underscores the need for reconfiguring the tenure process so as to be more inclusive of diverse academic women and mothers. To support women academic's career trajectory, Gabster, van Daalen, Dhatt, and Barry (2020) caution the academy to safeguard scholarly output against the effects of COVID-19 given that academic mother's publication rate suffered during the pandemic while academic men's publication numbers increased (Squazzoni, Bravo, Grimaldo, Garcia-Costa, Farjam, & Mahmani, 2021), particularly in the sciences (Madsen, Nielsen, Bjørnholm, Jagsi, & Andersen, 2022). In part, motherscholar's research productivity declined during the pandemic due to the exponential increase in unpaid care work (Laia da Mata & Samimi, 2022), both at work and in the home. This increase in unrecognized labor and decrease in lauded work resulted in a substantial negative effect on academic mother's mental health. Indeed, well prior to COVID-19 women in academia saw their "failure" to achieve work–life balance as being a personal rather than a societal issue (Toffoletti & Starr, 2016). Given that, Wagner, Pennell, Ellert, and Lim (2021) strongly advocate for more support and services from the institution for mother scholar and MotherLeader's social and emotional well-being. Perhaps the most comprehensive set of systemic solutions were put forth by Fulweiler et al.

(2021). In their research, they outline specific actions that academic mentors, university administrators, professional societies, publishers, and funding agencies can take to support academic mothers. These strategies include advocacy for others in the pipeline, relief from service work, affordable on-campus (and at-conference) childcare/daycare, invitations to and recruitment for women to publish in journals, and no-cost extensions on grant funding. Clearly, much research has been conducted with women in higher education and academic mothers during the COVID-19 pandemic and a wide array of supportive and useful conclusions, suggestions, recommendations, and solutions have emerged.

While the myriad of strategies listed here are practical, likely effective, and supported through research, to date, the literature reveals few to none have been implemented to help motherscholars or MotherLeaders in the current, waning, years of COVID-19. That's not to say that changes in higher education have not occurred as a result of the pandemic. Indeed, many adjustments and accommodations have taken root in the academy thanks to the new ways in which higher education had to go about its business during lock-down. Most of the changes affect teaching and instruction, and benefit student learning and experiences at colleges and universities. Unfortunately for academics, some of the post-COVID changes have blurred the line even more between work and personal life. For instance, meetings can now be beamed right into our homes, during many hours of the day. Expectations arise to be constantly virtually available, and the need for even quicker response times to emails and texts has become the norm. Flexibility to increase learning options via multi-modality courses has been a positive change for students, but made faculty lives more challenging (Ronkowitz & Ronkowitz, 2021). All of these new practices mix academic professional and personal lives even more than before the pandemic, and mixing the professional and the personal was the breaking point for motherscholars and MotherLeaders during the pandemic in the first place. While the refrain "getting back to normal" gives many people comfort, "normal" wasn't ever a great space for academic mothers in the first place.

CONCLUSION

"Plus ça change, plus c est la même chose" - the more it changes, the more it's the same thing. Has anything changed for motherscholars and MotherLeaders in higher education post-pandemic, or are we right back to where we left off? And, if nothing has truly changed, what does that mean or say about academic mothers and their value in the academy? Truly, if the work lives of motherscholars are to become more practicable and sustainable, action must be taken. Perhaps the most powerful way to implement solutions is to ensure that motherscholars and MotherLeaders are represented on groups and committees that make decisions about course schedules, campus-wide meeting times, course modalities, personnel policies, child-care services, tenure progression, parental leave, and a host of other work-related issues (LeBlanc, Spradley, Beal, Burrow, & Cross, 2022). In this way, the voices of motherscholars and MotherLeaders will be at the decision-making table from the outset, as challenges arise and solutions are crafted, rather than inheriting responsibilities, calendars, and timetables that continue the status quo and strengthen the patriarchal nature of colleges and universities. It's clear that academic mothers have to navigate a variety of obstacles in colleges and universities that are not present for male professors. This preceded the COVID-19 pandemic, and was brought to light during the crisis. It's time to make change, break traditions, alter the narrative and create a higher education system that embraces the complexities and richness of both mothering and professoring. If not now, then when?

REFERENCES

Aiston, S. J., & Jung, J. (2015). Women academics and research productivity: An international comparison. *Gender and Education*, *27*(3), 205–220. doi:10.1080/09540253.2015.1024617

Anderson, N. (2012). American University Professor Breast-Fed Baby in Class, Sparking Debate. *The Washington Post*. https://www.washingtonpost.com/local/education/american-university-professor-breast-feeds-sick-baby-in-class-sparking-debate/2012/09/11/54a06856-fc12-11e1-8adc-499661afe377_story.html?utm_term=.29c67ed75a81

Bailyn, L. (2016). *Breaking the mold*. Cornell University Press., doi:10.7591/9781501705045

Baker, M. (2012). Gendered Families, Academic Work, and the Motherhood Penalty. *Women's Studies Journal*, *26*(1), 11–24.

Bastain, T. M., Knapp, E. A., Law, A., Algermissen, M., Avalos, L. A., Birnhak, Z., Blackwell, C., Breton, C. V., Duarte, C., Frazier, J., Ganiban, J., Greenwood, P., Herstman, J., Hernandez-Castro, I., Hofheimer, J., Karagas, M. R., Lewis, J., Paglicaccio, D., Ramphal, B., & Margolis, A. (2022). Symptoms of pandemic-associated traumatic stress among mothers in the U.S. *JAMA Network Open*, *5*(12), e2247330. doi:10.1001/jamanetworkopen.2022.47330 PMID:36525271

Birken, S., & Borelli, J. L. (2015). Coming Out as Academic Mothers: What Happens When Two Highly Driven Women in Academe Decide to Have Children? *The Chronicle of Higher Education*. https://www.chronicle.com/article/Coming-Out-as-Academic-Mothers/151157

Bowyer, D., Deitz, M., Jamison, A., Taylor, C. E., Gyengesi, E., Ross, J., Hammond, H., Ogbeide, A. E., & Dune, T. (2022). Academic mothers, professional identity and COVID-19: Feminist reflections on career cycles, progression and practice. *Gender, Work and Organization*, *29*(1), 309–341. doi:10.1111/gwao.12750 PMID:34898865

Casteneda, M., & Isgro, K. (2013). *Mothers in Academia*. Columbia University Press.

CohenMiller, A.S., (2020). Spiraling. *Journal of the Motherhood Initiative: Academic motherhood and COVID-19, 11*(2), 9-20.

CohenMiller. A.S. & Loveto, J. A. (2022). Centering voices of motherscholars during the COVID- 19 pandemic shows overwhelming responsibilities, ingrained gender roles, and blurred boundaries. In CohenMiller, A.S., Hinton-Smith, T., Mazanderani, F.H., & Samuel, N. (Eds), Leading Change in Gender and Diversity in Higher Education from Margins to Mainstream (pp. 179-207). Taylor & Francis.

Collective, Motherscholar, Myles-Baltzly, C.C., Ho, H.K., Richardson, I., Greene-Rooks, J., Azim, K.A., Frazier, K.E., Campbell-Obaid, M., Eilert, M., & Lim, S.R. (2021). Transformational collaborations: How a motherscholar research collective survived and thrived during COVID-19. *International Perspectives in Psychology : Research, Practice, Consultation*, *10*(4), 225–242. doi:10.1027/2157-3891/a000029

Costa, K. (2020). Women's emotional labor in higher-ed and the COVID-19 crisis. *Women in Higher Education*. https://www.wihe.com/article-details/147/women-s-emotional-labor-in-higher-ed-and-the-covid-19-crisis

Crook, S. (2020). Parenting during the Covid-19 Pandemic of 2020: Academia, labour and care work. *Women's History Review*, *29*(7), 1226–1238. doi:10.1080/09612025.2020.1807690

Deryugina, T., Shurchkov, O., & Stearns, J. (2021). COVID-19 disruptions disproportionately affect female academics. *AEA Papers and Proceedings. American Economic Association*, *111*, 164–168. doi:10.1257/pandp.20211017

Fazackerley, A. (2020). Women's research plummets during lockdown—But articles from men increase. *The Guardian*. https://www.theguardian.com/education/2020/may/12/womens-research-plummets-during-lockdown-but-articles-from-men-increase

Flaherty, C. (2014). So Much to Do So Little Time. *Inside Higher Ed*. https://www.insidehighered.com/news/2014/04/09/research-shows-professors-work-long-hours-and-spend-much-day-meetings

Fulweiler, R. W., Davies, S. W., Biddle, J. F., Burgin, A. J., Cooperdock, E. H. J., Hanley, T. C., Kenkel, C. D., Marcarelli, A. M., Matassa, C. M., Mayo, T. L., Santiago-Vàzquez, L. Z., Traylor-Knowles, N., & Ziegler, M. (2021). Rebuild the academy: Supporting academic mothers during COVID-19 and beyond. *PLoS Biology*, *19*(3), e3001100. doi:10.1371/journal.pbio.3001100 PMID:33690708

Gabster, B. P., van Daalen, K., Dhatt, R., & Barry, M. (2020). Challenges for the female academic during the COVID-19 pandemic. *Lancet*, *395*(10242), 1968–1970. doi:10.1016/S0140-6736(20)31412-4 PMID:32563275

Gerwin, V. (2021). Pandemic burnout is rampant in academia. *Nature*, *591*(7850), 489–491. doi:10.1038/d41586-021-00663-2 PMID:33723408

Guarino, C. M., & Borden, V. M. H. (2017). Faculty service loads and gender: Are women taking care of the academic family? *Research in Higher Education*, *58*(6), 672–694. doi:10.100711162-017-9454-2

Harris, R. S. (2015). Childcare Shouldn't Be an Issue. *Inside Higher Ed*. https://www.insidehighered.com/views/2015/09/16/essay-says-child-care-shouldnt-still-be-issue-scholarly-meetings

Hartley, G. (2018). *Fed Up: Emotional Labor, Women, and the Way Forward*. Harper Collins.

Heath, M., Darkwah, A., Beoku-Betts, J., & Purkayastha, B. (Eds.). (2022). *Global feminist autoethnographies during COVID-19*. Routledge.

Hodge, D. M. (2017). Motherhood and Leadership in Academia: Getting Beyond Personal Survival Mode. In K. Cole & H. Hassel (Eds.), *Surviving Sexism in Academia: Strategies for Feminist Leadership* (pp. 1–8). Routledge., doi:10.4324/9781315523217-21

Hunt, A. N. (2015). The Role of Theory in Understanding the Lived Experiences of Mothering in the Academy. In A. M. Young (Ed.), *Teacher, Scholar, Mother: Re-Envisioning Motherhood in the Academy* (pp. 3–12). Lexington Books.

Isgro, K., & Casteneda, M. (2015). Mothers in U.S. Academia: Insights from Lived Experiences. *Women's Studies International Forum*, *53*, 174–181. doi:10.1016/j.wsif.2014.12.002

Jaschik, S. (2012). A Stop the Clock Penalty. *Inside Higher Ed*. https://www.insidehighered.com/news/2012/06/14/study-finds-those-who-stop-tenure-clock-earn-less-those-who-dont

Jaschik, S. (2017). But Will Her Husband Move? Study Suggests Women with Male Partners Face Bias in Searches for Junior Faculty Members. *Inside Higher Ed.* https://www.insidehighered.com/news/2017/10/27/hiring-junior-faculty-positions-study-finds-bias-against-female-candidates-who-have?utm_content=buffere28e6&utm_medium=social&utm_source=twitter&utm_campaign=IHEbuffer

Kalm, S. (2019). On academic housekeeping and its allocation. *Sociologisk Forskning, 56*(1), 5–26. doi:10.37062f.56.19503

Kim, E., & Patterson, S. Jr. (2022). The pandemic and gender inequality in academia. *PS, Political Science & Politics, 55*(1), 109–116. doi:10.1017/S1049096521001049

Laia da MataJ. A.SamimiS. A. B. (2022). Academic mothers during and post COVID-19 pandemic. *Revista Brasileira de Saúde Ocupacional, 47.* https://doi.org/ doi:10.1590/2317-6369000018121

Lantsoght, E. O. L., Tse Crepaldi, Y., Tavares, S. G., Leemans, K., & Paig-Tran, E. W. M. (2021). Challenges and opportunities for academic parents during COVID-19. *Frontiers in Psychology, 12,* 645734. doi:10.3389/fpsyg.2021.645734 PMID:34489778

Lapayese, Y. (2017). Mother-Scholars: Thinking and Being in Higher Education. Cole, K. & Hassel, H. (Eds.) Surviving Sexism in Academia: Strategies for Feminist Leadership. Routledge.

Laypayese, Y. (2012). *Mother-Scholar: (Re)Imagining K-12 Education.* Springer Publishing. doi:10.1007/978-94-6091-891-9

LeBlanc, S. S., Spradley, E. S., Beal, H. O., Burrow, L., & Cross, C. (2022). Being Dr. Mom and/or Mom, Ph.D.: Autoethnographies of motherscholaring during COVID-19. *New Horizons in Adult Education and Human Resource Development, 34*(3), 28–39. doi:10.1002/nha3.20360

Leonard, D. J. (2013). Blame the Institution, Not Just the Fathers. *Chronicle of Higher Education.* https://www.chronicle.com/article/Blame-the-Institution-Not/140405

Lim, S.R., Cerdeña, J.P., Azim, K.A., & Wagner, K. (2022). Motherscholars with disabilities: Surmounting structural adversity during COVID-19. *Snapshots of History: Portraits of the 21st Century Pandemic, 2021 American Educational History JournalSpecial Edition,* 133-140.

Lubrano, S. (2012). Tenure and Gender. *The Harvard Crimson.* https://www.thecrimson.com/column/exodoxa/article/2012/10/31/gender-tenure-women-professors

Madsen, E. B., Nielsen, M. W., Bjørnholm, J., Jagsi, R., & Andersen, J. P. (2022). Meta-Research: Author-level data confirm the widening gender gap in publishing rates during COVID-19. *eLife, 11,* e76559. doi:10.7554/eLife.76559 PMID:35293860

Matias, C. E., & Nishi, N. W. (2018). ParentCrit epilogue. *International Journal of Qualitative Studies in Education : QSE, 31*(1), 82–85. doi:10.1080/09518398.2017.1379625

McDermott, M. (2020). Learning from the experiences of mothers of school-aged children on tenure track during the COVID-19 global pandemic. *Journal of the Motherhood Initiative for Research and Community Involvement.* https://jarm.journals.yorku.ca/index.php/jarm/article/view/40618

Newman, J. (2014). There is a Gender Pay Gap in Academe But It May Not Be the Gap That Matters. *Chronicle of Higher Education*. https://www.chronicle.com/blogs/data/2014/04/11/there-is-a-gender-pay-gap-in-academe-but-it-may-not-be-the-gap-that-matters

Nora, K., Rochelle, G., Lopez, A.-M., & Williams, N. A. (2017). Surviving Sexism to Inspire Change: Stories and Reflections from Mothers on the Tenure Track. In K. Cole & H. Hassel (Eds.), *Surviving Sexism in Academia: Strategies for Feminist Leadership*. Routledge. doi:10.4324/9781315523217-13

Pascale, A.B., Ehrlich, S., & Hicks-Roof. K. K. (2022). The impact of COVID-19 pandemic on motherscholars: A comparative case study of United States and Australian higher education women faculty role strain. *Journal of Comparative & International Higher Education, 14*(3A), 53-68. (Part 1).3783 doi:10.32674/jcihe.v14i3

Pettit, E. (2021). Covid-19 has robbed faculty parents of time for research. especially mothers. *The Chronicle of Higher Education*. https://www.chronicle.com/article/covid-19-has-robbed-faculty-parents-of-time-for-research-especially-mothers

Platt, C., Goates-Jones, M., Maile Cutri, R., Fidalgo Wheeler, L., & Walden, T. (2022). Interrupted systems mitigating social gender roles: A Qualitative inquiry of motherscholars during a pandemic. *American Journal of Qualitative Research*, *6*(1), 153–177. doi:10.29333/ajqr/11645

Pokhrel, S., & Chhetri, R. (2021). A literature review on impact of COVID-19 pandemic on teaching and learning. *Higher Education for the Future*, *8*(1), 133–141. doi:10.1177/2347631120983481

Reister, M. (2022). *MotherScholar's perceptions, experiences, and impact on work-family balance*. Lexington Books.

Rhoads, S. E., & Rhoads, C. H. (2012). Gender roles and infant/toddler care: Male and female professors on the tenure track. *Journal of Social, Evolutionary, & Cultural Psychology*, *6*(1), 13–31. doi:10.1037/h0099227

Rivera, L. A. (2017). When Two Bodies are (Not) a Problem: Gender and Relationship Status Discrimination in Academic Hiring. *American Sociological Review*, *82*(6), 1111–1138. doi:10.1177/0003122417739294

Rodino-Colocino, M., Niesen, M., Noble, S. U., & Quail, C. (2017). Smashing the "Maternal Wall."". In K. Cole & H. Hassel (Eds.), *Surviving Sexism in Academia: Strategies for Feminist Leadership*. Routledge.

Ronkowitz, K., & Ronkowitz, L. C. (2021). Online education in a pandemic: Stress test or fortuitous disruption. *American Journal of Economics and Sociology*, *80*(1), 187–203. doi:10.1111/ajes.12377 PMID:34230669

Sabat, I. E., Lindsey, A. P., King, E. B., & Jones, K. P. (2016). Understanding and overcoming challenges faced by working mothers: A theoretical and empirical review. In C. Spitzmueller & R. A. Matthews (Eds.), *Research Perspectives on Work and the Transition to Motherhood* (pp. 9–31). Springer International., doi:10.1007/978-3-319-41121-7_2

Schnackenberg, H. L. (2018) motherscholar:MotherLeader. In Schnackenberg, H.L. & Simard, D.A. (Eds.), Challenges and Opportunities for Women in Higher Education Leadership (pp. 29-43). IGI Global.

Motherscholar and MotherLeader

Schnackenberg, H. L. (2020). motherscholar: MotherLeader and the Ethical Double-Bind. In Squires, M.E. & Yu, Y., & Schnackenberg, H.L. (Eds), Ethics in Higher Education (pp. 127-141). Nova Science Publishers.

Schnackenberg, H. L. (2021). motherscholar: MotherLeader and the Pandemic. In Schnackenberg, H.L. & Simard, D.A. (Eds), Women and Leadership in Higher Education During Global Crises (pp. 190-205). IGI Global.

Schnackenberg, H. L. (2022). Motherscholar and MotherLeader: Reflections from a little past the middle. In H. L. Schnackenberg (Ed.), *Women in Higher Education and the Journey to Mid-Career: Challenges and Opportunities* (pp. 259–274). IGI Global. doi:10.4018/978-1-6684-4451-1.ch013

Schnackenberg, H.L. & Simard, D.A. (2016) *Challenges Facing Female Department Chairs in Higher Education: Emerging Research and Opportunities.* IGI Global. doi:10.4018/978-1-5225-1891-4

Slaughter, A.-M. (2013). Why Women Still Can't Have It All. *The Atlantic.* https://www.theatlantic.com/magazine/archive/2012/07/why-women-still-cant-have-it-all/309020/

Spradley, E., LeBlanc, S. S., Olson Beal, H. K., Burrow, L. E., & Cross, C. (2020). Proving our maternal and scholarly worth: A collaborative autoethnographic textual and visual storying of MotherScholar identity work during the COVID-19 pandemic. *Journal of the Motherhood Initiative, 11*(2), 189–209.

Squazzoni, F., Bravo, G., Grimaldo, F., Garcia-Costa, D., Farjam, M., & Mahmani, B. (2021). Gender gap in journal submissions and peer review during the first wave of the COVID-19 pandemic. A study on 2329 Elsevier journals. *PLoS One, 16*(10), e0257919. doi:10.1371/journal.pone.0257919 PMID:34669713

Subbaye, R., & Vikthal, R. (2017). Gender, teaching, and academic promotions in higher education. *Gender and Education, 29*(7), 926–951. doi:10.1080/09540253.2016.1184237

Toffoletti, K., & Starr, K. (2016). Women academics and work–life balance: Gendered discourses of work and care. *Gender, Work and Organization, 23*(5), 489–504. doi:10.1111/gwao.12133

Turban, S., Freeman, L., & Waber, B. (2017). A Study Used Sensors to Show That Men and Women Are Treated Differently at Work. *Harvard Business Review.* https://hbr.org/2017/10/a-study-used-sensors-to-show-that-men-and-women-are-treated-differently-at-work

Wagner, K., Pennell, S. M., Ellert, M., & Lim, S. R. (2021). Academic mothers with disabilities: Navigating academia and parenthood during COVID-19. *Gender, Work and Organization, 29*(1), 342–352. doi:10.1111/gwao.12751 PMID:34898867

Ward, K., & Wolf-Wendel, L. (2012). *Academic Motherhood: How Faculty Manage Work and Family.* Rutgers University Press.

White, M. (2016). Academia and Motherhood: We Can Have Both. *Washington Post.* https://www.washingtonpost.com/news/grade-point/wp/2016/04/27/academia-and-motherhood-we-can-have-both/?utm_term=.2e95b36b4c60

Williams, J. C., & Jessica, L. (2015). It's Illegal, Yet It Happens All the Time: How Pregnant Women and Mothers Get Hounded Out of Higher Education. *Chronicle of Higher Education.* https://www.chronicle.com/article/Its-Illegal-Yet-It-Happens/233445

Young, A. M. (2015). *Teacher, Scholar, Mother: Re-Envisioning Motherhood in the Academy.* Lexington Books.

ADDITIONAL READING

American Council on Education. (2017). *American College President Study 2017.* ACE. http://www.aceacps.org

Baker, M. (2016). Women graduates and the workplace: Continuing challenges for academic women. *Studies in Higher Education, 41*(5), 887–900. doi:10.1080/03075079.2016.1147718

Bonawitz, M., & Andel, N. (2009). The Glass Ceiling is Made of Concrete: The Barriers to Promotion and Tenure of Women in American Academia. *Forum on Public Policy: A Journal of the Oxford Round Table, 5*(2), 1-16.

Gomez, M. L. (2017). "I have always felt like a trespasser": Life histories from LatinaaStaff members in higher education. In K. Cole & H. Hassel (Eds.), *Surviving Sexism in Academia: Strategies for Feminist Leadership.* Routledge.

Hochschild, A. (2012). *The Second Shift: Working Families and the Revolution at Home.* Penguin Group.

Kozma, M. M., & Schroer, J. W. (2017). For the Love of the Feminist Killjoy: Solving Philosophy's White Male Problem. In K. Cole & H. Hassel (Eds.), *Surviving Sexism in Academia: Strategies for Feminist Leadership.* Routledge. doi:10.4324/9781315523217-8

Marine, S. B., & Aleman, A. M. (2018). Women faculty, professional identity, and gender disposition. *Review of Higher Education, 41*(2), 217–252. doi:10.1353/rhe.2018.0002

Mason, M. A. (June 17, 2013). In the Ivory Tower, Men Only. *Slate.* https://www.slate.com/articles/double_x/doublex/2013/06/female_academics_pay_a_heavy_baby_penalty.html

Mason, M. A., Wolfinger, N. H., & Goulden, M. (2013). *Do Babies Matter? Gender and Family in the Ivory Tower.* Rutgers University Press.

McGranahan, C. (March 22, 2017). *Yes, You Can: Being an Academic and a Mother – Redux.* AllegraLab. https://allegralaboratory.net/yes-you-can-being-an-academic-and-a-mother

Rios, C. (2015). You Call It Professionalism; I Call It Oppression in a Three-Piece Suit. *Everyday Feminism.* https://everydayfeminism.com/2015/02/professionalism-and-oppression

Sepler, F. (2017). The Bullying We Don't Talk About: Women Bullying Women in the Academy. In K. Cole & H. Hassel (Eds.), *Surviving Sexism in Academia: Strategies for Feminist Leadership.* Routledge. doi:10.4324/9781315523217-31

Skurzewski-Servant, M., & Bugenhagen, M. J. (2017). Career Navigation of Female Leaders in Higher Education. In K. Cole & H. Hassel (Eds.), *Surviving Sexism in Academia: Strategies for Feminist Leadership.* Routledge. doi:10.4324/9781315523217-23

Stone-Mediatore, S. (2016). Storytelling/Narrative. In L. Disch & M. Hawkesworth (Eds.), *The Oxford Handbook of Feminist Theory*. Oxford University Press.

Ward, K., & Eddy, P. L. (December, 2013). Women and Academic Leadership: Leaning Out. *The Chronicle of Higher Education*. https://www.chronicle.com/article/WomenAcademic-Leadership-/143503

Wolf-Wendel, L., & Ward, K. (2006). Academic life and motherhood: Variations by institutional type. *Higher Education*, *52*(3), 487–521. doi:10.100710734-005-0364-4

KEY TERMS AND DEFINITIONS

Higher Education: Education beyond high school, typically provided by colleges, universities, and or professional schools.

Leadership: The position or function of one who guides or directs a group.

MotherLeader: The interwoven nature of a women, mother, and female guide, director, and/or manager; a powerful and nurturing female; an administrative position higher education.

Motherscholar: The interconnected, interwoven, seamless nature of a woman as both a mother and a scholar.

Pandemic: A widespread disease that is prevalent across the world at the same time.

Women: More than one adult, female, person.

About the Contributors

Heidi L. Schnackenberg, Ph.D., is a Professor and Department Chair in Education at SUNY Plattsburgh in Plattsburgh, NY. Specializing in educational technology, she currently teaches graduate courses on the use of technology to enhance teaching and learning in the P-12 classroom. Her various research interests include the integration of technology into pedagogical practices, the complexities of women in leadership in higher education, and the challenges faced by motherscholars and MotherLeaders in academia. She has published numerous articles on educational technology, co-authored Challenges Facing Female Department Chairs in Contemporary Higher Education: Emerging Research and Opportunities, and co-edited Best Practices for Education Professionals, Best Practices for Education Professionals Volume 2, The Ethics of Cultural Competence in Higher Education, Preparing the Education Space for Gen Z, Ethics in Higher Education, Challenges and Opportunities for Women in Higher Education Leadership, Women and Leadership in Higher Education During Global Crises, and Women in Higher Education and the Journey to Mid-Career: Challenges and Opportunities. Dr. Schnackenberg began her education career as an elementary music teacher.

Denise Simard, Ph.D., is presently the Interim Dean for the School of Education, Health, and Human Services at the State University of New York at Plattsburgh, in Plattsburgh, NY. She began her professional journey as a special education teacher. She then began collaborating with children and families to access technology devices and services to empower them to be more independent in their daily lives. She used those experiences to become an advocate for change and subsequently managed local and state professional development initiatives related to the infusion of technology into instructional practices to improve learning outcomes for all students, especially those with special needs. She also supported the strategic planning process, facilitation, and evaluation of online learning communities for education organizations on a local, state, and national level. Previously she served as an Associate Dean, taught undergraduate classes in the childhood education program and graduate classes in special education, and served as Department Chair in the Teacher Education Unit. Her areas of interest and research include multiculturalism, special education, assistive technology, online learning, and communities of practice. Through her various roles in higher education, she has had the wonderful opportunity to examine aspects of leadership and the nuances and intricacies involved.

***

Portia Allie-Turco is an assistant professor, program coordinator, and clinic director at the State University of New York Plattsburgh. She has over 20 years of mental health counseling experience in

About the Contributors

non-profit management, community mental health counseling, private practice, and university counseling. Her clinical experience fuels her passion to train and prepare students to make an impact in the world through their strong counselor identity and by embodying a commitment to social justice advocacy. Born during the segregation period of apartheid South Africa, Dr. Allie-Turco believes that education should be accessible to all and is invested in disrupting racial and social inequity to ensure that others succeed despite systemic barriers. Her research focuses on generational, historical, racial, and complex trauma and healing in counseling. Her teaching philosophy draws from the principles of existential and African-Centered theory as reflected in community building, meaning-making, and storytelling.

Dorothea Bowyer is a lecturer at Western Sydney University (WSU) School of Business, since 2004. Her research is threefold and focuses on a) infrastructure management and stakeholder accountability in the public sector b) gender equity in higher education, and c) graduates' career readiness. Dorothea is the chair of the WSU Engaged Parent Network and a member of her School's Equity and Diversity Working Party. A mother of three children, she actively seeks to advance the visibility of parenthood in the workplace. She was recipient and involved in Gender Equity Funded projects: "Returning to Work after Parental Leave: An Appreciative Inquiry" and "The Impact of Parenting on Careers". The latter project explored and reviewed gender equality policies across the tertiary and corporate sectors. Dorothea has assisted the WSU Student Parent Union to be founded and has undertaken a project on exploring flexible childminding options in the Higher Education sector. She has extended her work to investigate gender equity policies for student-parents in Australia, academic-motherhood and the impact of career breaks on professional identity.

Oindrila Chakraborty is a gold medalist in her MBA programme from University of Calcutta. She has 15 years of teaching experience in management education. She has completed her PhD from University of Calcutta and has several publications to furnish in National and International Journals of high repute.

Ivania Delgado, PsyD, MS, MSW, is a Social Work Core Faculty at Pacific Oaks College. Ivania has over 15 years of teaching experience in higher education. Her pedagogy is grounded in social justice, collaboration, and compassion. Before entering academia full-time in 2019, Ivania had experience working with individuals, couples, families, and groups in both public and private sectors in Miami-Dade County, Florida, providing trauma-informed mental health services. She is a proud mother, partner, hija, and community member.

Denise Demers is an Associate Professor and Department Chair for the Department of Health Sciences at the University of Central Arkansas. She avidly researches mother-students, motherscholars, and women in academia trying to find what helps them handle the stress, balance the multiple demands they face, as well as how to support them in higher education. She is a mother of four and an academic leader, in that order. She loves teaching and being in a place to empower others (especially women) to grow and succeed. If she is not at work, she is at a sporting event taking pictures of her children.

Luis Doña Toledo is an assistant professor at University of Granada. Previously associate professor at the University of Almería. and University of Sevilla. Member of the group responsible for the Graduates studies carried out by the University of Granada and other important reports. He has participated in 24 teaching innovation projects. He has published paper in scientific journals such as Journal of

About the Contributors

Marketing for Higher Education, International Review on Non-Profit and Public Marketing, Sustainability, or Revista Española de Documentación Científica. He has published 62 papers in national and international congresses and events. PhD. Marketing and Communication. Doctoral thesis on education in higher education marketing.

Nina Faraoni has a degree from the Università Degli Studi di Verona, Italy (equivalent to a university's degree in the area of knowledge of Social and Legal Sciences in the specific field of Business Education and Administration). Subsequently, she obtained a master's degree in Marketing and consumer behaviour and another in Economics and business organization, both from the University of Granada. She has a PhD degree in Economic and Business Sciences and she is Professor in the Department of Marketing and Market Research of the University of Granada. She participates in research projects, is co-author of scientific articles published in journals such as Studies in Higher Education, Journal of Marketing for Higher Education or Sustainability. She is also co-author of the book 'Universidad en el Espacio Iberoamericano: propuestas de futuro para la vinculación universidad-entorno y la promoción del posgrado' and the study of the economic impact of the University of Granada. She is the author and co-author of papers presented at conferences such as Aemark, Aedem, Cimas or Redue Alcue, and she works on topics related to universities, reputation management and results that are reflected in the positioning within rankings, as well as marketing audit.

Carlene Fider is a published scholar, prolific writer, diligent educator, a powerful leader, and is committed to providing and elevating the voices of minoritized, marginalized, and underrepresent groups through research. As a Professor, she is passionate about working with and supporting students in ways that allow them to engage in equitable practices, and become advocates for themselves and others.

Catherine Hayes is Professor of Health Professions Pedagogy and Scholarship at the University of Sunderland, UK. She is a UK National Teaching Fellow and Principal Fellow of the UK Higher Education Academy. As a graduate of Podiatric Medicine in 1992, Catherine was a Founding Fellow of the Faculty of Podiatric Medicine at the Royal College of Physicians and Surgeons (Glasgow) in 2012 and was awarded Fellowship of the Royal College of Podiatry (London) in 2010. She is currently Programme Leader of the University of Sunderland's Professional Doctorate pathways for the DBA, EdD, DPM and DProf.

Helen Hodgson is an expert in Taxation, based at the Curtin Law School. Her research is in the areas where tax and social policy intersect: superannuation; housing and inequality. Helen holds qualifications in accounting, business law and taxation and has been teaching taxation law in business and law schools since 1989. She has contributed significantly to policy review in the areas of superannuation, the tax and transfer system and housing, specifically examining these systems through a gender lens. In 2019 Helen was awarded a Provost Fellowship at Curtin University to identify the effects that career breaks have on staff; benchmark policies against other universities and make recommendations to address the negative effects of career breaks. She is a Director of the National Foundation for Australian Women and Chair of its Social Policy Committee.

Natasha N. Johnson is a Clinical Instructor of Criminal Justice and Criminology in the Andrew Young School of Policy Studies at Georgia State University. A career educator since 2001, her research

About the Contributors

focuses on critical theory, equity, and social justice leadership, particularly within the K-20 sector. Her other research areas include intersectionality, educational law, policy, and governance, and curriculum development. Dr. Johnson holds multi-state reciprocity and has previously worked as a teacher, guidance counselor, assistant dean, instructional leader, and curriculum developer domestically and abroad. She is a David L. Clark scholar, a CETLOE Faculty Teaching Fellow, and her work is published in SAGE, the Oxford Research Encyclopedia of Criminology and Criminal Justice, Taylor & Francis, the Routledge Focus series, Psychology of Violence, the popular press, and several highly acclaimed educational leadership journals.

Lolita L. Kincade, Ph.D., CFLE, PPS, NCC, LPC, is an Associate Professor and Chair of the Human Development and Family Relations Department at the State University of New York Plattsburgh in Plattsburgh, New York. She is certified as a Family Life Educator through the National Council on Family Relations (NCFR) and is also a Licensed Professional Counselor. Her professional interests include improving quality and standards of individual and family life. Dr. Kincade has published research on diverse topics, including the intersection of race and gender, and social justice education and advocacy. She has worked with diverse populations in academic, hospital and community settings, and is experienced in research consultation, program development and planning, non-profit administration and policy advocacy. Dr. Kincade is motivated to impact and transform institutions of higher education in the interest of students, faculty and leaders of color.

Teodoro Luque-Martínez is a professor of market research and marketing at University of Granada. Market Research and Marketing Department Chair (2002-04). Consumers' behaviour Master Program Coordinator (until 2011). He has more than 60 papers presented in international congresses and events. Director of ADEMAR Research Group. He has published more than 20 books in different publishing editorials such as Ariel Economía, Pirámide, Thompson-Civitas or Editorial Universidad de Granada. He has also published different articles in national and international journals such as Journal of Marketing Higher Education, Studies in Higher Education, Revista Española de Documentación Científica Journal of Interactive Marketing, European Journal of Marketing, Service Industries Journal, EPI, Public Relations Review, Information & Management, Scientometrics, Journal of Consumer Marketing, Cities, Quality and Quantity, Revista Europea de Dirección y Economía de la Empresa, Revista Española de Investigación de Marketing-ESIC, Distribución y Consumo or Investigación y Marketing. International stays: Oxford University (UK); Karlsruhe Institute of Technology (Germany); University of Texas-Austin (USA); Ottawa University (Canada); Indiana University, Bloomington (USA).

Maya A. Lynum-Walker currently serves as a Coordinator for a Doctoral program. She received her doctorate in Leadership with a concentration in Student Personnel Services at the University of the Cumberlands. She has a master's in Adult and Higher Education from Morehead State University and a master's in Athletic Administration and Coaching from Western Kentucky University. She is also an alumna of Kentucky State University, Frankfort, KY. Dr. Lynum-Walker's research interests include mentorship for minority women looking to move into leadership within higher education and mentorship impact for first-generation college students, specifically black students. She is also a member of Zeta Phi Beta Sorority, Incorporated., and enjoys spending quality time with her husband, daughter, and bonus daughter.

About the Contributors

Yaw Owusu-Agyeman is a Senior Lecturer at the Department of Adult Education and Human Resource Studies, University of Ghana. Before joining University of Ghana, Yaw served as a Postdoctoral Research Fellow at the Directorate for Institutional Research and Academic Planning, University of the Free State from December 2018 to November 2021.

Saudia Rahamat received her BA in Communication Arts from the University of Waterloo in 2018. In the wake of the COVID-19 Pandemic, she organized and managed a grassroots community of 8,500 in Waterloo, Ontario, to offset and build out resource gaps highlighted by the Pandemic. She also works as an Equity, Diversity, and Inclusion consultant with local and global mutual aid groups working to build a better post-lockdown society. She works with disenfranchised communities and individuals to restructure their opportunities and strategies as a Career Specialist.

Nafiza Spirko is an aspiring social worker and public health advocate who graduated with a Bachelor of Arts in General Studies, Concentration in Psychology from Southern New Hampshire University. With a passion for improving living and working conditions, she is currently pursuing a dual master's degree in social work and public health, utilizing both a macro and micro lens to identify and combat systemic oppression. She also works as a therapeutic art group facilitator for mental health clients. Nafiza's expected graduation date is December 16, 2023, and she is eager to utilize her education and experience to make a meaningful impact in her community.

Maureen E. Squires, Ed.D. is a Professor of Teacher Education at the State University of New York at Plattsburgh, in Plattsburgh, N.Y. She earned an Ed.D. in Educational Theory and Practice and a C.A.S. in Educational Leadership (2008) from Binghamton University, an M.S.Ed. in Special Education from LeMoyne College, and a B.A. in English with a concentration in Secondary Education from Nazareth College. She holds multiple New York State teaching and leadership certifications. Her professional career began as a high school English teacher. Currently, she teaches graduate cou rses and serves as a department chair in the Adolescence Education program and Special Education program. Her areas of interest and research include teacher preparation, special education, ethics and education, and MotherScholars.

Index

A

Academic Leadership 10, 20-21, 31, 71, 120, 149, 154-155, 157, 195, 253, 295
Academic Mother 284-285, 287
Academic Nurturing 143, 149-150, 154-156
Academic Parenting 259
Academic Rankings 193, 197, 205
Academy 17, 35, 51, 57, 59-71, 88-91, 94, 99-103, 106-109, 112-114, 116-117, 119-122, 125-134, 137-139, 141, 145, 159, 187, 208, 235-237, 239, 241-244, 246-247, 250, 253, 281-282, 284-288, 290, 294
Accessibility 45, 53, 72-73, 75-81, 83-84, 264
Agency 37-38, 41, 45-46, 48, 54, 147, 165, 168, 188, 218, 222-223, 225, 228, 245, 260, 282
Athena Swan 210-211, 257, 262-263, 271, 277, 280, 282

B

BIPOC 78-79, 112, 115, 122-123, 231-232, 238
Black Women Faculty 102, 106, 108-112, 114-116, 119-126, 137, 158
Black Women Stereotypes 106
Bottom-Up Processes 232

C

Capitalism 89, 100, 216, 219, 221-224, 230-233
Career Breaks 47, 257, 259, 263, 265-266, 275-276, 283
Career Progression 38, 43, 67, 143-150, 152-157, 257-259, 261, 263, 269-270, 277, 283
Caremongering 216, 226-230
Centering Women in Higher Education 8
college 7, 11, 13, 16, 21-23, 25, 34, 59, 70, 72, 74-75, 77, 81-83, 85, 90, 93-94, 98, 101, 104, 108-109, 111, 126-127, 130, 132, 135-136, 138-142, 166, 209, 216-217, 230, 235, 238-240, 246-247, 253, 255, 276, 285, 294

Community Building 1, 8-9, 223
Complex Ambiguity 37, 42-44, 48, 55
Conceptual Map 266-267, 271, 283
Covid-19 38-42, 45-46, 48-54, 64, 71-73, 75, 82-84, 106-107, 115-116, 120, 126, 129, 132, 135, 137, 140, 142, 190, 216, 218, 222, 225-227, 229-232, 234, 242, 245-246, 250, 252, 254-256, 259, 264, 275, 278-282, 284, 286-293
Critical Theory 221, 226, 230, 232

D

Decolonizing 142, 232
Dialectical 130, 232
Diversity 4, 8-10, 12-15, 17, 34, 38, 40, 45-47, 49, 53, 64, 68, 70, 87-88, 90, 93, 98-101, 104, 110-111, 118-121, 123, 126, 128, 131, 133, 137-139, 141-142, 167, 172, 178, 197, 209-211, 224, 230, 251, 262, 282, 289
Domestic 42, 58-60, 73, 89, 114, 165-166, 171, 180, 188, 194, 204, 223, 234, 252, 254, 276

E

Education 1-20, 23-25, 28-40, 42-43, 45-46, 48-54, 56-60, 63-94, 96-104, 106, 109, 111-115, 119-122, 124-136, 138-142, 144-146, 150-151, 155, 157-162, 165-169, 171, 176-182, 186-191, 194-197, 207-211, 213, 216-218, 221-222, 224, 226, 229-231, 234-235, 237, 241, 245, 249-258, 260-261, 263, 270, 276-282, 284-285, 287-295
Educational Leadership 15, 42, 52-53, 56, 67, 70, 130, 141, 208, 241
Empowering Women in Higher Education 1, 5-6, 10-12, 16-17
Empowerment 2, 6, 9, 11-12, 14, 17, 53, 61-62, 65, 83, 100, 102, 106, 109, 121, 123-124, 126, 129, 144-145, 159, 161-162, 165-172, 174, 178-183, 187-191, 228-229, 287

Index

Equality 4-5, 11-18, 27-28, 41, 46-48, 50, 53, 58, 65-69, 74, 122, 128, 138, 144-147, 155, 159, 165-168, 172, 179-183, 188, 190-191, 195, 205-207, 210, 260, 263, 280-282

Equity 2, 4-6, 8-14, 16-18, 33, 39-40, 42, 46, 48-52, 63, 65, 68, 73-75, 82, 84-88, 90-91, 98, 110-111, 118-124, 126, 128-129, 135, 138, 145, 151, 153-154, 157, 159, 162, 167, 194, 197, 207-208, 224, 228-229, 250-251, 253, 255, 257-258, 262, 275, 277, 281-282

F

faculty 1, 4, 6, 8-12, 15, 17, 29, 32, 35-36, 50, 53, 57, 59, 67, 84, 87-88, 90-92, 94, 96, 98-100, 102, 104, 106-142, 152-153, 155-156, 158, 162, 167, 173, 195, 207, 209-210, 216, 218, 221, 224, 231-232, 234-238, 240-242, 244, 246, 250-255, 270, 284, 286, 288, 290-294

Female Leadership 54, 56, 58

Feminist Institutionalism 143, 146-147, 156, 158

G

Gender 1-6, 8-18, 27-28, 33-53, 55-60, 62-68, 70-71, 73-74, 78, 84-87, 89-91, 93-94, 96, 98-99, 101-103, 108-111, 127-129, 131, 133-138, 141-151, 153-161, 165-169, 171-173, 176-181, 183-184, 186-191, 193-199, 203-211, 217-218, 222, 226, 234-236, 253, 255, 257-265, 271, 275, 277-282, 289-294

Gender Equity 2, 6, 8-10, 12, 16, 39, 42, 49, 51, 73-74, 84-86, 145, 151, 153-154, 157, 159, 167, 197, 207, 255, 257-258, 262, 275, 277, 281-282

Gender Gap 11, 15-16, 35, 47, 56-57, 64, 84, 166, 189-190, 236, 291, 293

Gender Inequality 14, 17, 42, 50-52, 70, 143-145, 149, 159, 165, 168, 173, 176, 184, 191, 194-196, 235, 253, 291

Gender Inequity 37, 41, 45, 55, 66, 259

Gender Norms 6, 51, 56

Gendered Practices 143-145, 147-149, 152, 155-156

Glass Ceiling 27, 38, 40, 49, 69, 100, 103, 161, 236, 294

Great Resignation 216, 218-219, 233

H

Higher Education 1-20, 24, 28-38, 40, 42, 45, 48-54, 56-60, 63-78, 81-94, 96-104, 106, 109, 111-115, 121, 124-131, 133-134, 136, 138-141, 144-146, 150-151, 155, 157-160, 162, 166, 176-179, 186, 188, 190, 194-195, 197, 207-211, 213, 218, 221-222, 224, 226, 230-231, 234-235, 237, 241, 249-254, 256-261, 270, 276-278, 280-282, 284-285, 287-295

Higher Education Leadership 42, 53, 56, 68, 70, 87-88, 91, 159, 209, 256, 292

I

Inequality 14, 17, 27, 38, 42, 46, 48, 50-54, 70, 78, 89, 128, 139, 143-145, 149, 153, 155, 157, 159, 161, 165, 167-168, 171, 173, 176, 184, 191, 194-196, 207, 217, 235-236, 253, 291

Internationalisation 193-194, 204-205, 207

Intersectionality 3, 12-13, 15-16, 78, 85, 87, 89, 99, 101, 103-104, 139, 178, 216-217, 227-229, 233

L

Leadership 3-17, 19-21, 28, 31, 33-34, 37-43, 45, 47-64, 66-71, 80, 86-88, 91, 93-94, 101, 103-104, 109, 116, 120, 128, 130, 141, 143-146, 148-149, 153-157, 159-162, 165-167, 169, 172, 176, 181, 185-191, 195-196, 208-209, 217-218, 227, 229, 232, 235-237, 241, 249, 251-253, 255-256, 275, 277, 282, 286, 290-295

Leadership Capacity 37, 55

Leadership Development 53, 56, 67

Leximancer 257, 264-266, 271, 278-280, 283

M

Material Conditions 218, 221, 226, 233

Mental Health 11, 19, 29, 31, 42, 74, 92, 97, 118, 125, 129, 131, 134, 137, 177, 216, 219, 221-222, 226, 228, 231, 286-287

Metacognition 37, 42, 55

Misogyny 37, 48, 55

MotherLeader 234, 237-238, 256, 284, 287, 292-293, 295

Motherscholar 19, 30, 234, 237-238, 246, 250, 254, 256, 284, 287, 289, 292-293, 295

O

Online Education 72-73, 75-76, 79-83, 85, 292

Organization 31, 33, 50, 54, 67, 71, 99, 101, 128, 131, 133, 138, 161, 173, 184, 188, 206-207, 210, 217, 219, 227-228, 245-246, 259-260, 277-282, 289, 293

Organizational Theories 216-217, 219

Index

P

Pandemic 19, 33, 38, 41-42, 45-46, 48-49, 52, 64, 73, 82-83, 85, 106-107, 110, 113-117, 120, 126, 131, 133, 135, 137, 140, 218, 222, 225-230, 234, 239, 242, 250, 252, 254-256, 258-259, 261, 276, 278-282, 284-293, 295

Peer Mentoring 69, 99

Policy 17-18, 32, 46-47, 51-52, 70, 83-85, 88, 96, 100, 129-130, 136-138, 140, 143-145, 148, 150-151, 153, 158-159, 179, 181, 188, 208-210, 219, 223, 232, 246, 250, 253, 257, 262-264, 268, 271, 273, 275-276, 279, 281, 284-285, 287, 294

Power 3, 13, 18, 26, 42, 49, 52-54, 58, 61, 65, 68, 83, 90-91, 94, 100, 103, 108-109, 120, 122-123, 133-134, 141, 144-147, 150, 152, 155, 159, 161, 180, 190-191, 196, 199, 205, 218, 220-221, 224, 226, 232, 249, 251

Profit Over Life 233

Q

Quiet Quitting 216-218, 228

R

Reflection 18, 32, 37, 43, 45, 55, 217, 240, 279

Reflexivity 43, 45, 55, 159

Relational Leadership 57-58, 62, 68-71

Role Incongruence 59, 65, 70-71

ROPE 32, 257, 262, 275-277, 279, 283

S

Same-Gender Mentoring 61, 65

single parent 234, 237, 256

Situational Specificity 42, 44, 48, 55

Social-Ecological Theory 87, 94

solo-mother 234

Stabilizing Women in Higher Education 5

STEMM 257, 261-262, 283

Stereotype 3, 14, 16, 55, 90, 94, 108, 115, 127, 137

Student Loan Debt 11, 221

T

Traditional Learning 72

U

university 1, 7, 12-16, 19, 23, 27, 29, 32-34, 36-37, 47, 49-50, 52-53, 56-60, 66-68, 75, 79-82, 84-86, 90, 93-94, 98, 100-104, 112, 114-115, 120, 126-127, 129, 131, 133, 135-136, 138-139, 141, 143-146, 148-157, 159, 166-167, 186, 191, 193-201, 203-210, 212-214, 222, 224, 229-230, 234-235, 251-254, 257, 260-265, 269-272, 274-279, 281, 283, 288-289, 293-295

University Segmentation 193

University Women 15, 56-60, 66, 68, 103, 193, 235, 253

V

Violence 6, 8, 13, 42, 54, 92, 139-140, 161, 169, 171, 180-182, 187-188, 191, 221, 224

W

Women 1-19, 21, 26-28, 30-43, 45-54, 56-74, 78-94, 96-104, 106-149, 151-160, 162, 165-174, 176-183, 185-196, 198-210, 217, 229, 235-238, 241, 246, 250-251, 253-256, 258-259, 261-262, 265-267, 269-271, 276, 278-283, 285-295

Women academic 147, 153, 287

Women in Higher Education 1-14, 16-19, 30, 32, 49, 53-54, 56-58, 65-66, 68-70, 72, 111, 127, 131, 176-178, 194, 210, 253, 256, 270, 285, 288-289, 292-293

Women of Color 12, 70, 78, 80, 83-84, 87-94, 96-102, 104, 111, 114, 120, 126, 128, 131, 134, 136-137, 139, 141

Women's Empowerment 2, 83, 145, 159, 161-162, 165-169, 171-172, 178-182, 187-191

Work-life Balance for Women 177, 192

Recommended Reference Books

IGI Global's reference books are available in three unique pricing formats:
Print Only, E-Book Only, or Print + E-Book.

Order direct through IGI Global's Online Bookstore at
www.igi-global.com or through your preferred provider.

Online Distance Learning Course Design and Multimedia in E-Learning

ISBN: 9781799897064
EISBN: 9781799897088
© 2022; 302 pp.
List Price: US$ **215**

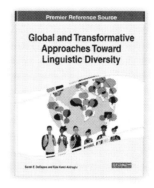

Global and Transformative Approaches Toward Linguistic Diversity

ISBN: 9781799889854
EISBN: 9781799889878
© 2022; 383 pp.
List Price: US$ **215**

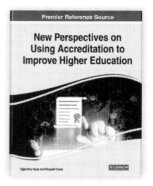

New Perspectives on Using Accreditation to Improve Higher Education

ISBN: 9781668451953
EISBN: 9781668451960
© 2022; 300 pp.
List Price: US$ **195**

Impact of School Shootings on Classroom Culture, Curriculum, and Learning

ISBN: 9781799852001
EISBN: 9781799852018
© 2022; 355 pp.
List Price: US$ **215**

Modern Reading Practices and Collaboration Between Schools, Family, and Community

ISBN: 9781799897507
EISBN: 9781799897521
© 2022; 304 pp.
List Price: US$ **215**

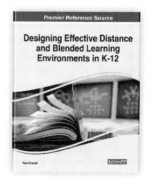

Designing Effective Distance and Blended Learning Environments in K-12

ISBN: 9781799868293
EISBN: 9781799868316
© 2022; 389 pp.
List Price: US$ **215**

Do you want to stay current on the latest research trends, product announcements, news, and special offers?
Join IGI Global's mailing list to receive customized recommendations, exclusive discounts, and more.
Sign up at: **www.igi-global.com/newsletters**.

Publisher of Timely, Peer-Reviewed Inclusive Research Since 1988

www.igi-global.com   Sign up at www.igi-global.com/newsletters   facebook.com/igiglobal   twitter.com/igiglobal   linkedin.com/igiglobal

Ensure Quality Research is Introduced to the Academic Community

Become an Evaluator for IGI Global Authored Book Projects

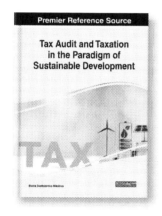  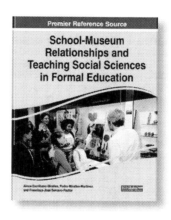 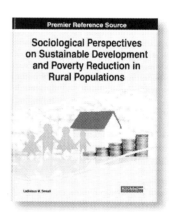

The overall success of an authored book project is dependent on quality and timely manuscript evaluations.

Applications and Inquiries may be sent to:
development@igi-global.com

Applicants must have a doctorate (or equivalent degree) as well as publishing, research, and reviewing experience. Authored Book Evaluators are appointed for one-year terms and are expected to complete at least three evaluations per term. Upon successful completion of this term, evaluators can be considered for an additional term.

If you have a colleague that may be interested in this opportunity, we encourage you to share this information with them.

Easily Identify, Acquire, and Utilize Published
Peer-Reviewed Findings in Support of Your Current Research

IGI Global OnDemand

Purchase Individual IGI Global OnDemand Book Chapters and Journal Articles

For More Information:
www.igi-global.com/e-resources/ondemand/

Browse through 150,000+ Articles and Chapters!

Find specific research related to your current studies and projects that have been contributed by international researchers from prestigious institutions, including:

- Accurate and Advanced Search
- Affordably Acquire Research
- Instantly Access Your Content
- Benefit from the InfoSci Platform Features

"*It really provides an excellent entry into the research literature of the field. It presents a manageable number of highly relevant sources on topics of interest to a wide range of researchers. The sources are scholarly, but also accessible to 'practitioners'.*"

- Ms. Lisa Stimatz, MLS, University of North Carolina at Chapel Hill, USA

Interested in Additional Savings?

Subscribe to
IGI Global OnDemand *Plus*

Learn More

Acquire content from over 128,000+ research-focused book chapters and 33,000+ scholarly journal articles for as low as US$ 5 per article/chapter (original retail price for an article/chapter: US$ 37.50).

7,300+ E-BOOKS.
ADVANCED RESEARCH.
INCLUSIVE & AFFORDABLE.

IGI Global e-Book Collection

- Flexible Purchasing Options (Perpetual, Subscription, EBA, etc.)
- Multi-Year Agreements with No Price Increases Guaranteed
- No Additional Charge for Multi-User Licensing
- No Maintenance, Hosting, or Archiving Fees
- Continually Enhanced & Innovated Accessibility Compliance Features (WCAG)

Handbook of Research on Digital Transformation, Industry Use Cases, and the Impact of Disruptive Technologies
ISBN: 9781799877127
EISBN: 9781799877141

Handbook of Research on New Investigations in Artificial Life, AI, and Machine Learning
ISBN: 9781799886860
EISBN: 9781799886877

Handbook of Research on Future of Work and Education
ISBN: 9781799882756
EISBN: 9781799882770

Research Anthology on Physical and Intellectual Disabilities in an Inclusive Society (4 Vols.)
ISBN: 9781668435427
EISBN: 9781668435434

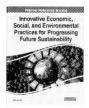

Innovative Economic, Social, and Environmental Practices for Progressing Future Sustainability
ISBN: 9781799895909
EISBN: 9781799895923

Applied Guide for Event Study Research in Supply Chain Management
ISBN: 9781799889694
EISBN: 9781799889717

Mental Health and Wellness in Healthcare Workers
ISBN: 9781799888130
EISBN: 9781799888147

Clean Technologies and Sustainable Development in Civil Engineering
ISBN: 9781799898108
EISBN: 9781799898122

Request More Information, or Recommend the IGI Global e-Book Collection to Your Institution's Librarian

For More Information or to Request a Free Trial, Contact IGI Global's e-Collections Team: eresources@igi-global.com | 1-866-342-6657 ext. 100 | 717-533-8845 ext. 100